THE
FIRST GREAT
CIVILIZATIONS

THE HISTORY OF HUMAN SOCIETY

General Editor: J. H. Plumb, LITT.D.

Christ's College, Cambridge

ALREADY PUBLISHED

Prehistoric Societies   *Grahame Clark and Stuart Piggot*

The Dutch Seaborne Empire 1600–1800   *C. R. Boxer*

The Spanish Seaborne Empire   *J. H. Parry*

Pioneer America   *John R. Alden*

The Greeks   *Antony Andrewes*

The Romans   *Donald Dudley*

The Portuguese Seaborne Empire 1415–1825   *C. R. Boxer*

Imperial China   *Raymond Dawson*

The First Great Civilizations   *Jacquetta Hawkes*

IN PREPARATION

The British Seaborne Empire 1600–1800   *J. H. Plumb*

The Jews   *Cecil Roth and Simon Schama*

The French Seaborne Empire 1600–1789   *Leo Gershoy*

The Medieval Mediterranean World   *Arthur Hibbert*

Britain, the Industrial Empire   *John Vincent*

India and the West   *Anil Seal*

Africa   *J. D. Fage*

Japan   *Marius Jansen*

China and the West   *Jerome Ch'en*

JACQUETTA HAWKES

THE

FIRST GREAT
CIVILIZATIONS

LIFE IN MESOPOTAMIA, THE INDUS VALLEY,
AND EGYPT

HUTCHINSON OF LONDON

HUTCHINSON & CO (*Publishers*) LTD
3 Fitzroy Square, London W1

London Melbourne Sydney Auckland
Wellington Johannesburg Cape Town
and agencies throughout the world

First published 1973

*Printed in Great Britain by litho on antique wove paper
by Anchor Press, and bound by Wm. Brendon,
both of Tiptree, Essex*

ISBN 0 09 116580 6

CONTENTS

ILLUSTRATIONS

DRAWINGS

MESOPOTAMIA

THE INDUS VALLEY

EGYPT

PLATES FOLLOWING PAGE 130

MESOPOTAMIA

War scenes from the 'standard' of Ur. (Mansell)
Phalanx of Sumerian soldiers. (Mansell)
Enemies held in the net of Ningirsu. (Tel-Vigneau)
Battle stele of Naram-sin of Akkad. (Mansell)
Attack on a city, showing battering rams, archers, impaled captives. (Mansell)
Riding camel and horse in battle. (British Museum)
Uranshe the singer. (Max Hirmer)
Goddess with flowing vase. (Schneider-Lengyel)
Carved steatite bowl, showing humped bull and possible rain-making rite. (John R. Freeman)
Libation cup of Gudea of Lagash. (Mansell)
Head thought to represent Sargon the Great. (Max Hirmer)
One of the many statues of Gudea of Lagash. (Mansell)
Group of 'worshippers'. (Oriental Institute, Chicago)
An offering to the goddess. (Franceschi)
Goddess seated under a tree. (Franceschi)
Tablet with pictographic script. (Franceschi)
Cuneiform tablet, with envelope. (Mansell)

THE INDUS VALLEY

The 'priest-king' from Mohenjo-daro. (Mansell)
Bronze statuette of a girl dancer. (Mansell)
A Shiva-like divinity. (Mansell)
A humped bull. (Mansell)

PLATES FOLLOWING PAGE 290

EGYPT

Carved ivory handle of a flint knife. (Mansell)
Votive slate pallet of King Narmer. (Mansell)
Relief symbolizing unity of the Two Lands. (Max Hirmer)
Amenhotep, son of Hapu, as a scribe. (Max Hirmer)
Menkaure and his queen. (Museum of Fine Arts, Boston)
Statue of Ramesses II. (Hubertus Kanus/Barnaby's)

MAPS

INTRODUCTION

BY J. H. PLUMB

1

Over the last fifty to a hundred years, man's belief that the historical process proved he was acquiring a greater mastery over nature has received a brutal buffeting. In his early youth H. G. Wells, a man of vast creative energy, of rich delight in the human spirit and of all-pervading optimism, viewed the future with confidence—science, born of reason, was to be humanity's panacea. When, in the years of his maturity, he came to write his *Outline of History*, his vision was darker, although still sustained with hope. World War I, with its senseless and stupid slaughter of millions of men, brought the sickening realization that man was capable of provoking human catastrophes on a global scale. The loss of human liberty, the degradations and brutalities imposed by fascism and communism during the 1920s and 30s, followed in 1939 by the renewed world struggle—all these events finally shattered Wells's eupeptic vision, and in sad and disillusioned old-age he wrote *Mind at the End of Its Tether*. His hope of mankind had almost vanished. Almost, but not quite: for Wells's lifetime witnessed what, as a young writer, he had prophesied—technical invention not only on a prodigious scale but in those realms of human activity that affected the very core of society. And this extraordinary capacity of man to probe the complexities of nature and to invent machinery capable of exploiting his knowledge remained for Wells the only basis for hope, no matter how slender that might be.

If the belief of a man of Wells's passionate and intelligent humanism could be so battered and undermined, it is not surprising that lesser men were unable to withstand the climate of despair that engulfed the Western World between the two World Wars. The disillusion of those years is apparent in painting, in music, in literature —everywhere in the Western World we are brought up sharply by an expression of anguish, by the flight from social and historical reality into a frightened, self-absorbed world of personal feeling and expression. Intellectual life, outside science, has pursued much the same course as artistic life, although it has shown greater ingenuity and a tougher-minded quality. Theology, philosophy and sociology have tended to reduce themselves to technical problems of exceptional professional complexity but of small social importance. Their practitioners have largely ceased to instruct and enliven, let alone sustain the confidence of ordinary men and women.

In this atmosphere of cultural decay and of professional retreat, history and its philosophy have suffered. As in so many intellectual disciplines, its professional workers have resolutely narrowed the focus of their interests to even more specialized fields of inquiry. The majority of historians have withdrawn from general culture in order to maintain, at a high intellectual level, an academic discipline. They have left the meaning and purpose of history to trained philosophers and have spent their leisure hours tearing to shreds the scholarship of anyone foolish enough to attempt to give the story of mankind a meaning and a purpose—writers as diverse as H. G. Wells and Arnold Toynbee have been butchered with consummate skill. The blunders of scholarship and the errors of interpretation have counted everything; intention nothing. Few academic historians, secure in the cultivation of their minute gardens, have felt any humility towards those who would tame the wilderness. In consequence, an atmosphere of anarchic confusion pervades the attitude of Western man to his past.

A hundred years ago, in the first flood of archaeological discovery, scholars possessed greater confidence. The history of mankind seemed to most to point to an obvious law of human progress: the past was but a stepping-stone to the future. First adumbrated by the philosophers of the late Renaissance—Bodin in France and Bacon in England—the idea of progress became an article of common faith during the Enlightenment. And progress came to mean not only the technical progress that had preoccupied Bacon but also moral progress. By the nineteenth century the history of man demonstrated for many an improvement in the very nature of man himself as well as in his tools and weapons. Such optimism, such faith in man's capacity for rational behaviour, was shaken both by discoveries in science and in history and by events. By the middle of the twentieth century man's irrational drives appeared to be stronger than his intellectual capacities. Freud and Marx laid bare the hollow hypocrisy of so-called rational behaviour either in individuals or in society. Also, the rise and fall of civilizations that had been laid bare by the spade seemed to point to a cyclical pattern in human destiny which made nonsense of any idea of continuous progress; and this naturally attracted the prophets of Western doom. Yet more persuasive still and, perhaps, more destructive of confidence in human destiny, was the utter loss of all sense of human control brought about by global wars and violent revolutions. Only those men or societies who felt life was going their way—the revolutionaries and, above all, the Marxists—believed any longer in the laws of historical progress. For the rest, retrogression seemed as tenable a thesis as progress.

This disillusion in the West suited academic historians. It relieved them of their most difficult problems. If they happened to be religious, they were content to leave the ultimate meaning of history to God; if they were rationalists, they took refuge either in the need for more historical knowledge or in the philosophic difficulties of a subject that by its very nature was devoid of the same objective treatment that gave such authority to scientific inquiry. In the main they concentrated upon their professional work. And this was an exceptionally important and necessary task. What the common reader rarely recognizes is the inadequacy of the factual material that was at the command of an historian one hundred years ago or even fifty years ago. Scarcely any archives were open to him; most repositories of records were unsorted and uncatalogued; almost every generalization about a man or an event or an historical process was three-quarters guesswork, if not more. Laboriously, millions of facts now have been brought to light, ordered and rendered coherent within their own context. Specialization has proliferated like a cancer, making detail vivid, but blurring the outlines of the story of mankind and rendering it almost impossible for a professional historian to venture with confidence beyond his immediate province. And that can be very tiny: the Arkansas and Missouri Railway Strike of 1921; the place-names of Rutland; seventeenth-century Rouen; the oral history of the Barotse; the philosophy of Hincmar of Rheims. And so it be-

comes ever more difficult for the professional historian to reach across
to ordinary intelligent men and women or make his subject a part of
human culture. The historical landscape is blurred by the ceaseless
activity of its millions of professional ants. Of course, attempts at
synthesis have to be made. The need to train young professional
historians, or the need to impart some knowledge of history to students of other disciplines, has brought about competent digests of
lengthy periods that summarize both facts and analysis. Occasionally
such books have been written with such skill and wisdom that they
have become a part of the West's cultural heritage. A few historians,
driven by money or fame or creative need, have tried to share their
knowledge and understanding of the past with the public at large.

But the gap between professional knowledge and history for the
masses gets steadily wider: professional history becomes more accurate, more profound, while public history remains tentative and
shallow. This series is an attempt to reverse this process. Each volume
will be written by a professional historian of the highest technical
competence; but the books will not exist *in vacuo*, for the series is
designed to have a unity and a purpose.

But, first perhaps, it is best to say what it is not. It is not a work
of reference: there are no potted biographies of the Pharaohs, the
Emperors of China or the Popes; no date lists of battles; no brief histories of painting, literature, music. Nor is this series a Universal
History. All events that were critical in the history of mankind may
not necessarily find a place. Some will; some will not. Works of reference, more or less factually accurate, exist in plenty and need not be
repeated. It is not my intention to add yet another large compilation
to what exists. Nor is this a 'philosophic' history. It does not pretend
to reveal a recurring pattern in history that will unveil its purpose.
Fundamentally philosophy, except in the use of language, is as irrelevant to history as it is to science. Nevertheless, this history has a
theme and a position in time.

The theme is the most obvious and the most neglected; obvious
because everyone is aware of it from the solitary villages of Easter
Island to the teeming cities of the Western World, neglected because
it has been fashionable for professional and Western historians to
concern themselves either with detailed professional history that cannot have a broad theme or with the spiritual and metaphysical
aspects of man's destiny that are not his proper province. What, there-

fore, is the theme of *The History of Human Society*? It is this: that the condition of man now is superior to what it was. That two great revolutions—the Neolithic and the industrial—have enabled men to establish vast societies of exceptional complexity in which the material well-being of generations of mankind has made remarkable advances. That the second, and most important, revolution has been achieved by the Western World; that we are witnessing its most intensive phase now, one in which ancient patterns of living are crumbling before the demands of industrial society; that life in the suburbs of London, Lagos, Jakarta, Rio de Janeiro and Vladivostok will soon have more in common than they have in difference. That this, therefore, is a moment to take stock, to unfold how this came about, to evoke the societies of the past while we are still close enough to many of them to feel intuitively the compulsion and needs of their patterns of living.

I hope, however, in these introductions, which it is my intention to write for each book, to provide a sense of unity. The authors themselves will not be so concerned with the over-riding theme. Their aim will be to reconstruct the societies on which they are experts. They will lay bare the structure of these societies—their economic basis, their social organizations, their aspirations, their cultures, their religions and their conflicts. At the same time they will give a sense of what it was like to live in the societies. Each book will be an authoritative statement in its own right, and independent of the rest of the series. Yet each, set alongside the rest, will give a sense of how human society has changed and grown from the time man hunted and gathered his food to this nuclear and electronic age. This could only have been achieved by the most careful selection of authors. They needed, of course, to be established scholars of distinction, possessing the ability to write attractively for the general reader. They needed also to be wise; to possess steady, unflickering compassion for the strange necessities of men; to be quick in understanding, slow in judgement; and to have in them some of that relish for life, as fierce and as instinctive as an animal's, that has upheld ordinary men and women in the worst of times. The authors of these books are heartwise historians with sensible, level heads.

The range and variety of human societies is almost as great as the range and variety of human temperaments, and the selection for this series is in some ways as personal as an anthology. A Chinese, a

Russian, an Indian or an African would select a different series; but we are Western men writing for Western men. The Westernization of the world by industrial technology is one of the main themes of the series. Each society selected has been in the main stream of this development or belongs to that vast primitive ocean from whence all history is derived. Some societies are neglected because they would only illustrate in a duller way societies which do appear in the series; some because their history is not well enough known to a sufficient depth of scholarship to be synthesized in this way; some because they are too insignificant.

There are, of course, very important social forces—feudalism, technological change or religion, for example—which have moulded a variety of human societies at the same time. Much can be learnt from the comparative study of their influence. I have, however, rejected this approach, once recorded history is reached. My reason for rejecting this method is because human beings experience these forces in communities, and it is with the experience of men in society that this series is primarily concerned.

Lastly, it need hardly be said that society is not always synonymous with the state. At times, as with the Jews, it lacks even territorial stability, at least until the foundation of Israel; yet the Jews provide a fascinating study of symbiotic social groupings, and to leave them out would be unthinkable, for they represent, in its best-known form, a wide human experience—a social group embedded in an alien society.

As well as a theme, which is the growth of man's control over his environment, this series may also fulfil a need. That is to restore a little confidence not only in man's capacity to endure the frequent catastrophes in human existence but also in his intellectual abilities. That many of his habits, both of mind and heart, are bestial needs scarcely to be said. His continuing capacity for evil need not be stressed. His greed remains almost as strong as it was when he first shuffled on the ground. And yet the miracles created by his cunning are so much a part of our daily lives that we take their wonder for granted. Man's ingenuity—based securely on his capacity to reason—has won astonishing victories over the physical world, and in an amazingly brief span of time. Such triumphs, so frequently overlooked and even more frequently belittled, should breed a cautious optimism. Sooner or later, painfully perhaps and slowly, the same intellectual skill may be directed to the more difficult and intransigent problems of human living—man's social and personal relations —and this may perhaps be accepted as the proper way of ordering human life. The story of man's progress over the centuries, studded with pitfalls and streaked with disaster as it is, ought to strengthen both hope and will.

Yet a note of warning must be sounded: the history of human society, when viewed in detail, is far more often darkened with tragedy than it is lightened with hope. As these books will show, life for the nameless millions of mankind who have already lived and died has been wretched, short, hungry and brutal. Few societies have secured peace; none stability for more than a few centuries; prosperity, until very recent times, was the lucky chance of a small minority. Consolations of gratified desire, the soothing narcotic of ritual, and the hope of future blessedness have often eased but rarely obliterated the misery which has been the lot of all but a handful of men since the beginning of history. At long last that handful is growing to a significant proportion in a few favoured societies. But throughout human history most men have derived pitifully little from their existence. A belief in human progress is not incompatible with a sharp realization of the tragedy not only of the lives of individual men but also of epochs, cultures and societies. Loss and defeat, too, are themes of this series, as well as progress and hope.

Ω

THE UNCOVERING OF THE CIVILIZATIONS DESCRIBED IN THIS REMARKABLE book has taken place during the last hundred and fifty years, and even now much of the material still awaits detailed and scholarly study; almost certainly the spade will uncover more tombs and more fragments of papyri in Egypt, more royal graves and clay tablets in Mesopotamia, and the language of Mohenjo-daro and Harappa may yet yield its secrets. If so, fresh light will be thrown on one of the most creative of all periods of human history. What we already have, however, is more than sufficient to give us an insight into ways of living very alien to our own and yet of exceptional and direct importance to our own way of life; indeed, they are fundamental to it, for the technical achievements of Egypt and Babylonia enter directly into the mainstream of European history, and so do many themes of their art as well as their life-style.

True, these great civilizations were not alone in making the discoveries that have so greatly influenced our world. The Chinese developed writing as well as cities; urban life and the complexities of social organization which it created developed in the New World—in Central America and Peru—as well as in the Old. But both China and the New World suffered to some degree from the restrictions of geographical barriers that were always likely to make diffusion of their cultural developments slow and uncertain; less so, of course, with China than the New World. Egypt and Mesopotamia, however, lay at the crossroads of the world's greatest landmass, with relatively easy means of communication even for the most primitively equipped people. At the same time, the great geographical complexity of the crescent of the Near East created a challenge for all new techniques. And the diversity of physical terrain was matched by the ever-shifting nature of its peoples. Studying so seminal a period for Europe's history requires not only a strong intellectual grasp of social relationships and historical development, but also delicate imagination and subtle empathy; otherwise, the whole way of life of these fascinating peoples would be distorted. For it is essential not to impose upon the civilizations here described later uses of techniques or of ideas of our own that seem to resonate with theirs. Miss Hawkes avoids such pitfalls in this great synthesis. She is as alert to what is alien as she is to those themes that touch our common humanity.

What did these peoples achieve? They created monarchy and the first great cities; they invented writing; they developed institutionalized religion. Their food surpluses sustained not only priests, but lawyers, scholars and warriors; for the first time whole classes of men were freed from the direct necessity of raising their own food or hunting for it. They developed architecture and monumental sculpture and raised these to sophisticated arts. From their preoccupation with measurement, mathematics took its first stumbling steps; from their preoccupation with the stars for purposes of divination began the long road that was to lead to the science of the universe. They conquered metals and made them mankind's most efficient tool—of death as well as life. And with them medicine begins.

Above all, these peoples created easier methods of social evolution, by writing and the development of libraries, particularly in Babylonia. Knowledge required a more permanent base; the oral tradition, by which knowledge had been transmitted, was by its nature more fragile, more open to the winds of chance, to modification and to loss. Baked on clay, inscribed in stone or painted on the hidden walls of tombs, the chances for the survival of fact became infinitely greater. In a very deep sense, an epoch which has lasted until the dawn of our own new world of scientific industry was born in these civilizations of some four to five thousand years ago.

And yet, there is a great need for caution in isolating those inventions and institutions which possessed social dynamism for subsequent generations from the way the society which brought them into being used them. All the social and technical developments that occurred in Mesopotamia, the Indus Valley and Egypt flowed— as did the civilizations of China and the New World—from the neolithic revolution. That revolution created a vast range of new opportunities in which intensively creative and highly intelligent human beings could work, invent, and express themselves. Hence, the early centuries covered by this book were some of the most creative in the history of man—as vital, as vivid, as original in thought and invention as the last two hundred years of human history. Fortunately, with the invention of writing we are given for the first time an opportunity to reach through to the thoughts, the hopes, the fears of individual men and women and also to obtain some insight into the way their beliefs, traditions and social forces helped to adjust them to the world in which they lived and to explain it to them satisfactorily. And although at times their own world seems strangely alien to our own, we recognize at once that the men and women who lived in it were like ourselves, sharing similar hopes and fears, alive to aspiration, depressed by transgression, full of love, capable of hate, enraged by jealousy, obsessed by habit, capable of dedication and self-sacrifice. So near to us they are that it is easy to imagine being one of them. And this book illuminates their common humanity as well as their strangely different societies. Hence, the book possesses extraordinary fascination—the beginnings, remote though they may be, of what could grow into our own world. We can, when guided by so skilled and perceptive a scholar as Miss Hawkes, reach through with empathy and understanding to the first complex civilizations, and yet to men and women like ourselves.

It must be emphasized that neither the institutions nor the inventions of the early creative phases of these civilizations released a chain of continuous development. Many remained potential and seemed quickly to freeze into a timeless and static world. Let us take only two which have—in the fullness of time—deeply influenced the world's history: writing and urbanization. A vast quantity of written material has, of course, vanished or lies buried beneath the desert, but there remains sufficient, certainly in Mesopotamia, to assess its social function, which indeed was very limited. In Egypt all that we have for most of the dynasties is ritualistic writing—intended for gods, most of it indeed never intended, never written, to be seen again by the human eye. There may, indeed, have been considerable writing on leather or on papyrus which has almost disappeared and which may have fulfilled the same social function that writing possessed in Mesopotamia, but in Egypt the scribal class never seems to have been so numerous or so important. From the paucity of written material, largely cylinder-seal inscriptions, writing seems to have played an even smaller part in the mysterious Indus civilization.

In Mesopotamia writing quickly became highly complex and very difficult to learn beyond the limit required for bureaucratic administration—the listing of goods, the payment of rents and taxes, the obligations of labour—and which the administration of large temple estates or of a royal palace required. Even this moderate literacy demanded a very considerable apprenticeship, so that literacy was always for hundreds and hundreds of years confined to a small class of scholars and priests.

Apart from administrative purposes, the major use of writing was in divination. Tens of thousands of baked-clay tablets record the state of the liver of the animal sacrificed in order to know how propitious were the times for action or inaction. This was the major social function of the scribes, not the creation or transmission of literature or knowledge. To enter into this world of divination, this daily attempt to know the minds of the gods, is very difficult for anyone educated in the monotheistic religions of later European and Islamic societies. Yet in these earlier civilizations gods were everywhere: ruling cities, fighting amongst themselves, marrying and breeding and absorbing each other in the most bewildering way. In Mesopotamia gods faded as cities fell; even Marduk of Babylon failed in the end. This kaleidoscopic world of ever-changing gods—always present, always unpredictable, usually implacable, occasionally benign—needed constant ritual, constant sacrifice and constant interpretation. In a generation that has drawn away from close living with a nature whose moods and tantrums have become increasingly explainable, it requires intense empathy to realize how god-ridden the life of men in these early civilizations was. And yet it would be wrong to consider these old civilizations fear-ridden; men learn to live with divination as easily as with tabus or puritanical repression. What is fascinating is the amount of social energy and social wealth, as well as literary effort, divination demanded and that such effort and such expenditure of social wealth was acceptable to generations of men and women. It obviously created a sense of deep security.

Bureaucracy and divination being the scribal functions that came after the long apprenticeship of learning, what literature there was—largely religious ritual—was a minor part of writing, even though it is one that resonates in our own age with peculiar force. The *Epic of Gilgamesh*, which possesses a haunting appeal today, was only of moderate interest to the Babylonians. It exists only in a few copies or scraps of copies and is very seldom referred to, unlike many other texts. It would therefore be most dangerous to regard Gilgamesh as a towering folk hero, or to build upon his epic any interpretation of the feeling and attitudes of the Sumerians.

Although there are many moving and fascinating literary works from both Egypt and Mesopotamia, when spread over two and a half millennia they add up to a small corpus, and it would be difficult, almost impossible, on literary evidence alone to reconstruct in depth these first civilizations as Jacquetta Hawkes has done. For this period the work of the archaeologist is critical to our understanding of what, so often, the written records do little to reveal. What is so difficult in these early societies is to glimpse the daily life of ordinary men and women or to catch even an echo of their hopes, fears and aspirations. After all, the scribes worked for the kings, the priests, the merchants. True, the great codifications of law give us some insight into social valuations, but law and living are often at variance —an interpretation of present-day social history, based on modern statutes, would give a strange picture of our contemporary society. Perhaps a better example is the difficulty of deriving the diversity of human relationships in slave societies by considering the slave codes. And so, in the reconstruction of these societies a great intellectual delicacy is required in order to use the difficult materials available. Similar care must be used in commenting on their relationship with the societies that followed them.

One feature, I believe, must be stressed. Historians are rightly impressed by the social stability of China, which withstood political and dynastic upheavals with ease—in marked contrast, it seems, with Europe and its revolutions, rapid social change, decay and growth of empires, and constant intellectual ferment. And so historians tend to ignore the remarkable social stability achieved on Europe's doorstep by the early civilizations, at least in Egypt and Mesopotamia, where a similar life-style, modified it is true from time to time by technical and intellectual as well as political change, remained fundamentally the same for well over two thousand years. After the first creative burst of the early centuries that saw the rise of Sumer and the birth of Pharaonic Egypt until these civilizations were overwhelmed by Greece and Rome—a time longer than has elapsed since the birth of Christ—the patterns not only of living but also of thought changed little: empires came and went, cities rose and fell, but social structure, the ways men earned their livings, even the ways they thought about life and destiny, changed so slowly, so imperceptibly, that to the majority of men and women the world was a *given* environment, often disturbed by the displeasure of the gods and sometimes rendered benign by their satisfaction, but changeless. In such a world the inertia of social institutions was formidable—immense both in Egypt and in Mesopotamia—yet neither civilization was very historical-minded in the sense that it required written history to support government or to justify political change as the Chinese required it. Had they been historically-minded, this volume would have been far less difficult to write.

Tradition-bound, yet nonhistorical, god-ridden yet secure; these are the difficult hurdles that a modern reader must overcome to obtain a feeling for the life of these people. There is a great deal of both Egyptian and Mesopotamian civilization that is very remote from our own ways of thinking and of living. And yet the two civilizations are linked with our own world in a most formidable sense. We witness in them, as we do also in Classical China, the establishment of those social institutions which were to dominate the civilized world until our own time. The rise of organized religion, with complex sources of wealth and authority and embracing a considerable segment of society, was a new and dramatic feature of human devel-

opment that emerged in these centuries—an aspect of social life that
has lasted until our own day. Equally significant was the emergence
of the concept of kingship and all the complex forms of ritual and of
art that went with it. Sometimes, as with the Pharaoh, king and high
priest were united in the same person, who acquired god-like attributes, and so god-like power. But kings were always law-givers, the
final power in a society, no matter how complex its individual or
corporate rights. And kingship was to persist for millennia, like
organized religion.

More important even than these, however, was the growing
strength of the unitary family and the strengthening of the authority
of the father over wife and children—marked, indeed, by the ever-
growing ferocity in Mesopotamia of the punishments to be inflicted
on adulterous wives or disobedient children. Indeed, the family
became powerful for economic as well as social reasons. After all,
the family was the most economical work force either in crafts or in
farming, as well as a natural and simple educational unit in which
the techniques of agriculture and commerce and industry could be
taught; and it was the natural base for all law and order. Again, it
is only in very recent times that this social institution, which acquired
so much of its legal and moral authority at such early times, began
to crumble.

A sharply defined warrior class was another new feature of human
living that was to have a long and sinister history. In fact, the steady
differentiation of human functions in society was perhaps the most
remarkable feature of these civilizations, made possible by greatly
enhanced wealth as well as population and the far greater security
of human life which complex civilization brings. And these people
also developed social memory—their greatest single achievement—
through the art of writing, used at first maybe oddly; nevertheless,
the capacity to store knowledge and to impart it to others distant in
space and time has made social evolution more possible and more
probable. True, the systems of writing here described were lost and
the knowledge they stored largely forgotten, and it would be unwise
to exaggerate their direct contribution to human history. The techniques of these skills, however, were never lost: men continued to
devise systems of writing to store their knowledge and to impart it.
And for Babylon as well as Egypt much was imparted before the
knowledge of cuneiform and hieroglyphic was lost.

These civilizations, therefore, have two aspects of great fascination:

one witnesses the emergence of those social institutions which have so profoundly influenced all human history for these last ten thousand years and at the same time one enters imaginatively into a world which in thought and in living is distinct from our own. For this we could have no better guide than Jacquetta Hawkes.

PART I

THE BEGINNING
OF CIVILIZATION

IT WAS THE GOD ENKI, THE SUMERIANS KNEW, WHO HAD TAUGHT MEN
the arts of writing and geometry, how to build cities and temples. He
had also filled the Tigris and Euphrates with sparkling water and
stocked them with fish. Moreover:

> *The plough and the yoke he directed*
> *The great prince Enki.*
> *Opened the holy furrows.*
> *Made grain grow in the perennial field.*

Confronted with one of the great moments in the history of human
achievement, the first creation of civilized life, this is perhaps the
most wholesome way to begin to apprehend it. The descendants of
those who had created Sumerian civilization, seeking for an explanation of their inheritance, found their answer in these mythopoeic
terms. They were appropriate, for they too sprang from the human
psyche just as the forms of civilization had done—and were for ever
to do, as grain grows in the perennial field.

This primacy of the creative psyche has to be insisted upon at the
outset because its obviousness appears to be so truly overwhelming
that it is not seen. At the present time, when man's thinking has
flowed into narrower and more consciously directed channels, many
people are engaged in attempts to fit the whole glorious, unconfined,
indefinable growth of civilization into various precise intellectually

conceived shapes. There are the ecological, the economic-materialist, the political, the social and the moral shapes. The fact that these various explanatory forms often conflict is a useful reminder of their artificiality.

That they are artificial does not mean that they are useless. It is only that in them the whole flow of life has been forced into various moulds, just as the mud of the Valley of the Twin Rivers was forced into brick-moulds and hardened in the sun. Such blocks are good intellectual building material, but it must never be forgotten that it was the human mind, and above all the amazing energy of its image-making capacities, that raised civilization and its greatest monuments. Good soil, agriculture, some elementary technology, social stratification may have made the necessary groundwork, but what except imaginative power lifted inert mud into the fantastic ziggurat with its crowning temple, or the resistant mass of rock into a gleaming pyramid? This should be very plain today, when hitherto unimagined material wealth, specialization and techno-logical ability show signs of failing to maintain civilization or to create nobly imaginative monuments.

The first difficulty in the way of any more analytical approach to the nature of civilization is that of defining the meaning of the word itself. In its original sense, of course, it referred to the quality of citizens, and it is therefore to be expected that the Greeks, as exemplified by Strabo, classified peoples who had no cities as uncivilized.

The Romans certainly maintained this assumption, making the foundation of cities an essential part of their conscious plan to impose civilization throughout the provinces of their empire. It has remained with Western man until very recent times. It is evident, for instance, that when the Spanish conquistadors stumbled upon the Aztec capital of Tenochtitlán, it was above all the size, wealth and exquisite amenities of this city that led them to feel that they had discovered a true civilization and one which could be compared favourably with that of Europe.

Now that our own disintegrating cities become increasingly barbarous, while at the same time new modes of travel and communication have made it possible to enjoy almost all that has been meant by a civilized life far away from their streets, sociologists are ready to say that civilization cannot be identified with urban living—and, moreover, that it never should have been. It has been claimed that not only in pre-Columbian Middle America but in Egypt too, civilizations came into being without true cities.

However, if we turn to our immediate historical objective, man's first creation of civilization in the great valley of the Tigris and Euphrates, it becomes clear why the identification was made not only by the Greeks and Romans, to whom it was self-evident, but also among those moderns who first began to put a social interpretation upon the revelations of archaeology. Gordon Childe, making a close study of the rise of Sumerian civilization, came very close to identifying the establishment of such cities as Uruk, Lagash and Ur in the fourth millennium B.C. with the dawn of civilization.

This rise of city life with its social and economic changes he styled the urban revolution. It is true that on occasion he used this term and 'civilization' as equivalents. When, however, he was sharpening his focus, he saw the city as 'the resultant and symbol' of the urban revolution. This view logically implied his acceptance of the historical fact which, as we shall see, archaeology has demonstrated—that his own criteria for civilization had already evolved before the appearance of the fully fledged city. This is 'what happened in history', yet it can be accepted that in Mesopotamia the urban revolution followed so closely and, it seems, inevitably on the heels of civilization that they can be accepted as a single process. Indeed the whole argument might well be condemned as one of the follies forced upon us by our attempts to impose intellectual analyses on the organic flow of life.

Today the most acceptable interpretations of the development of civilization and its essential criteria are primarily social and economic. The first necessity was for a greatly increased food supply. The adoption of farming many millennia before had produced a variety of self-contained communities winning their subsistence from agriculture and herding. Now productivity had to be increased far beyond subsistence level. The regions where this was attainable to the extent demanded for the support of high civilization were the flood plains of the three great river valleys of the Tigris-Euphrates, the Nile and the Indus. These level valley floors offered an unlimited water supply and the feasibility of irrigation; and alluvial soil which, once drained, was immensely fertile and, more unusual, maintained in fertility by floods that every year spread fresh silt on the fields. They also offered long-distance water transport for travellers and for goods.

When the cultivator could produce far more food than was needed for his own family, the way was open for considerable sections of a rapidly increasing population to give part, or even the whole, of their time to the practice of crafts and professions. This specialization of skills and knowledge, together with larger communities, profoundly altered the social structure. In precivilized times the social order was based on kinship, with its inturned, emotional bonds. Now people were ordered by the place where they lived and the work which they did.

This degree of social evolution was still not enough for the higher flights of civilization. It might have led to nothing more ambitious than the economy and cultural attainments of a market town. The next necessity was for the food surplus, or its equivalent in other forms of wealth, to be transferred from the producers to a ruling élite who would use it to satisfy, with ever greater magnificence, the prompting of human imagination and love of power. Temples, palaces, citadels, city walls and the equipment of armies were all made possible by the work of the peasantry and the excellence of their soil.

Whether the élite is held to have extorted wealth from its producers or to have received it in order to fulfil the desires of the people depends to some extent on the political sympathies of the historian. It can be assumed that what began as spontaneous tribute to the gods and their earthly representatives hardened with the centuries into the more or less reluctant payment of taxes. There is no reason to doubt that the normal ambiguity of the situation can be illumined by thinking of the attitudes to taxation in a modern social democracy.

If craftsmen, sculptors, architects, fighting men and a luxury-loving élite were to have their needs and desires satisfied, one other broad economic advance had to be made. The vast, monotonous silt plains of southern Mesopotamia—even more than the other river valleys—were lacking in natural resources. No civilization could have flowered there without a merchant class able to import metals, woods and stone as well as such precious rarities as lapis lazuli, turquoise and sweet gums. For long-distance trade some easily portable medium of change had to be devised. So it was that measures of silver and copper began their long career as common tender.

Gordon Childe, as a materialist historian, gave first place to these social and economic criteria of civilization. He summed up,

'The story is one of accumulating wealth, of increasing specialization of labour, and of expanding trade.' He added to them two further criteria that could be seen as economic in origin but that were loaded with significance for man's mental growth. These were writing and numbering and the beginning of a kind of exact observation and calculation that could be called scientific.

To keep and transmit to successors some account of the stores of barley, the cattle, sheep and other wealth that poured into the central treasury the administrators needed durable records. Moreover, the calculation of crop areas, of the volume of grain, of bricks and the like certainly added a stimulus to mastering elementary geometry and arithmetic. For the measurement and forecasting of time so valuable for the management of the agricultural year, exact observation of the stars and planets brought gifts of foresight that must have appeared magical to the ignorant. So, as man's first venture in civilization advanced, its leaders added knowledge and intellectual craft to the other powers of rulership.

One of the underlying effects of this materialist interpretation of the birth of civilization is its apparent inevitability. Every stage comes pat upon the one before and the whole chronicle seems to advance with perfect logic and good sense. Yet one knows that it was not inevitable, for on the one hand men have lived on well watered and fertile land without creating civilization, and on the other have created civilizations in apparently poor environments. As for the logic and good sense, was not all this effort from surplus food-growing onwards and upwards to be devoted to the wildest imaginative fantasies—to raising artificial mountains for men-gods and building millions of tons of rock into a perfect geometric form to receive the corpses of god-men?

With all these orderly economic and social constructions we seem to be confronted with something like a motor car without an engine or a suit of armour without a knight. The dynamic is missing.

Various emendments have been suggested by historians who accept, fundamentally, the materialist chain of causes and effects. Robert Adams suggests that models for the growth of civilization may have been too much inclined to show only internal order and relatedness and to ignore the creative energy that could have come from the clashes and rivalry of increasingly varied classes and interests. Lewis Mumford, considering particularly the rise of cities, sees as the source of energy working upon a productive peasantry the institution of kingship from origins in the Palaeolithic chieftain-ship. He sees the citadel, where the king in his palace, the priests in the temples and the administrators of the royal granaries lived within a container of high walls, as the controlling nucleus of the city cell. For him the citadel and not the market place symbolizes the heart of ancient civilization.

The apparent logic and inevitability of the materialist interpreta-tion produces a deep reluctance to recognize the presence of an-other dynamic. Robert Adams writes of the development of civiliza-tion in Mesopotamia: 'Apparently the first specialized administrative group, or ruling stratum, was composed of hierarchies of priests. These priests were associated with monumental temples and were in the service of gods who were regarded as resident in the individual communities. *Why the initial emphasis should have been placed on a priesthood, as indeed also seems to have been the case in the formative stages of other early civilizations, remains a matter of conjecture.*' Adams goes on to argue that it may have been to meet the need for social cohesion in a more diverse society. Yet he would probably not feel the same puzzlement or put forward the same kind of explanation for the very similar manifestation in early mediaeval Christendom.

The need to give due weight to an interpretation of civilization opposite and complementary to the economic and social has, of course, been recognized, particularly by those anthropologists who favour the 'culture pattern' rather than the 'social structure' school of thought. There have indeed been most elaborate theoretical sys-tems, culminating in the 'culturology' which assigns to culture its own independent life and evolution.

Here the simple statement will be preferred that the dynamic within civilization was the human psyche and what Suzanne Langer has recognized as its innate image-and-symbol-making drive. The material advances in food production, technology and the rest make it possible for these mental forms to find a new magnificence of ex-pression—to be royally dressed. That they were not new and that they were to a very large extent universals of human self-conscious-ness responding to what it found in its inner and outer worlds, can hardly be doubted in the face of the evidence.

The same drives, to some extent even the same symbolic forms, can be seen already in the first ascendancy of *Homo sapiens* in late Palaeolithic times. We can see that the same excitement and concern roused by birth and fertility which found expression in the female figurines of the hunters was also celebrated in the great temples and cult figures of Ninhursag, Inanna and other versions of the Mother Goddess of ancient civilization. We can see how the emotions roused by death and the desire to defeat its sting which caused the Palaeolithic peoples to bury their dead with care and give them valuable tools and food were, when social wealth permitted it, to swell to such extravagances as the royal graves of Ur and the pyramids. We can be reasonably sure from cave art and analogy that the hunters early promoted shamanlike go-betweens to link them with the spirit world, who corresponded in this function to the civilized priesthoods. As Mumford and others have suggested, we can see the Palaeolithic hunting chieftain writ large in the divine king. We can see how in the Palaeolithic Age there was a tremendous urge to symbolize in the visual forms of painting and sculpture. That shrines were the first form of public building is suggested by the one that underlay all other buildings at Jericho, and by the number and elaboration of those at Catal Huyuk—a settlement which in many ways still embodies Palaeolithic tradition. Moreover, the animal painting and carving in the shrines at Catal Huyuk tends to confirm what had already proved an irresistible conclusion—that the painted and sculptured caves were sanctuaries and the scene of magico-religious rites. We can see, then, that the temple, embellished by art and a ritual theatre, was an enlargement and formalization of the hunters' shrines and sanctuaries.

It is not difficult to list these things—the embodiment of birth and fertility, the ritualization of death, the priestly go-between, the chieftain-king, visual symbols and the containing sanctuary—which reveal to what a great extent the early civilizations provided cultural expression for the same drives which had dominated human life since the emergence of *Homo sapiens*. It is easy to expose the universality not only of these drives but of the course of their fulfilment by appealing to Middle and South America. After the deepest fission in world history, conquistador could meet Inca or Aztec king among palaces, temples and ceremonies that seemed essentially familiar.

It is infinitely more difficult to account for the origin and nature of these drives or the underlying common force that makes them all 'religious', bathes all that concerns them in the light of the numinous. What has been said, that they represent human self-consciousness responding to what is found in the inner and outer worlds, may be a right beginning. More exploration is called for, particularly of that inner realm.

As consciousness heightened in our kind and the sense of I-ness strengthened with it, this I sought to relate itself to the world-apart through symbol, image, metaphor. At the same time forces from the unconscious could invade the conscious mind charged with tremendous psychic force. If this still happens today, and everyone who has experienced creation through the arts or religious obsession knows that it does, it happened far more readily in the millennia before the cultivation of the detached intellect. Emotions of fear, of love and hate, of wonder at the tremendous features of the outer world, could release the archetypal invaders. Their expression then became a matter of compulsion rather than of purpose.

As for their origin, we have to imagine individual experience running back into the inherited experience of the species—of light and darkness, of birth, sex and death, of the mother, of the father-leader. Now that it is being recognized that animal nature is subject to formal laws of hierarchy and territory and group responsibility, it appears that a transformation of these instinctive behaviour patterns may lie behind the urge to ritual. The enactment of ritual, it is well known, can itself give birth to gods.

The story is one of such complication and subtlety, involving such an interplay between inner and outer, between conscious and unconscious, between the individual and society, between present and past, that we are unlikely ever fully to apprehend it.

HERE, THEN, ARE THE TWO ASPECTS OF THE BEGINNING OF CIVILIZATION —roughly to be called the materialist and the psychic (which would once have been called the spiritual). Are we to say in the beginning was the food surplus, or in the beginning was the word? To Gordon Childe and his followers it has been obvious that the economic and technological progress and the elaboration of social structures were primary. But it can also be made to seem obvious that man's desire to clothe his psychic image-and-symbol-making drives in more and more splendid dress impelled the material revolution. It was a peasantry and not an agricultural folk culture that could be counted upon to produce the food surplus. It is not altogether irrelevant to look forward to the next 'revolution', the industrial, and observe that it followed after the more purely intellectual adventures of the seventeenth century. We can quite simply agree that economic conditions and technical inventions provided both the limitations and the range of opportunities within which the mental dynamic could work. The two together could create an almost infinite variety of results.

The three river valley civilizations with which the rest of this book will be concerned cannot fail to appear as living examples of this variety. With many of the same limiting factors and opportunities, with so much shared in common both through historical contact and, it seems, innate human tendencies, the three emerge each with its own coherence and its own brilliant individuality. Although analogies between society and persons are notoriously dangerous, it is tempting to make a very simple one, not less significant because it is obvious. One can take an individual artist. He will be endowed with bodily parts not identical with but overwhelmingly similar to those of his contemporaries; his face will have the same basic features but so distinctively arranged that he can be instantly recognized from among all other men on earth. He will have been taught a common language and yet his voice will be almost equally distinguishable, he will have been taught a common script and yet his handwriting on an envelope can always be identified. Above all, he will have been taught painting and may very well belong to a school of painters, yet his subjects, his constructions, every mark left by his brushwork will be so much his own that his pictures can be recognized from afar— or from a small fragment.

The correspondingly vital identity of a civilization Henri Frankfort has called its 'form'. He says, 'We recognize it in a certain coherence among its various manifestations, a certain consistency in its orientation, a certain cultural "style" which shapes its political and judicial institutions, its art as well as its literature, its religion as well as its morals.' He sees the emergence of this 'form' not as a slow evolution but the 'outcome of a sudden and intense change producing a rapid maturity.' This Athena-like birth is followed by a long period of internal development, more or less affected by outside influences.

An attempt to sketch 'forms' of the Mesopotamian, Egyptian and Indus valley civilizations at this point can be no more than an apéritif to sharpen the attention for what is to come.

Fundamental to the personality structure of the Sumerians and their inheritors was a tendency to pessimism and insecurity. They believed that the gods had created mankind to slave for them; they lived in the expectation of disaster and a return to primeval chaos. It was characteristic that Enlil, lord of storm, should be a supreme deity.

Gilgamesh, the greatest literary epic of Mesopotamia, developed into a tragedy. It taught that struggle as he would, man was helpless, his fate and death decreed by the gods. Nor was there any hope of bliss to come. Death led only to an Underworld of dusty gloom. Moreover, although the gods might show justice on occasion, men were usually at the mercy of the arbitrary tempers of their greatest divinities. The humbler people, too, were much concerned with demons, far more often harmful than kindly. Individual human life was insignificant if not futile. If anything redeemed the existence of mankind as a whole, it was the gods' need of men to maintain the divine order. Every New Year the victory of the god—Enlil, Marduk or another—representing that of dynamic authority and order over the powers of inert chaos was celebrated and the people shared in the victory. Their king represented the god, and their state the divine cosmos.

That the Valley of the Twin Rivers came to be divided into city-states maintaining rivalries that often flared into warfare and destruction is in keeping with this psychological character. There was good reason for insecurity and for the fear of the return of chaos—and the internal threats were enhanced by those of external aggressors. At the same time there was good reason for strong authority and for man to endure his fate in carrying out the will of the gods.

It was perhaps this last aspect of life in Mesopotamia that is most clearly expressed in its art. From the earliest time this is almost exclusively in the service of religious cult. The figures are powerful, aloof, severely formalized and generally impersonal. Above all they are isolated. Even in reliefs where ritual scenes are shown, each figure seems to be indeed an island, utterly unrelated.

The 'form' of Egyptian civilization contrasted with that of Mesopotamia in all these characteristics—of psychology, religion, politics and art. The great personality difference lay in the fact that the Egyptian was secure, based on an ideal of changelessness, of the eternal cycle. Western historians show prejudice when they judge Egyptian civilization a failure because it did not progress but maintained an intense conservatism through two thousand years. This was success, the fulfilment of the ideal. Similarly, of course, the popular notion that the Egyptians were a gloomy people, weighed down by death, is a misconception. Death being the great enemy of their idea of continuance, a tremendous effort had to be made to defeat it by rejecting its reality.

Although with death the man's 'soul' left the body, if it was to enjoy an afterlife in any of its supposed forms the body had to be preserved—as well as handsomely housed and supplied. All this is in complete contrast with the Mesopotamian resignation so well expressed in *Gilgamesh*: 'For when the gods created man, they let death be his share, and life withheld in their own hands.'

The hope of resurrection was inevitably tied up with the other great distinguishing characteristic of Egyptian civilization: the existence at the heart of society of the divine Pharaoh. If at first immortality could be assured only for the king and his immediate followers, the cult of Osiris was soon to offer this happy prospect to the common man. Yet as Osiris was identified with the king or kingship, the role of Pharaoh in securing the afterlife of his subjects remained as important as it was for their life in this world.

Psychologically and theologically, Pharaoh was distinguished from his Mesopotamian contemporaries by his divinity. The rulers of Sumer and Akkad were seen as stewards of the gods: their title, of *lugal*, means 'great man'. Pharaoh was above humanity, he was Horus himself, universally portrayed on equal terms with the greatest divinities. As these divinities stood for nature and her powers and the order of the universe, Pharaoh's membership in the pantheon enabled him to maintain a harmonious and secure relationship between man and nature. He brought his people confidence in place of *angst*, faith in eternal continuance in place of the more dynamic uncertainties of Mesopotamia.

Politically the distinction was at least as sharp. The Egyptian had his security at the expense of any degree of liberty. The Predynastic Egyptians are assumed to have shared in typically African traditions of divine kingship. The crucial time when the 'form' of Egyptian civilization sprang to maturity came when one of these kings became powerful enough to bring the delta lands and the valley lands together under his own absolute rule. So at the time when the Valley of the Twin Rivers was dividing into separate city-states of modest size, one thousand miles of the Nile and its delta mouths became a single united kingdom, safe from internal strife and largely protected from external attack by flanking deserts. If this unity came readily to people used to absolute kingship, it was strengthened and made real by the great thoroughfare of the river. Pharaoh's subjects could float northward with the current, sail southward with the wind.

At least as significant as this political contrast between Meso-potamia and Egypt was the difference of economic structure that went with it. As we shall see, the true urbanization of Sumer and Akkad was not matched in Egypt, where there were ceremonial and royal cities, but none based on manufacture and commerce. The Egyptians remained essentially a rural people.

Finally the two 'forms' are distinguished by their art. Almost from the beginning Egyptian sculptors and painters made naturalistic portraits of individual men and women and loving studies of animals, birds and plants. Moreover, the individuals could be related: men and women were shown holding one another with a certain re-strained but very real tenderness; scenes of daily life, men doing all manner of things together, were full of lively observation. The artists had their conventions, such as the only too well known squar-ing of the torso, yet except for certain portrayals of Pharaoh their work had none of the tense, impersonal formalization of Meso-potamia. The difference is almost as great as that between the representational forms of Egyptian hieroglyphs and the severe ab-straction of cuneiform. It seems as though the Egyptians, secure in their faith that all was right with the world, were relaxed enough to be able to see and enjoy one another and the one thousand and one things of life by the Nile.

The third of the river valley civilizations was as true to its 'form' as the other two. Yet because they wrote little and none of that little has been deciphered, and because of an exceptional dearth of surviving representational art, the people of the Indus civilization remain more remote.

Their culture was remarkably uniform over the whole of its vast area. This suggests that it came closer to that of the Egyptians in being in some sense a unified state. It appears to have been ruled not from one capital but two, Mohenjo-daro and Harappa. On the other hand it was genuinely urbanized in the Mesopotamian manner. These and other smaller cities or towns were genuine centres of economic life. Moreover, their strong defences and dominating citadels have something in common with the cities of Sumer and Akkad.

Yet aesthetically and in spirit they were very unlike. In place of the organic, unplanned growth of the Mesopotamian cities, these of the Indus were laid out with Roman precision on a grid plan. Building lines were strictly observed. The streets must have been grim, fronted with expanses of brickwork unornamented and almost without the relief of window openings, as the houses were inward-looking, turning blank walls to the passer-by.

All this and much more has suggested that the Indus civilization was authoritarian, stereotyped, inflexible. Archaeologists do not often allow themselves value judgements, yet Stuart Piggott wrote, 'I can only say that there is something about the [Indus] civilization that I find repellent.'

It is principally in its religious life that this civilization seems already to possess something that could be called distinctively Indian. Phallus worship, concern with ritual bathing, a reverence for bulls, and above all a god with recognizable features of that sombre destroyer, the Hindu Siva, all tell us that deep-seated elements of the Indus tradition survived the Indo-European conquest to come into their own once more in historic Hinduism.

AT THE VERY BEGINNING OF THE HUMAN EXPERIMENTS IN CIVILIZED living, we find these three essays so similar in many essentials, so utterly different in imaginative expression and in all those features of the cultural style that Frankfort identified with the 'form' of civilization. If one wishes, with dangerous over-simplification, to sum up these prevailing characters in single words, one could say that in their formative ages conflict-torn Mesopotamia was progressive, Egypt conservative, north-west India static.

From its very beginnings human culture was various. In earlier Palaeolithic times, however, these distinct cultural traditions extended over vast stretches of time and space. During the Neolithic age, on the other hand, there were a great many local cultures, sharply defined and relatively short-lived. Now men showed the same gift for variety in their creativeness but were able to give it expression in all the new ways that came with civilization.

These cultural differences which have done so much to enrich and enliven our history (but which may never again appear in their essential spontaneity) remain largely inexplicable. In part—and most conspicuously in the arts and other fruits of the imagination—

the sources were innate, springing from still mysterious roots in the psychological inheritance of peoples and in individual men and women of genius.

At the same time, of course, the natural environment and the aspects of life that were dictated by it were powerful influences. The three earliest high civilizations all came into being in immense river valleys that offered their inhabitants many of the same opportunities and challenges. Yet they were also sufficiently different to have been able to play some part in determining the distinctive 'forms' of the civilizations they nourished.

PART II

FROM PEASANTS
TO CITIZENS

THE TIGRIS-EUPHRATES VALLEY

THE GREAT GEOGRAPHICAL SYSTEM DOMINATED BY THE EUPHRATES, THE Tigris and their tributaries has to be understood from two points of view. First there is the introverted view. Here was the container of the first-born civilization—call it wombland or cradleland according to historical perspective and taste in metaphors. Second there is the view of extroversion. This mighty river system was a branching central nerve sending impulses to the most vital areas of the ancient world: India, Persia, Anatolia, the Levant, and by way of the Mediterranean, Egypt and southern Europe.

The name of the Twin Rivers sometimes given to the Euphrates and Tigris is at least partially justified, for from their sources to their 'Siamese' junction over a thousand miles away they are closely related. They are, however, very far from being identical twins. Because of its contrary start and mighty windings the Euphrates traverses some 1800 miles on its way to the Persian Gulf, while the more direct Tigris takes only 1150 miles.

The mountainous upper valleys of the Euphrates are of great significance from the point of view of external relationships. An easy pass leads from the western arm of the Euphrates (the Firat) over to the Aras, which flows eastward into the Caspian. This has made a natural route from northern Persia to the west, and especially Asia Minor—it was in fact the route followed by Turks, Mongols and

Tatars, and must have been of significance even in prehistoric times.

In the middle valley below Samsat, where the river flows through a rocky but habitable valley a few miles wide, its north-south course is only some hundred miles from the coast, providing a region which from ancient times saw a give and take of influences between Mesopotamia and the Mediterranean.

Further downstream, when the Euphrates has already set its main course towards the Gulf, there is an important route from Damascus by way of Palmyra converging with another from Mosul along the always important route of the Khabur valley. Further down again was ancient Mari, a city that certainly had contacts with the Mediterranean world.

Below Mari the Euphrates flows through harshly barren land, with the Syrian desert to the west and the steppe of the Al-Jazira to the east. Here the valley was only cultivable in a chain of river oases such as the modern Ana. Today Al-Jazira is still a land of nomads, the Shammar Arabs pitching their black, goat-hair tents among its wastes.

It is at Ana that date palms become abundant, while olives disappear—where in fact the Syrian type of climate that permits rain cultivation gives way to the Mesopotamian climate, with so little rainfall that crops must depend on irrigation. At Hit, a hundred miles north-west of Baghdad and 550 miles from the Persian Gulf, the Euphrates leaves the rock-cut middle reaches of its valley, where it had flowed above a stony subsoil, and enters the true alluvial plain. Round Hit are large deposits of the bitumen so much used by ancient builders.

The corresponding middle reaches of the Tigris, from the Taurus mountains in the north to the Hamrin hills in the south, formed the land of Assyria. Most of the fertile country lay to the east of the river between it and the great Zagros range, but the narrow strip to the west widened at Mosul—or ancient Nineveh. While the Euphrates receives no major tributary after the Khabur, the Tigris is fed by four very considerable rivers rising in the Zagros range—the Great and Little Zab, the Adhain and the Diyala—as well as lesser ones even further south. These tributaries, particularly the Diyala, made links with Iran that were being used by traders from prehistoric times.

At various periods both in prehistoric and historic Mesopotamia there was a clear cultural break between north and south. From the Great Zab down to Tikrit the Tigris flowed through desert lands, corresponding to the Mari to Hit stretch on the Euphrates. This desert belt across the valley, although of course penetrated by the rivers themselves, served as a partial barrier, or at least a filter between the fertile and densely populated alluvial plain that immediately adjoined it to the south-east and the middle valley. It also served as a homeland and strategic base for nomadic infiltrators and invaders.

When the Twin Rivers reach this plain at Hit and Tikrit they are on a convergent course, but from the region of Baghdad they straighten out to run roughly parallel for about a hundred miles, before diverging once more. This strip of country where the Tigris and Euphrates approach to within thirty miles of one another was known after about 2400 B.C. as Akkad. Here powerful cities were to grow, for it was a natural area for cross traffic and also a strategic point for the control of both northern and southern Mesopotamia.

The southernmost part of the alluvial plain where the rivers enclose a wide oval of territory was Sumeria proper, the setting of the very first cities. Three of the most ancient were in the extreme south, Uruk just within the oval and Ur and Eridu to the south of the Euphrates. In this region the Euphrates splits into several branches, and owing to the slightness of the fall (only 100 feet from Baghdad), both rivers have been inclined to shift their courses and are subject to annual floods. In ancient times the whole of the alluvial plain was elaborately irrigated, the building of major canals being the pride of powerful kings. Irrigation, enabling cultivators to make full use of the wonderful fertility of the soil, has had two climaxes, the first under the great dynasties of Babylon, the second under the Abbasid caliphs of the early Middle Ages. It was broken by the irruption of the Mongols in A.D. 1258—a disaster which can also be said finally to have shattered a social structure that had persisted since the Sumerians.

In their lowest reaches the rivers are involved with wide areas of marsh and lakes. United at last after so long a journey side by side, the Twin Rivers flow into the Persian Gulf as the Shatt-al-Arab. It has been thought that in ancient times the head of the Gulf reached much further inland, approaching Ur and the other southern cities, but this is now very much in doubt. Whatever the relation between land and water at that time, it seems certain that the marshlands were already inhabited by peoples living in much the same way as the modern Marsh Arabs.

The geographical picture cannot be left with the Twin Rivers brought at last to the sea. To the north Sumeria merged without break into the coastal plain below the Zagros range—that province of Iran called Khuzistan, the ancient Susiana or Elam. From the first, Sumerian culture profoundly affected it, and although Elam lagged behind we shall find it developing into a powerful enemy of Mesopotamia.

Throughout the greater part of their length the Tigris and Euphrates are swift and sometimes turbulent rivers. From their vast catchment area in the northern and eastern mountains, melting snow and spring rains sent a huge volume of water, brown with silt, down their upper reaches, to flood and shed its burden when it reached the plain. Violent floods could also be caused by spring tides and gales in the Gulf, or by landslides temporarily damming the narrow defiles in the Zab and Khabur valleys. The Euphrates could spend some of its force in the Syrian desert, but the Tigris, with its straight descent, tended to be swifter and more dangerous. A cloudburst in the northern mountains could raise it twenty feet in a few hours.

By their nature, then, the Twin Rivers were far from ideal for water transport. The journey upstream was always a struggle, and traffic up the valley was probably dominated by land routes along the river banks. Downstream transport of such heavy goods as timber, stone and copper ores was, as we shall see, of great importance. Although today sailing vessels ply the lower Tigris and Euphrates, and steamers and barges use the Tigris from Basra to Baghdad, traffic in the upper valley is still mainly downstream by raft.

The annual flooding of the Euphrates takes place erratically between April and May, that of the Tigris about a month earlier. The waters begin to recede in June. While men still lived in lightly built villages, violent floods and shifts of course were of no great significance, but once they had created cities, the Twin Rivers were tyrannical adversaries, able to destroy the work of generations in city and irrigated fields alike. Moreover, as the time of the floods meant that the agricultural season had to continue through the summer months, when the rivers were back within their banks, the plain dwellers had to labour to conserve water for irrigation in reservoirs, canals and ditches. In spring they had to struggle to protect themselves against excess of water, in summer to conserve it.

As for the climate of Mesopotamia, most of its features are abominable to man. It is simply divided between a fiercely hot summer and a winter that is cold and even frosty. It is true that in the mid-valley, in the land that was to be Assyria, height, the proximity of the mountains and a winter rainfall produce a fair spring with cultivable fields, natural pasture and carpets of wild flowers. But after May even these uplands are burnt brown. In the south the sun strikes the vast, monotonous plain with seemingly vindictive ferocity, winds pick up the dry soil and choke men and all their works with dust, while rain is so scanty and irregular that farming has always been impossible without irrigation.

Anyone travelling in ancient Sumeria today and experiencing these hateful conditions—not greatly changed since the fourth millennium —must wonder with a kind of dismay at the thought that this was where high civilization began. It is certainly proof of the importance of an abundant food supply that this land and not one more congenial to the spirit of man should have played this leading role in our history.

The difficulty and frequent insecurity of the environment seems to have affected the 'form' of Mesopotamian civilization to its psychological roots. The ceaseless, often frustrated, efforts to maintain the irrigation system on which each town, and later city, depended could help to inspire the vision of man as a slave of higher powers. The uncertainty and occasional violence of the necessary flood, and shifts in river beds, could ruin a city in a few days, and have helped to arouse the sense of insecurity, the prevailing awareness of threat from careless gods, so characteristic of the Sumerians and those who inherited the colour of their thought.

These direct effects of nature upon the valley dwellers were only enhanced by threats from their fellow men. Their valley was open to attack by mountain men from the north, still more by nomads from the deserts to the south and west. So began a long and now familiar process: the rough, virile, boldly led barbarians, or 'have-nots', emerging from their particular wilderness to seize what they could not create, the delicious fruits of civilization. That they in turn might settle, weaken, but learn to create did not lessen the apprehension, the knowledge of ceaseless enmity, in the minds of the civilized.

In this account of the valley of the Twin Rivers, proper names have been used from time to time without clear definition. As both geographical and historical complexity make nomenclature difficult, it will be as well to adopt fixed conventions. When the Greeks devised the name of Mesopotamia they had a more limited territory in view, but nowadays it can be applied to all the country dominated by the Tigris and Euphrates—and therefore including some fringes of Syria, Turkey and Iran as well as the whole of Iraq. The upland area between the great ranges and the alluvial lands will be called the mid-valley, unless Assyria is being more precisely intended. The real complexity begins in the south. The great stretch of alluvial lands can first be called Sumeria, then (after Sargon) Sumer and Akkad, and finally Babylonia. Unless the particular historical context makes these names appropriate it will be referred to as the Plain.

THE NILE VALLEY

THE GEOGRAPHICAL SETTING OF ANCIENT EGYPTIAN CIVILIZATION IS simple in comparison with the complexities of the Tigris and Euphrates. By far the greater part of the Nile's immense length lay beyond the southern frontiers of the pharaonic kingdom. The upper part of the river system has to be considered only as the source of the life-giving waters and their silty flood.

The White Nile is fed from the central African lakes, emerging finally from Lake Albert, the last of this series of natural reservoirs, to pour down into the Sudan. Here live the cattle-herding Shilluk, Nuer and Dinka, three Nilotic peoples whose culture and social forms appear to preserve something of the archaic substratum of Bronze Age Egypt.

The Blue Nile has covered nearly a thousand miles since leaving Lake Tana 5800 feet up in the mountains of Abyssinia. It is usually assumed that it is the blue-grey silt brought down by the Blue Nile during the flood months from July to October that has fertilized the fields of Egypt through the millennia. Nevertheless, the mud of the steadier White Nile may also make an important contribution.

Below Khartoum, flowing through open stone desert, the united Nile soon crosses the first of the six 'cataracts' that disturb its course through Upper and Lower Nubia. These are low ridges of tough igneous rock that the river has not as yet quite worn down but flows over in broken rapids. As they were numbered by explorers pushing upstream, the First Cataract is at Aswan, the Sixth at the Sabaloka Gorge.

Between the Fourth and Third Cataracts stands Gebel Barkal, an historic point for this was the boundary of the Pharaohs' Egypt at its greatest extent in New Kingdom times. Far more imposing as a natural boundary, however, is Semna, above the Second Cataract, the frontier of the Middle Kingdom period. Here two rock masses (crowned by forts and temples) used to confront one another like lions, the Nile deep and violent pouring between their paws. Semna was the site of the oldest Nile dam, built by a Pharaoh in about 1800 B.C. From here to Aswan the river was always navigable and the Nubians were able to cultivate large stretches of fertile soil. All this part of the valley is now under the waters of Lake Nasser.

Near the Second Cataract and not far above the modern frontier between Sudan and Egypt stood Buhen, one of the massive mud-brick forts built by Pharaohs of the Middle Kingdom to control the Nubians. Here was the boundary between the domains of Kush and Wawat, corresponding roughly with Upper and Lower Nubia.

The original southern frontier of Egypt, maintained all through the centuries of the Old Kingdom, was at the First Cataract by Aswan. Here the river has forced its way through a ridge of red granite much quarried for obelisks and other monuments. It comes near to satisfying the ancient Egyptians' ideal of a substance that would endure for ever.

Below Aswan (formerly so much graced by the isles of Philae and Elephantine) the Nile still flows for some seventy miles between sandstone cliffs, and the people and their culture are still essentially Nubian. Then, at Edfu, the rock changes to a soluble limestone and the water runs in a well-defined channel. The valley, nearly six hundred miles to the Delta, is a trench from two to twelve miles across, its walls formed by limestone bluffs. Virtually all the people of Upper Egypt lived, and still live, on the winding ribbon of irrigated alluvial soil lining both banks of the river. The break between the outermost field and the desert is often so sharp that a donkey can straddle from the desert to the sown. As the soil is too precious to be lost under buildings, most settlements, ancient and modern, stand on the rocky verge.

Beyond the western bluff the expanse of the Libyan desert, with

its shifting lines of sandhills, is broken by a chain of oases fed
underground from the Nile waters. All these were fertile and made
small centres for trade and a meeting and mingling of peoples. The
large Fayum Depression with its lake lying below sea level can be
seen as the northernmost member of this chain, although it is much
closer to the Nile valley. It was always very fertile and was considered to have an ideal climate.

To the east of the Nile the Arabian desert is dominated by a range
of harsh mountains, with peaks of over 7000 feet, that divides the
river from the Red Sea. Sometimes in winter or spring, storms break
over these mountains and then the dry side valleys, or wadis, leading
down towards the Nile may carry sudden torrents. Afterwards the
desert will blossom for a while. In imagining conditions in ancient
Egypt it must be remembered that these wadis, and to a lesser extent
those to the west of the Nile, were far less barren than they have
since become. They supported trees and pasture and were the home
of wild asses, cattle and sheep, ibex, antelope and lions.

The ribbon of fertile land widens at Luxor and Karnak, the site of
Thebes, and at this point the Nile is already making an eastward
loop that brings it within about ninety miles of the Red Sea. Here,
from near Koptos, runs the Wadi Hammamat, an important route
between sea and river that was certainly used by Asiatic traders and
perhaps sometimes by invaders. Here also were famous quarries for
the greywacke much prized by sculptors and architects.

About 650 miles from its natural frontier at the First Cataract,
the valley of Upper Egypt gives way to the Delta, the huge fan of
alluvial soil that constitutes Lower Egypt. Because it was the best
place from which to command both together as the united Kingdom
of the Two Lands, a new capital, Memphis, was founded here, a
little to the south of modern Cairo. Across the river the stony floor
of the valley, now nearing its end, supports the heaviest buildings
in the world, the Giza pyramids. Just to the north of Cairo was the
holy city of Heliopolis, standing where the Wadi Tumilat reached
the Nile. This wadi, which runs north-east, parallel with the edge
of the Delta, made a route from Sinai that must often have been followed by Asiatic peoples drifting into Upper Egypt. The main land
route between Egypt and the Levant, however, was by the El-Auja
road across northern Sinai.

The deltaic Nile is now largely canalized into the two branches of

Rosetta and Damietta, but in the Bronze Age it reached the Mediterranean through seven main channels and five minor ones, and was traversed also by innumerable rivulets. Thus, while the river gave Upper Egypt a geographical unity, it tended to divide Lower Egypt into sections. There were, in fact, a dozen little principalities, each administered from its capital town or village.

The Delta was bordered on both sides by stretches of meadowland offering good pasture to flocks and herds. The best royal vineyards were in its western region, and the whole watery land was probably more given to meadows, gardens and vineyards than to cereal crops. Unfortunately little is known of its physical condition, as of its history, because the evidence has been buried below the vast deposits of silt brought down by the annual flood.

Although the coastlands of Lower Egypt catch some Mediterranean rainfall, it does not amount to more than eight inches in the year, and rapidly decreases inland. At Cairo it is less than two inches, while throughout the whole of Upper Egypt it is negligible. Unlike Mesopotamia, therefore, Egypt depended wholly on irrigation for her agriculture. On the other hand, the distances that the water had to be led were not nearly so great, and the systems were correspondingly less complex and less liable to collapse with the weakening of central government.

The Nile flood rose with extraordinary regularity. With a sowing season in the autumn, the Egyptians did not have to labour through the heat of summer to maintain the irrigation of their fields. Thus they did not have to confront the double-headed bugbear that always threatened the Mesopotamians. It was as though they lived within a vast and on the whole efficient hydraulic machine.

Moreover, the Egyptians could expect to live their lives in exceptionally regular and comprehensible surroundings. They could look across the river and see the limits of human habitation. With the easy two-way water transport provided by wind and current, they could know neighbouring communities and all that lay above and below them on the river. Every day the sun sailed across blue skies from desert cliff to desert cliff with nothing more to vary its passage than the presence or absence of a few freckles or wisps of cloud. The gods had given them the Nile; it was only the strangers, the foreigners, who had need of rain. And those strangers, at least in the formative early days, seemed far away and harmless. The wide deserts to east and west brought a sense of isolation and wholeness. Once Upper and Lower Egypt had been united, peace and security appeared to be, and for a long time were, complete.

The natural conditions of the Nile valley were dependable, and its people felt secure from foreign attack. The natural conditions of the Tigris-Euphrates valley were uncertain and difficult, and its people lived always with hostile neighbours. The Egyptians were confident in their relationship with nature and the gods, and their civilization exalted changelessness. The Mesopotamians' outlook tended to be anxious or fatalistic; they took a gloomy view of death and man's enslavement to the gods. These facts appear to reinforce one another in support of the view that the total environment deeply affected the psychology of peoples and hence the 'form' of their civilizations.

This judgement has sometimes, perhaps rashly, been extended to include artistic forms. It has been claimed that the box-like constructions that tend to dominate Egyptian art and architecture were inspired by the typically rectangular, containing form of the Nile valley itself. These rectangular constructions have then been contrasted with the conical forms often favoured in Mesopotamia— the creations of a once mountain people who still worshipped their gods on high peaks even when they had to build them in mud-brick.

THE INDUS VALLEY

VIEWED AS A WHOLE FROM ITS GLACIAL SOURCE TO STEAMING DELTA, the Indus can certainly claim to be the most spectacular of the three historic rivers with which we are concerned. It rises at an altitude of no less than 17,000 feet, below the clustering Kailas peaks of Tibet. Like the Euphrates, it sets off in a direction quite different from that of its lower valley. For 650 miles it flows northwest through some of the most awe-inspiring mountain scenery in the world. It next breaches the Himalayas in a series of great gorges, is joined by the Kabul descending from Afghanistan, and reaches the plain at Attock. The Indus is now well within Pakistan, and remains within it for the rest of its journey.

Once on the plain, the river begins to lose its velocity and wanders with braided channels through the Thar desert before receiving its last major tributaries. These are the Five Rivers of the Punjab. In former times another river, the Ghaggar, ran to the south of the

Sutlej. Its dry bed can be traced for a long distance before it dies out in the Bahawalpur deserts.

This river system of the Punjab is of great significance for the Indus civilization. Harappa, the northern capital, was on the Ravi, while a number of settlements, including some sizeable towns, stood by the Ghaggar and immediately to the south of it in Bahawalpur. This area, in fact, formed that northern part of the 'kingdom' which was centered on Harappa. In some respects it can be likened to the place of Assyria within the Tigris-Euphrates system.

The Indus itself not only has no site of the Indus civilization down to its junction with the Panjnad, but none for the next two hundred miles where it runs by the Thar, or Indian, desert. There is, in fact, a wide sterile gap between the northern Punjab territories of the Indus civilization centred on Harappa, and the southern Sind territories centred on Mohenjo-daro.

Mohenjo-daro stands towards the northern limits of these southern territories, near Sikkur. It is just 350 miles from Harappa. Over a dozen lesser settlements are known, most of them below Mohenjo-daro on the western bank of the river.

The delta, which covers some three thousand square miles, is still a maze of shifting channels, lagoons and mangrove swamps. At this point, where the many little mouths empty into the Arabian sea, the Indus has lost about one half of its volume through evaporation and has covered two thousand miles.

For a long time after the original discovery of the Indus civilization, it was thought to have been confined to the Indus valley system. More recently it has been discovered that Indus settlers pushed right down the coast as far as the east side of the Gulf of Cambay, giving them command of eight hundred miles of coastline. Even more unexpectedly, it has also been found that they crossed the watershed from the Indus system into that of the Jumna. This bold eastward movement is as yet represented by a single site lying about thirty miles north of Delhi. More may well come to light.

Although there is an appreciable rainfall on the Punjab plain, its present prosperity as a great corn-growing area has been brought about by irrigation. As for the alluvial lands of Sind, they are now quite arid and no crops could be raised without river water. At present agriculture is made possible only by elaborate mechanized barrages and canals, unirrigated land producing no more than poor pasture and scrub.

Because these present conditions made it seem incredible that huge cities could have been supported without a more favourable climate, until recently it was claimed that rainfall must have been much greater in the Bronze Age, the subsequent change having been caused by an eastward shift of the south-west monsoon. A number of secondary arguments were accepted as a further proof of a wetter climate. The use of fired rather than sun-dried mud-bricks for building the Indus cities seemed to suggest a need to resist rain, while the drainage system of the cities was thought to have been intended to carry off storm water. The huge number of fired, or burnt, bricks was seen to demand far more fuel than could be provided by the present tamarisk and scrub, while the animals living in the valley also indicated a far more abundant vegetation. (There were rhinoceros and tiger, elephant, water buffalo and crocodile, while smaller animals included bear, monkey, squirrel, wolf and many kinds of deer.)

Of late, however, scientific opinion has swung against the idea of any considerable climatic change. It is claimed instead that the nature of the Indus alluvium would have made it possible for the edges of the flood plain to support woodland and grasses that would have provided a suitable home for the animals as well as fuel for the brick kilns. This native vegetation and the additional soil fertility it must have brought were destroyed not by a loss of rainfall but by tree-felling and the grazing of goats and sheep. As for the drains, they were designed only for domestic purposes.

It is now accepted, then, that the Bronze Age agriculture of the Indus valley depended upon irrigation and the annual silt-bearing floods. These, like their counterparts in Mesopotamia and Egypt, are caused by the melting of the snows and glaciers. They are at their height in March, the waters receding to their lowest in September. It seems that the extent of the flood was very erratic, more like that of the Tigris and Euphrates than the steady pulse of the Nile. Indus cities and towns were protected against them by banks and platforms but were still often inundated. They were also probably often ruined by changes in the river's course—another anxiety that their people shared with the citizens of the Sumerian plain.

We know too little of the Indus civilization to be able to make any profound judgement of the effect of the natural environment upon its 'form'. We can only say that if the Indus environment shared some characteristics with that of the Tigris-Euphrates, they did not produce very similar results. It might be hazarded that if it, too, caused stress, the dangers and anxieties were countered in a different way—by an authoritarianism as uniform as it was uninventive. If at first the state had the drive that can come from totalitarianism, it fell into inertia. It does not seem surprising that the third high civilization of the world was destroyed when the other two, already its elders, had nearly another millennium of life before them.

MESOPOTAMIA

OF THESE THREE RIVER SYSTEMS THAT OFFERED THE POSSIBILITIES FOR the growth of high civilization, the Nile valley was certainly the most friendly for human life. Why, then, did this growth, with all its exhilarating promise for the future, in fact begin on the dismal and hostile plains of the Tigris-Euphrates? For once the answer is relatively simple and certain. It was due to the historical geography of the end of the late Neolithic age.

That age had ended with village communities thriving on all the uplands enclosing the valley of the Twin Rivers from the north-west round to the south-east. In Syria, in northern and eastern Iraq by way of the Elburz and Zagros mountains to Elam and the Iranian plateau, the progressive agriculture and stock breeding of thousands of these villages were leading to a continuous increase in population. Although each community could provide itself with all the essentials of life and was in that sense self-supporting and isolated, they were in fact culturally and therefore presumably socially interrelated over wide areas—represented by the 'cultures' of the archaeologists.

In this way population pressure must have given a stimulus to improved ways of doing things on a practical level. It also meant larger labour forces ready to carry out any of the odder promptings of the human mind. There must at the same time have been some pooling of ideas among the abler individuals, occasional concentrations of exceptional energy and ability. If, as we know, exquisite and exactly particular ways of painting decorative designs on pottery could spread and be adopted from village to village over hundreds of miles, it is impossible to doubt that other forms of mental intercourse were equally active. Such communication would have speeded the spread of a wider range of domestic animals, which had come to include goats, sheep, cattle and dogs, and of cultivated plants, which now included lentils, peas, vetch and flax and possibly also grapes, olives and other fruits.

While many of these advances helped to feed the ever-growing numbers, an even more important means of meeting the problem was by the settlement of new territories. One obvious and inviting area was the upper valley of the Tigris and Euphrates down to about the Diyala river. As we have seen, this was an area where rain agriculture was possible. By the mid-sixth millennium there were large and flourishing settlements throughout this agreeable region. Further south, however, the whole of the lower valley was still empty except, perhaps, for a few marsh dwellers and a scatter of nomads. Much of the southernmost part of the country near the head of the Persian Gulf was too marshy for immediate settlement, but the reason why the future cradle of civilization remained empty for many centuries after the upper valley was being cultivated was simply the lack of rain. The whole Plain was far too arid for crops to be grown without irrigation. The need for more fields must have been urgent, and experiments may have shown that with water the soil was amazingly fertile. By about 5000 B.C. farmers were beginning to move down to build simple dykes and canals and so at last to bring into food production the soil that Pliny was to describe as 'the most fruitful land of all those in the Orient'.

It is reasonably certain that most of these pioneer irrigators came from the hills to the north and east—from Elam and the fringes of the Iranian plateau. It might be thought that this would mean a change of environment of intolerable violence, but at that date southern Iran was less arid than it has since become, and some of its valleys had marshy conditions not altogether unlike those that the immigrant encountered between the Tigris and Euphrates.

At much the same time as the northern hill folk were beginning their struggle to drain and solidify the wet lands and lead water to the dry lands, smaller numbers of emigrants may have drifted down from the middle valley, making a minor, but still recognizable, contribution to the cultures that were to develop in the new country. From the very first, then, it seems that this country knew the mixture of peoples and traditions that was to remain one of its characteristics.

However modest the first attempts at irrigation may have been, it is very probable that exodus from Persia was to some extent planned and carried out by groups of settlers under their own leaders. Many settlements were made on sites so well chosen that they remained to grow into the cities of historical times. We can imagine the immigrants coming down from the hills by slow stages, driving their flocks and herds, possibly with donkeys loaded with possessions and with grain that had to serve both for food by the way and seed for the crops of the hoped-for, if not promised, land. If they came in anything of the frontier spirit of the American pioneers, they were at least as abundantly rewarded.

The cereals that they brought from their native uplands did prodigiously well in the rich silt and heat of the valley. The barley in particular appears to have mutated from its original two-row form to produce a six-row variety of far higher yield. In time this new gift of the gods was to be adopted throughout the ancient world.

That grain had been introduced from the northern mountains was never forgotten. Its true history became incorporated in Sumerian myth and written down thousands of years later. The story tells how the supreme sky-god Anu brought down wheat, barley and hemp from his own heavenly domain onto the earth. Then Enlil, his son, lord of storm and therefore ruler of the air, stored it up in the hills, 'barring the mountains as with a door'. At last Ninazu, a god of the underworld, and Ninmada, goddess of the earth, willed that the seed should be given to the people of the valley. Their decree was to allow 'Sumer, the land that knows no grain, [to] come to know grain.' It was in this fashion that the founders of civilization recorded the vital first steps of their forebears and left the story for us to discover.

Another tradition that may be no less reliable was that the date palm, a valuable new crop which the settlers soon learnt to exploit to the full, had come originally from Dilmun—the island of Bahrein in the Persian Gulf. Apart from the addition of dates, and the loss of the olive, which could not grow in so arid a climate, the domestic animals and cultivated plants were those they had raised in their homeland. The Twin Rivers and the Gulf, and in time the irrigation channels, increased their protein supply with an abundance of fish. Fishermen were recognized as an important class in the population.

The whole of the Plain came to be settled, which means also irrigated, during the fifth and fourth millennia. We do not know

how dense the population was, nor how large the individual settlements. Many people lived in reed huts not unlike those still woven
by the Marsh Arabs of southern Iraq. Other huts were of compacted
mud or of sun-baked mud-brick, and in time these were improved
into more regular houses. In Elam and Persia copper had been in
use, but here there was none, nor was there sufficient social organization to import it. Ingenuity had to be used instead. These people
had good kilns to fire their fine and elegantly decorated domestic
vessels, and they were, therefore, able to fashion choppers and
sickles of clay and fire them at a high enough temperature almost
to vitrify them and give a fair cutting edge. With implements so
cheap in terms of labour, it did not matter if they smashed as easily
as they were made.

The size of the main prehistoric settlements is not known because many have probably been buried below alluvial silt, while
a number of others lie at the base of massive *tells* formed by the
accumulations of later city life. Probably they grew quite large
but remained essentially rural communities based on kinship. On
the other hand, from the earliest days the need to construct and
maintain an irrigation system must have demanded more organization and advance planning than had been needed for rain agriculture. As numbers grew and the area to be cultivated extended
further and further from the rivers, a central authority must presumably have been accepted. To judge from what was to follow
but from nothing else, there may well have been a headman for
each community with sufficient power to have some of the ceremonial and material endowments normally granted to men of
authority. That authority may already have been tempered and
supported by a council of elders, the beginning of the assembly
that existed under the early Sumerian kings.

This is no more than guesswork based on backward projection.
Yet this process is at least partially justified by the undoubted continuity that existed beween prehistoric villagers or townsmen and
historic citizens. This can be seen most clearly in their religious
worship and its setting. The most important building in each prehistoric settlement was a temple. It seems often to have stood on the
same site that was to be occupied by the great buildings of later
times and may have been dedicated to the same, or a similar, divinity.

Among the prehistoric settlements that grew into royal or sacred cities—and the fact that they did so is, of course, evidence for some sort of continuity—were Eridu, Ur, Uruk, Nippur and Girsu. Of these Eridu gives the surest proof of a continuance of worship from the first peopling of the Plain through historic times. Eridu, the home of Enki, god of wisdom and sweet waters, was the southernmost of all the important Sumerian cities. It lay some twenty-five miles south-west of Ur.

The prehistoric temple builders chose the site that was later to be occupied by the great Abzu, Enki's house of the abyss or watery deep. Here they raised a series of temples, each standing above the foundation of its predecessor. At first they were content with modest, single-roomed buildings. Yet already they had devised the oblong plan with the god's altar at one end and the offering table near the other that was to be the basis of Sumerian religious architecture.

By about 4000 B.C. the Eridu architects had begun to develop almost all the main features of that tradition. It seems that having initiated the idea that their god should be nobly housed, an idea that may well have gone with seeing him for the first time in magnified human form, they were set on a course for increasing and elaborating it with all the energy and ingenuity that men have always shown once the first step has been taken and the means are there.

The temple now measured as much as eighty by twenty feet, and its mud-brick walls were strengthened by a running series of buttresses that were to produce the pilastered effects of later times. The building interior was now divided into a central *cella* with altar and table, and a pair of side chambers. Even more significantly it was raised on a substantial platform—the first stage towards the lofty ziggurat.

In one of this later series of prehistoric temples the offering table was caked with a six-inch layer of fish bones. The historic Enki was often to be portrayed with fish swimming in streams of water flowing from his shoulders, and it was said of him (in characteristic Sumerian mood):

> When Enki rose, the fish rose and adored him.
> He stood a marvel unto the Apsu. . . .
> To the sea it seemed that awe was upon him,
> To the Great River it seemed that terror hovered about him
> While the south wind stirred the Euphrates to its depths.

Enki, God of Wisdom; from an Akkadian seal.

It is an irresistible conclusion that if Enki was not worshipped in prehistoric Eridu by name, then his predecessor already possessed his attributes and character.

The temple building itself has obvious social implications. Its size and its complex, presumably liturgical plan, the dominance secured by raising it above the houses of the people, seem to announce higher ambitions than are to be expected of an ordinary village community. Those who directed its construction and served in it, whether or not they as yet represented a distinct class of priests and rulers, had power to command considerable labour and material resources. Although knowledge of these prehistoric centres of population is fragmentary, it looks as though by the fourth millennium all was ready for the 'take-off' of civilization. The power that was to drive it was man's religious obsession.

The take-off was, in fact, somewhat delayed. During the middle period of the fourth millennium there was probably a steady increase in population and some development in housing and technical skills. But it was not until the last two centuries of the millennium that there was a sudden spurt and Sumerian civilization rose and its true form took wing.

Was this extraordinary rush of achievement, one of the great moments of history, given impetus by the arrival of a new people in the valley? The archaeological evidence suggests that the pre-historic culture had developed consistently, and that villages grew into towns and cities without any sharp break. On the other hand there were changes in the last phases—conspicuous only in that sensitive plant of the archaeologist: pottery. The elegant painted pottery that had been manufactured in the valley since its settle-ment was replaced by plain wares, turned out in a wide range of useful forms. The main consensus is that the Sumerians were in fact newcomers, and that they arrived not later than 3500 B.C. Some authorities believe that they came as conquering nomad shepherds establishing themselves at once as a ruling élite; others think instead that, like their predecessors in the valley, they were ordinary farmers. Certainly they settled in the southern part of the Plain round the head of the Gulf, later spreading to dominate the whole of the lower valley but never extending further north.

The origins of this most gifted people remain obscure. It seems sure enough that, like the prehistoric folk, they moved down from the eastern or northern uplands of Persia or Elam. As we shall see, their agglutinative language is without known relatives. The vast majority of the early farming peoples were of the slight, neatly featured stock usually referred to as Mediterranean, and there is nothing to show that the Sumerians were markedly different from them. Their sculpture, though too highly stylized to be altogether reliable, suggests that they were round-headed, with large noses slightly convex in profile, and with well-shaped lips of medium breadth. We know from their own words (when they had invented a way to write them down) that they called themselves the black-headed people.

In early historic times there were Semites in Sumeria in sufficient numbers to thrust loan words into the language. It is not known, however, how long they had been there or whether they had moved down the valley or come more directly from Arabia.

The dramatic advance towards civilization of the late fourth millennium was led in the name of the gods and through religiously inspired organization. It has already been shown how difficult it is to know just what this came to mean in the minds of those involved —from highest to lowest. There is no mistaking the material facts. The first steps to civilization were made visible in large-scale, truly monumental architecture, fine representational sculpture, the acceptance of powerful leaders and the invention of writing. The architecture was devoted to temple buildings—the leaders were greatly concerned with religious ceremonial and were certainly by now well on the way to divinely inspired kingship; the sculpture was exclusively religious, often portraying these leaders or the gods themselves; and writing was invented solely to keep account of the wealth of temples that evidently already dominated the economic life of the whole land.

This 'Protoliterate' period that saw civilization beginning to shed its light on this one very small patch of the earth's surface was a prosperous one. Life was still based on the cultivation of barley and wheat in irrigated fields. The demands of the gods and their earthly representatives and the central direction they provided must have made it more productive. The workers in the fields were equipped with ploughs, sleds and carts. Barley was probably already, as it was to remain, the basis for exchange.

Yet cattle, and perhaps sheep even more, were evidently of great significance. They were often shown in relief sculpture that decorated temple walls, and on the cylinder seals which now began to be used as marks of ownership. In the earliest script there were no fewer than thirty-one characters for sheep and goats, all derived from the sign for sheep. As soon as we can read about them, too, rulers may be referred to as 'good shepherds'. This preoccupation with flocks in the minds of the Sumerians could be used to support the view that they were once a pastoral people.

Pigs were kept and often served as scavengers. Although pork was to be taboo as food for the gods, and probably (as in Egypt) for priests and other exalted persons, it may well have been the meat most often available to the poor.

While this ancient life of the fields and pastures, and of the fresh and sea waters, went on much as before, the society that it supported was changing drastically. The villages or country towns of late prehistoric times had grown into cities. Sometimes it seems groups of villages coalesced—just as they were to do so often in the future history of cities: typically in Rome and in London.

Yet the countryside and its cultivators were not cut off from the city dwellers after the fashion of industrial societies. On the contrary, many workers woke in the cramped little rooms of houses in the city and walked or trotted on donkey-back through the streets on the way to field and byre. Others continued to live in villages, but the villages themselves fell within the orbit of the city. The inhabitants must often have gone to town with produce for market or temple store, to visit relatives, to join the throng bringing offerings to the gods, and above all to involve themselves in the festivals and processions that were now such an exciting and necessary part of life.

All these food-producers had in fact now become true peasants in the sense that their labour supported urban life and the social pyramid that went with it. Many artisans, and even minor officials or other superior persons, may not only have owned fields (which they certainly did) but themselves worked in them. In so far as they did so they were peasants. In the land of Sumer the independent, self-sufficient communal village was a thing of the past.

There were now very many cities of the Plain, but how many is uncertain. Probably all those that are known to have been flourishing in the fully historical time of the second half of the third millennium were already in existence. Beginning in the south, which in fact led the way with Uruk as greatest among them, these cities were Eridu, Ur, Uruk, Badtibira, Lagash, Nina, Girsu, Umma and Nippur. A more northerly trio were Kish, Sippar and Akshak.

Each city must already have been the focus of the territory, with its contributory villages, that was to emerge as the true city-state. No doubt the boundaries were ill-defined and beginning to cause the disputes that were to provoke so much litigation and warfare in time to come.

The cities themselves were truly urban in the sense that they were centres of economic production and commerce. Artisans occupied many of the mud-brick houses that lined the narrow alleys and the crooked thoroughfares, crowded organic growths full of energy and devoid of plan. Among them were many stone masons, mainly kept busy shaping blocks and cones for the temples. After the mediaeval fashion we should probably associate with them the artist-craftsmen who carved still rather simple figures in the round, reliefs, and ornamental stone vessels. Also there were seal-cutters, not many of them as yet, who were beginning to perfect the exquisite art of miniature sculpture in reverse, the intaglio work that was to spread and flourish for thousands of years. Another large group were the brickmakers, who turned out from their moulds vast quantities of mud-bricks (and some to be fired) for the building and incessant repair of the temples. They also produced the fired clay cones needed for the temple mosaics. The potters had, of course, a long-established craft that was now becoming more commercialized. The product was plain, utilitarian, bulk-produced stuff. Although we know nothing of them, presumably there must have been some specialist weavers of textiles—both in linen and wool. However, perhaps most spinning and weaving for ordinary domestic use was done at home. Spinning was also done by girl slaves in the temples.

Pride of place among all craftsmen must surely have gone to the metal workers, who by this time were turning out not only tools and weapons but also substantial and well proportioned copper vessels, toilet articles, and animal figures. It is true that the composition of bronze was not understood, and the small amount of tin sometimes present was an accidental element in mixed ores. Nevertheless the whole process of producing metal involved rare and exotic materials, and a range of esoteric knowledge and special skills that must have given smiths an exalted and probably mystery-laden reputation among their fellow citizens.

When to these leading crafts are added those of the leather-workers, basket-makers, and carpenters, it is plain that a stratified and subdivided urban society had come into being during Protoliterate times. Whether or not these craftsmen might work their own fields, or at least be called upon to turn out to help the farmers at sowing time or harvest, their skills were professional and their goods intended for society at large and not for their own families. It is not known if already each group of craftsmen lived and worked in its own section of the city, but it seems probable that they did. Such arrangements are practical and convenient, and also satisfying to civilized man's love of forming inturned groups within larger social classes. Uruk and her sister cities probably had quarters that stank of tannery or retting flax, and others sweet with freshly cut cedar wood. There must have been alleys that knew the glare of the smiths' furnaces and the sound of their hammers, or the blowing dust and ceaseless tap-tap of the masons.

Several of these crafts depended on the existence of another class of specialists—the merchants and dealers who imported and supplied the raw materials. Of these the most important were copper, wood and stone. The trickle of foreign trade of prehistoric times had now become an essential flow. However, the lines which it followed are not certainly known for this time and can only be inferred from what was to be recorded later.*

The same is true of details of temple life and administration, yet these oldest cities cannot be left without some mention of the temples that dominated them and whose servants were already occupied by the greatest achievement of the time—the invention of writing.

In general they were developed from the plan already established at Eridu, but they were very much larger and might be complicated by a T-shaped central nave and additional cult chambers. Temples of this type were built as far north as Khafajah in the Diyala valley and Brak on the Khabur, striking proof of the extent of Sumerian influence even in Protoliterate times.

These pioneers of the architectural profession showed sure instinct for heightening the external effectiveness of the houses of the gods. The facades were often composed of flat buttresses or pilasters alternating with recesses that must have made bold stripes of light and shade in the glare of the Mesopotamian sun. An extraordinary technique for the decoration of walls and columns was popular among Sumerian builders but was used also at Brak. Tens of thousands of conical nails of burnt-brick (or more rarely of stone), their heads coloured red, black or buff, were driven into a matrix of plaster to make simple geometrical patterns—lozenges, triangles, zig-zags. This curious variety of mosaic not only had a bold polychrome effect but also served as a waterproof skin protecting the mass of mud-brick behind.

The finest and most numerous examples of temple architecture have been found at Uruk, on the site of the later Eanna of the city's patron goddess, Inanna. The complex of buildings referred to as the Pillar Temple included a platform and courtyard faced with cone mosaic leading to a raised portico with eight massive round columns in two rows and corresponding half-columns on the adjacent walls. These giants, nearly six feet in diameter and constructed of fired segmental brick encased in cone mosaic, are the earliest-known example of columnar architecture on a monumental scale.

One of the flanking temples, standing on a platform of limestone that had to be transported over thirty miles, measured 248 by 96 feet. When, as often happened, another temple was later built over it

* See Part IV.

these dimensions were extended to 275 by 176 feet. This was architecture on a very different scale from that of prehistoric Eridu.

On another site within the city a temple belonging to the supreme deity, Anu, had white-washed walls and was raised on a forty-foot-high pilastered platform—or elementary ziggurat. The expenditure of labour, raw materials, technical and administrative skill and brilliant new invention involved in this whole complex of sacred buildings was quite prodigious. True that Uruk was the greatest of cities in these Protoliterate days, but all the rest made comparably great efforts. The Sumerians certainly saw to it that men were the slaves of the gods.

It seems that at this early period in each of the emergent city-states there was an assembly consisting of all adult free males and a body of elders. How far these institutions can be said to represent actual political power vested in the citizens, and therefore a form of democracy, will be discussed later.* Whatever answer is given to this very difficult question, it is certain that assembly and elders had no monopoly of power even in these early days. Far from it. Scenes depicted on cylinder seals show that each city must have had its man of authority, a figure whose dignity and importance is manifest both in his leaderly functions and in the magnified stature given him by the artists.

This great man is usually bearded, with long hair held by a prominent head band and fastened in a chignon at the back. He most often wears a full skirt bearing a reticulated design. On relief carvings as well as seals, he can be seen leading religious processions to the goddess or her priestesses, or offering branches (of the tree of life?) to vigorously nibbling goats. Already, too, he is shown hunting lions (with both spear and bow), beginning an association of rulers with the king of beasts that continues yet.

How far this dominating figure from Protoliterate art can be identified with the Sumerian *en* and *lugal* is doubtful. Yet it seems very likely that these offices had already been instituted at this time. The title *lugal* appears in one Protoliterate document from Uruk. Those who believe in the democratic government of the earliest cities are convinced that the *ensi* and *lugal* were originally elected to temporary office, the first to take quick decisions in times of public crisis, the second to lead the army in war. According to this view, in the innocence of a civic dawn, the citizens could not

* See Part IV.

know how strong were the hidden forces that would cause their chosen leaders gradually to combine their offices and make them hereditary, until they were ready to suppress the institutions of the people, or leave them with only a ghost of power.*

Frankfort wrote of the institution of assembly and elders, in which he was prepared to see real power vested, as follows:

It is well to recognize the extraordinary character of this urban form of political government. It represents in the highest degree the intensified self-consciousness and self-assertion which we recognize as distinctive of the Protoliterate period. It is a man-made institution overriding the natural and primordial division of societies in families and clans. It asserts that habitat, not kinship, determines one's affinities.

Here is a most successful evocation of the psychological transformation of becoming civilized that man was now experiencing for the first time. On the other hand, although family and clan organization must indeed have been primordial, the prehistoric people of the valley had long been developing the kind of rural society that has often produced institutions of the assembly and elders type combined with some form of chiefly leadership. It seems probable that the young cities developed their systems of government out of older village tradition, just as surely as in many places the cities themselves grew out of, and upon, the fabric of the villages.

Meanwhile, the temple chiefs and their underlings in southern Sumeria were making one of the greatest inventions in world history —a step beside which the first taken on the surface of the moon was unimportant. It is right to call the earliest writing an invention, for it is clear that the scribes were consciously seeking a practical system for setting down records. The fact that they were pushed into doing so is in itself a sufficient proof that the development of the temple state was already far advanced.

The lead may well have come from Uruk. Here the controllers of the temple estates found themselves being overwhelmed by the growing complexity and amount of their work. Year by year the quantities of grain, sesame seed, vegetables, dates, cattle large and small, preserved fish, wool, skins and the rest brought to the temple stores increased, as did the numbers of citizens bringing them. Who could remember in his head how much was stored or whether it would meet the need when the time came for its distribution?

* See Part IV.

If a rogue claimed to have brought in his dues, who could prove that he had not? Who could remember with certainty just how much sesame had been issued to the oil makers, barley to the brewers or wool to the spinners? How many sheep and goats did the god own at any one time? How much seed corn was needed for the common lands and how much for the ploughing oxen? What was needed for the grain allowance for the temple's own functionaries and how great were the total incomings to be set aside for offerings to the divine owner of all? How could the information be brought together for the future planning of sowings and yields? Past and future became a blur; the possibilities for cheating, thieving and disastrous forgetfulness were infinite. Something had to be done.

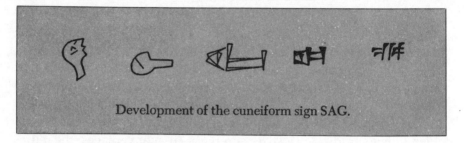

Development of the cuneiform sign SAG.

Perhaps it was an individual of genius who, towards the end of the fourth millennium, first thought of representing things and numbers by symbolic marks. If so, the idea soon spread. These pioneer scribes chose for their materials two of the most abundant: reeds and clayey mud. At first the reed stylus was used on the flattened lump of clay only to make standardized pictures of the things concerned, perhaps together with numeral signs and the impressions of the cylinder seals of the individuals concerned in the transaction. The most advanced attempts made during these birth throes of literacy were wage lists—signs representing individuals followed by an indication of daily pay in terms of bread and beer. Writing was invented in Sumeria solely for the administration of the temple economy.

It is significant that from the first, however, a kind of shorthand was used—that is to say the pictograms were not only standard but much conventionalized. For example, women were represented by the pubic triangle, oxen by a triangular face and V of horns. There was absolutely no connection here between writing and art or decoration. The aim was so practical and so well defined that progress towards it was bound to be rapid. Schools were established where ambitious young men could learn word-lists and all scribal skills. Within a few generations the crucial steps had been taken from signs representing *things* to signs representing *sounds*. By the end of the Protoliterate period the script that had begun in numbering sheep was almost ready to be used to set down the creations of the human imagination. It was to prove so flexible that it could be adapted to many languages, and so durable that it remained in use for three thousand years.

So with the opening of historic times in about 2800 B.C. the 'form' of Sumerian civilization and the way of life of its city-states had been established. Although, unlike the Egyptian, it was to suffer some major modifications, such as the change of language, it was astonishingly tenacious. Sumerian culture was strong enough to be transferred intact to another people, the Semites, to withstand the impact of invasions and conquests, to spread northward from the Plain into the vast territories of the mid-valley. The Babylon of Nebuchadnezzar still owed much to Eridu, Uruk, Ur and all the ancient cities of the Sumerians.

EGYPT

IN EGYPT THE PROGRESS FROM PREHISTORIC 'BARBARISM' TO CIVILIZAtion followed a rather different and simpler course. The fundamental distinction lay in the historical fact that innovation tended to begin in south-west Asia, later to be introduced to the Nile valley when already some way advanced. In this limited sense, Asia can be seen as the seed-bed of new ideas, Egypt the plot to receive the transplanted seedlings.

The Neolithic age had opened in Egypt only in about 5000 B.C. Thus the earliest farmers began to discover the rich possibilities of Nilotic soil only when in Mesopotamia the Plain was being settled by people with some two thousand years of farming behind them. The prehistoric Egyptians were still camping at the edge of the reed beds, or at best living in little villages of flimsy huts and depending to a considerable extent on hunting wild game, when Eridu was a substantial settlement of mud-brick houses with a modestly dignified temple lifting its roof above them.

They were of mixed stock, for people had drifted towards the

river from east and west during the millennia after the end of the
Ice Age when northern Africa became increasingly desiccated and
grass lands turned to desert. Predominantly they were of the Hamitic
branch of the Mediterranean stock: slightly built, long-headed,
brown-skinned and with black wavy hair, they may have represented
a blend of southern or Ethiopian Hamites with other western Hamitic stock from Libya. Their way of life has often been related to
that of the surviving tribes of the Upper Nile. Frankfort has written
of the several earlier prehistoric cultures:

Together they represent the African substratum of Pharaonic civilization,
the material counterpart of the affinities between ancient Egyptian and
modern Hamitic languages; of the physical resemblances between the
ancient Egyptians and the modern Hamites; and of the remarkable
similarities in mentality between these two groups which make it possible to understand ancient Egyptian customs and beliefs by reference
to modern Hamitic analogies.

During the first half of the fourth millennium, the Early Predynastic period, there was a gentle progress in skills and amenities.
Villages were rather more substantial; they included a chief's house
that was rectangular in plan and a little larger than the round huts
of the others, and a shrine for the local god graced by flags on poles
—a feature that was to continue and appear in grandiose style on
the great gateways of pharaonic temples.

The villagers also manifested what is sometimes too easily taken
for granted, man's normal urge towards making himself and his
possessions finer than nature or practical use demand. They wove
linen for garments, carved stone, shell and ivory for all manner of
personal ornaments, and softened their skins with castor oil. Already malachite was being imported and ground on ornamental
palettes for a green eye-shadow that was surely intended more for
allurement than for ophthalmic health.

The potters had left far behind the clumsy old baggy forms of the
fifth millennium and now showed an aesthetic sense equal to their
technical skill. The glossy red vessels, their tops so simply yet
effectively blackened by the prevention of oxidization, showed a
mastery of form—some simple, some of extraordinary sophistication.

Their fellow craftsmen, the cutters and polishers of stone vessels,
rivalled them in producing perfection of form and finish. These
men worked entirely with flint, and the hours that they must have

devoted to cutting and polishing a footed vase or slender flagon—perhaps during the undemanding months of the summer inundation—is something now almost unimaginable. They were the founder members of a craft that was to develop and flourish amazingly all through pharaonic times, and to stock the museum shelves of the twentieth century.

Equally prodigal of time and skill were the flint workers—knappers seems too rough a word for their exquisite productions. Some of these were certainly intended for display rather than use; the patience and minute physical control needed to detach the tiny spalls of the ripple flaking were extraordinary. Their craftsmanship was unrivalled except among the obsidian workers of Middle America.

These efforts to refine and enhance the human body, to give weeks or months to making fine things where hours or days would have done for practical purposes, found among a people still elementary in their domestic and social organization, speaks eloquently of man's innate love of exercising creative skill, as well as of his aesthetic sense, so mysteriously brought to him, it seems, from his own remote associations with the harmonies of the universe. It is well to remember these innate urges that pushed men and women to 'work' when they might have been idle. In the subsequent centuries, when thousands of men worked for the glorification of Pharaoh, it would evidently be wrong, as some moderns have done, to see all their labours as forced on them from above. Not only must they have been convinced that it was for their own well-being but also to some extent they were satisfying this love of making things. Maybe it was more wholly satisfying to sit quietly and use one's skill for the family or the village, but some of the same satisfaction must have come from temple and pyramid.

During the two centuries (3600–3400 B.C.) of what is known as the Middle Predynastic period the unambitious way of life of the little village communities, so characteristic of Neolithic cultures in their self-supporting economy, showed signs of more rapid change. Hitherto cultivation had been mainly of a shifting kind, with such irrigation as there was organized locally. Not that there was any shortage of food. The Predynastic villagers probably enjoyed easy lives. Wheat and barley yielded them a good return even with the simplest ways of cultivation. They had goats and sheep, cattle and geese—and in the north, pigs as well. To hunt and fish and go wild-fowling was a pleasure in itself as well as providing a variety in diet. In the summer months when cultivation was at a standstill and men could only wait for the floods to go down, food was still easily come by. Hippopotamus, wild boar, water birds—and fish as well—invaded their fields in large numbers.

Yet even in these conditions the increase in their numbers seems to have exceeded the food supply, and it may well have been in this progressive Middle Predynastic phase that concerted efforts were made to reclaim the marshes, to grow grain where before there had been sad, soughing reed beds and ever-changing watercourses.

Land reclamation and the extended irrigation system that went with it needed wider and stronger governmental power. The basis of political life in the Nile valley was still the tribal area centred on its large village or market town and ruled by its chieftain as son of the tribal deity. These areas were to become stabilized as the nomes of historical times, and their gods became the nome gods— many of them to win a place in the national pantheon.

Religious cult and political organization could no more be separated than warp and woof. As tribal territories were brought by conquest into larger groupings, myths developed to express the relationships of their gods. Moreover, while the chieftain was ruler and presumably source of justice for his people, his office still kept its darker meanings drawn from the depths of the prehistoric past. He remained the embodiment of the fertility and well-being of the tribe. The man who in some of his functions might have looked to us like a powerful mayor might perhaps have ended his term of office in ceremonial execution, his flesh and blood returned to the tribesmen's fields.

If such rites, memories of which still seem to haunt some of the Pyramid Texts, did indeed last into this age, they were already near their end. By about 3400 B.C. the land was stirring with the vigour of coming civilization. Culturally it was the Delta people of the north who were in the lead, probably because of their direct contact with the Levant. It is now of all times that the loss of evidence for developments in the Delta is most damaging. It accounts for many of the uncertainties that still blur our understanding of this lively age of transition.

Foreign trade was increasing significantly. Unlike the Tigris-Euphrates, the Nile valley had good building stone in abundance, but otherwise was almost as poor in raw materials. Copper was imported from Sinai in such quantities that it could be freely used not only for weapons but for tools for the common man. From the same quarter, too, came malachite and turquoise and stones for vessel-making. Timber was probably already being shipped from the forests of the Lebanon and Syria. Transport for these raw materials, however, remained archaic. Perhaps because of their easy dependence for internal trade on the highway of the Nile, together with the peculiar conditions of desert routes, the Egyptians did not early build carts, but depended upon pack animals and sledges.

Politically it has to be assumed that ambitious rulers were beginning to weld the tribal areas into larger blocks and then into principalities. This would seem to be the likely preparation for the emergence of the two well-organized monarchies of Upper and Lower Egypt that certainly existed for some generations before their union was to bring the historic Egypt of the dynasties into being. Although Frankfort denied it, there no longer seems much doubt that these kingdoms were strong political entities and struggled for supremacy. The Delta, with its cultural superiority, may have had the best of it for a time, but in the end it was the southern kings of the valley who proved to have greater political coherence and military might. By 3200 B.C. the northerners had been violently conquered and the first kings of the first dynasty had begun their rule over the Kingdom of the Two Lands.

In the period immediately before the unification, the northern capital seems to have been at Sais and the southern at Thinis or Abydos. Even if these and other leading cities were essentially market towns serving the needs of the rural areas, they must have been places of some size and dignity. The royal courts were well established, even in some ways luxurious. From beginnings in Late Predynastic times such essentials of civilization as monumental architecture and writing rushed into flower with the first dynasty.

Only a few centuries before, the Nile valley had been a land of tribal villages and rustic craftsmen. Now it was a civilized kingdom with one authority recognized from Aswan to the Mediterranean. The dramatic speed of this transformation has encouraged Egyptologists to look for something in the nature of a magic wand.

It has, in fact, been very generally agreed that the flowering of Egyptian civilization was speeded by a foreign stimulus that, whatever its immediate source, came ultimately from Mesopotamia. The means by which this stimulus was administered, however, remains very much a matter of dispute.

Many Egyptologists attribute it to a gradual infiltration of peoples and individuals from the Levant. Some would relate it more particularly to the development of sea-going ships and of trade with such Levantine ports as Byblos. Others, perhaps few in number but including such a high authority on the period as W. B. Emery, are convinced that Egypt fell to an invading horde entering either by the Wadi Hammamat or down the eastern side of the Delta by the Wadi Tumilat. They identify the invaders with a 'dynastic race' taller and with larger, rounder skulls than the native stock, whose remains have been found in certain Late Predynastic cemeteries— possibly also with an increase in the Semitic component in the Egyptian language thought to have occurred at about the same time. According to this theory, after a period of struggle the 'dynastic race' can be recognized in the 'Followers of Horus' who composed the royal houses and nobility of both Upper and Lower Egypt.

Whether by conquest, infiltration or trade, there can be no doubt that the temporarily more advanced culture of Mesopotamia did make itself felt in the Nile valley during the crucial centuries after 3400 B.C. On the other hand it is equally certain that Egypt was already in a progressive phase, open and ready to respond to new ideas and to adapt them through her own genius for her own needs.

From the first there was nothing inferior in the Egyptian performance. The debt to Asia is most apparent in the fact that several elements of civilization appear suddenly, without the gradual development that led up to them in Mesopotamia. The most important of these elements were architecture, writing and the use of cylinder seals.

In the first of these the pupils immediately surpassed the masters. Yet the abrupt appearance by the Nile of an advanced monumental architecture is one of the best of the cultural arguments for the arrival of a 'dynastic race'. While it is not impossible to imagine immigrants and traders inspiring the Egyptians to be dissatisfied with the poor old ways and to put up great buildings like those then rising between the Tigris and Euphrates, it is a great deal easier to attribute the change to powerful new overlords.

The new architecture was clearly based on designs and techniques that we have seen being perfected in Asia since the long-ago days of Enki's temple at Eridu. In place of wattle and daub, rushes or matting of the prehistoric village, it employed the Asiatic device of sun-dried mud-bricks turned out from standardized wooden moulds. These were even laid in the same way, usually with three rows of headers alternating with one of stretchers. In the composition of their facades the Egyptian architects from the first produced the subtle vertical emphasis of alternating pilasters and recesses which the Asians had developed out of simple buttressing.

While this monumental architecture was evidently introduced ready-made, the distinctive Egyptian social and religious values at once put it to different uses. In the Mesopotamian cities the first great buildings were city temples; here in Egypt they were royal tombs and royal fortresses.

The introduction of writing followed an altogether different course and one that could easily be accounted for without any appeal to invasion. It would be meaningless to say it was a new course, for everything in the way of communication between civilizations was then being experienced for the first time. It is, however, one for which it is quite difficult to find later analogies. The pioneer scribes of Asia had advanced from pictograms to wholly abstract cuneiform at the same time as they had advanced from representing things to representing sounds. The Egyptians came in at the phonetic stage, but evidently determined to ignore the script in which writing had been brought into being, and instead to devise one entirely their own. The style that they chose was not abstract and practical, but included a large proportion of lifelike pictorial forms of the kind dear to the Egyptians. It was, and remained, determinedly decorative.

It is hard to imagine just how this conversion came about. It appears astonishingly deliberate for the opening phases of so subtle and complicated an invention as writing. It is true that the first Egyptian hieroglyphics of Late Predynastic times were still rather clumsy and probably limited in their use. Yet in a very short time, with the first dynasty, hieroglyphic writing was freely used and was in exactly the same stage of development and complexity, with a blend of ideograms, phonetic signs and determinatives that had been slowly and gropingly achieved in Mesopotamia. In Egypt there is no sign of a pre-phonetic script. It looks as though Egyptian intellectuals must have grasped the theory of rendering sounds by signs, rejected the tablet and the reed and with them cuneiform itself, and consciously devised an Egyptian counterpart. With such evidence for directed intelligence, it is not surprising to find that while the dignified hieroglyphs were to remain in use for some 3000 years, already by the first dynasty the manufacture of paper out of papyrus pith had been invented, together with a simplified cursive script suitable for writing upon it in ink. The borrowers had quickly surpassed the inventors. While in Mesopotamia and all neighbouring countries within her sphere of influence scribes would always have to struggle with the awkward art of their wedge impressions and the cumbersome storage of heavy tablets, their Egyptian colleagues could write fluently on a material that was tough, light and easily stored.

The original Egyptian seizure upon the idea of writing free from the particular form seems to have more general implications. It suggests that disembodied theoretical information could spread in the ancient world and give rise to action just as it can today. This is a possibility that will prove to be of some relevance when we come to consider the origins of the Indus valley civilization.

The third of Egypt's main cultural borrowings from Asia, that of the cylinder seals, is relatively straightforward. Actual Sumerian seals were brought into Predynastic Egypt—three have come to light there, all dating from the Protoliterate period of Mesopotamia. The Egyptians quickly copied them, preferring hieroglyphic titles to the Mesopotamian pictorial designs, and often cutting them in wood instead of stone. They used them, like the Sumerians, for marking the clay sealings of jars and other goods, but also sometimes as funerary amulets. (The cylinder seal, so well adapted to making impressions on clay, was unsuitable for use with papyrus and was later replaced by the simple scarab stamp.)

Over exactly the same period of time, the last centuries of the fourth millennium, Asian influence strongly, if briefly, affected Egyptian artists. Both motifs and style that were undoubtedly derived from the Protoliterate art of Sumeria appear in their work. Most striking are the weird composite beasts that were such typical creations of the Sumerian imagination. Winged griffons and confronted serpent-necked lions, their grotesque necks intertwined, certainly both originated in Sumeria. Even more unmistakable is the figure of a man mastering a pair of confronted lions on the famous Gebel el-Arak knife-handle. The composition itself was a favourite one in Mesopotamia, and the man is the Sumerian ruler; his garment, his beard, his distinctive chignon hairstyle, and even the manner of depicting the muscles of his legs are reproduced exactly.

In several other works of art of the period, Egyptian motifs were executed under the unmistakable influence of Sumerian style. Yet the artists were undoubtedly Egyptian. They worked on such typically Nilotic products as the ceremonial palette and mingled characteristic Egyptian motifs and style with the exotic. Very soon, too, all alien influences had been absorbed or discarded. If there were indeed invading 'dynasts', they cannot have been very numerous—or they were solely concerned with power and left cultural development in their subjects' hands. Their impact would certainly be judged much less than that of the Normans on Anglo-Saxon England, and its effects lasted a shorter time and were more completely absorbed.

NORTH-WEST INDIA

IN EGYPT THE RISE OF CIVILIZATION WAS SUDDEN ENOUGH FOR THE notion of an invading 'dynastic race' to have been put forward to explain it. Yet there was a very real continuity in cultural traditions between the village communities of late prehistoric times and the civilized societies that followed them. In north-west India the division between the two appears to have been more nearly complete.

When the first known Indian cities were built there were plenty of settled villages among the mountains and hills to the west and north of the Indus, and others spilling down on to the Indus plain itself. Most of them continued to prosper side by side with the Indus cities. In some places the villagers seem to have been dispossessed and Indus settlements were built over the village sites. Yet there is no sign of continuity between them. The birth of the Indus civilization has too often, but not inappropriately, been likened to that of Athena: so far as we have been able to discover it appears suddenly and fully formed. For this reason it is only necessary to give a brief account of the various agricultural village societies as part of the total environment in which that civilization existed.

These first farming communities of India were the easternmost of a vast range of peoples living in more or less similar fashion over much of south-west Asia. While their traditions still had something in common with those of the much earlier prehistoric communities of northern Mesopotamia, their more immediate cultural ties were with the intermediate lands of Elam and Persia. Various links can be found with such places as Susa, the ancient capital of Elam, with Sialk and Hissar in Persia, and with Turkmenian Anau.

While it would be a grave mistake to give an impression of an advancing tide of farmers moving to the east, while in fact most of the Indian villagers would have been of native stock, it can hardly be denied that the spread of farming skills and settled habits, and to some extent of the biological continuum of livestock and grains, did involve the percolation of people through these harsh territories of mountain and desert. Some may have pushed gradually through the valleys and passes south of the Elburz mountains, while others may rather have extended south of the Zagros and along the coastal routes above the Persian Gulf.

There was ample time for such a gradual percolation. The prehistoric cultivators of Mesopotamia, who can be recognized as remote cultural ancestors of the Indian villagers, were already flourishing well back in the sixth millennium B.C. The earliest dates at present known for Indian agriculture are at least two thousand years later. On the other hand the fact that there was always adaptation to local conditions and resources is satisfactorily proved by the very early appearance of humped zebu cattle (*Bos indicus*) in place of the old western breeds.

Most of the Indian villages were among the foothills and mountain valleys of Baluchistan and Sind, reaching as far north as the Sulaiman range and the Quetta region. Southward they extended into the Makran on either side of the present Pakistan-Persian frontier. Other villages were set among the foothills to the east of the river Hab, and it was in this area that they spread down on to the alluvial plain of the Indus.

At Rhana Ghundai in the Shob valley, one of the very few sites where a number of superimposed settlements have been explored, it was thought that the first had belonged to semi-nomadic herdsmen who had not built substantial houses. Most unexpectedly, remains of domesticated horses were found in this encampment. The inference is that as early as the mid-fourth millennium B.C. Asian pastoralists were already herding on horseback. Whether this represents a pastoral phase that preceded village life throughout this part of north-west India it is too soon to say.

The permanent villages were not very large, seldom covering more than two acres, but they were occupied long and continuously enough to form quite massive *tells*, sometimes as much as forty feet in height. The houses had small rectangular rooms and were commonly built of *pisé* or moulded mud-brick on a stone footing. They had window openings and wooden doors, and the walls of the rooms might be plastered. The burnt-brick so characteristic of Indus architecture was virtually never used, even by villagers who must have been familiar with the output of the Indus kilns. Nor, so far as is known, were there any temples, citadels or other public or chiefly buildings.

The modest prosperity of the village folk depended on mixed farming. They cultivated both wheat and barley, but probably their cattle, sheep and goats were more important to them. Pride of place went to the zebu. These strong and noble-looking animals must presumably have been domesticated from some wild species that has not been identified. Their actual remains have been found at Rhana Ghundai, but their presence, and the villagers' reverence for them, is far more widely revealed to us through their portrayal on painted pottery. That the bulls were the subject of a cult seems plain enough, and this form of worship was to have a significant place also in the Indus civilization and to persist through all the vicissitudes of Indian history.

The use of oxen as draft animals has not been proved. Clay models of two-wheeled carts have been found in the villages, but they may have come from the Indus cities—where such models were very popular. The villagers, however, would hardly have been so dull as not to make use of carts wherever the terrain made it worth while.

To get a better idea of the life of these village communities we can look more closely at one area: southern Baluchistan and the Makran. It merits special attention because the prevailing culture, named after the settlement of Kulli, was rather livelier and more advanced than the rest, and its creators had trading contacts with Sumeria. This culture was largely contemporary with the Indus civilization but may have had earlier origins.

The Kulli people usually built their houses of stone, and although a rough masonry set in mud usually satisfied them, they occasionally produced good ashlar work. Interior decoration, too, might run to a finish in white plaster. Their potters turned out neat shapes on the wheel and were exceptionally fond of decorating them with zebu, goats, lions, sacred pipal trees, painted in a style that was lively and engaging if not of the highest aesthetic merit. The potters may have been villagers working part time, or specialists hawking their wares from market to market (as in present-day India and Ceylon). A hawkers' circuit might explain the distinctive regional styles, of which the Kulli is only one.

That part of the Kulli people who lived in the Makran had learnt to make one fine product that lifted them above the normal village level. This was a substance, probably some form of scented unguent, that they put up in well-finished stone jars. This product, as we shall see, was in such demand that the luxury trade carried it as far as Syria, and at least one jar is known to have reached the dressing table of a Sumerian queen.

The Kulli women themselves were far from being village hoydens. Little pottery figurines were probably goddess idols from household shrines, but there is no need to doubt that, as in most times and places, divine and human ladies were dressed alike. If the cosmetic jars suggest care of the complexion, the figurines are proof of elaborate hairdressing. Like most Indian women today, these of Kulli seem to have had long, thick hair. The front locks were piled high behind a fillet, while at the back the hair was either allowed to lie in a heavy loop on the nape of the neck or brought forward over the shoulders in two braids. The women also smothered themselves with beads, some at least made of lapis lazuli, agate or other semi-precious stones. They wore them from high on the neck to well below the bosom, and often further weighted them with large pendants. Their arms, and especially their left arms, were heavy with bangles. The fact that the English word 'bangle' is derived from Hindi serves to remind us of the long life of this Indian fashion.

Like other villagers, the Kulli folk had some copper utensils and even a little bronze—indeed they could probably afford rather more metal than most of their neighbours. It is appropriate that the finest copper object to have come from Kulli territory is a circular mirror with a handle in the shape of a woman's body. When the possessor looked into the mirror, her reflection provided the little figure with a face. Although it may be true that no village society would have achieved such charm and sophistication had it not known something of cities, it can also be claimed that feminine fancy of this kind does not agree with our idea of the Indus civilization. Moreover, the mirror itself appears to be unique. We can look into it and see the reflection not of a naked ape but of a species clad from head to foot in originality and imagination.

While a very loose network of mountain trade ways may have kept the northern villages of Baluchistan and Sind in occasional touch with Persia and even Mesopotamia, there is some evidence for closer and more direct maritime ties linking South Baluchistan and the Makran with the civilized lands to the west. It is at its most positive in the stone unguent jars already mentioned. Considerable numbers of these have been found in Mesopotamia, including one in the grave of Queen Shub-ad in the famous royal cemetery of Ur. Others come from Mari on the 'Mediterranean bulge' of the Euphrates, a remarkably cosmopolitan city that can thus be said to have consumed the products at one time of the Kulli people, at another of the Cretans—a trading span of nearly three thousand miles.

All the evidence agrees with that of Queen Shub-ad's grave: this trade was at its height during the Early Dynastic period of Sumeria, that is to say round about the middle of the third millennium B.C.

From an economic point of view it might be expected that wealthy and well organized Sumerian merchants would have fitted out trading ships to sail down to Makran and bring back unguents and any other exotic goods that would find a market in their home cities. Yet there are hints that this was not so, that on the contrary there were little colonies of Indian traders living in Ur and other Sumerian cities —and perhaps also in Susa. It looks as though they lived in an enclave maintaining native ways such as the worship of bulls. One of these hints will lie in the palm of the hand. It is a cylinder seal from Ur undoubtedly engraved by an Indian gem-cutter with a fine, round-eyed zebu bull.

Recent archaeological discoveries made on an island off the Oman peninsula and inland at Buraimi suggest that the inhabitants there had contacts of some kind with the Kulli region. These may well have been involved with the trade in Oman copper.

The Indus civilization did not grow directly from any of the known village cultures. That has already been stated. What, then, was the relationship between them? The first cities are thought to have been built about the middle of the third millennium when many of the villages were already long established in their own simple but effective way of life. No one need doubt that the communities living far up in the isolated mountain valleys would have maintained a sturdy independence. The same could be said, though

with less conviction, of the Kulli people whose lands lay well to the
west of the Indus realm. The problem becomes sharper with the
inhabitants of the Sind villages on the Indus plain. Some of these
were no more than a day's walk from Mohenjo-daro itself. In the
present state of knowledge all judgement must be hazardous, yet it
appears that even here villagers were not peasants in the sense that
has been defined—they were not an integral part of the Indus
economy as were the peasantry of the Mesopotamian city-states.

There were contacts between them, of course. Sometimes the
villages were affected by the cities. In some regions the Indus
civilization expanded at their expense or set up trading posts among
them. Conversely, no doubt some of the villagers left home and
adopted city life. Country girls may have gone to town as folk
dancers and entertainers. For the most part, however, the old village
culture in its regional variation seems to have maintained its independence, and many of the villages were destroyed only when the
Indus civilization itself was destroyed, and by the same invaders.

We have seen how in Mesopotamia and in Egypt the last centuries
of the fourth millennium B.C. saw the creation of literate civilization.
Although the Early Dynastic period is not allowed to have begun in
Sumeria much before 2800 B.C.—four centuries after the unification
of Egypt—both countries had in fact left their primitive past behind
them before even the earlier date. The long delay was in the appearance of civilization in the Indus valley, a country offering almost as
good opportunities as those of the Nile and the Twin Rivers, but
separated from them by appallingly difficult country and by a
swampy and incultivable delta.

When, according to present information, the citizens of Mohenjo-
daro first raised their great citadels and began to write their still
undeciphered script, the magnificent fourth dynasty of the Pharaohs
was coming to an end, their never-to-be-rivalled pyramids already
built. In Sumeria kings were living in the wealth and luxury that we
can at least dimly perceive through the dusty death of the Royal
Tombs of Ur. At this moment in the mid-third millennium all three
river valley civilizations were flourishing according to their distinctive forms. Great things were being accomplished, and although the
Sumerians understood the cruelty of the human lot and always feared
the return of chaos, no one could yet know from experience that
the civilization given to them by the gods could also be taken away.

PART III

KINGDOMS AND CONQUESTS

A HISTORY OF THE VALLEY OF THE TWIN RIVERS

EARLY DYNASTIC PERIOD

THE CENTRAL INTEREST OF THIS BOOK IS WITH UNFOLDING SOCIAL CON-
ditions, and it would be agreeable to ignore political history altogether. It would also be blameworthy. We are concerned with the
peoples of a vast river system over some two thousand years of
their history. Changes in political power between one area and
another, frequent foreign infiltrations, the seizure of sovereignty by
invaders, even the rise and fall of dynasties, deeply affected social
and cultural life. This was even truer for Mesopotamia than for the
more secure and isolated Egypt.

Then, too, although the nature of the everyday life of the humbler
people was not greatly changed by the doings of their rulers, and
although the cultural traditions created by the Sumerians showed an
astonishing persistence through all vicissitudes, it would be impossible to understand the experience and outlook of the population
without some knowledge of the often violent political events in
which their states were involved and which were a matter of life and
death to countless families.

The earliest fully historical phase in Mesopotamia is known as the
Early Dynastic period. It begins in about 2800 B.C. or a little sooner,
and ends with the accession of the first great empire-builder, Sargon
of Akkad, in 2340 B.C. These dates are approximate only, for there is
no quite securely fixed point within the period. Even its opening,

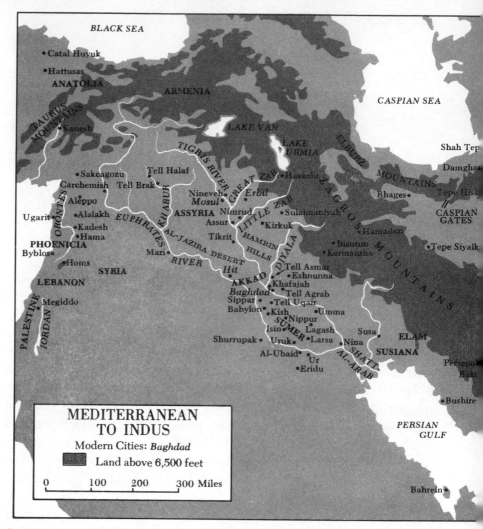

MEDITERRANEAN
TO INDUS

Modern Cities: *Baghdad*

Land above 6,500 feet

0   100   200   300 Miles

that is to say its separation from Protoliterate times, is partly arbitrary. We have seen that Sumerian cities ruled over by *ensis* were already flourishing in the earlier age, and that the leading city of Uruk already had a *lugal* or king.

The reason for distinguishing the Early Dynastic period from what had gone before lies less in any break in the historical evolution of Sumeria than in the nature of our knowledge of it. Now at last the nameless world of prehistory is left behind, and, in spite of vast uncertainties, we can know something of individual men and women and of the events that they felt worthy of record.

Although archaic cuneiform was still a very crude instrument, there do now begin to be numbers of royal inscriptions, treaties, administrative accounts, and word lists compiled by scribal schools.

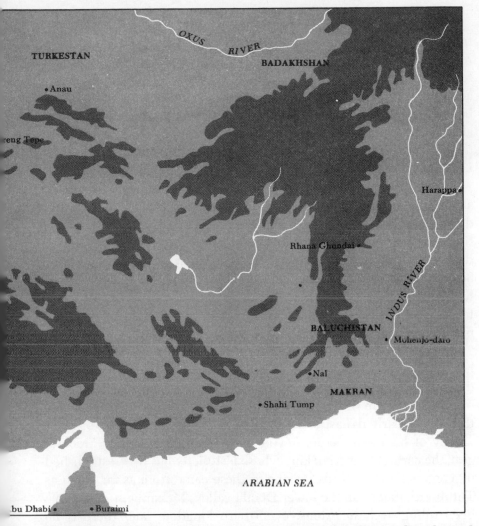

These contemporary documents, together with other archaeological findings, serve to correct, expand and make historical sense of the second main written source of information: the *Sumerian King List*.

This *King List* was compiled early in the second millennium, during the dynasty of Isin, but draws on much older sources. It consists of a series of royal dynasties of city-states, with the names of the kings, the length of their reigns and occasional brief notes on their most celebrated doings. Unfortunately it is quite useless for chronological purposes because not only are the earlier reigns quite fantastically long, but also the scribes have adopted the convention that the dynasties succeeded one another, whereas in fact many of them were contemporary. After kingship had first 'descended from heaven' (an event which for the Sumerians was of the essence of civiliza-

tion) the *King List* gives five dynasties that are separated from the
rest by the Flood which 'swept over the land'. These dynasties last
for well over 250,000 years and it is likely that most of the kings are
as legendary as their years. It is possible that some of them may have
been those *ensis* and *lugals* of Protoliterate times, but it is noticeable that their cities do not correspond at all closely with those
proved by archaeology to have been of importance at that period.
Uruk, for example, is not among them.

As for the Flood itself, although silt deposits have been discovered
at Ur and several other Sumerian cities, they belong to different
dates and it has proved impossible to establish a single great inundation affecting the whole land. Presumably floods were a familiar
dread that produced in men's minds the myth of the Great Flood.
Some authorities have been bold enough to suggest that the word
had become synonymous with disaster and was used in this sense
to refer to the flow of Semites into the Plain that seems to have
marked the end of the Protoliterate period.

When, after the destruction of the Flood, kingship descended from
heaven for the second time, the *King List* assigns the first post-
diluvian dynasty to the city of Kish. The reigns are still of preposterous length, yet in other respects this dynasty begins to emerge into
the light of early dynastic history. Twenty-second in the list of kings
(many of his predecessors having had Semitic names) is Mebaragesi, the earliest Sumerian king whose historicity has been established
by contemporary records. As one of these came from as far north as
Tutub (Khafajah) in the lower Diyala valley, Mebaragesi must have
been ruling over an extensive northern kingdom, and there is no
need to doubt the note in the *King List* that he 'despoiled the
weapons of the land of Elam'. This is the first glimpse of what was
to be a long enmity between Sumeria and her eastern neighbour.
The significant reign of Mebaragesi has been assigned to round about
2700 B.C. His son Agga is recorded as the last of the Kish dynasty.

From this point reigns cease to be impossibly long, and the *Sumerian King List* becomes a more nearly reasonable chronicle. From
now onwards, too, inscriptions not only emend the *King List*, making
it possible to establish many synchronisms between one dynasty and
another, but also add much information not known to the scribes.
Most important are the names of rulers of Ur found in the 'Royal
Cemetery' of the city, who reigned before the first dynasty of Ur in
the *King List*, and the succession of seven kings of Lagash altogether

overlooked in the scribal lists. The fine series of inscriptions recording this Lagash dynasty have played a great part in making the last phase of Early Dynastic history more or less coherent. They are also remarkable in themselves, including such notable monuments as the 'Vulture Stele' of Eanatum.

The two written sources taken together have made it possible to reconstruct a considerable part of the dynastic histories of some half-dozen cities of the Plain, including Ur, Umma, Lagash, Uruk and Kish. The *King List* also assigns one dynasty to Mari, and here again excavation has confirmed that this Semitic city away to the north on the Middle Euphrates was indeed an outpost of Sumerian cultural influence in Early Dynastic times.

One further general point has to be made about the *King List*, because it is fundamentally concerned with constitutional practice. The work rightly assumes that although composed of many city-states, Sumeria had a kind of unity, but wrongly that at all times the royal house of one of these states had a hegemony over all the rest, that there was never more than one true *lugal*. Thus at the end of each dynasty the *King List* has the formula 'City A was smitten with arms, the kingship was taken to city B'. As a matter of political history it has already appeared that the pretence that all dynasties were successive is one of the basic failings of the *King List* from our point of view. Nevertheless, there is no doubt that from the Early Dynastic period, if not before, the city-states did fight one another not only over rights and frontiers but also for dominion. Towards the end of the period we shall find an emergence of national kings that was to lead directly into the still wider powers of Sargon. Thereafter it was a common assumption that the supremacy of one city with its god and its king was part of the tradition of the land.

To turn now from the sources of political history and their implications to that history itself, we can see that the basic political fact was the confirmation of the pattern of separate city-states. True, they might be held together from time to time (and later more regularly) by royal overlords, but the reality of the pattern remained, providing the greatest political difference between Mesopotamia and Egypt.

Most of the Sumerian cities of history had already been established during the Protoliterate centuries. A few, such as Shurrupak, only rose to importance in Early Dynastic times. Ancient Nippur was peculiar in that it seems to have been decided that it should never compete for any form of political supremacy but remain a holy city where supreme kings sought the endorsement of Enlil. Each city continued to control its surrounding territory of irrigated fields and villages. Each was normally separated from its neighbours by a fringe of unirrigated waste land that could be used for grazing. It is a surprising fact that there is as yet no evidence of the cities being walled before the fortification of Uruk, perhaps during the twenty-seventh century B.C.—yet the idea of town walls had emerged in south-west Asia far back in prehistory. Some have taken this to mean that inter-state wars did not begin until well into Early Dynastic times. Yet the human condition, certain Protoliterate carvings, and the tradition of early hegemonies are against this belief in peaceful co-existence. Certainly for the rest of the Early Dynastic period border disputes and other petty wars were frequent and sometimes protracted. When royal overlords were in power they might attempt to fix disputed boundaries between subject states.

Another element in a repeating pattern already beginning in Early Dynastic times was, as we have seen, fighting the Elamites, a people who owed much of their culture to Sumer, emulated her, and yet were often to be her enemies. Yet another, and one far more important for the future, was the first major penetration of Sumer by Semites, the outcome of one of the most persistent features in all history: the drift of tribes from the western deserts into the settled land of Mesopotamia.

Whether or not there were Semites among the original settlers of the Plain, some were undoubtedly there from the dawn of history, for the earliest texts contain Semitic names and words. A falling off in the work of Sumerian artists and craftsmen at the end of Protoliterate times has been attributed to an influx of Semites—who by now can be called Akkadians. Indeed, as has been said, some scholars have identified their arrival with the devastating Flood of the *King List*.

Even these forerunners of later Akkadian power did not arrive among the civilized Sumerians of the Plain as nomads. The story seems to be that by the opening of the third millennium Semites were drifting into the mid-valley of the Euphrates from the Arabian and Syrian deserts. Some perhaps continued their nomadic existence for part of the year while turning to agriculture for a season. Others made their way into the cities and soon adopted the values of city dwellers. Mari was one of the places where they settled. There, before 2500 B.C., they had advanced so far as to be adapting cuneiform to the Akkadian language.

There must have been a continuous shift of Semites southward down the Euphrates. They came to dominate the land that was to be Akkad, and in the Diyala region developed Sumerian cultural traditions in ways of their own. The city of Kish, where, according to the *King List*, most rulers before Mebaragesi had Semitic names, must have become a power centre for their thrust into ancient Sumer itself.

It is difficult to judge how, in political terms, the Akkadians and Sumerians conducted their affairs as they met and mingled on the Plain. There is no evidence either in archaeology or epic tradition that they clashed on racial lines. In petty wars between states they must sometimes have fought one another, but on terms of neighbourly enmity, not as Semites against Sumerians.

Sumerian language and culture remained entrenched in Uruk, Ur and all the old southern centres. If at first the Semitic penetration had a disintegrative effect, it was temporary. In time the stimulus of cultural exchange, combined perhaps with a beneficial mingling of genes, reversed the downward trend. By the later pre-Sargonid centuries the revivified Sumerian cultural tradition was again making itself felt as far as the Diyala. The same reaction was to be repeated when, after the collapse of Sargon's Semitic empire, the Sumerians were to enjoy a last experience of creativity and power under the leadership of the Third Dynasty of Ur.

These, then, were the main trends of the age. There is no space to do more than touch on a few of the main events of the reigns of the kings who ruled and contended for power after Mebaragesi of Kish. According to Sumerian story it was his son Agga who fought against Gilgamesh, finally, it seems, submitting to him and allowing the supreme kingship to pass to his city of Uruk. The historicity of Gilgamesh, who was to be the hero of the great Akkadian epic, has not as yet been substantiated, but it is very probable indeed that he did exist, and even that, as the epic says, he built the first walls of Uruk.

In spite of its eclipse, the prestige of Kish, and perhaps, too, its command of Semitic influence, counted for so much that 'King of Kish' was adopted as an honorific title by rulers of other states who had succeeded to the hegemony. Probably in about 2500 B.C. (though some would now date it much earlier) this title was claimed by Mesanapeda, whose name heads the first dynasty of Ur in the *King List*. This overlordship of the great southern city probably represents the height of the Sumerian resurgence after the Semitic penetration.

However, Ur was not able to keep the hegemony. Not very long after Mesanapeda, the title 'King of Kish' had gone to Eanatum I of Lagash. He subjected not only Ur, but Uruk, Kish and Akshak, and then further north again fought successfully against Mari, which at this time was threatening Akkad. He also claimed the conquest of Elam, calling himself 'He Who Subjects All the Lands'. The victories of this ambitious conqueror are recorded on the great 'Vulture Stele' he set up in his home city. It shows him leading his phalanx and driving a war chariot, while a huge figure of the city god, Ningirsu, in whose name he fought, holds his puny enemies jumbled in a net.

The last of these overlords before all were eclipsed by their far greater successor, Sargon, was Lugalzagesi of Umma. For the best part of two hundred years Umma had carried on a feud against the adjacent state of Lagash. It was probably typical of the small struggles that racked the Sumerian people, the irritants being disputes over the grazing lands lying between the two states and the water channel that they shared. For a long time victory wavered from side to side, with neither ever wholly crushing the other. Then in about 2360 that Urukagina who is famous for the record of his social reforms seems to have come to the throne of Lagash as a popular usurper. By ill luck, he had as his near contemporary on the throne of Umma another usurper, and one more interested in conquest than reform. This was Lugalzagesi, the son of a princely priest of the local goddess, and possibly an Akkadian. From the first he may have intended to clear the way for greater projects, for when he led his army against the traditional enemy, Lagash, he broke the rules of the war game. He sacked the city and looted the temples of their treasures before setting them on fire. Urukagina survived to evoke the divine punishment of his enemy, but it was of little help. Lugalzagesi went on to conquer Uruk and to claim the overlordship as 'King of the Land of Sumer'. In what is the oldest Sumerian royal inscription in full literary style, he related himself to the divinities of the many subject city-states of the Plain—including Enlil of Nippur.

His inscription also makes what appears to be a far wider claim: 'From the Lower Sea along the Euphrates and Tigris to the Upper Sea, Enlil made all lands go directly to him.' It seems that these words do not mean that Lugalzagesi was claiming a political control from the Persian Gulf to the Mediterranean, but only the establishment of direct trading relations. Yet it must be significant that he already had a grasp of this extended realm of the Twin Rivers which was soon to be ruled as an empire by the man who wrested all power from him and led him in fetters to Nippur—Sargon of Akkad.

FIRST SEMITIC EMPIRE

THE WORLD'S FIRST CIVILIZATION HAD BEEN CREATED IN MESOPOTAMIA under Sumerian leadership. Now, about one thousand years later, the world's first empire was to be created under Semitic leadership. Just as urban life had quickly assumed characteristics that are still familiar to us all, so Sargon and his empire appear at once as the model for many successors down to recent times. He and his descendants shared many of the virtues and triumphs, the temptations, difficulties and final failure of Napoleon and his. The Akkadian empire, however, lasted for 180 years.

The man himself was probably even more humbly born than the corporal from Corsica. He may have been the child of semi-nomadic pastoralists in the region where the Khabur joins the Euphrates. If so, like other ambitious young Semites, he must have travelled down river to seek his fortune in the wealthy cities of the Plain. He became cup-bearer to a king of Kish, but how he rose from courtier to king is not known. Perhaps his first step was to carve out a neighbouring domain for himself and there to found the city of Akkad (Sumerian Agade). The exact site has not been identified, but it is thought to have been on the Euphrates at no great distance from Kish. It was to remain his capital, and he was always to place 'King of Akkad' first of his many titles.

Once Sargon had won control over the north of the Plain as King of Akkad and of Kish, he was ready to turn southward against Lugalzagesi, who had already loaded himself with titles and was claiming the overlordship of the Land of Sumer. Some inscriptions suggest that it cost him three campaigns and thirty-four battles to overthrow this rival and the fifty governors supporting him. At last 'he conquered Uruk and broke down its walls . . . Lugalzagesi, King of Uruk, he took prisoner in battle and brought him in fetters to the gates of Enlil' (that is, to the Ekur, the national shrine at Nippur).

Probably it was Sargon's moment of purest triumph, but it was by no means the end of his ambitions. Two campaigns to the north-west

took him first as far as Mari and then on to the Cedar Forest of
Lebanon and the Mediterranean. He may even have entered Anatolia. To the east he defeated the Elamites and their allies, and he
occupied Subartu, a realm which probably included Assyria and
the adjacent flanks of the Zagros. He even marched along the Persian
Gulf, and, like Lugalzagesi before him, claimed close trading relations far to the south. His victory inscription states, 'At the wharf of
Agade he made moor ships from Meluhha, ships from Magan
[Makan] and ships from Dilmun.' These places, as we shall see, were
probably the Indus region, Oman and Bahrein.

Sargon's likely conquest of Assyria calls for a mention of this
hitherto neglected region. Owing to its isolation by hills and deserts,
it had remained something of a backwater in Early Dynastic times.
Semitic nomads had made their way there and settled among the
prehistoric inhabitants. According to tradition their rulers lived as
tent-dwellers for many generations, but before the middle of the
third millennium they had founded Assur, naming it after their
supreme deity. It was to remain the religious capital of Assyria (to
which it gave its name) for two thousand years. Although some
Sumerian cultural influences had penetrated there much earlier, the
art of writing seems to have been unknown in Assyria before the
time of the Sargonid empire.

In organizing his subject lands, Sargon did not normally expel
the native rulers but installed officials to represent his rule. He himself seems to have been constantly on the move about his realm. It
is said that Sargon's main motives for the exhausting and bloody
business of carving out this first empire were economic, that he was
after wood, stone, metals and trade monopolies of all kinds. In one
sense this is evidently true. Yet there was nothing inevitable about it.
Scores of other kings before him had not been so impelled by economic circumstances. There is the same ambiguity that surrounds
the beginning of civilization. Surely the prime mover was again
psychological, a demonic energy within this self-made man that
drove him on until the need to pit himself against the Enemy, to
conquer and subdue became irresistible.

It is interesting to find that in later times the Babylonians were
not altogether happy about Sargon; he was not their kind of hero.
One story that was partly, but probably not wholly, fictitious accused him of a dreadful act of sacrilege that caused the god to
destroy him and his people. The theme expresses the Babylonian's

sense that he had been guilty of *hubris*. In contrast, the Assyrians, that most martial of Semitic people, were able to identify with him, accepted him as a hero figure and revived his royal name.

Sargon in fact enjoyed an immensely long reign—there is no need to doubt the fifty-six years assigned to him in the lists. Probably, however, the later chroniclers are right in saying that because of his immoderacy he knew revolts and even disasters in his own life-time. Certainly his descendants did. The two sons who succeeded him one after the other had to fight ferocious wars against Elam and Warahshe with much sacking and slighting of cities. Sumeria also rose, and her cities had to be subdued again one by one. The brothers may have campaigned in Assyria, for one founded a city in the north of Nineveh, while the second established the famous temple of Ishtar at Nineveh itself.

It is said that greatness often misses a generation. Sargon's grand-son, Naram-Sin, the fourth in the dynasty, must have inherited much of his grandfather's drive and ambition. He came to the throne in about 2260 B.C. and was to rule for thirty-seven years. Although faced with rebellions in all parts of his realm, he put them down and even extended his frontiers, until he made himself master of 'lands that no king before had ever conquered'. It is tempting to identify this claim with a rather dubious record that he marched against Magan and himself captured its king. It may also refer to his northern frontiers, for he went up into the Zagros to subdue a mountain peo-ple, the Lulubum (neighbours of the Gutians). His famous stele was carved to celebrate this victory, and a crude copy was sculptured on the rocks in Lulu-land itself—at Qara Dagh, south of Sulaimaniya.

Before marching against the Lulubum, Naram-Sin made a treaty with the king of Elam as with an equal. Perhaps this was a sign that his empire was already stretched to danger point. It was, however, under his son Shar-kali-sharri (2223–2198 B.C.) that the real crack-up be-gan. Elam gained its independence, and it seems that Uruk also rebelled and carried much of Sumeria with it. Shar-kali-sharri also had to deal with an attack in the north-west from the Amurru, a Semitic people from the western desert, better known as the Amorites, whose great days still lay ahead. The more immediate dan-ger came from the opposite flank—the Gutians of the Zagros moun-tains, a relatively fair-skinned, barbarous people whom the Sumerians referred to as the 'mountain dragons'.

Naram-Sin may have been the first to fight against them, but now their savage raids became far more menacing. The King of Akkad (Shar-kali-sharri's modest title) claimed a victory over them, but a letter of the time, addressed apparently to a provincial governor, gives a very revealing picture of the true condition of the land. 'You shall plough the fields and look after the cattle. It is no good saying "yes, but there are Gutians about and so I cannot plough my field." Set up patrols of watchmen every half mile and then plough your field. If armed bands advance there will be local mobilization, and you must then have the cattle driven into the city.'

According to literary tradition, the luckless Shar-kali-sharri, last of Sargon's line, was murdered in a palace intrigue. Among the four contenders for his throne, one was a Gutian king. No doubt he had already been ruling over some part of the old empire. It was a sad state of affairs. As the author of the *King List* put it, 'Who was king, who was not king?' Although a remnant of the old domain may have rallied under Dudu of Akkad, by about 2159 B.C., with the death of his son, this first of empires had faded into air.

The Gutians were now ruling over a considerable part of Meso-potamia, including the northern Plain. They adopted the cuneiform script and Akkadian language for their official inscriptions, but these 'mountain dragons' appear to have remained essentially barbarous. They are known to have destroyed much, including the city of Assur, and to have created nothing. No temple or palace, no style of art, no valuable innovation of any kind has been attributed to them. Al-though at one time they may have pushed as far down as Nippur, happily the old Sumerian south held out against the mountain men and was able at last to take the lead in their expulsion.

Among the city-states to do so, one was Lagash, which the second dynasty had again raised to pre-eminence. Outstanding among this line of *ensis* was Gudea (2143–2124 B.C.), whose calm, strong face is so well known to us from the many fine sculptures unearthed from his capital city. Lagash and all the southern cities were profiting from the fact that the Gutians had ruined Sargon's river port of Akkad. Gudea, indeed, seems to have built up a peaceful commercial empire comprising nearly all the lands which the Sargonids had won and held by force. Even the black diorite in which Gudea's features were recorded for posterity had been shipped up the Gulf from Makan.

In fact as well as in his own inscriptions, Gudea must have been a wise ruler who restored Sumer to political health and cultural vitality. He was a great builder of temples, devoted to civic improvement, canal-making and drainage works. Above all he was not aggressive. A defensive campaign against Elam is the only word of war coming from his prosperous reign.

Yet it was not to be given to Lagash either to free the north from the Gutians or to preside over the last flare of Sumerian greatness before the centre of power shifted irrevocably to the north. Within a decade of Gudea's death his city seems to have been losing ground, and a place in history as the liberator of the land from the mountain dragons went instead to Utuhengal of Uruk. After having seized Ur, this king marched against the Gutians and gave them battle in the extreme north of Sumer, near the limits of their own territory. His victory must have been complete, for the Gutians were thrown out of Mesopotamia and never again played any significant part in her history.

Utuhengal did not have long to enjoy his triumph. He had indeed already prepared the way for his own downfall when he appointed one of his generals to be governor of Ur. This Ur-Nammu, able and ruthless, seems first to have made himself king of Ur and then moved swiftly to destroy his former master the king of Lagash as well. Probably Lagash had retained much of the trade with the Gulf, for after this victory Ur-Nammu celebrated 'The return of the ships of Magan and Meluhha into the hands of Nanna' (the moon god of Ur).

This memorable founder of the Third Dynasty of Ur was now able to impose his rule over Akkad and far beyond. His name is found as far north as Tell Brak on the Khabur. He devised for himself the new title of King of Sumer and Akkad, a term long to remain in use. His regime was essentially Sumerian, centred as it was in the deep south and conducting all its affairs in the ancient tongue.

Like Gudea before him, Ur-Nammu was active in temple-building and irrigation works. He must have been an excellent administrator, and, so far as is known at present, was the first king to draw up a code of laws. So long as they prospered, he and his line ruled as absolute monarchs with an imperialist outlook. The king was now the supreme judge, the head of every service; *ensis* had become no more than governors with delegated powers. Indeed, kingship was recognized as divine. Hymns were addressed to the king, shrines dedicated to him, sacrifices made to him, and from the reign of Ur-Nammu's son, Shulgi (2093–2046 B.C.), his name was written with the divine determinative. (Yet even now these Sumerian kings were far less exalted in the hierarchy of gods than the Pharaohs in Egypt.)

In their assumption of divinity, in the political domination and centralized administration of their realm, the monarchs of the Third Dynasty of Ur resembled those of the Akkadian empire rather than those of Lagash. The men of Ur had in fact learnt much from the Semites.

The actual extent of their realm, which can properly be called an empire, is rather uncertain—and indeed was probably always shifting. The dynasty seems to have been in permanent control of Sumer and Akkad, of Elam and the Diyala region, of the mid-valley as far as Mari (and sometimes the Khabur) and Assur. In all these inner territories the empire of Ur was greatly superior to that of Akkad in that it was peaceful—wonderfully free from internal dissension. On the other hand the kings fought imperialist wars on their frontiers. Shulgi in particular, who revived the ambitious title 'King of the Four Quarters', led many campaigns in the north.

These campaigns were not altogether aggressive. The lands to the east of the Tigris were suffering a dangerous influx of foreigners. These were the Hurrians from the northern mountains. They had been entering peacefully for a century and more (there was even an enclave of them in Nippur as early as 2200 B.C.) but now they came in larger numbers. It was probably due to the strong military policy of Ur that they did not penetrate the Plain and repeat the success of the Gutians.

For eighty years the empire of Ur maintained its inward stability, and its downfall when it came was largely due to attack from without. The Hurrians had been held in check, but now the pendulum of invasion was to swing back to the west—from mountain enemy to desert enemy.

The Amorites (Sumerian Martu and Akkadian Amurru) had been drifting into Mesopotamia since the days of Sargon. These nomad Semites can in fact be seen as successors to the Akkadians, but they appear to have been less ready to settle and become good citizens. Efforts had been made to draw them into society as landowners and office holders, yet now they were becoming a threat to the realm. Very soon after the accession of Ibbi-Sin in about 2027 B.C. they began to harry Akkad and Sumer in force.

The Diyala region seems to have been the first to be lost, then Elam, and probably Assur also, took advantage of Ur's difficulties to break away. Marauding bands of Amorites were beginning to reduce the empire to chaos; the king, probably with reason, suspected some of his *ensis* of not opposing them whole-heartedly. With the central government weakened, city-states were reverting to their ancient rivalries, and in some Amorite sheiks seized power.

The man to take most advantage of an unhappy situation was one of Ibbi-Sin's own commanders, but himself an Amorite from Mari. There was a famine in the south and the king sent his general to collect grain in the central Plain. This he did, storing much of it in Isin, but when Ibbi-Sin proved unable to provide transport to carry it to Ur, he seems to have decided to set himself up as an independent ruler. Opinions differ as to how far Ishbi-Erra was a traitor, and how far his policies were forced upon him by circumstances. Certainly he took over control of the north and centre of the Plain and from his capital at Isin was soon claiming the imperial title of King of the Four Quarters.

Ibbi-Sin, however, continued to rule over Ur and the south for a number of years, and when at last, in about 2003 B.C., he and his proud and venerable city fell, it was not at the hands of Isin, but of Elam. It was an historic tragedy, fittingly commemorated by the Sumerian *Lamentation over the Destruction of Sumer.* The Elamites had no imperial ambitions in Sumeria, but contented themselves with garrisoning the town and carrying booty and captives home to Susa—including Ibbi-Sin himself and the cult figure of Nanna.

Ur could be restored, Nanna returned to his temple (no one knows what happened to Ibbi-Sin), but Sumer had lost its greatness. Civilization had been kindled there, sparks had leapt to Egypt and to India. Now, so far as Mesopotamia was concerned, its heat and light, its main centres of creative energy and their resulting worldly power, were to shift northward, leaving the south as something of a burnt-out land.

The causes included such mundane matters as soil pollution, but they were also historical and racial. While the Sumerians had never been reinforced since their first settlement of the Plain, more and more Semites had been arriving over the centuries. Geography, and the Sumerian presence, had determined that their focus of strength should be to the north of the Plain in the area which they had made Akkad and which was soon to be Babylonia.

During the two centuries that followed the fall of Ur, usually known as the Isin-Larsa period, Sumerian is thought to have died out as a spoken language. For a long time it had been absorbing more and more Semitic words, and now it succumbed altogether. Semitic Akkadian, adopted also by the Amorites, became the dominant speech of Mesopotamia. Yet Sumerian had immense prestige. Rather as Latin remained the unifying medium of learning and religion long after it had ceased to be spoken, so Sumerian continued to be used by priests and scribes, and to be taught in scribal schools, for as long as Babylonian civilization endured. It was indeed studied well beyond the boundaries of Mesopotamia—in Egypt and in Anatolia, and even in the Hittite capital as late as 1200 B.C. As might be expected, it kept its classical purity longest in holy Nippur.

For a time Sumer and Akkad appear to have been tolerably secure and even prosperous under the hegemony of Isin, but by the time towards the end of the first century of the second millennium, when Larsa began her gradual rise, they relapsed into a chaos of warring states. The Akkadian omen texts give a fearsome impression of the endless petty wars and *coups d'état* that were assumed to be the normal conditions of life and death in the little kingdoms of the time. The priestly readers of sheeps' livers or of oil on water expected to find signs of princes killing their fathers for the throne, of treacherous officials and regicides of every kind.

Among several states vying with Isin and Larsa for supremacy was one that had only recently lifted itself from obscurity. This was Babylon, a humble but ancient settlement on the banks of the Euphrates in the land of Akkad. Its first independent dynasty was established in 1894 B.C. by a prince of Amorite stock who was soon able to annex Sippar and Kish. Babylon was on its way.

This increasing sway of Babylon was in fact part of a general trend towards larger political units apparent by the late nineteenth century B.C. Eshnunna had periods of hegemony in the Diyala country, and Assur was celebrating its independence of the south by reviving the great names of Akkadian empire. The prosperity of all Assyria was increased by the development of trade with Anatolia, which was led by the active trading colony of Kanesh. Mari, now chief among a chain of Amorite kingdoms along the Euphrates and in Syria, was also booming at this time. It throve as a centre of caravan and boat traffic along the river and a link with the Mediterranean.

Mari was to become much involved in the mounting ambitions of Assyria. The interest of this phase in her history has been magnified by one of the chances of archaeology. The vast and richly decorated palace was famous in its day, and it was in its ruins that a complete royal archive, covering the years from about 1810 to 1760 B.C., came to light. It includes letters, domestic and foreign, received by the kings of Mari, copies of their own outgoing letters, administrative texts and legal documents. They range over the greater part of the civilized world, from Crete to Dilmun, and from the Zagros to Hattusas and to Galilee. On the political side the letters show a mixture of good sense and responsibility, expediency and cynicism that would be closely matched in any modern diplomatic bag.

Of all the varied contents of this marvellous archive, one situation in particular brings the characters and doings of the Bronze Age kingdoms to life. For this reason as well as others, what is sometimes called the 'Assyrian interlude' at Mari is well worth attention. The story begins with Shamshi-Adad, one of the most active of the throne snatchers who are so characteristic a part of the Mesopotamian way of political life. His family had been expelled from their little Amorite kingdom by Mari, and this once dispossessed princeling had succeeded by tenacity of purpose, probably helped by Amorite mercenaries, in winning his way to the throne of Assyria. This was in about 1814 B.C. His plans did not stop there, and it can be assumed that most of all he was determined to avenge himself on Mari.

When the personal story begins to emerge from the intricate impressions on the little clay blocks of the Mari archive, Shamshi-Adad had installed one of his sons, Jasmah-Adad, as his viceroy in Mari and another, Ishmo Dagan, as ruler of a small state within Assyria, and he had killed the King of Mari with all his sons save one. The daughters were differently disposed of: Shamshi-Adad wrote to Jasmah, 'Jahdunlin's young daughters whom I gave to you—these daughters have now grown up. . . . you shall have them delivered to Shubat-Enlil [his new capital] where they shall live in the house that belongs to you. They will be trained in singing and when you come . . .'

There are hundreds of letters exchanged between the father and his two sons, and in this triangle poor Jasmah-Adad emerges as the weakling who is always humiliated by the high-powered father and the brother who evidently took after this parent. One letter told him, 'While your brother has won a victory here, you remain there, reclining among women', while another asked, 'As to you, how long will it be necessary for us to guide you all the time? How much longer will you be unable to administer your own house? Do you not see your brother commanding far-flung armies?'

Shamshi-Adad campaigned to hold and extend his frontiers, while still finding time for an astonishing number of practical affairs, down to the supply of new ploughs and bronze nails. Gradually, however, his good son, Ishme-Dagan, who had battled so hard against the tribesmen always threatening Assyria from east of the Tigris, took over his responsibilities and at last his throne. He wrote to Jasmah, 'I have ascended the throne in my father's house. That is why I have been extremely busy and have not been able to send you news of my well-being. You must not be anxious. Your throne is and will remain your throne. . . . Let us swear a binding oath to each other by the life of the gods. . . .'

It seems as though in a ruthless world where so many kings were driven out or murdered, Ishme-Dagan had developed a protective attachment to his inadequate brother. It was of no use. Within a very short time the surviving prince of Mari, Zimri-Lim, succeeded in ousting Jasmah-Adad and began a long reign that was to be maintained by exceptional diplomatic agility. Ishme-Dagan was able to hold his throne in a much reduced Assyria, and it can be hoped that his brother had been able to escape there and to end his days in thankful obscurity.

Both kingdoms were in the end to fall to the great man who had been gradually building up his power in Babylonia. Hammurabi is one of very few monarchs of Bronze Age Mesopotamia to have won a place in the gallery of world figures. He had every gift, and perhaps the most valuable of them all was a long life. He reigned nearly sixty years.

As sixth king of the Amorite dynasty of Babylon, he had succeeded in 1792 B.C. Unlike most other famous conquerors and empire builders, his ambitions appear to have ripened slowly. This fact is in harmony with his general character: he was politician, diplomat and administrator of rare ability, and moreover was genuinely concerned to bring social justice to his subjects.

When Hammurabi had done no more than annex Akkad and Assyria, he was still only one successful king among a number. A letter of Zimri-Lim's written at this time has often been quoted, but is so revealing that it must be quoted again: 'There is no king who of himself is strongest. Ten or fifteen kings follow Hammurabi of Babylon; the same number follow Rim-Sin of Larsa; the same Ibal-pi-El of Eshnunna; the same Amut-pi-El of Qatahum, and twenty kings follow Yarim-Lim of Yamkad.' The two last ruled in Syria; some of their vassal 'kings' can have held no more than small sheikdoms.

Now, in 1763 B.C., Hammurabi turned against Larsa and on Rim-Sin's surrender assumed his hegemony in the south. Using an old formula he claimed to have 'established the foundation of Sumer and Akkad'. A few years later even Zimri-Lim's long diplomatic struggle for survival came to an end when Hammurabi took Mari by force of arms and won control of the vital trade route into Syria.

When Hammurabi came to draw up his great Code, he listed in the prologue twenty-four major cities that were subject to him in these last years of his reign. They range from Eridu and Ur to Mari, Assur and Nineveh—corresponding quite closely to the empire of the Third Dynasty of Ur, except that Elam was not included. With some justification it has been said that as Sargon represented the final political fulfilment of the Akkadian penetration of Mesopotamia, so Hammurabi represented the Amorites. There were significant differences. The many Amorite ruling houses did not bring anything so momentous as the Akkadian change of language; they did not even conspicuously affect art forms. On the other hand, as we shall see, Hammurabi's empire saw the culmination of profound social changes that must greatly have altered the outlook and opportunities for most citizens in the valley of the Twin Rivers.

There was something about Hammurabi and his imperial reign that charged it with more importance than can easily be accounted for from the historical facts. He was a great soldier, administrator, law-giver; he strengthened and beautified Babylon and presided over a period of great material prosperity. All this is true, yet the lasting impact of an empire which, after all, began to collapse very soon after Hammurabi's death seems hardly accounted for. Shamshi-Adad had shown most of these virtues, yet he and his new capital were ephemeral. Edzard wrote of the re-unification of Sumer and Akkad after 1763 B.C., 'The empire thus formed was of short duration, but its significance for the later history of Mesopotamia knew no limit in time. Babylon became the metropolis of Sumer and Akkad: the whole country took its name. . . . Babylon had become the symbol of the Semites of southern Mesopotamia.' This significance is still, of course, recognized today and accounts for the fact that the time from the beginning of the first dynasty down to its fall in the sixteenth century B.C. is known as the Old Babylonian period.

OLD BABYLONIA TO THE FALL OF ASSYRIA

HAMMURABI'S BABYLONIA, IN WHICH SUMERIAN CIVILIZATION HAD BEEN completely absorbed by the Semites and now flourished under their political domination, completes the most essential part of this survey of the historical background to Mesopotamian social and cultural life.

Internally the most important events that remain to be told concern the rise of Assyria, the kingdom that was to dominate the ancient world during the first half of the last millennium B.C. Equally significant was the change in Mesopotamian external relationships. Foreign trade had always been important, but from the time of Hammurabi onwards the Land of the Twin Rivers lost much of its old self-containment and entered more and more into a political world which embraced all south-west Asia and Egypt.

At the beginning of the second millennium, Europe and western Asia were being disturbed by the migrations of peoples speaking Indo-European languages. The story of their probable dispersal from homelands between the Dnieper and the Don was told by professors Piggott and Clark in the first volume of this series, *Prehistoric Societies*. There is no question of any 'pure' or coherent Indo-European race. Yet it does seem to be true that there were related peoples of nomadic and pastoral origins who combined strongly patriarchal social organization, strongly masculine deities and exceptional fighting qualities that went with the use of the heavy battle axe and of the horse—later the horse-drawn chariot. They expanded in a series of explosive movements that in the end were to cause the Indo-European language to be spoken all the way from Ireland to India and from the Eurasian steppes to the Mediterranean.

One of the earlier results of this expansion was the penetration of Anatolia by the Hittites. Their language had some special affinities with Latin and they worshipped Indo-European gods. At a time when they must still have been living peacefully among the Hatti and other native populations, Hittite names appear among the commercial texts of the Assyrian merchants at Kanesh. Gradually, however, their kings, ruling from the old Hattic city of Hattusas (now Boghazkoy), developed an aggressive imperialist policy. By the middle of the seventeenth century B.C. they had conquered as far as northern Syria, winning control of the trade routes to the Euphrates.

We shall find these conquests troubling the Egyptians, and they must certainly have had some ill effects on Assyria and Babylonia. Then suddenly the Hittites struck at Mesopotamia itself. Presumably as a show of his imperial might, in 1595 B.C. King Mursilis I led a sudden raid down the Euphrates, captured Babylon itself and ended the Amorite dynasty of Hammurabi. This feat shook the whole ancient world. Its direct effect might not have been very great, for Mursilis had to withdraw his army and soon after was assassinated. Yet the fall of the dynasty and the subsequent confusion may have opened the way for the seizure of lasting power by the Kassites.

For another intrusion of Indo-European history into that of Mesopotamia we have to return to the Hurrians, last seen being held in check by the Third Dynasty of Ur. These people, whose original home was probably in the Armenian mountains, spoke a language that was neither Semitic nor Indo-European. The eastern tribes that harried Shamshi-Adad and his son were probably predominantly Hurrian, and Hurrian texts of about this time are known from Mari. After the reign of Ishme-Dagan, Assyrian history sinks into obscure doldrums, and it seems that this was due to a great influx of Hurrians—who were actually in a majority in some cities and were very numerous in Assur itself. A large force of them also swept across northern Mesopotamia, reaching the Syrian coast and influencing the petty states of Palestine.

Perhaps from the first it was pressure from Indo-European peoples that caused these incursions by the Hurrians, and they may soon have acquired chariot-driving Indo-European leaders. Certainly when, rather before 1500 B.C., Mitanni emerged into history as a centralized Hurrian state, it was dominated by such an Indo-European ruling aristocracy. Names of Mitannian kings can be derived from Sanskrit, while the alien divinities they introduced into the old Sumerian-cum-Semitic pantheon had names well known from the Vedic literature of India. It is therefore assumed that these rulers were a branch of the Indo-Iranian group who chose a westerly route into Mesopotamia when the majority moved eastward to Persia and India.

In the fifteenth and fourteenth centuries B.C., Mitanni extended from the Zagros to the Mediterranean and the kings of Assyria were no more than her vassals. It was the hostile policy of Mitannian kings against Egypt that provoked Thutmose III to march to the Euphrates. Later they made friends with the Egyptians and three generations of princesses, with hundreds of followers, made the hazardous journey to Thebes, where they were given in marriage to Pharaoh and lived out their days in the royal harem.

A fresh phase of Hittite expansion caused Mitanni to fall even more swiftly than she had risen. By the middle of the fourteenth century the kingdom had ceased to exist as a great power. Yet the Hurrians did not disappear from history. Away to the north in their Armenian homeland they entrenched themselves and built up the kingdom of Urartu. Here something of their culture, and an Urartian language very close to the Hurrian of Mitanni, was preserved.

The third of the barbarian peoples to impinge upon Mesopotamia were the Kassites. Like the Hurrians, they swarmed down from the eastern mountains and seem to have been led by a chariot-driving Indo-European aristocracy. Since the eighteenth century B.C. they had been settling more or less peaceably in the middle Euphrates region. Then, when Babylon had been shattered by the Hittite raid of 1595 B.C., Kassite rulers took the chance to assume the kingship. From that date for no less than four centuries Babylonia was ruled by a Kassite dynasty. Unhappily the king lists for the earlier Kassite period are so obscure as to form what has been called a chronological dark age. It is this obscurity that still makes it impossible to be certain of absolute dates for the preceding Babylonian and Akkadian dynasties.

Although no Kassite king achieved personal fame, they were not altogether unworthy successors of the line of Hammurabi. Nor is it any longer thought that theirs was a time of total cultural decadence. The Kassites may have been uncreative, but as guardians of the ancient traditions of the land they were impeccable. From the first they adopted the Akkadian tongue, while Sumerian was maintained as the language of religion and learning. When they built a new capital at Dur-Kurizalgu, its temples and palaces were in the Babylonian style.

The later decline of Babylonia was less due to her Kassite rulers than to the rise of Assyria. When Mitanni collapsed, the Assyrians were quick to assert their independence and presently annexed what remained of the Mitannian kingdom. In general their policy towards Babylonia was a moderate one, although late in the thirteenth century B.C. an Assyrian king captured Babylon itself. In this period of her Middle Kingdom (1350–95 B.C.) Assyria was emerging as one of the great powers of the ancient world. Yet her ascendancy was to be curiously inconstant, with phases of militant expansion broken by recessions.

With the end of the thirteenth century there came another age of violence and ethnic instability comparable to that caused by the Indo-European movements many centuries earlier. The upheavals associated with the western drive of the 'Sea People' will be more fully described in Part V. Egypt herself was so gravely threatened that she could no longer keep any control of the petty states of Palestine or southern Syria. Hittite power was shattered and the political order that she had imposed on Anatolia and northern Syria collapsed in chaos. With the political framework in ruins, the trade routes also collapsed. This situation is referred to in the *Book of Judges*, where it is said, 'In the days of Shamgar . . . caravans ceased and travellers kept to the by-ways . . .'

Babylonia suffered less from these disturbances than her more exposed northern neighbour, and for a time was once again supreme in Mesopotamia. Yet by the time Tiglath-Pileser I came to the throne in 1115 B.C., Assyria had recovered her authority, with flourishing trade supporting her military might. The re-opening of the old diplomatic channels between the great powers is well represented by Tiglath-Pileser's approach to Egypt. It seems that the Pharaoh of the day sealed the alliance not with the hand of a princess but with the gift of a live crocodile.

Tiglath-Pileser was already beginning to have trouble with another surge of desert Semites from the west. These Aramaeans set up small independent states in Syria, but in Mesopotamia, although their coming caused dislocation, they accepted its civilization so completely as to leave no conspicuous cultural mark. Yet they were numerous enough to make one great change. During the last millennium B.C. Aramaic became the spoken language of the people over most of the valley. Meanwhile the southern marshlands of ancient Sumeria were settled by yet other Semitic wanderers, the Kaldu or Chaldeans.

In the mid-tenth century B.C., after the main impact of these newcomers had been absorbed, the Neo-Assyrian age saw the northern kingdom become the dominant force of the civilized world. The Assyrian army became an almost irresistible machine, splendidly armed and equipped, and with cavalry now beginning to supplement the weight of the chariotry. Assurnasirpal, one of the leading monarchs of the ninth century, built up a mighty capital at Kalah (Nimrud) on the banks of the Tigris. The gates of his vast palace were guarded by gigantic man-headed winged bulls—the first of their kind.

Hitherto Assyrian conquests had been mainly concerned to win booty and tribute, but now a true imperial system was to be imposed. This new concept is particularly associated with the strong man who seized the Assyrian throne in 740 B.C. under the name of Tiglath-Pileser III—the Pul of the Old Testament. His policy (followed also by his successors) was to master western Asia and its trade routes by securing his own always exposed northern and eastern frontiers, and controlling Babylonia, Syria, Palestine and the rich Phoenician cities. Conquered lands were placed under provincial governors and obliged to pay a fixed tribute. Rebellion was ruthlessly punished by brutalities that included the deportation of peoples to distant parts of the empire. Well known instances were when Sargon II captured Sumeria and carried off nearly thirty thousand Israelites and when his son Sennacherib apparently deported much larger numbers after his campaigns against Hezekiah of Judah. Vast numbers of domestic and transport animals might also be taken as booty and tribute in gold, silver, precious stones and ivory demanded.

The profits of the Assyrian war machine during the climax of its power in the eighth and seventh centuries must have been enormous. The wealth poured in, much of it going to enrich successive royal capitals—Dur-Sargon (Khorsabad) following Kalah and being followed by Nineveh. The war gain was tremendous, but so, too, was the war strain. Assyria's aggressiveness caused all her enemies, including Egypt, to attempt defensive coalitions against her. They were seldom successful, yet fighting was incessant.

The empire approached its peak under Esarhaddon, who won the throne in 681 B.C. He was a brilliant soldier, but also a statesman of sense who was prepared to follow conquest by conciliation. One of his first acts was to restore Babylon, wantonly destroyed by his father, Sennacherib. He made it, indeed, an alternate capital of his empire. This king's most momentous deed was his annexation of Egypt. His campaigns against the Nile culminated in 671 B.C. when Memphis fell and the Nubian Pharaoh fled. The new province was divided into satrapies, each with its governor, native or foreign. Egypt was to be held for only fifteen years, but before her liberation, Esarhaddon's son, Assurbanipal I, had fallen upon Thebes. He did his best to destroy its colossal temples and carried off two obelisks to Nineveh—the first of many instances of these weighty monuments serving as trophies of war.

In the earlier years of this reign, Assyria's might seemed as absolute as it had ever been. Elam had been conquered at last, her kings made to drag Assurbanipal's chariot through the streets of Nineveh. The king himself, leaving the battlefield largely to his generals, felt secure enough to make himself a patron of learning and to build up the great library of Nineveh. Yet well before his death, and faster still under his two inadequate successors, the empire was disintegrating. Egypt's breakaway was followed by that of Babylon, when Nabopalassar seized the throne with the support of the Chaldeans. A new and worse threat was developing in the eastern mountains. Among the Indo-European peoples who had penetrated there were the Medes and Persians. Assyria had had dealings with them in the past, but it was only now that their old tribal structure was consolidated by ambitious kings.

Once the Medes had allied themselves with Nabopalassar, Assyria's position was hopeless. In 614 B.C. the allies sacked Assur and Kalah, and two years later they succeeded in destroying Nineveh itself and in killing the Assyrian king. Within a few more years, in spite of Egyptian aid, all resistance was at an end: the most martial of empires had fallen from its zenith in less than fifty years. The biblical *Vision of Nahum* gives a superb poetical account of the fall of Nineveh, the mightiest city in the world.

> *Woe to the bloody city!*
> *It is all full of lies and robbery;*
> *The prey departeth not;*
> *The noise of a whip and the noise of the*
> *   rattling of wheels,*
> *And of the prancing horses, and of leaping*
> *   chariots.*
> *The horseman lifteth up the bright sword*
> *   and the glittering spear;*
> *And there is a multitude of slain. . . .*
> *They stumble upon their corpses.*

Such was the poet's vision: at Kalah when the archaeologist's spade uncovered the main fort it was six feet deep in the ashes of the final conflagration. Among them lay exquisitely carved ivory inlays from the priceless furniture that had been stored there. The looters had no eyes for art, but had stripped off the gold leaf covering the ivories, leaving a few scraps clinging round the nail heads to tell the tale of their greedy violence.

Assyria had gone down, and now with the last swing of the pendulum, Babylon rose once more. Nabopalassar's son, Nebuchadnezzar, took most of Assyria (leaving the north to the Medes) and created what is now known as the Neo-Babylonian Empire.

Nebuchadnezzar's Babylon was, of course, the city that has remained famous for all time. He rebuilt her temples and palaces, and constructed the Ishtar gate and the great processional way that can still be seen among the sad, dusty mounds. The way led to the temple of Marduk that was the religious centre of the empire. The whole of the main chapel, over 130 feet long, the king had plated with gold.

The wealth of Babylon depended in large part on trade, and here she was handicapped by the Medean control of the north. Nebuchadnezzar knew that he must hold his western lands and keep back the Egyptians in that quarter. Hence the capture of Jerusalem and the 'Babylonian Captivity' that was to bequeath to Christendom the image of the Whore of Babylon.

His reign was followed by a period of civil war and assassinations, but Babylonia was to enjoy a last burst of glory under Nabonidas (Banu-na'id). However, as is well known, the handwriting was on the wall. The Persians, who had hitherto been subject to their neighbours the Medes, now rose against them under Cyrus II. Nabonidas sided with the Persians. This paid for a time, but as soon as Cyrus had secured Anatolia he was ready to turn against his ally. Babylonia had inherited the unpopularity as well as much of the wealth of Assyria, and probably Isaiah's view of Cyrus as the chosen of the Lord was by no means limited to the Jews. Even at home Nabonidas had many opponents, probably enough to weaken resistance. The Babylonians were defeated at Opis, and when Cyrus marched on to Babylon the gates were opened. Babylon remained the capital of a province of the Achaemenid Empire, rich but subject.

Nabonidas and the surrender of Babylon are a familiar chapter of world history. One of the king's activities that may be less well known has a special meaning for this book. This was his restoration of the famous ziggurat of Ur—by his day Ur of the Chaldeans. On the cuneiform cylinders that he had buried in each corner of the monument he recorded how he had learned from their inscriptions that Ur-Nammu, 'a king before me', and his son had built the ziggurat. 'Upon the ancient foundations whereon Ur-Nammu and his son Dungi had built I made good the structure of that ziggurat, as in old times.' There could be no finer demonstration of the continuity of sentiment and of culture that linked the last independent king of Babylonia with a predecessor of nearly two thousand years before. In spite of the invasions, revolutions and upheavals of all kinds chronicled in this chapter, Nabonidas saw Ur-Nammu simply as 'a king before me'. Moreover, he (or his scribes) could read what that king had written.

PART IV

LIFE IN
THE VALLEY OF
THE TWIN RIVERS

1. THE MATERIAL WORLD

AGRICULTURE

To BEGIN WITH THE FARMER AND SHEPHERD, WITH THE PRODUCERS OF food, is in no way to retreat from the claim for the primacy of the psyche in the creation of culture. Men painted and carved, decorated themselves and their possessions, worshipped, sacrificed, gave themselves to rites and festivals, as much when they were hunters and food gatherers as when they became producers of food. It is right to begin with peasant farming because as a matter of everyday fact this was the foundation on which all higher or more complex achievements of Bronze Age civilization were built. It is a question of hierarchy, of starting with the simplest thing, at the base of the human pyramid.

In contemplating the last chapter, it is painful to think of the long-suffering peasants who over a period representing nearly a hundred generations supported the pride of kings in their endless military adventures. As though the toil, the natural threats of flood or drought, of famine or disease were not enough, they had to fear the trampling or requisitioning of precious crops, the driving off of flocks and draft animals, the burning of villages, looting, raping, and, for many, the obligation to fight and to die—sometimes in a neighbour state, sometimes far from home. The *Lamentation over the Destruction of Sumer* in Ibbi-Sin's day makes many references to the cruel effects of war in the countryside. For example:

That stalls be destroyed, that sheepfolds be wiped out,
That [Sumer's] oxen no longer stand in their stalls,
That its sheep no longer spread out in their sheepfold,
That its rivers flow with bitter water,
That its cultivated fields grow weeds,
That its steppes grow wailing plants,
That the mother cares not for her children,
That the father says not 'Oh my wife' . . .
That the young wife rejoices not in his lap . . .

It is very difficult to estimate how great were the losses of men and produce caused by warfare of all kinds. Famines certainly occurred, and although in the earlier days of fighting between small city-states losses of men may have been slight, from Sargonid times onwards armies ran into tens of thousands and then hundreds of thousands, and the slaughter must have been correspondingly great. It is quite possible, in fact, that the repeated declines in the military fortunes of Assyria were at least partly due to the exhaustion of the supply of good fighting men for her armies. However, although it is right to remember this aspect of life in Mesopotamia, particularly since it contrasts with its more peaceful tenor in Egypt and India, the fact remains that for most of the country folk most of the time the cycle of the farming year turned steadily, food was produced, dues and taxes paid, the gods served and celebrated.

From the point of view of the crops they grew, the animals they reared and the methods they used, there was no very great difference between the peasants of dynastic times and those who had returned to dust in the prehistoric past. For us, however, there is a revolutionary change. The inferences of archaeology are now enhanced and brought to life by written documents of many kinds.

Irrigation and the management of the irrigated fields were, of course, at once the most fundamental and the most exacting of all agricultural labour. It has already been seen how from the first the making and maintenance of the network of irrigation channels must have led to a strengthening of social organization and authority. This became more pronounced as the number and size of cities mounted and every available one of the 11,500 square miles of the alluvial soil of the Plain had to be brought under cultivation. The construction of the main canals, that might be twenty-five yards wide and run for many miles, was indeed so great a task that it was a royal respon-

sibility. Most of the kings of Sumer and Akkad who had any claim
to greatness built or restored canals. Next to victorious campaigns
or the building of temples, it was these hydraulic achievements that
they most loved to boast of.

The first recorded canal in all history is still in partial existence.
This is the Al-Gharrif, an apparent branch of the Tigris at Kut. It
was in fact cut by a governor of Lagash before the middle of the
third millennium B.C., as we know from a surviving account of his
project. For a later example it is recorded under the ninth regnal
year of Hammurabi, 'The canal [called] Hammurabi-hegal [was
dug]'; under the twenty-fourth year, 'he redug the "Flowing-Vase"
canal for Enlil, and also [the bed of] the Euphrates', while the entry
for the thirty-third year reads, 'He redug the canal [called] Hammurabi [spells] abundance-for-the-people, the Beloved-of-Anu-and-
Enlil, [thus] he provided Nippur, Eridu, Ur, Larsa, Uruk and Isin
with a permanent and lasting water supply.'

It is important to remember that when kings made canals they
were providing main arteries not only for irrigation but also for
transport. Produce could be shipped to the capital and to town
markets from all parts of the state. Often the monotony of the endless flat fields and lines of date palms must have been enlivened by
the sight of sails gliding serenely across the land.

Irrigation on the Plain was of a distinctive kind. Natural conditions determined that it should be perennial. By the time the floods
began in late March or April the winter-sown crops were already
greening the fields and the summer sowing was done. It was, therefore, impossible to allow the water freely on to the land as could
be done in Egypt. Some of the flood water could be immediately
used under strict control, while some was stored in reservoirs, natural
depressions and in the irrigation system itself. This could be used
during the following summer months. Probably rather more important was the water that could be led off from the rivers themselves
all through the year. The silt brought down from the hills and mountains by the floods was deposited when the current slackened on the
Plain, and gradually built up the bed and banks until the river
flowed well above the level of the fields. This was particularly true of
the Euphrates, always of far greater importance than the Tigris for
the watering of the Plain. To prevent disastrous breaching at flood
time, the banks had to be perpetually strengthened and repaired.
This was immensely laborious, as was also the building up of the

main canals to a level corresponding with the river bed in order to avoid an excessive rush of water when the sluices were opened. On the other hand the high level of the river made it possible, even in summer time, to lead water over long distances and with a minimum of hoisting. Such perennial irrigation enabled the farmers of the Plain to raise two crops a year, reliably brought to harvest beneath the summer sun.

There was one very serious problem of soil conservation. The silt fertilized the fields, but the water also carried salt and gypsum. If it was allowed to lie in stagnant pools and evaporate, it caused salinization of the soil that greatly reduced its yield. Drainage channels were therefore needed to lead away surplus water, a process made very difficult by the high water table. The fact that barley is more tolerant of salinity than is wheat was one of the reasons why it was always the principal crop and seems in time to have replaced wheat altogether. Inevitably, in spite of all efforts, salinization increased through the centuries of cultivation, and loss of fertility in the old Sumerian countryside of the southern Plain was probably one of the reasons for the northward shift of the focus of power.

Strabo has left us a wonderfully accurate account of Babylonian irrigation and its problems. Although when it was written during the first century B.C. the country had lost its greatness, governments had remained strong enough to maintain irrigation, probably very little changed from what it had been in the Bronze Age kingdoms:

The Euphrates rises to floodtide at the beginning of summer, beginning first to rise in the spring when the snows in Armenia melt, so that of necessity it forms lakes and deluges the ploughed lands, unless the excess of the stream, or the surface water, is distributed by means of trenches and canals. Now this is the origin of the canals; but there is need of much labour to keep them up, for the soil is so deep and soft and yielding that it is easily swept out by the streams and the plains are laid bare, and the canals are easily filled and their mouths choked by silt; and thus it results again that the overflow of the waters, emptying into the plain near the sea, forms lakes and marshes and reed beds, which last supply reeds for all kinds of crafts. . . .

It is impossible perhaps to prevent overflows of this kind, but it is the part of good rulers to afford all possible aid. The aid required is this: to prevent most of the overflowing by means of dams, and to prevent the filling up with silt . . . by keeping the canals cleared and the mouths opened up. Now the clearing of silt is easy, but the building of dams requires the work of many hands; for, since the earth readily collapses and is soft, it does not support the silt that is brought upon it, but yields to the silt and draws it on along with itself, making the mouth hard to dam.

And indeed there is also need of quick work in order to close the canals quickly and to prevent all the water emptying out of them. For when they dry up in the summer they dry up the river too; and when the river is lowered it cannot supply the (?) sluices with water at the time when it is most needed—in summer when the country is fiery hot and scorched. It makes no difference whether the crops are submerged by the abundance of water, or are destroyed by the thirst for water. At the same time, too, the voyages inland, with their many advantages, were always being thwarted by the two above-mentioned causes, and it was impossible to correct the trouble unless the mouths of the canals were quickly opened up and quickly closed, and unless the canals were so regulated that the water in them neither was excessive nor failed.

In addition to this late but most telling account of the difficulties of working the endless, structureless alluvium of the Plain, 'so deep and soft and yielding', and of defeating the twin demons of flood and 'thirst', we have inherited an extraordinarily full account of the subsequent stages in the agricultural year. This is no text of classical times, but a contemporary *Farmer's Almanac*. The tablet (from Nippur) mainly used for translation was inscribed a generation or two after Hammurabi but has earlier origins. It is given a literary form, beginning 'In days of yore a farmer gave [these] instructions to his son', and evidently became a respected Sumerian text, often copied by the scribes. As such, in spite of its lack of poetic feeling, it can be seen as a counterpart for Sumerian readers to Hesiod's *Works and Days* for the Greeks and Vergil's *Georgics* for the Romans.

The almanac tablet is not in perfect condition, and Professor Kramer has slightly modified his earlier versions. The gist of the paternal instructions on how to grow the heaviest possible crop of good barley is as follows. The field had first, of course, to be irrigated, great care being taken not to allow the water to rise too high. After the field had been drained, specially shod oxen were to be driven in to trample the weeds (and presumably to supply a certain amount of manure?). The trampled surface was then to be twice worked over with narrow mattocks of a certain weight, then smoothed by some form of harrow. Next the field had to be ploughed, it seems by two types of implement, and any remaining clods broken up with hammers. This preparation of the seed bed was expected to take ten days, working hard by day and by starlight. The young farmer was exhorted to keep his labourers always under his own eye.

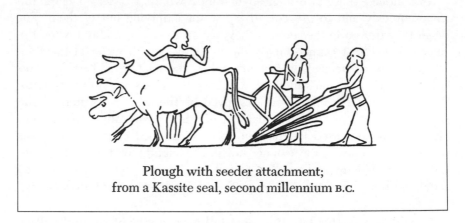

Plough with seeder attachment;
from a Kassite seal, second millennium B.C.

The sowing was to be done with an instrument that may perhaps have been invented in early historic times. This was a plough with a funnel to drop seed at a steady rate and depth behind the 'tongue' that was opening the furrow. The funnel itself was kept supplied by a man with a bag of barley walking alongside. When the whole field was sown it appears that the furrows had to be cleared of any new clods—a perfectionism that shows concern for every blade of barley.

At the next stage divine help was sought to reinforce human carefulness: the farmer was bidden to offer a prayer to Ninkilim, goddess of field mice and vermin, as soon as the corn began to sprout. He was also to 'shoo away the flying birds'. (The still abundant, mellifluous but greedy pigeons of the country would certainly have been after the tender blades.) At least three further irrigations were advised, one when the furrows were filled by the young barley, one when it covered the ground 'like the mat in the middle of a boat', and a third when it had reached full height. This was the moment of danger from the much-feared *samana*, an equivalent to rust. If this was escaped and the barley could still develop, a fourth watering might bring a ten percent increase in the yield.

Even so, the young farmer was instructed not to delay until the barley bent under the weight of the ears, but to harvest it 'in the day of its strength'—a phrase that brings a breath of poetry to this Sumerian *Works and Days*. The harvesting was to be done by a reaper, a binder and a third man who perhaps piled the stocks. The reaped grain stalks were to be taken to the threshing floor and the grain loosened by driving a threshing sledge over them during a period of five days. The final process, the winnowing, was to be done by two workers designated 'barley lifters', who were to throw the product of the threshing floor into the windy air so that unwanted chaff, husks and other litter might be carried away. It is an astonishing example of the conservatism of peasant life that threshing and winnowing are still done in precisely this way in many parts of the Near and Middle East—including lands so near to modern cities as central Anatolia and Crete. If the implements have also remained the same, then the sledge was a slightly up-curved board like a heavy surfing board, set underneath with flints or other sharp stones, and the tossing of the grain was done with flat wooden shovels —that could afterwards be used to pile the grain in golden heaps on the threshing floor. Presumably, too, on days when the gods did not provide a wind, wicker or basketry winnowing fans were used.

In the mid-valley the almanac would have had to be considerably modified. In Assyria hope and anxiety must have been focussed on the erratic rainfall. Then, as today, it would have varied from four inches in the Jazira to fifteen inches on the plains east of the Tigris —and forty inches up in the Zagros. It seems that all through history the eight inch rainfall line has usually divided the farmers from the nomad pastoralists. In times of strong government, at least, the fields were pushed southward to this limit. (At the present time the Bedouin have taken over most of the country west of the Tigris.) Assur itself lay very near the limits of cultivation and for this reason often suffered from drought. It may be that the imperialist kings of the first millennium B.C. built their new capitals further to the north and east of Tigris in order to escape this threat and to have a good supply of grain always available for their armies.

Along the mid-Euphrates the rainfall was normally too scanty to allow cultivation, but here irrigation was well developed. For example, Mari seems to have depended for its main grain supply on an irrigated strip three or four miles wide extending along the south bank of the river for the greater part of the two hundred miles of the kingdom. In the days of Jasmah-Adad, one of the king's governors refused to come to the capital when bidden because he was needed to supervise the irrigation. He told his sovereign, 'If the waters are interrupted, the land of my lord will starve.'

Barley, then, more or less supplemented by wheat and millet, provided the main energy-producing food for the peoples of Mesopotamia. Most of the grain went into little cakes or loaves, some was eaten as porridge and some went to the brewers. Other crops were also grown. The food lists most often mention onions, garlic, cumin, coriander, mustard and watercress. Leeks, cucumber and melons were grown as well. Lettuce, which evidently had a tender sexual association, is often mentioned in love poems and must have been popular. Beans are mentioned as part of the farmers' regular produce in the *Dispute* to be referred to below. Peas and lentils had been raised on the upland farms from the earliest times and were certainly known to the later peoples of the valley. It has been said that these legumes were of little importance to them, yet it seems unlikely that so valuable a source of protein was neglected by the poorer folk. It may be that the food lists neglect them because these lists represent the consumption of palace, temple and mansion. Surely in the reed and matting huts of the countryside and the mud-brick hovels of the city back-streets, hot, mushy bowls of pulse must have been enjoyed for wintertime dinners?

Already the Sumerians had discovered the secret of shade gardens, and it is likely that from that time many vegetables were raised in them. A garden of this kind forms the setting of a myth of the goddess Inanna. The gardener Shukalletuda, having failed in his horticulture and suffered torment himself through the ravages of dust and wind, one night looked up and 'from the inscribed heavens learnt the omens'. These star-written 'decrees of the gods' told him to plant five places in his garden with trees.

The tree's protecting cover, the sarbatu *tree of wide shade—*
Its shade below, dawn,
Noon and dusk did not turn away.

As a result his garden flourished and grew green—and the fact that he later involved the country in terrible plagues by copulating with Inanna when she lay down to rest near this delectable spot is no part of horticultural history.

Mesopotamian gardens were enriched by orchards of many kinds. Figs, grapes, apples, plums, peaches and cherries were all grown. The Assyrians seem to have been particularly fond of pomegranates and knew both a bitter and a sweet variety. On the Plain, however, by far the most important fruit tree was the date palm. It was grown both in orchards and along canal banks. From quite early times the cultivators had discovered the need to practise artificial fertilization if a good crop was to be had. Dates were not only eaten as fruit, but made into a sweet substance referred to as honey, and also into date wine. The tree itself was valuable as a source of wood, fibres and matting.

The texts tell us almost nothing of the growing of sesame—perhaps because this tropical plant (now thought to have originated in Africa rather than India) throve easily without need of special skills. Certainly it was a most important crop for the people of the Plain, where olives could not be grown. The oil pressed from its many-coloured seeds was used for cooking, lighting and presumably cosmetics. It was one of the three basic rations issued to workers of all kinds.

Except for the few Semitic tribesmen who may have maintained a wholly nomadic life in the wastes of the mid-valley, the peoples of Mesopotamia practised mixed farming with a sound, flexible balance between plant and animal husbandry. Sheep and goats were the most important of the domestic animals, at any rate for ordinary people. They were certainly the most numerous. At the time of the Third Dynasty of Ur flocks of sheep numbering tens of thousands were recorded. No doubt the shepherds often led mixed flocks of sheep and goats—as they still do today beside those grass-grown mounds that once were Assyrian cities.

There is disagreement between scholars as to the extent to which the many names for sheep represent distinct breeds. Certainly there were both black and white breeds, and the fat-tailed variety (*Ovis platyra*) was kept. In the north of the valley mountain sheep were probably driven down seasonally from their upland valleys as is still the practice among the Kurds.

The meat of lambs, kids and young adult animals was enjoyed at least by the well-to-do. Care was taken to produce good fattened meat for those who could afford it. Thus in the instructions for the sacrifices to be offered to the gods in the city of Uruk mention is made of rams that have been fed for two years on barley, and others that were milk-fed. Curiously, there is also special mention of 'fat rams that have not been fed on barley'.

It can be assumed that both ewes and she-goats were milked. In the literary *Dispute* between the shepherd god Dumuzi and the farmer god Enkimdu (referred to as 'king of dyke, ditch and plough'), Dumuzi boasts of the various types of milk and fat and small cheeses he can supply, yet says nothing to suggest that he tended any stock other than sheep and goats. Probably poor families were often able to keep a few goats and depended heavily on their milk and cheese.

The Sumerians traditionally wore the *kaunakes*, a sheepskin kilt with the fleece outside. To judge from the long, curling tails of wool sometimes shown on these kilts, sheep had already been carefully bred for their fleece. Later, woollen textiles became an important part of the economy and huge quantities of wool, usually still plucked and not shorn, were produced for the industry. Many thousands of tons were used every year at Ur alone. Dr. F. E. Zeuner made an interesting observation concerning the origins of the use of wool. He pointed out that wild sheep living in the surrounding hills of Mesopotamia shed their woolly winter coat in the spring. Masses of this moult hang in the thorny shrubs and must always have attracted attention. Anyone with an understanding of fibres would have seen the possibility of spinning it, but felting would have been an even more obvious way of utilizing the wool. If the valley dwellers themselves did not use felt, it seems very likely that the invaders from the mountains and the invaders from the deserts both did so.

Goat hair was also used for cords, carpets and other textiles. Some goat-hair cloth seems to have been employed for packaging. Was it also already woven, as it still is in remote regions today, to make the low, long black tents of the nomads?

The *Dispute* of Dumuzi and Enkimdu, with its foretaste of Cain and Abel, can be best seen as reflecting the division of function within the mixed farming economy of the valley. The shepherd's was a distinct calling. The laws of Hammurabi contain severe penalties against the shepherd who 'has pastured sheep on the field without consent of the owner of the field'. Unlike the more violent Hebrew story, the Sumerian *Dispute* ends in reconciliation. The pacific Enkimdu exclaims:

> *I against thee, O shepherd, against thee O shepherd,*
> *I against thee*
> *Why should I strive?*
> *Let thy sheep eat the grass of the river bank,*

In my meadowland let thy sheep walk about,
In the bright fields of Erech let them eat grain
Let thy kids and lambs drink the water of my Unun canal.

This charming pastoral scene illumines the economic fact that there was close interdependence between plant and animal husbandry.

The Sumerians, like the prehistoric peoples before them, kept pigs, enjoying pork and pork fat and making use of pigskin. They not only had specialized swineherds but also pork butchers to see to the slaughtering and preparation of the meat. With the dominance of the Semites, pork-eating evidently became taboo, and so far as is known pigs were no longer kept on the farms.

Although perhaps less important than sheep and goats, cattle were an essential part of the Mesopotamian economy. The usual breed was a good solid animal, with wide upcurving horns. Seals and reliefs sometimes show cattle with smaller or larger humps. Although in a few instances these may have been the work of Indian artists, it looks as though a zebu strain was present in Mesopotamia. In the torrid climate of the Plain, stock tended to deteriorate and needed an infusion of genes from outside. An instance is known of a stud bull being imported from Elam.

Beef and veal were eaten: the sacrificial animals prescribed for the temple at Uruk included milk-fed bullocks as well as large bulls. The cows were milked and butter and cheese made. A charming dairying scene on a mosaic 'cut-out' from Al-Ubaid, near Ur, shows the milker sitting well aft of the cow and reaching the udders from behind the back legs. This scene also shows a variety of large pottery containers, and a liquid, presumably milk, being poured from one into another through a funnel.

The hides had many uses. One of the most curious and best recorded was the covering of sacred temple kettle-drums. Instructions for the ritual to be followed start with the selection of a bull which on scrutiny 'from head to tip of tail' proves to be 'black as pitch' all over, with perfect horns and hoofs. It must never have been struck by a staff or touched by a goad. After this paragon of sacrificial beasts has been led (on an auspicious day) into the temple and bound, there must follow all manner of purifications, censing, subsidiary sacrifices and pouring of libations in beer, wine and milk. The bull itself is to be subject to the 'washing of the mouth', then one incantation is to be whispered through a reed into his right ear and another proscribed incantation into his left ear. After the skin has been removed it is to be subject to a variety of treatments, some evidently magical, others practical—including rubbing with gall-nuts and 'alum from the land of the Hittites'. Among the gods invoked for the closing rites is the Divine Kettle-drum himself.

It is worth recalling this exceptional and religiously charged use of the hide of a black bull without blemish because in a society where farming has become almost wholly economic, is losing its last faint breath of the numinous and symbolic, it is important to remember that it was quite otherwise in the high days of Bronze Age civilization. Then, as we shall see, the bull was one of the supreme symbols of divinity; the bull, the cow, the ram, the lamb and the good shepherd permeate all the imagery of religious and moral teaching. The farmer in his daily life and work naturally combined all his practical skills with appropriate rites, prayers and magic spells. For him each would have been vain without the others: this was the way of doing things taught him by the gods, the right and only way.

The Mesopotamian peoples might have been able to dispense with the bull, the cow and their offspring as sources of food, drink, hides and hair, but they could not have flourished without that source of energy, the castrated male. Ox-power was essential for heavy transport. The slow and stupid, but strong and tireless oxen, guided by nose-rings and their strength quite efficiently harnessed through yoke and pole, drew solid-wheeled wagons of various kinds—from the grandest vehicles used for the royal funerals at Ur to the roughest serving the needs of farmers or builders. It was usually oxen, too, that plodded along canal tow-paths pulling deeply laden boats. They were equally indispensable in the fields. Ever since the time, probably before 3000 B.C., when the plough displaced the hoe, oxen had served as tractors. We have already encountered them dragging the threshing sledge, trampling the newly watered earth.

When greater speed was necessary, the Sumerians succeeded in harnessing that intractable beast, the onager. Then at the beginning of the second millennium the onager began to be replaced by the horse. Here was a change in livestock that profoundly affected Mesopotamian history, but it belongs with military affairs, not with the unhurried, unaristocratic life of the countryside and market.

One other beast of burden that very much did belong to it was the ass. The donkey or ass, coming originally from North Africa, was everywhere used, and probably heartlessly exploited, for carrying goods in paniers or packs, for drawing small carts, and as a mount for the common man. Man's use of the donkey has not changed through the millennia. Anyone today who has been to a land where the relationship still prevails and has seen men and boys trotting into market from distant villages, either with legs wide apart over their packs or poised with uncanny skill on the haunches of their beasts, then has seen the jostling and thwacking as they converge upon the market place and knows something at least of country life in ancient Mesopotamia—or indeed in Egypt and all the Middle East.

The camel was known to the Sumerians, for they gave it the preposterous name of 'ass of the sea'—which probably means they associated it with Arabia. However, as it never seems to have come into general use in the valley but remained a creature of the desert caravans, it will find its place in a discussion of trade.

That the labour of their farmers produced a good and varied diet for the peoples of Mesopotamia is already apparent. It was, however, increased and made more interesting and full of variety by the gifts of nature. Above all rivers, canals, lakes, and in the south the sea provided great quantities of fish. The Euphrates in particular swarmed with them, and there a lucky fisherman might sometimes land a two-hundred-pounder. Together with the leguminous vegetables this abundance of fish (eaten both fresh and salted) must have meant that even the poorest need never go short of protein. If the livers were eaten, they also supplied vitamins A and D. Fish, however, was considered worthy of the best occasions: ten thousand were supplied for Assurnasirpal's great feast at Kalah.

This famous banquet also helps to show how far hunting and fowling added to the pleasures of the table. Deer and gazelle were on the menu, together with a great variety of birds. Presumably there were few game animals to be had on the Plain, but for Assyria and other parts of the mid-valley they were probably quite plentiful among the deserts and foothills. As for birds, there were pigeons and partridge in abundance, wild geese came to Mesopotamia on migration, and in time the goose was domesticated, providing rich fat and eggs as well as succulent meat. Cranes were eaten; they appear in the list of sacrifices offered at the temples of Uruk. So, too, do ostrich eggs.

Honey was, of course, the best sweetener available in the ancient world. In Mesopotamia it was taken from the nests of wild bees, but, in contrast with Egypt, bees do not seem to have been kept until quite late in her history. Yet beeswax was also needed by the bronze-smiths for lost-wax casting. There are always a few such national idiosyncrasies to defeat any economic determinism. Perhaps the date 'honey' did well enough to satisfy man's sweet tooth. Yet true honey was certainly esteemed. Just as in the United States, it could stand for the sweets of love—but seems to have been applied to the man rather than the woman. In a love song probably used in the rites of the Sacred Marriage, the king is addressed as 'My Lord, the "honey-man" of the gods . . . whose hand is honey, whose foot is honey, sweetens me ever. Whose limbs are honey sweet, sweetens me ever.'

CRAFTS

NOT ALL THE BARLEY AND DATES THAT GREW SO WELL IN SUMERIAN and later fields went into foodstuffs. Like all that have succeeded it, man's first civilization gave great place to intoxication. Long before there was decadence or world-weariness, men and women wanted to change their response to the planet on which they had evolved to self-consciousness.

True wine was being drunk in Sumeria by Early Dynastic times. The best vintages, however, came from the cooler lands to the north. Date wine was also a popular drink, particularly after the end of the Kassite period when, for a time, beer seems to have fallen out of favour. The Greeks were to find it 'a pleasant drink causing headaches'! Wine shops were often kept by women. One of the laws of Hammurabi decrees that if a woman wine seller fails to hand over outlaws sheltering on her premises then 'that wine seller shall be put to death.' Even worse is the fate decreed for a priestess who goes into a wine shop for a drink—or so much as opens the door: 'They shall burn that woman.'

In the days of Sumer and Akkad beer must have been the most universal drink, and the one most closely related to the agricultural life of the countryside. Brewing became an increasingly subtle and skilled business. There were many named varieties of beer—seemingly far more than our light and dark ales, stouts and lagers, mild and bitter and the rest. Moreover, individual brewers were noted for the distinctive flavour and quality of their product.

Beer drinking through reeds; from a seal of c. 2500 B.C.

As with wine-selling, women played a large part in the business. This is true in many of the non-industrial societies of the world today—for example among the maize and manioc beer-makers of Brazil. In Mesopotamia itself it is well exemplified by the tale, popular until the time of Hammurabi, of a woman who, with her husband, brewed a special beer and sold it in her tavern. No doubt it was partly due to the fact that brewing could be seen as a form of cooking, and also involved much use of great earthenware containers —embodiments of the feminine principle.

This female supremacy appeared also in the magical and religious aspects of beer-making. Alone among the craftsmen of Mesopotamia, the brewer enjoyed the patronage of a goddess. She was Ninkasi, the Lady Who Fills the Mouth, deity of strong drink. She is evoked in a fine Sumerian hymn where she herself appears as performing every act in the brewing process. In the last stanza, when the beer is ready, she shares her joys with Inanna herself:

> *Drinking beer in blissful mood*
> *Drinking liquor, feeling exhilarated. . . .*
> *The heart of Inanna is happy again,*
> *The heart of the Queen of Heaven is happy again.*

The technical details of the craft have proved difficult to follow, chiefly because they are obscured by many specialist terms, Sumerian and Akkadian, that changed over thousands of years of brewing history. The main processes, however, are clear enough.

The most subtle and important of them was the preparation of the malted beer-bread, or *bappir*. The grain, usually barley, but sometimes emmer wheat, was soaked and allowed to germinate and sprout. At the moment when its sweetness and flavour were judged to be at their best, it had to be spread out to dry. At this stage the sprouted grain was vulnerable and might be protected by guard dogs. A Sumerian saying equivalent to our 'bull in a china shop' is 'The elephant tramples the sprouting greenmalt.'

The malted grain was now crushed, flavoured with a choice of herbs, spices, honey and dates and either used at once or made into cakes for storage or transport. (Malt bread of this kind had long been used as a highly nutritious foodstuff particularly valuable to travellers.) The hymn describes the last part of the process: 'You [Ninkasi] are the one who handles the beer bread . . . with a big shovel, mixing in a pit the *bappir* with sweet aromatics.'

In the next stage soaked *bappir* and hulled grain were mixed together, warmed in a slow oven until the right moment (again a matter of careful timing), and the mash spread on a large mat to cool. Some sugary substance was added to aid fermentation and the mash put with water into the vat. This had a perforated base allowing the beer to drip through into another vessel below. In the early days, at least, yeast does not seem to have been used, but rather other micro-organisms more able to survive the warmth of the oven. These could survive in the crannies of the brewing vessels. In this way, unknowingly, each brewer would have maintained his own brand of ferment with its special flavouring. The whole brew must have seethed with magic potency. This final stage is clearly conjured up by the hymn.

> *The fermenting vat, which makes a pleasant sound,*
> *You place as it should be above the great collector vat.*
> *Ninkasi, . . .*
> *You are the one who pours out the filtered beer . . .*
> *It is (like) the onrush of the Tigris and Euphrates.*

The pleasant sound is, of course, that of the fermented beer dripping through the filter—a fine contrast with the gush when the collector vat is poured out.

In all the existing texts of the Ninkasi hymn it is associated with a unique Sumerian drinking song. This has no more rational meaning than most drinking songs, yet it has a value for us. It can act as a grain of yeast in the imagination to make us fully aware that life

for these men and women of Sumer and Akkad felt just as it does
to us—in all its overwhelming reality and immediacy. An obvious
truth, perhaps, but not one that all historians seem to appreciate.
Imagine, then, country folk, after all day in the fields, sitting out
in the sweet warm night below the divine moon and stars—or, for
contrast, townsfolk in winter, the crowded tavern lit by firelight and
an oil lamp or two. Their song is:

> *The* gakkul *vat, the* gakkul *vat,*
> *The* gakkul, *the* lam-sa-re *vat,*
> *The* gakkul *vat, which makes the liver happy,*
> *The* lam-sa-re *vat, which rejoices the heart,*
> *The* ugur-bal *jar, a good thing in the house,*
> *The* sa-gub *jar, which is filled with beer. . . .*
> *The beautiful vessels are ready on their stands!*

Although brewing required traditional knowledge, care and some
judgement, it can hardly qualify as a skilled or highly specialized
craft. In every kingdom it must, in fact, have been carried on
in scores of premises both rural and urban. Thus it provides a sound
link between the ancient, slow-changing life of the fields and that of
the city workshops with their evolving skills. The fully urbanized
life of Sumerians, Akkadians and Babylonians, reinforced by ambitious and competitive royal houses, must have acted as a magnet
for fine craftsmen and a stimulus to experimental advances.

While most people would probably judge that the extraordinary
wealth of the Pharaohs and their royal cities produced finer and more
freely used art, Mesopotamia generally led the advance in technical
skills. Nowhere was this more obviously true than in metallurgy, the
central and most significant technological achievement of Bronze
Age man.

The first steps were not, of course, taken in Mesopotamia, but very
probably in the uplands to the north, somewhere between Anatolia
and the Caspian where copper ores and fuel were both plentiful. It
may have been here that the first stages of hammering up native
copper into small objects, and then later the use of heat for anneal-
ing, were successfully mastered. The next advance, that of reducing
copper ores in the presence of charcoal, was probably also made
there, by about 4000 B.C. A groping appreciation of the fact that an
admixture of other ores, and particularly tin, produced a metal that

was at once harder and more readily cast than pure copper was spreading by the end of the millennium. We have seen that in later Protoliterate times metal was already being used for a variety of objects, including vessels. Craftsmen were prepared to tackle a work as elaborate as the great Ibn-Dugud panel from Al-Ubaid, with its antlered stags, before 2500 B.C. The advance to the use of bronze, however, was probably as tentative and uncertain for the ancient metal workers themselves as is the historical reconstruction of the process for us today. The sources of uncertainty are twofold. One is that copper ores usually contain impurities of various kinds, sometimes including tin. Metal containing 2 percent or less of tin is usually written off as representing a natural, unintentional adulteration of this kind. On the other hand, of course, the metal workers may have learnt to prefer ores coming from regions where tin was present because they observed that they produced better results.

The second source of uncertainty is past and present ignorance about tin itself. There are no ancient accounts to tell us anything about where it was obtained or how it was prepared. Nor is it ever found separately (as copper may be) in bronzesmiths' 'hoards'. Cassiterite or tinstone occurs in quartz veins in volcanic rocks, where it may be associated with gold. Both ores were often washed out and redeposited by streams. It seems that men seeking the bright specks of gold in the streams came across heavy dark nuggets of tin and recognized them as metallic. Metal workers were already experimenting with alloying copper with lead, arsenic and antimony— and it is known that tin was at first held to be a form of lead. However, it is obvious that they would soon have recognized that this version of 'lead' gave them a finer product than any other. Whether inquiring minds came to realize that the new alloy could be identified with the copper ores naturally adulterated with tin we are unlikely ever to discover.

The earliest Mesopotamian artifacts that can be called bronzes date from about 3200–3100 B.C. However, as they contain only about 4 percent tin and also yield lead and iron, it is very probable that the tin was present as a natural impurity. It was in the Early Dynastic period that the controlled and deliberate production of bronze really got under way. It then developed with the speed often released when men clearly recognize a problem or a need and so can set themselves to meet the challenge.

In the early stages of this most significant technological advance, the alloying was probably done by mixing the unreduced ores of copper and tin and smelting them with charcoal. This rough method would account for the wide fluctuation in the percentage of tin found in the earlier bronze. By about the middle of the third millennium, however, bronzesmiths had realized that about 10 percent of tin was the ideal proportion for most purposes. They now probably were able to control this proportion more exactly by reducing the tinstone in the presence of smelted copper. By this time craftsmen could cast very fine objects indeed—well represented by the many splendid vessels and other bronzes from the Royal Cemetery of Ur (c. 2600 B.C.) A still more perfect specimen of bronze casting is the noble bearded head from Nineveh—which if it does indeed represent King Sargon, must date from about 2340 B.C.

Soon after this the bronzesmiths must have faced an economic crisis in their trade. During later Sargonid times axes were again being made of hammered copper. Presumably either all the easily accessible sources of stream tinstone had been exhausted, or some political disturbance had cut off supplies. The former is more likely, particularly as there is evidence that prospectors now began to explore westward to discover new sources of supply. A late advance in the production of bronze, which was to mean plentiful metal resources during the last centuries of the Bronze Age, was accomplished before the middle of the second millennium B.C. At about this time the metal workers learnt how to smelt the sulphides of copper which were to be obtained by deeper mining. Hitherto they had depended on the oxides and carbonates (malachite) to be found in surface deposits. Tin supplies were now well organized throughout Europe and western Asia, and it became the practice to reduce the pure metal instead of relying on tinstone. Now that the alloying could be made with pure copper and pure tin, proportions could be controlled with a new precision, and it was possible to produce a range of bronzes from soft (about 5 percent) to hard to suit different purposes.

It is thought that in the early days of metallurgy pure copper was first produced in the pottery kilns of the time, which readily commanded the temperature of 1085° C., the melting point of copper. Later special furnaces were developed. The simplest form may have been a clay-lined pit, then an earthenware pot sunk in the earth. This pot furnace was then further evolved by building a shaft and chimney above it, reducing the ores themselves in a crucible where they need no longer be interspersed with the charcoal. An early Sumerian ideogram for furnace shows a shaft furnace of this kind. In all furnaces the necessary heat had to be raised by draft, supplied either by simple blowing through clay-tipped reeds or, as the scale increased, by the employment of bellows with long clay nozzles. At Girsu in the city-state of Lagash a pot furnace was found complete with two of these nozzles designed for a pair of bellows. It had been in use in about 2500 B.C.

A parallel evolution in casting can be followed from the simple open mould used for flat copper axes, through moulds of stone or (rarely) bronze made in two or more parts, to the ingenious lost-wax or *cire perdue* process. In this method, reserved for the finer castings only, a core in the form of the object was modelled, then coated with beeswax, which was in turn coated with fine clay reinforced with a porous bricky clay. The wax was then run off through carefully designed vents, and the molten bronze poured into its vacant place. *Cire perdue* was a time-consuming method, since each mould could be used only once.

Complex moulds and *cire perdue* were already employed by the Sumerian bronzesmiths. They also were skilled in sheet metal work with its complexities of rivetting and surface finishing. In almost all these and other related techniques we shall find that the Mesopotamian bronze workers were from the first, and remained, much in advance of their Egyptian contemporaries.

While the early development of metallurgical skills is of interest to us, especially as a proof of how far man could progress in empirical knowledge and technical ability without any 'scientific' understanding of the nature of the processes involved, the bronze industry is of greater significance here for the very high degree of organization that it involved. While Assyria and other mid-valley states were somewhat better placed, the Plain was far removed not only from tin and copper ores, but also from the good-quality charcoal necessary as the reducing agent. Every foundry and workshop was at the centre of a web of trading relationships and supply lines.

Early supplies of copper probably came from Iran and the other mountain territories to the north that are thought to have been the birthplace of metallurgy. In the Old Babylonian period, Kanesh, as has already been seen, became a trading colony for the supply of Anatolian copper to Mesopotamia—and handled finished metal goods in exchange. Copper was also coming by the Gulf route through Dilmun (almost certainly Bahrein). The ultimate source of at least a part of this southern copper was Makan—now usually identified with the Oman. By a happy chance we have intimate knowledge of the affairs of one Dilmun trader. This was Ea-nasir, of Ur, who was carrying on his import-export business in the years on either side of 1800 B.C.—when Abraham may have been a fellow citizen.

Ea-nasir's letters and accounts, inscribed on tablets found in his house, show how sophisticated the trade had become and what substantial quantities were handled. He evidently acted as a copper broker, undertaking to deliver agreed quantities of copper from the holding of one individual into the possession of another. He seems not always to have behaved with perfect probity. One of his clients, Nanni, complains: '. . . you said, "I will give good ingots to Gimil-Sin." That is what you said, but you have not done so; you offered bad ingots to my messenger, saying, "Take it or leave it." Who am I that you should treat me so? Are we not both gentlemen?' Another tablet, which is also of interest in relating the different standard weights prevailing in Dilmun and in Ur, reveals that one shipload of copper was as much as eighteen metric tons—out of which Ea-nasir's share was over five tons.

The sources of tin remain obscure. Probably Iran and Caucasia at first largely supplied Sumeria, but it is quite conceivable that so valuable a substance may have trickled through from further east—even from so far as Lake Baikal. Strabo mentions tin ores from Transoxiana. In the second millennium western sources, including central Europe and Spain, seem to have been tapped.

In a land so short of timber, even the supply of charcoal required organization. Poor-quality dry wood, reed bundles and shrubs could be used for the furnace, but for the charcoal reduction agent fresh wood was needed—and in very large amounts. It seems to have been brought down from the northern valleys. Hammurabi, instructing an agent, specifies Kusabku wood and continues, 'Every lot of three hundred logs shall be loaded on a freighter and brought to Babylon. Among the firewood that will be cut there shall be no wood that died in the forest. They shall cut green wood only. This firewood shall be brought quickly, lest the metal workers sit down empty-handed.' Presumably they *were* sometimes held up in this way, and the supply of charcoal was as much a limiting factor in the output of bronze as the supply of the ores themselves.

It seems that, sometimes at least, the same workshops that made bronze goods also worked in gold and silver. Many of the skills would have been shared—although the production of the precious metals was much easier owing to their lower melting point and the smaller quantities involved. The advanced techniques of the Sumerian gold- and silversmiths are brilliantly exemplified in the treasures of the Royal Cemetery of Ur. In gold there were the beautifully fluted beakers, the ceremonial weapons and helmets, the intricate if somewhat flimsy female headdresses and necklaces; in silver great numbers of shapely vessels. All these show the mastery of the Early Dynastic craftsmen—which included the special skills of soldering, filigree and granulation.

Mesopotamia, lacking the abundant gold supply of Egypt, probably obtained it from a number of sources, often coinciding with those of tin. Alluvial gold could have come from Caucasia and Iran, and some certainly came from Anatolia, particularly perhaps from the torrent beds of the Anti-Taurus range. When more local stream beds were exhausted, the Mesopotamian princes' appetite for gold may have been satisfied by supplies brought by caravan from western Arabia and even the Yemen. Small quantities almost certainly arrived from India.

Silver production was always associated with that of lead, as the two metals are together in the bright, eye-catching mineral galena. Here one source overshadowed all others: Anatolia, and particularly the mountains of the Taurus and Armenia. Classical tradition was to recognize northeastern Anatolia, the Land of the Chalybes, as the home of silver. Sargon of Akkad and Gudea of Lagash sent expeditions to secure the products of the mines of the Silver Mountain. This natural wealth of their land must have added immensely to the economic power of the Hittites: the name of their capital, Hattusas, was written with an ideogram signifying silver. The Assyrian merchants who lived among them at Kanesh and elsewhere bought the metal in both its crude and refined states.

This metal of the moon god, Sin, had a special importance as one of the main bases of currency. Obedient to the laws of supply and demand, in Mesopotamia silver was always worth much less than gold. In the time of Sargon of Akkad gold was eight times more valuable, in the Mari records only four, yet for the greater part of the ancient history of the Valley of the Twin Rivers the ratio seems to have been about ten to one. In Egypt, on the other hand, where gold was plentiful and the silver mines far away, silver was at times worth up to twice as much as gold.

Although its use falls outside the main period of our concern, a word must be said about the latest addition to the metallurgy of the ancient world—iron. Early metal workers familiar with the marvellous properties of those blue and green minerals that gave them copper must have experimented with the red minerals that could in fact have yielded them iron. Iron oxides reduce at about the same heat as those of copper, but owing to the much higher melting point, the experimenters were not rewarded with a flow of metal. The small lumps of metal were lost in the spongy mass of the 'bloom'. It is hardly surprising that millennia went by before men discovered the many processes needed to produce an iron that was superior to bronze—the heavy work of extracting the metal by much heating and hammering was not enough, for this wrought iron remained soft. It was more fit for ornaments than for tools or weapons.

It was not until the second half of the second millennium B.C. that the essential process of carburizing, or steeling, by repeated heating in the presence of charcoal, and hammering was fully mastered. It seems to have been accomplished by those famed metallurgists, the Chalybes, then subject to the Hittites. For some two centuries (1400–1200 B.C.) the Hittites held a near monopoly. Then with the collapse of their empire and the general ethnic upheaval of the time, the blacksmith's art was spread rapidly in all directions. Mesopotamia, however, was slow to adopt the new metal. Although it had been known and sparingly used centuries earlier, it can be said that there was no true Iron Age there before the ninth century. From that date the Assyrian kings used great quantities for their armies. Hard iron and the Assyrian empire were well suited to one another. Sargon II was particularly lavish, and it is appropriate that 150,000 kilograms of iron bars were found in his palace. The Assyrians seem to have imported the iron ready-made from Anatolia and Syria, the state keeping central stores in each city and issuing it to smiths to forge under contract.

The blacksmith, even more than earlier metal makers, was a man set apart in society. Working among smoke and fumes with his huge hammers and tongs at the bloomery, or by the glaring red eye of his forge, with the many mysterious processes (increased when quenching and tempering were added to carburizing) that he took care to keep secret, he filled his fellows with awe.

One other craft almost equal to metallurgy in economic import-ance was that of the spinners and weavers of textiles. In social psychology it was at the opposite extreme from smithing, for it grew gradually out of a simple prehistoric craft practised by the women of the house by the fireside or outside the door. Yet in Sumeria already before the end of the third millennium it was a highly organized industry, much of it carried on in near factory conditions. As has so often happened when a skill or craft passes beyond the domestic scale, men began to take part in what had been women's work, though women were still employed in larger numbers. Weav-ing was a hereditary profession and there was much specialization. Not only were there spinners, weavers, dyers and fullers, each or-ganized into a guild-like group with an organization man at its head, but even the weavers seem sometimes to have been specialists —as for example in coloured cloths. It is not surprising to learn that there were also linen weavers, for this involved distinct techniques. In sharp contrast with Egypt, however, flax was not much grown in Mesopotamia and the output of linen must have been very small.

The reason for the large scale of the woollen textile industry was, of course, that it formed the backbone of Mesopotamia's export trade. Without it the peoples of the valley could hardly have im-ported the wood, the minerals and other raw materials that they lacked. Northward, for example, it was largely woollens coming up from Assur that the merchants of Kanesh could offer against Ana-tolian metals; southward it was woollens (and wool) that enabled merchants of Ur, like Ea-nasir, to import copper through Dilmun. Tablets from Ur specify various numbers of garments and quantities of wool shipped to Dilmun from the Nanna temple of Ur: in one it is stated that this merchandise was 'for buying copper from Makan'.

We have, in fact, a unique knowledge of the organization of crafts, and particularly of textile manufacture, preserved for us among the archives at Ur, many of them dating from Third Dynasty times. Some of the ateliers belonged to private merchants (these became rela-tively commoner in later times as part of the general swing to private enterprise associated with Semitization). More belonged to the king and temples. In the temple shops both men and women were em-ployed, with the women probably always outnumbering the men. Though a large proportion were slaves, there were also free citizens, and it seems that they may sometimes have taken spun wool home to weave, bringing it back to the temple as finished cloth. Weaving of wool was probably usually done on vertical frame looms, as these gave more tension to the warp threads, which would otherwise be inclined to stretch and sag. Horizontal looms were also in use and may have been preferred for weaving linen, where there is not the same need for tension.

This cloth-making was a slow process. Professor Kramer has calculated that it took a team of three women eight days to spin and weave a piece measuring 3½ by 4 metres. When it is remembered that every year many thousands of tons of wool were worked up at Ur alone it is evident how very many hands must have been employed. They and their work were supervised with the bureaucratic thoroughness of a welfare state. Not only were detailed accounts kept of all individuals, their pay and output, but also of deaths, absences and stand-ins for the sick. Women were evidently debarred from work during menstruation. One entry reads, 'payments for the sick, for the days of absence (when unclean) and sundry expenditures of female workers for one month'.

When the weaving was done the lengths of cloth went to the fuller to be steeped in his alkaline vats and afterwards trampled under foot. Natural wool could be selected to produce whitish, brown and black tones, but dyes were used for coloured cloth or for ornamental woven borders. Among dyes used in early times were woad for blues and a concoction of pomegranate rinds for yellows. Mesopotamian customers seem to have recognized that for luxury cloths their workshops were far surpassed by those of the Levant. The Syrians in particular were renowned. Assyrian kings on their campaigns to the west were always ready to carry off fine cloth as booty.

Among the more important of the other craftsmen, working mainly for the home market rather than for export, were the leather workers, the carpenters and the potters. Of these the first were perhaps economically the most important as leather was used in large quantities for military equipment—shields, helmets, slings, chariots and chariot tyres—as well as for more usual domestic purposes such as shoes, sandals, bags, water-skins and furniture seats. In the account of the drum membrane, mention has been made of the alum and gall-nuts that were brought 'from the land of the Hittites' employed in the tanning. Fine leather might be dyed, and one worker at Ur is recorded as using 'powder of gold' for decoration. The skins of bulls, calves and pigs were regularly employed, but by far the largest number came from those vast flocks of sheep that were kept principally for their wool. Hides were in fact among Sumeria's exports. In some of the accounts of the 'Dilmun traders' of Ur, hides were listed in the same cargoes as the wool and cloth.

In spite of the absence of good local woods, there were plenty of carpenters working in Sumer and throughout Mesopotamia. The bronzesmiths furnished them with the tools of their trade, which included saws, hammers and drill bits. They turned out such goods as house doors and plough frames, boats and waggons. That was the everyday trade of the average carpenter. The best craftsmen made fine furniture for the gods, the royal apartments and the wealthy. In the surviving woodwork from the Royal Cemetery at Ur there are examples of one wood inlaid with another; Queen Shub-ad's big wooden chest had a single band of mosaic inlay. The superb ivory-covered couches and chairs from the Assyrian palaces fall into a different category and will be considered as works of art. In general it can be supposed that Mesopotamian furniture, though perhaps rather heavier in style, was no less rich or beautifully made than that of Egypt—where so many actual specimens can still be admired.

Much of the wood came down river from the mountain valleys to the north. This was the source for oak, walnut and fir. All of these were in use in the Ur workshops, as was also ebony. The famous cedar wood of the Lebanon, the object of so many royal expeditions to the Amanus range, was used for furniture, but the greater part of it must have gone into the architectural woodwork of temples and palaces. In spite of all these imports, fine woods were too valuable to be wasted. The accounts of a carpenter's workshop at Ur, dating from the reign of Ibbi-Sin, tell us that three old tabletops and four chests were broken up and their wood used to make one table, two beds and a small box.

Among humbler local woods employed by the carpenters were mulberry and tamarisk. In that characteristic example of a literary genre, the *Dispute Between the Tamarisk and the Date Palm*, the tamarisk boasts:

> *Pay attention, O lunatic. What of mine is in the king's palace? In the king's house the king eats off my table, the queen drinks from my cup, with my fork the warriors eat. . . .*

And in another place:

> . . . *from the trough made of me the baker scoops*
> *out the flour.*

Like the craft of the cloth maker, that of the potter was an ancient one growing from the domestic skills of the prehistoric past. But whereas when textiles had been commercialized in large ateliers, spinning and weaving remained home crafts and women everywhere went on making materials for family use on simple looms, commercially produced pottery seems completely to have displaced the home-produced wares. It happened just as today factory plastics have displaced local types of container even in the most out-of-the-way markets of the world. It is easy to understand why this should be so. For one thing the firing of pottery was always a difficult, dirty and space-demanding business, and for another the bulk-produced vessels of the professional potters were presumably very cheap and within the reach even of the poorest.

As has been described, bulk production had already developed in Protoliterate times and, already by the time of the arrival of the Sumerians, was associated with a sharp decline in the artistic quality of the ceramics. This was not reversed—although the palace ware of the Neo-Assyrians was a superior product. Unlike the Minoans, Mycenaeans and Greeks—or for that matter the peoples of Middle and South America—the Mesopotamians of historic times never made potting into a high art form. This has sometimes been explained by saying that as the privileged could afford to have vessels in precious metal or decorative stone they had no need to patronize the potters. Yet this was no less true of the élite of the Aegean world.

The Mesopotamian potters continued to turn their pots on the socket-and-pivot wheels that had been adopted before the end of the fourth millennium. They fired them in domed ovens with a perforated floor above the fire. They made a good range of quite sound and practical shapes in a hard and pervious ware, and of every size from neat tableware to large storage jars, vats and other functional vessels for the handling of milk, beer and wine. If not artists, the Mesopotamian potters were sound craftsmen who supplied customers at all levels with the cheap containers they needed.

ARCHITECTURE AND THE CITIES

THE MAJORITY OF ALL THESE CRAFTSMEN, AS WELL AS OTHERS, LESS important, with whom there is no space to deal, lived and worked in the cities that were so distinctive a creation of Sumerian civilization. In their physical aspect, their fabric and design, cities can be viewed in two ways. They can be seen, narrowly, as the containers of a social organism, created almost as unconsciously as (we assume) a coral reef or termitry is created. The fantastic skyscrapers of the termites are in fact stupendously centralized: millions of years of termite-living evolved the vast queen who breeds subjects by the million. The whole pillar city evolved to contain this function, to serve the queen and the rigid hierarchy of her subjects in their divergent ranks.

It has always been too easy to liken the human city focussed on palace and temple to the anthill or termitry focussed on the royal cell. There is, of course, some meaning in the likeness. The crowded residential areas in Sumerian and other agglutinative cities, where the little cellular houses and their alleys have grown spontaneously with the increase of the human entities serving the central power, have indeed much to link them with the cells and galleries of the insects. Yet essentially how different the meaning is. In their queen the ants created a quintessence of pure function, while in deity-cum-royalty men were expressing an idea, giving body to an image. The contrast becomes precisely explicit if we take as an instance a town, such as Al-Ubaid, where the temple was built as the house of Nin-hursag, the most ancient mother-goddess. Where in the royal cell of the termitry we have motherhood incarnate, fertility in physical being, in the temple we have the idea of motherhood and fertility; while in the cell the new units of life arrive by the million, in the temple there is no birth, only worship of an image.

Before going on to describe cities of Sumeria and Assyria, something should be said of the technical advances in building made in historic times. While kiln-fired bricks (burnt-brick) were in occasional use in the Protoliterate period, by Early Dynastic times they were becoming much commoner, being used for pavements and for architectural facings where buildings were most exposed to the rain. They came in time to be used in enormous quantities, particularly in the facades of the fully developed ziggurats. Here (as at Ur) they might be set in bitumen to make a tenacious and durable skin to the mass of sun-dried mud-brick within.

The use of burnt-brick contributed something to an important advance of the Early Dynastic age. This was the invention of the true arch. In face of the persistent popular belief that the self-supporting arch was invented by the Romans, it cannot be too firmly stated that the idea had already dawned in the minds of Sumerian builders before the middle of the third millennium B.C. Leonard Woolley believes that it may have been suggested to them by the laying of mud-brick over the roofs of the reed buildings which had such a considerable influence on the early architects.

However this may be, the doorway of one of the tombs in the Royal Cemetery at Ur had an arch of burnt-brick, and others of a humbler kind (over drains) were constructed in mud-brick at much the same time. The Ur tombs show another ingenious Sumerian invention— the barrel vault constructed by leaning each arch of bricks at an angle against the next, the final support being provided by the end wall, which had to be strengthened to bear the thrust. This method, which was to continue for over three thousand years, made it unnecessary to use expensive wooden centring to support the vault while it was being built.

Brick arched vault; method used from Third Dynasty of Ur onward.

Although the Sumerians invented the arch and barrel vault (later imitated by the Egyptians) they were never able to span spaces much wider than 1.5 metres, even though the use of wedge-shaped voussoir bricks was understood by about 2000 B.C. For the wider spans of public buildings imported timber must often have been used, but an alternative was the primitive corbelled vault. This construction was used for domed tomb chambers in limestone rubble in the Royal Cemetery, while by the Third Dynasty of Ur the chambers in the royal mausoleum had corbelled vaults of burnt-brick set in bitumen that held up over a span of 3.6 metres.

Nevertheless, Sumerian and later architects maintained a preference for long, narrow rooms that was probably due to an inability to roof larger spaces. Here were buildings of a monumental grandeur and scale still cramped by technical weakness. The same contrast is even more striking in the Mayan architecture of Middle America.

There is one other development in brickwork that might be ignored as having no more than archaeological interest. Yet it has wider significance as an example of the odd variations that can crop up even in material culture—that offer themselves in fact as modest examples of human free will that could not occur in anthills. Whereas the Protoliterate mud-brick makers filled their rectangular moulds and smoothed off the open face before turning out the brick to dry, those of the Early Dynastic period took to mounding up the mud on the open face and then denting it with their finger tips. The loaf-like 'plano-convex' bricks that emerged were also laid in a very distinctive way. They were set on edge at an oblique angle, each row leaning in the opposite direction from the one below. This herringbone walling in plano-convex bricks is a distinguishing feature of Early Dynastic times, persisting until the rise of Akkad.

While these technical advances or changes had some effect on the configuration of Sumerian cities, the conspicuous and important developments in historic times came with the increase in size of the towns and of the monumentality of temples and palaces, and the introduction of massive walls and gates. At the same time regular provision seems often to have been made for harbours and quays, while private houses became more elaborate and roomy and better provision was made for public health.

The Protoliterate temples at Eridu and Uruk were already imposing, already with many features of architectural subtlety and enrichment, already raised above all human dwelling on substantial plat-

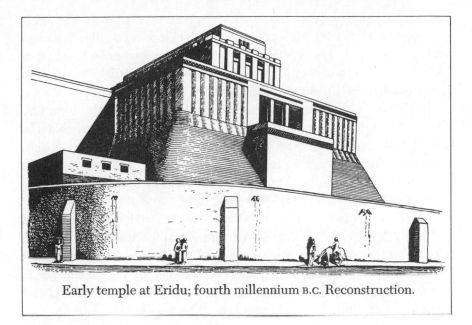

Early temple at Eridu; fourth millennium B.C. Reconstruction.

forms. During the second half of the third millennium, however, all these features were greatly enhanced, reaching a most impressive climax under the Third Dynasty of Ur.

Most dramatic of all, and most distinctive, was the evolution of the platform into the ziggurat. These huge, multi-staged, pyramidal temple-mounts dominated almost all Mesopotamian cities just as their surviving mounds dominate the dusty ruins of today. The ziggurat was built solely to raise the temple and shrine of the presiding deity, that stood on the topmost platform, as high as possible above his domain. In this as in the long stepped ramps that gave access to the superimposed platforms, they much more nearly resembled the Mayan temple-pyramids than the tomb pyramids of Egypt. Inside the ziggurat was a solid mass of mud-brick, divided only by layers of reed matting used for binding and drainage and to discourage subsidence. The facades of each stage or platform (of burnt-brick, as has been said) were treated with the same alternating recess and pilaster effect always characteristic of Mesopotamian architecture. These verticals, together with the inward batter of the walls, led the eye up to the crowning temple. In the best preserved ziggurat, that built by Ur-Nammu for the moon god Nanna at Ur, an astonishing degree of architectural sophistication is manifest. In order to give a greater effect of solidity by defeating the effect of perspective, the builders made each facade very slightly convex—to the extent of 1:125 horizontally, and 1:100 vertically, between base and parapet. The Sumerian architects of about 2000 B.C. had in fact discovered the principle of entasis always so greatly admired in the Athenian Parthenon.

Ur-Nammu's ziggurat measured 72 by 54 metres at the base and rose to a height of about 26 metres. It has been estimated that the one at Mari may have been nearly 50 metres high. Later monarchs commanded the power to magnify them further still: the ziggurat at Assyrian Kalah probably topped 60 metres and we shall see that Nebuchadnezzar's fantastic 'Tower of Babel' rose to over 90 metres.

While the main shrine of the supreme city god was often lifted towards the heavens in this way, other temples were not built on ziggurats. In many ways the temples of historic times could hardly be more impressive than the great Protoliterate Inanna fane at Uruk, but they became far more numerous and often formed part of a vast complex of buildings—including several temples, housing for the priests, offices and stores—that might be enclosed by massive walls and cover a very large area indeed. To give two examples covering the north and south, the Early Dynastic *temenos* of Khafajah in the Diyala valley, an oval enclosed by double walls, covered about 7 acres; the Third Dynasty, rectangular *temenos* at Ur measured 270 by 190 yards—and was later enlarged.

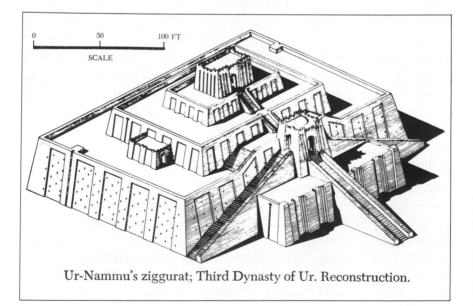

0   50   100 FT

SCALE

Ur-Nammu's ziggurat; Third Dynasty of Ur. Reconstruction.

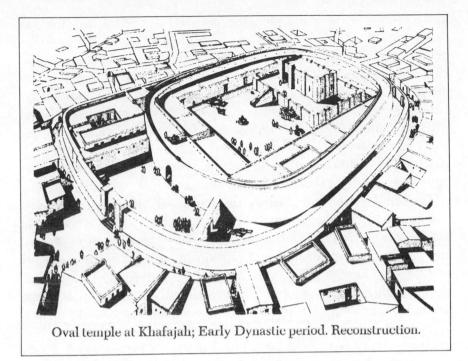

Oval temple at Khafajah; Early Dynastic period. Reconstruction.

Again, although architectural enrichment could hardly be more striking and brilliant than the cone mosaics on facade and columns at Uruk, the embellishments might now involve more costly materials. So soon as the Early Dynastic period and in the small town of Al-Ubaid near Ur, the temple was extravagantly ornamented with copper figures—bulls on the walls, lions at the entrance and the famous relief of Ibn-Dugud and the stags above the door. In addition it had an open portico with palm trunk columns sheathed in copper or set with mother-of-pearl mosaic. The heads of the cones still used for wall decoration were now fitted with rosettes of coloured stone, and use was made of shell cut-outs to make friezes of white figures against a black background.

If so much craftsmanship, such a weight of metal, could be expended on a small building in a minor provincial town, it is fair to assume that far greater riches have been plundered from the great city temples.

Another development that, as far as is known, began in the Early Dynastic period, and certainly grew with time, was the building of royal palaces separated from the temples. The oldest examples that have as yet come to light are at Kish and Eridu, both probably built in the middle of the Early Dynastic period, about 2600 B.C. It seems that before this time the king was so far identified with the god that he had his quarters within the temple area. Now in Sumeria the king's house was built as a separate entity; it might adjoin the main temple, as it did at Ur, but was apart from it within its own enclosure. Oddly enough, we shall find that in later times in Assyria the palaces, while remaining separate residences, were again more directly related to the temples, being enclosed with them in a single lofty citadel. The political and social implications of these building patterns can be left to the next part.

Throughout their long history the houses of Mesopotamian kings had much in common with the houses of the gods. Normally the palace was centred on the throne room where the king sat to receive ambassadors, tribute bearers and suppliants. Throne room and royal seat were within the palace very much the counterpart of the inmost shrine (*cella*) and dais of the god within the temple. Both alike fronted on to a main courtyard and were approached through a monumental gate.

Most palaces also contained a lustration room for the royal rituals set near the throne room, a large banqueting hall, the private apartments of the royal family, a harem, kitchens and pantries, administrative offices and stores, workshops, and accommodation for a household of several hundred. All these quarters were ranged round open courtyards.

Among palaces older than those of the Neo-Assyrian capitals, one of the largest and best preserved is that at Mari. Dating from the beginning of the second millennium, it became the home of the Assyrian underling Shamshi-Adad before being wrecked by Hammurabi. Because of Mari's position at a meeting place of international thoroughfares, this palace probably received an exceptional number of visiting big-wigs—ambassadorial, mercantile and high official. It had three hundred rooms and covered six acres. The discovery of walls still standing almost to their full height has given us a new understanding of the ornate interior decoration of these royal houses.

In Sumer and Akkad the great mass of the temples and palaces normally stood near the centre of the city. All round them crowded private houses with unpaved alleys and cul-de-sacs running erratically among them. At Ur, Woolley identified alleys that had been screened by awnings and lined with open booths—just as in the souks or bazaars of many Asian or North African towns today.

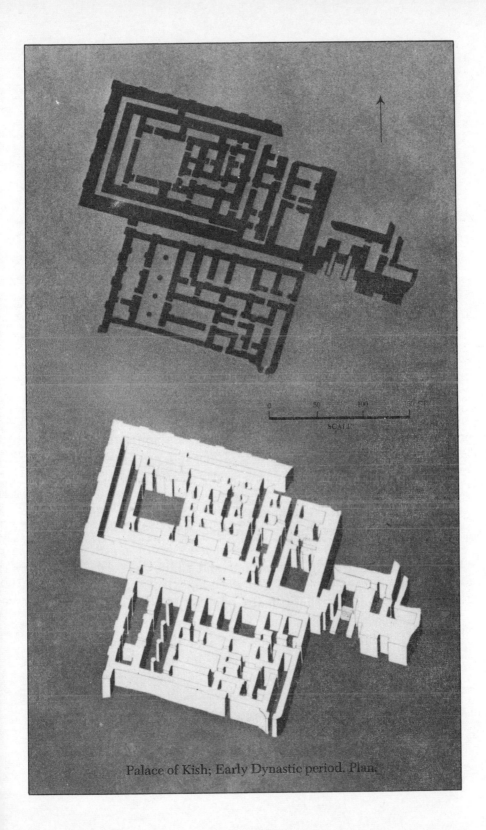

Palace of Kish; Early Dynastic period. Plan.

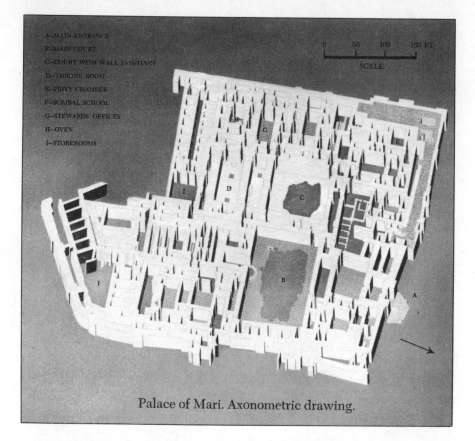

A—MAIN ENTRANCE
B—MAIN COURT
C—COURT WITH WALL PAINTINGS
D—THRONE ROOM
E—PRIVY CHAMBER
F—SCRIBAL SCHOOL
G—STEWARDS' OFFICES
H—OVEN
I—STOREROOMS

0   50   100   150 FT.
SCALE

Palace of Mari. Axonometric drawing.

Wedged in between the houses he found 'little public chapels dedicated by pious citizens to the minor deities'.

The private houses were of assorted sizes but of generally similar plan. A few were small, flat-roofed and single-storeyed, but most had an upper floor, and some may even have had three storeys. This majority of larger dwellings had fronts built of burnt-brick for the first storey with mud-brick above. The street door (occasionally arched) led through an anteroom into a central open courtyard. The ground floor rooms, guest chamber at the back, kitchen, servants' sleeping room and other staff accommodation opened on to the court. A stairway with lavatory below led to a wooden balcony supported on four corner posts, and this gave access to the family rooms. The house roof was wide enough to cover the balcony, and sloped inwards with gutters designed to shoot rainwater into the court below, whence it was drained into a sump. Attached to the back of the house were the family chapel and burial vault.

Houses of this kind must have been as cool and airy as possible, and prove high expectations of domestic comfort among ordinary private citizens. For their owners were not of the élite, or even exclusively well-to-do merchants like Ea-nasir. Tablets show that many of them belonged to shopkeepers, traders—and a few scribes. At Ur there was, however, an unmistakable slum quarter adjoining the *temenos*. There the poor quality, single-floored dwellings may have been occupied by temple slaves. To judge from some Sargonid houses

Ur, a private house. Reconstruction.

at Eshnunna, domestic architecture in provincial towns was much simpler than in the great cities.

At Ur, as at other ancient foundations, the *temenos,* palace and crowded residential districts forming the city proper were raised above the Plain on a mound of ruined mud-brick buildings accumulated over the centuries. The whole area was enclosed by lofty and immensely thick walls set with imposing gates. They separated the inner city from outer suburbs where families lived among gardens, orchards and small farms.

The idea of defending an urban settlement with walls was by no means new. Jericho had walls and towers several thousand years before there was a single city on the Plain. Yet the clustering of so

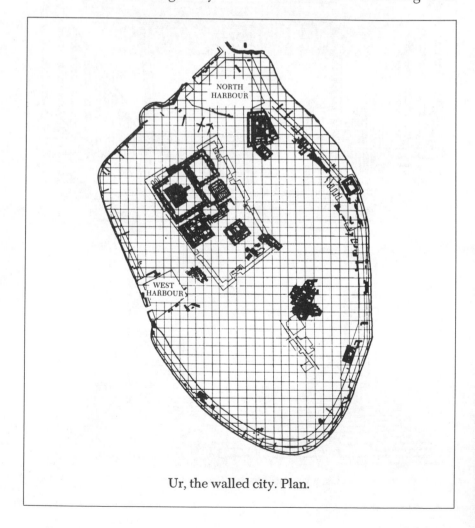

Ur, the walled city. Plan.

many strongly fortified cities—so numerous that some were within sight of one another—was characteristic of Sumeria.

Fortification can, of course, be quite readily explained by the basic political pattern of the small sovereign state. At first the walls were raised against attack by the hostile neighbour. Later, all too often vainly, they had to be manned against ambitious conquerors. It has already been recorded that the first known wall-building was supposed to have been executed by Gilgamesh somewhere about 2700 B.C. It was always one of the king's duties to build, maintain and restore the fortifications of his city, just as it was the victor's crowning satisfaction to tear down those of the vanquished.

To live below the towering seat of divinity and royal power and at the same time to be enfolded by stout walls must have imbued the citizens with a deep sense of security and togetherness. Psychologically speaking the unity, and perhaps even the feeling of security, would only have been intensified by the threat of danger from without, the sight of the enemy city on the skyline. It was a formal context of living that was to be approximately repeated in many parts of the Old World over the next four millennia. It disappeared only when men's faith in divine power crumbled even while their armaments passed the point at which defensive walls had meaning.

The gates of Mesopotamian cities were large and elaborate, and, as we shall see, served a special function as the civic centres of their own quarters. Very probably, too, they would often have served as informal market places. Leo Oppenheim has insisted that the earlier Mesopotamian cities had no markets for the exchange of products between town and country, attributing this to the citizens' personal links with the countryside. It seems unbelievable that they should have been so uniquely deprived. While the gates, whither all footsteps must converge, would be expected to have attracted booths, and that familiar figure, the poor old lady seated behind her tiny piles of fruits and vegetables, the harbour areas would seem likely places for more formal produce markets. Ur was situated at the junction of a large canal with the Euphrates, and a harbour serving both was enclosed within the northern tip of the city walls. It would be surprising if produce were not offered for sale there.

Certainly there were public squares where people expected to enjoy themselves. In the story called *A Scribe and His Perverse Son* the father commands his boy, 'Don't stand about in the public square or wander about the boulevard.' Laws refer to 'a harlot from the pub-

lic square'. Again, in a song concerning the love of Inanna and
Dumuzi, the shepherd god persuades Inanna to deceive her watch-
ful mother by telling her, 'My girl friend, she took me with her to
the public square, there a player entertained us with dancing, his
sweet chant he sang for us.' It is rare for a resort of this kind never
to have stalls—but this, of course, is pure surmise. It is certainly
true that for Mesopotamian cities their market places cannot have
had any of the commanding importance of the Greek *agora*. One has
to remember that so far as consumer goods were concerned its place
would have been taken by the bazaar.

Ur is generally representative of the cities of the Plain. Further
north, and particularly in Assyria, a slightly different plan was
sufficiently established for Leo Oppenheim to distinguish the 'citadel
city'. Here the ziggurat, temples, and the palace, the treasury
and royal barracks were closely associated and enclosed together
within a wall. This citadel was typically raised high above the rest of
the town, either on a debris mound, as at Assur itself, or on an artificially constructed platform. The mass of citizens lived at its foot
in a lower town, which was usually also walled. Whereas the older
cities had the citadel more or less centrally within the walled lower
town, in the new royal capitals of Kalah, Nineveh and Dar-Sargon
(Khorsabad) the citadel was on the circumference of the city walls,
its platform lifting the base of the citadel buildings about to the
level of the wall top.

Kalah (to use the biblical name of Assurnasirpal II's capital,
anciently known as Kalhu and now as Nimrud) is a fine example of
this Neo-Assyrian type of city. Here the great square of the walls
of the lower town enclosed nine hundred acres, but this area was
partly open with parks, gardens, farms and an arboretum and zoological garden founded by Assurnasirpal himself. The citadel rose
above the Tigris in the south-west corner of this vast fortification. It
was approached from the lower town by a cobbled street which
passed through an east wall that was no less than one hundred feet
thick and probably about sixty feet in height. On the opposite, western, side were palaces overlooking massive stone-built quays on the
Tigris. As their foundations were as much as forty feet above the
river, their towering walls and crenelated roof line, with the huge
mass of the ziggurat beyond to the north, must have struck awe into
the minds of disembarking travellers.

The citadel itself covered sixty acres and contained as many as

MESOPOTAMIA

Milking and dairying;
Sumerian limestone reliefs from a temple
at Al-Ubaid, first dynasty of Ur,
third millennium B.C.

RIGHT: Carpenter and
his adze; terracotta plaque,
Uruk, early
second millennium B.C.
FAR RIGHT: Harpist;
terracotta plaque, Uruk, early
second millennium B.C.

LEFT BELOW: Round skin boat on the Tigris, carrying building material for Sennacherib's palace; Assyrian relief, Nineveh, 704–681 B.C. BELOW: Round boats on the Euphrates in recent times.

ABOVE: Assurbanipal and his queen feasting in the garden,
with the head of his enemy hung in a tree;
Assyrian relief, Nineveh, 668–627 B.C.
LEFT BELOW: Seal impression—
goddess introduces worshipper to a seated god;
late third millennium B.C.

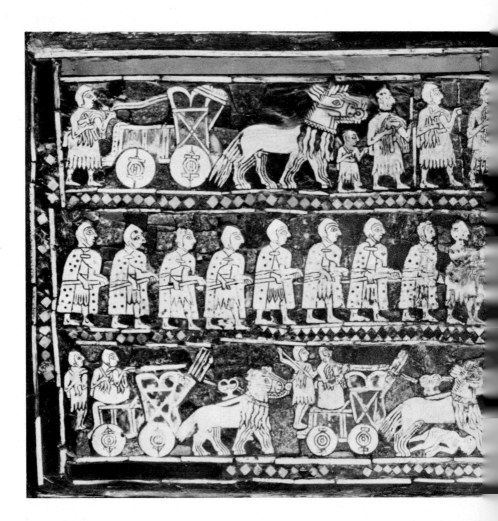

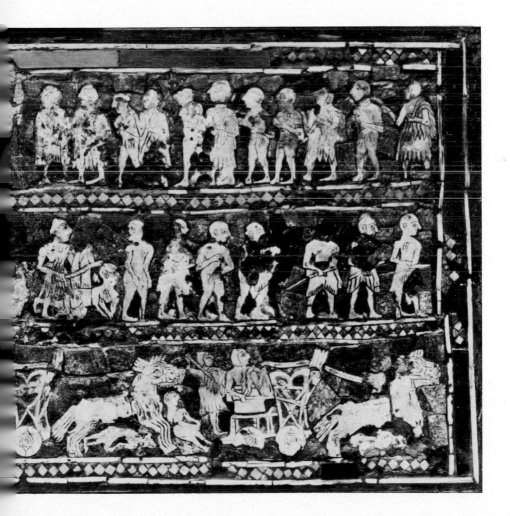

ABOVE: Phalanx of Sumerian soldiers; from the 'Vulture Stele' of Eannatum of Lagash, mid-third millennium B.C.
FAR RIGHT ABOVE: Enemies held in the net of Ningirsu; from the other side of the 'Vulture Stele'.
RIGHT: Battle stele of Naram-sin of Akkad; c. 2260–2223 B.C.
FAR RIGHT CENTER: Attack on a city, showing battering ram, archers, impaled captives; relief from the bronze gates of Balawat, ninth century B.C.
FAR RIGHT BELOW: Riding camel and horse in battle; Assyrian relief, Nineveh, 668–627 B.C.

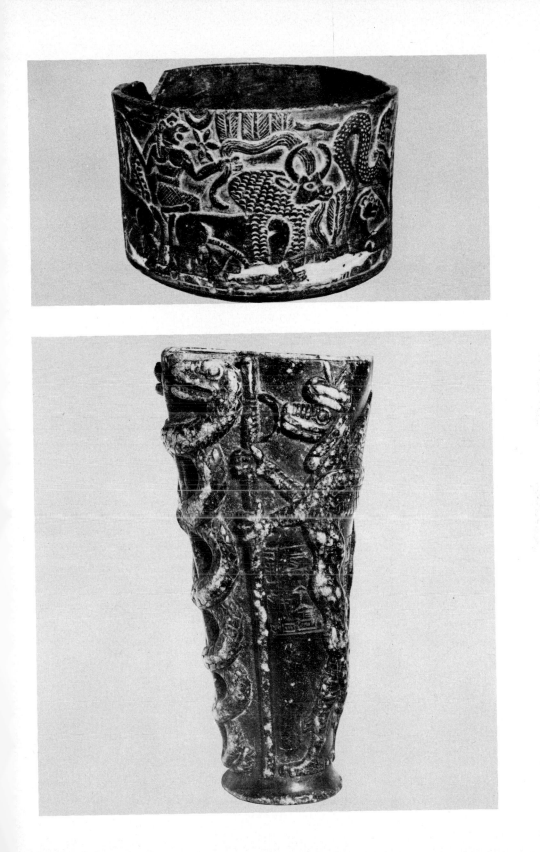

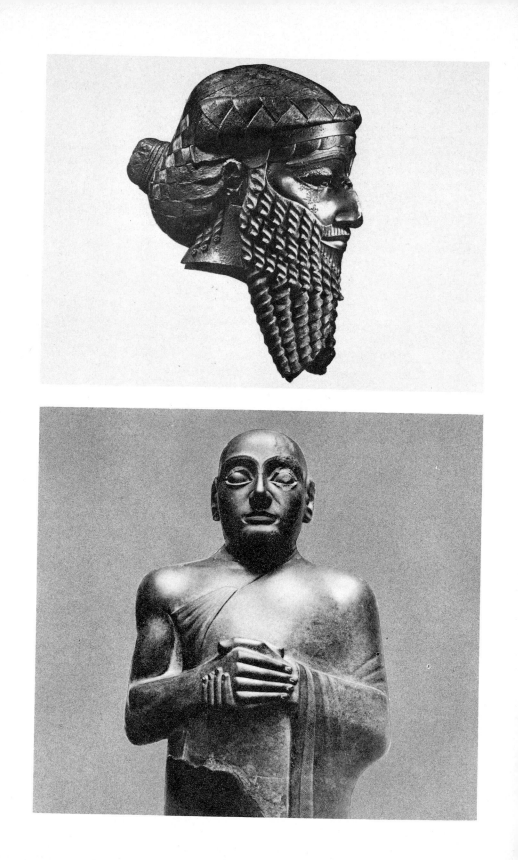

FAR LEFT ABOVE: Head thought to represent
Sargon the Great; bronze, Nineveh, c. 2340–2284 B.C.
FAR LEFT BELOW: One of the many statues
of Gudea of Lagash; c. 2144–2124 B.C.
ABOVE: Group of 'worshippers'; votive statuettes
from the Abu temple at Tell Asmar,
second quarter of third millennium B.C.
LEFT BELOW: Seal impression—an offering to the goddess;
second half of third millennium B.C.
RIGHT BELOW: Seal impression—goddess seated under a tree;
second half of third millennium B.C.

ABOVE: Tablet with pictographic script;
Sumerian, late fourth millennium B.C.
BELOW: Cuneiform tablet, with its envelope
showing impressions of a cylinder seal;
Old Babylonian period.

THE INDUS VALLEY

The 'priest-king' from Mohenjo-daro.

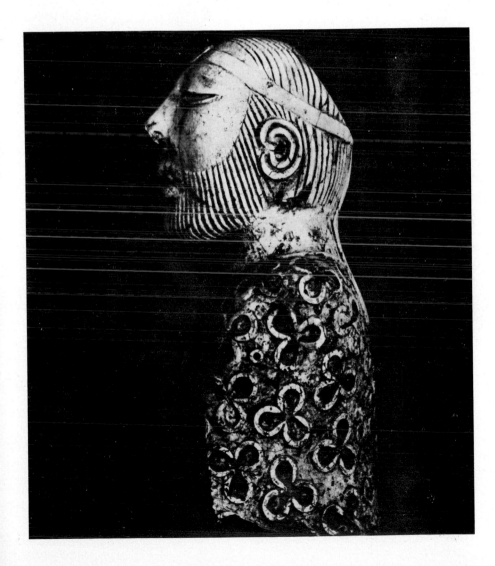

ABOVE: Small bronze statuette of a girl dancer;
Mohenjo-daro.
LEFT BELOW: Seal impression—a Shiva-like divinity;
Mohenjo-daro.
RIGHT BELOW: Seal impression—a humped bull;
Mohenjo-daro.

nine temples, the most important being the ziggurat and the temple of Ninurta, god of war and hunting, at its foot. There were also several palaces built by Assurnasirpal and his successors. That of Assurnasirpal himself was a truly enormous pile, its great throne room (45 by 15 metres) approached through two gates with the colossal stone man-headed monsters so characteristic of Neo-Assyrian architecture. Bas-reliefs on the facade portrayed lines of foreign tribute-bearers, a scene gazed upon by uncounted numbers of living tribute-bearers as they waited to approach the throne of the most powerful monarch on earth.

The citadel also gave shelter to the spacious courtyard houses of important officials. Originally most public buildings seem to have been within its walls, but after 800 B.C. space was short and several were built in the lower town.

By far the most important building outside the citadel, however, was of earlier date: the enormous palace-cum-fortress put up by Assurnasirpal's son, Shamaneser III. Tucked into the south-east corner of the city walls, and entered through its strong towered gate, it contained barracks and arsenal and voluminous magazines, as well as a throne room and other palatial accommodation. One of its several huge courtyards was furnished with a saluting base where the king reviewed his bodyguard and world-conquering troops. Fort Shamaneser was in fact the largest military establishment of the Assyrian empire. It remained a great centre of power until that day in 614 B.C. when it, together with the whole of Kalah, fell to the Medes.

Kalah is an outstanding example of the citadel-type foundation of the Neo-Assyrian age. Unfortunately little is yet known of the layout of the lower town. It might be expected that cities such as this one established as new capitals on virtually virgin sites would give an opportunity for town planning and formal layout. To judge from the somewhat haphazard arrangement of the temples and palaces within the citadel, and from the modest and irregular design of the approach road from the lower city, this opportunity was hardly taken further than the regularity of the city walls. On the other hand Sennacherib had the streets of Nineveh straightened, and enlarged one narrow one to make a royal road. In general it seems that the Assyrians, at least in their earlier days, followed the old Meso-potamian tradition: they lavished their wealth on grandiose in-dividual buildings; but showed no concern for great vistas, sym-metrical layout or other features of monumental city planning. We shall find that the Egyptians surpassed them in monumentality, while the Indus people from the first disciplined their building to the geometric regularity of the gridiron plan.

The lack of desire for great vistas shows itself even in the *Via Sacra,* or processional way, which was a feature of at least some Mesopotamian cities. Its primary purpose seems to have been to carry the procession of the city god at each New Year festival. On this, the greatest occasion of the sacred calendar, the divine image was borne from its main shrine to another situated outside the walls. One such *Via Sacra* has been found at Assur, and another is recorded in the texts for Uruk, but the most famous was that at Babylon.

Babylon is the city with which to end this outline, linking as it does the high days of Babylonia with its end, and the ancient with the modern world. Most of the surviving fabric dates from the time of its last splendour under Nebuchadnezzar II, but it seems that in its main dispositions it followed the lines of the Babylon of Hammurabi and the restorations of the Assyrian conquerors. Therefore, in spite of the vast increase in scale and of the introduction of Assyrian features and of a new splendour of colouring given by the glazed and relief-cut bricks, the city visited and described by Herodotus, the city where Alexander the Great died, still had some of the character of its first days as a great capital.

The old city stood on the east bank of the Euphrates, but a new town developed on the west bank, and the bridge linking the two sides across the wide, tawny waters became one of the many famous sights of Babylon. Nebuchadnezzar proudly recorded, 'That no assault should reach Imgur-Enlil, the wall of Babylon [the inner fortification of the old city] . . . I did what no earlier king had done . . . I caused a mighty wall to be built on the east side of Babylon, I dug out a moat and I built a scarp with bitumen and bricks. . . . Its broad gateways I set within it and mounted within them double doors of cedar-wood overlaid with copper. In order that the enemy . . . should not press on the flanks of Babylon, I surrounded it with mighty floods, as is the land with the wave-tossed sea.' This wall was indeed worth boasting about, for along the top ran a causeway so broad that a chariot could be galloped along it, four horses abreast, and two chariots could even pass one another. For the later city at least, the grandest approach was from the north. Here the processional way, for two hundred yards passing between high walls embellished with coloured reliefs of lions of most ferocious aspect, led up to the even greater magnificence of the Ishtar gate—where the place of the lions was taken by bulls and strange, attenuated dragons. Through this gate into the inner city, the *Via Sacra* had the temples of Ninurta and Ishtar on the left, and on the right, between it and the Euphrates, the lofty citadel with the royal palaces, the hanging gardens, the colossal ziggurat (the 'Tower of Babel') and beyond it the Esagila, temple of the Lord Marduk. The way, in fact, turned westward to run between the ziggurat and Esagila, and so down to the river bridge. An inscription of Nebuchadnezzar's cut on every paving slab records how the king had paved Babil street 'for the procession of the great Lord Marduk'.

This street was indeed monumental, an enormous raised causeway flanked by noble buildings, yet it remains true that it was not laid out for vistas or for symmetry. Not only did it turn at right angles, but other view lines seem to have been off centre or blocked.

According to Herodotus, here in the inner city the houses were two or three storeys high and the streets all quite straight, 'not only those parallel to the river, but also the cross streets which led down to the waterside'. As it would be wrong to disbelieve an observant visitor on such a point, it may be concluded that like Sennacherib at Nineveh, the last kings of Babylon imposed a degree of town planning that was alien to the older Babylonia or Sumeria.

Babylon had a citadel in the sense that temples and palaces were raised and strongly fortified. It was not, however, a 'citadel city' in the specialized sense, for these temples and palaces formed quite distinct units. Presumably this was so from the first, and Nebuchadnezzar spoke of maintaining the division as though it had special significance: 'My dwelling place in Babylon grew insufficient for the dignity of my Majesty. Because the fear of Marduk my lord dwelt in my heart I did not change his street in order to widen my fortress . . . the seat of my Majesty in Babylon. I did his sanctuary no damage, nor did I dam up his canal, but I sought at a distance room for myself.' He goes on to describe the riches of the new palace, its doors of cedar, cypress and ivory inlaid with gold and silver.

Nebuchadnezzar also vaunts the superhuman size of the palace: 'I grounded the foundations on the bosom of the underworld, and raised its summit high like mountains.' Yet of all the buildings of the citadel block that the thousands of pilgrims saw from afar, it must have been the Tower of Babel itself that reached closest to the heavens. According to a tablet, this ziggurat was nearly three hundred feet high. Some accounts mention seven stages, but Herodotus allowed it eight. He says after mentioning the palace:

. . . in the other was the sacred precinct of Bel, the Babylonian Zeus, a square enclosure two furlongs each way, with gates of solid bronze, which was also remaining in my time. In the middle of the precinct was a tower of solid masonry . . . upon which was raised a second tower, and on that a third, and so on up to eight. The ascent to the top is on the outside, by a path which winds round all the towers. When one is about half way up, one finds a resting place and seats, where persons are wont to sit some time on their way to the summit. On the topmost tower there is a spacious temple, and inside the temple stands a couch of unusual size, richly adorned, with a golden table by its side. [Bel, meaning lord, was, of course, an epithet name for Marduk.]

There can be no doubt that this latest form of the ziggurat stood on the same site as its predecessors dating back to the first dynasty, and probably even before. No doubt, too, much of the mud-brick of the earlier phases was incorporated in this Tower of Babel, the greatest wonder of the Babylon that Herodotus was still able to say 'surpasses in splendour any city of the known world'. Yet this huge pile was to be so thoroughly destroyed and plundered for building material that now its site, among all the shapeless mounds of Babylon, is marked by a large hole with stagnant water.

TRADE

For egypt foreign trade was of secondary importance. for Mesopotamia it was an essential source of raw materials and of wealth, without which high civilization could hardly have been created. The stark fact, already so often mentioned, that the whole alluvial plain had no metals, no stone and no good timber meant from the first that the cities had to import in bulk. It meant also that they had to produce desirable goods for exchange exports—a challenge to the skill and productivity of their craftsmen as much as to their merchants. Foreign trade also served to stimulate the development of an astonishingly sophisticated financial system based on capital loans and interest payments that greatly encouraged the enterprise of merchants and traders.

In the laws of Hammurabi, the many provisions concerning merchants' loans to 'gentlemen' (*awilum*) based on the security of

arable fields and date plantations, and their loans to travelling traders
in cash or goods, make plain how at the bottom of the financial
structure and the merchant venturing lay the fertility of Mesopotamia's fields. Where barley could be expected to yield a hundred-
fold shrewd men could afford to invest and pay interest and brave
men, the travelling merchants, could set off to the four quarters of
their known world.

Trade routes might indeed be said to have run towards the four
quarters. The importance of these routes severally has already become apparent: south-eastward down the Persian Gulf to the Indus,
north-eastward by the tributaries of the Tigris to Persia, Afghanistan,
northern India and inner Asia, north-westward by the upper valleys
of the Tigris and Euphrates to Armenia and eastern Anatolia, and
westward by the vital routes from the Euphrates bulge across Syria
to the ports and seaways of the Mediterranean.

Mesopotamian merchants and traders made some part of their
wealth by a carrying trade between foreign cities or with unorgan-
ized 'barbarians' on the fringes of civilization. These activities
helped to spread the influence of Sumerian culture, but of far
greater significance internally was the main import-export trade.
Here the pattern was a curious and interesting one, highly favourable to the peoples of the Valley of the Twin Rivers.

So far as the import of bulk raw materials was concerned, and the
sending of manufactures in exchange, north-western routes involving the use of the Tigris and Euphrates were dominant, and followed a skiing model. That is to say, traffic could come hurtling
down on a water surface, but had to plod up on hard, dry land.

Pine wood and other timber and metal ores were shipped down
the Tigris. The original name of the Euphrates, the Urudu or copper
river, is a sign of its early use for bringing down ores; it was also
used for timber and fine stones and wine. Part of its course carried
bitumen from Hit. Most spectacular, however, and a marvellous
instance of what man will do for aesthetic ends, was the import of
the famous cedarwood from the Amanus range—the 'Cedar Mountain'. This beautiful, workable and aromatic wood was going also
to Egypt and indeed was in demand throughout the ancient world,
but at that time the supply of the noble trees darkening vast mountain slopes seemed inexhaustible. In Mesopotamia every ambitious
monarch had to acquire cedar for the roof beams, great gates and
panelling of his new temple or palace. The logs were first dragged

by ox teams by way of Alalakh on the Orontes (where there were probably agents from Mesopotamia) and over the Aleppo plateau to the Euphrates near its westernmost point, whence they could be floated downstream. The journey is vividly described in Gudea's account of his temple building at Girsu: 'Gudea . . . made a path in to the Cedar Mountain which nobody had entered before. He cut its cedars with great axes. . . . Like giant snakes cedar rafts were floating down the water . . .'

For marbles, ores, bitumen—everything other than floatable woods—boats had to be provided. Three kinds of craft were used, all of them still to be seen on the river today. One was a heavy wooden keeled vessel, up to nine metres long, broad in the beam and provided with a lateen sail and oars. These could be built in the north of mountain timber. When they had unloaded at the quays of the cities of the Plain, they might be used for local canal traffic, or possibly on the Gulf, but far more came down than were needed in the south, and as they could not go upstream beyond Hit, most were broken up and the wood sold.

The second type of boat, a coracle, greatly excited Herodotus. They had been riding the Euphrates for two and a half millennia before his visit and they have survived as long after it. His description cannot be bettered:

These boats are circular in shape and made of hide; they build them in Armenia, to the north of Assyria, where they cut withies to make the frames and then stretch skins taut on the underside for the body of the craft; they are not fined-off or tapered in any way . . . but quite round like a shield. The men fill them with straw, put cargo on board—mostly wine in palm-wood casks—and let the current float them downstream. . . . Every boat carries a donkey—the larger ones several—and when they reach Babylon and the cargoes have been offered for sale, the boats are broken up, the frames and straw disposed of and the hides loaded on the donkeys' backs for the return journey overland to Armenia. It is quite impossible to paddle the boats upstream because of the strength of the current. . . . Back in Armenia with their donkeys, the men build another lot of boats to the same design.

The third class of vessels utilizing the forces of gravity to supply the cities of the Plain were large rafts made of timbers buoyed up on inflated skins. They were uncouth, but could carry the heaviest loads—such as the eleven-metre block of stone shipped by a king of Babylon in the eighteenth century B.C. The rafts, too, were dismantled when they reached their destination, the wood sold and the deflated skins returned to the north on donkey-back. Following the same routes up the river banks must often have gone merchant caravans loaded with the textiles and garments that were the staple exports of Mesopotamia.

The Gulf route cannot have carried anything like the bulk of goods that came down by the Twin Rivers. Yet evidently this trade with the Orient was much esteemed and held to be important. It was certainly one source of the wealth of Ur, the readiest port of disembarkation for shipping from the Gulf. Sargon, it will be remembered, was proud to claim that 'at the wharf of Akkad he made moor ships from Meluhha, ships from Makan and ships from Dilmun', while Ur-Nammu with equal pride proclaimed their return to Ur. Jasmah-Adad of Mari wrote to Hammurabi about a caravan he had sent to Dilmun and which was on its way back—a double journey of some 3200 kilometres.

In the mention of Sargon's conquest it was accepted that Dilmun was situated in Bahrein Island, that Makan (also written Makkan and Magan) was a part of the Oman territory and that Meluhha in some sense represented the Indus valley. Recent excavations in Bahrein and Oman make the first identification virtually certain, the second very probable. It is less sure that Meluhha can be identified with a port or district within Indus territory. It may be that when people in Mesopotamia spoke of Meluhha they had very little idea of what it meant more precisely than somewhere far, far away in the lands of the rising sun. A place, indeed, that might well have been affected in their minds by the strange, mythical aura that continued to invest the name of Dilmun.

The name matters little, however, for there is much to show that from Early Dynastic times until the rule of the Kassites, Mesopotamia was in touch with the Indus world, Dilmun being an important link between them. Before the end of the third millennium Dilmun was a walled city about two-thirds the area of Ur itself. Its island site and its marvellous springs of fresh water made it an ideal depot and port of call for all the traffic moving up and down the Gulf. Commercially its people seem to have been closer to India than to Mesopotamia, for they employed a type of seal believed to have originated in the Indus cities and, more significant still, used the Indus system of weights and not the Mesopotamian. Dilmun also had an outpost near Kuwait, presumably the last stopping place before boats entered the marsh-fringed river mouth en route for Ur. There at Ur, in the foreign settlement near the harbour, were Indian residents, probably agents for home interests, and no doubt waiting to ship back their own bales to Dilmun, Makan and Meluhha.

In the last section it was made clear that the staple trade for Dilmun was in Makan copper for Mesopotamia. We encountered Ea-nasir, the Ur copper dealer of Old Babylonian times whose shipments on his own behalf or for clients were typical of the *alik Dilmun*, or ship-masters guild, which by then probably had a near monopoly of the Dilmun trade in the city. It seems that in earlier centuries and indeed down to the end of the Third Dynasty, the temple and palace had been much involved, but in Old Babylonian times when private enterprise was everywhere in the ascendancy, the guild merchants had taken over, paying customs dues to the palace and a tithe to the temple.

It is, as it happens, in tithe lists from the temple of Ningal in Ur, dating from about 1900 B.C., that we get the best idea of the trade in luxury goods that went on side by side with that in Makan copper. It was in this luxury trade via Dilmun that India almost certainly played a leading part. It is worth quoting one of the tithe lists in full (in so far as it can be translated): it gives an idea of the rich variety of goods handled—and how like they were to the fine things that the rich were always to seek through foreign trade. After some fairly weighty items of copper and bronze there follow:

3 kidney-shaped carnelian beads; 3 'fish eyes' [almost certainly pearls]; 9 *sila* of white coral; 5½ minas of ivory rods; 30 pieces of tortoiseshell; 1 wooden rod with copper; 1 ivory comb; 1 mina of copper in lieu of ivory; 3 minas of *elligu* stone, 2 measures of antimony [for eye paint]; counting board [?] of Makan reed [possibly bamboo]; from an expedition to Dilmun, tithe for the goddess Ningal from individual shareholders.

In addition there were two other items of unknown stones and some untranslatable substances that could be gums or spices. Other lists included lapis lazuli that must have come from Afghanistan.

There was Dilmun, then, a Bronze Age Singapore on a trade route which (through Mari) linked India stage by stage with Crete and the Aegean. One discovery made in the town brings its men and their traffic to life with all the intensity of the minutely particular. Here were material remains as illuminating in their different way as the written records of Ea-nasir. Just inside the main sea gate was a small square with a well and a drinking trough. Fronting the square were two buildings that contained seals and a set of Indus-type weights. Here in the square the drivers must have unloaded and watered their donkeys, then perhaps squatted in the shade sampling the beer or some of Dilmun's famous dates, while their master struggled with the officials in the customs office. There would be all the weighing to be done, dues to be calculated, bills of lading to be stamped, and perhaps seals on the bales themselves. Sometimes there would be language difficulties. There were plenty of excuses for argument and delay, especially if the local bureaucrat on duty that day happened to be pompous or aggressive or corrupt. Then at last the packs would have to be heaved up once more and the string of donkeys either thwacked up into the town or down to the quays—quays where there might be big Indian dhows as well as ships from Makan and the cities of the Plain.

It is just possible that outside the gate they might pass a little encampment of desert people and their camels. Seeing the party coming out of the gate these men would draw their headcloths closer and look away; they were Bedouin, a people apart.

The question of camels and their part in the trade of the Bronze Age world is curiously obscure. There is no doubt that the pack-ass carried virtually the whole of the goods that went overland on all the routes that have so far been considered, not least, presumably, on the difficult mountain ways through Iran to India. Yet there is no doubt either that already in the third millennium the people of all three river valleys knew of the dromedary of southern Asia. The Sumerians, as has been said, had a word for it implying that they associated it with the south—presumably Arabia. Thereafter written references and portrayals are extremely rare until about the eleventh century, when the Assyrian army is found using camel transport. In Egypt the situation is almost exactly the same: the camel was about but people saw it only out of the corner of their eyes, as it were. A few camel bones were found in Mohenjo-daro and a second millennium portrayal of a riding animal at a site in Persian Makran. There is also the fact that in contrast with Mesopotamian and Egyptian literature, the Old Testament has a number of references to camel-owners from Abraham onwards.

Now, quite unexpectedly, large quantities of camel bones, apparently food remains, have been found in a settlement in Abu Dhabi, and a carving of one animal, a dromedary, on a nearby tomb.

The people in this settlement were among those who had contact with the Kulli folk of Baluchistan, and they would certainly have been within the area of influence from the Makan copper mining. They may have eaten camels, but it would be surprising if they had not tamed them for transport use as well.

It seems that from the third millennium nomads were already crossing the Arabian and Syrian desert tracks, perhaps already building up a carrying trade, including the myrrh and spices that were to make the fortunes of the camel breeders of the Minyean kingdom of Arabia by the fourteenth century B.C. The city people and the Bedouin despised and distrusted one another; the camel trains never entered the cities, never became the concern of the bureaucrats or got on to their files. It was probably only with the coming of the Aramaeans that dromedaries began to be a familiar sight to the peoples of Mesopotamia.

The physical courage and enterprise that went into trading ventures in foreign lands were remarkable enough, yet perhaps the business astuteness and financial skills that lay behind them were even more astonishing. Mesopotamia must always have been at the centre of this commercial progress.

We have to think first of the organizations of the merchants themselves, communities as internationally minded as their counterparts in the modern world. At home they had their merchants' guilds with overseers who were likely to be very wealthy men. The guild life would be centred on the *karum*, which can be recognized as both a merchant quarter and a merchant corps. At Ur, probably typically, it was situated outside the city walls and seems to have had its own administration. Members of the *karum* were expected to behave *mar awilum*, 'like gentlemen', and to keep them up to the mark their agreements and contracts were deposited under the eye of Shamash, god of justice, whose temple was in the vicinity. The laws of Hammurabi make it plain what enormous importance was attached to all agreements being officially witnessed and set down in writing. Without the tablet the deal could be void in law and the investor or creditor forfeit his rights.

Above all the *karum* served as an exchange for interstate and international trade. It can be supposed that the Ur merchants met their brethren from India and other foreign agents there. It seems likely that members of the *alik Dilmun* such as Ea-nasir would sometimes have frequented the *karum* to find backers and partners, arrange cargoes and so on. Whether the merchants who worked for the temple and palace would be members on an equal footing with the rest is not known, but seems to be probable.

To us it is amazing that commerce and finance should have gone so far without coinage, yet so it was. Currency was originally based on barley, and grain always remained an acceptable medium of exchange. In time, equivalents were made in copper, silver and gold, but always the value was calculated by weights—although the precious metal might bear royal stamps as a mark of purity. The names of the shekel and the mina were in general use in centres of civilization other than Egypt, but they applied to widely varying systems of weights. The Mesopotamian shekel was of 129 grains (based on the barley grain) and the mina was sixty times as much—while sixty minas went to the talent, the heaviest of the standard weights. Different peoples gave their weights different shapes: the Sumerians and the Babylonians employed a sleeping duck of excellent design, while the Assyrians preferred a lion. The maintenance of correct weights and measures, like that of pure metals, was a royal responsibility.

Although the ratios of value between one metal and another varied, they were always agreed. Silver was the normal standard of exchange for all considerable merchant dealings—silver that had to be weighed out on the scales at each transfer. Grain remained in use for agricultural wages and other country dealings. It is probably significant that in the provision on forced sales in the Urukaginan reforms the price of the donkey, a movable and to some extent international type of asset, was quoted in silver, that of the house in barley. Yet in some circumstances the idea of barter in any substance at a fair rate of exchange was evidently maintained, for a

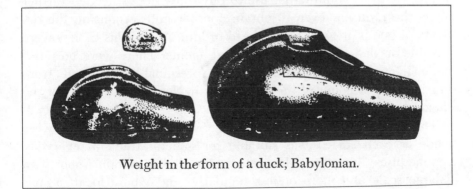

Weight in the form of a duck; Babylonian.

law of Hammurabi reads: 'If a gentleman borrowed grain or money [silver is implied] from a merchant and does not have the grain or money to repay . . . he shall give to his merchant whatever there is in his possession, affirming it before witnesses that he will bring it, while the merchant shall accept it without demur.'

Much of the power that drove Mesopotamian trade so forcefully along the land and water thoroughfares was the institution of credit, and particularly credit at interest. It was in this way that the merchant capitalist financed the merchant adventurer. The king attempted to stabilize interest rates. Referring again to Hammurabi, we find him laying down 20 percent for both silver and grain—but such decrees had little force in practice. In earlier times at least temples sometimes served almost as community banks, making loans to citizens. They may have tried to serve the state by keeping interest relatively low: there is an instance of the temple of Shamash at Sippar lending barley at 20 percent and silver at 6¼ percent.

The Old Testament has made us familiar with the Hebrews' disapproval of loans at interest 'between brethren'—though of course interest could be charged to foreigners. The Babylonians' lack of inhibitions towards usury was yet another of the reasons for the Hebrews' condemnation of them. Mesopotamian merchants did on occasion finance one another as 'between gentlemen'—interest free.

For inter-city or international trade by land routes, when carrying a great bulk of goods was impossible and much silver sometimes risky, a system amounting to letters of credit was devised. It involved the presence of known agents along the trader's route. Setting out with a pack-train of goods, say wool or grain, he could dispose of them at a city in need, receiving for them signed tablets with the value set out probably in terms of shekels or minas of silver. These he could either use to buy other goods needed further along the route, or even to obtain another note promising the delivery of goods at some point ahead of him. Always his tablets were payable on demand by his accredited agents. There were no international currency difficulties—except, presumably, on some frontiers, to keep account of the differences in the actual weights of the shekel.

This kind of commercial travelling (when of course profits were made at each stage) was suitable for general trade in everyday commodities, but when Mesopotamia needed to obtain imports on a large scale and more or less regularly, and where local organization was required in obtaining them, then it was evidently desirable to have merchants established in or near their place of origin. This was true particularly of the trade in cedar wood from Syria and metal ores from Anatolia. For the first there was probably a Mesopotamian presence in the little royal capital of Alalakh, in northern Syria, directly commanding the approach to the Amanus range. There may also have been Mesopotamians at Quatna, further up the Orontes, engaged if not in timber then in other forms of commerce with Syria. Far better known, however, are the Assyrian trading posts in eastern and central Anatolia, of which the most important was that at Kanesh—already quoted for its admirable self-government as well as for its trade. There were some nine other merchant settlements, including one at Hattusas (Boghazkoy). The larger settlements had the name of *karum*, but naturally, unlike the *karum* at home, these had a residential quarter—although still, as at Ur, outside the city wall. As we have seen, the merchants of the Kanesh *karum* were largely concerned with obtaining copper and other ores for Assur and bringing in textiles in exchange. Although they had to pay various dues to the local rulers, they succeeded in accumulating much silver and gold as the profits of their enterprise. Among their archives were business letters, accounts, contracts and court records. Kanesh in fact was the seat of the central court for all the Anatolian settlements and there they administered law according to Assyrian custom, both among themselves and occasionally for suits between Assyrians and natives.

Everything at Kanesh implies excellent order, great freedom and safety of movement, and a determination, in spite of human frailty, to maintain probity in business affairs. To an impressive extent these things prevailed throughout the vast network of Bronze Age trade. States and their rulers knew how much advantage they got from commerce, both directly through their own dealings and from taxes and levies. Private merchants could make fortunes. All were anxious to keep the waterways and the land ways open and secure. When disaster caused them to be blocked and overgrown, it was a subject for bitter lamentation. On one occasion a Babylonian caravan bearing gold was robbed on its way through Canaan. King Burna-buriash of Babylon sent a stern order to the Canaanite ruler that the brigands must be executed and the gold recovered or 'trade between us shall stop'. He had no doubt, evidently, about the compelling force of this threat.

2. THE SOCIAL AND POLITICAL WORLD

STATE AND GOVERNMENT

QUESTIONS OF MATERIAL CULTURE, OF ALL THE THINGS GREAT AND SMALL made by human brains and hands out of the raw materials of nature, have a blessed simplicity. The objects, the buildings, the farmlands, the plants and animals were substantially there, and their discovery by archaeology, much enriched by texts and works of art, leave us with only the most particular doubts as to how they were produced and what they were.

With the social affairs of lost civilizations we are, of course, plunged at once into a quagmire of uncertainties and complexities from which there is no escape. Except for the few broad hints given by such material facts as the relation of temple and palace, the lay-out of cities, and the pictorial record of works of art, information comes down to us only through the written word. In Mesopotamia, all the way from Sumerian to Neo-Babylonian times, this means overwhelmingly the word as written on clay tablets.

The quag really is deep and wide. First there is the changing nature of the finding of the tablets and other inscriptions. Because one kind of building happens to be excavated and not another, the tablets may give a partial and, therefore, false view of the total scene. Many authorities are becoming convinced that selection of this kind has long given us a wrong picture of the structure of the

Sumerian state. Then again, there are the variations that existed between one state or region and another. In a civilization growing from millennia of prosperous prehistory, and involving many peoples, such local differences were considerable and we are too prone to generalize. Similarly, just as there were variations in space, so too there were differences in time—changes that took place between one age and another during the long course of Mesopotamian history.

Finally, there are all the difficulties caused by the nature of the tablets themselves. Even the best preserved are hard to read and interpret; many of the longer texts are badly enough damaged to leave us with uncertain readings and baffling gaps. So far as social history is concerned, decipherers are often confronted with thousands, indeed tens of thousands of administrative and business notes from which general meanings can only be extracted by a combination of dull labour and keen penetration. There are not so many people in the world able and willing to decipher cuneiform, and in fact only a small proportion of vast collections of tablets already unearthed have as yet been deciphered, let alone fully studied. In a book of moderate length, then, it is impossible to treat either the facts or the uncertainties with the subtlety and thoroughness they demand. In these limiting circumstances the best policy would seem to be to pay most attention to Sumer and Akkad down to the end of the Third Dynasty of Ur, making only the briefest references to the later changes brought about by internal evolution and foreign conquest.

In addition to all the difficulties of using the written word of cuneiform as a basis of understanding the social life of Bronze Age Mesopotamia, there is one all-pervading element that makes such understanding hard for modern man. Only by humble open-minded self-examination and strenuous exercise of the imagination can we begin to achieve it. This is the strange interpenetration of the divine with human affairs.

Something has already been said about the apparently universal tendency of human societies when lifting themselves to civilization to see the universe as created and dominated by gods, their own rulers as either divine or divinely appointed, and their own structures and functions as reproducing those of the divine society. More will have to be said about the faith and the worship implicit in this outlook when discussing religion. Meanwhile this interpenetration cannot be ignored in any attempt to understand societies and their government. The secular and the religious were inseparable—in authority and the individual offices representing it, in everyday life and in social values.

Most of all, perhaps, we today should like to know how far people at all social levels really believed in the divine control of their affairs, how far cynicism, deliberate exploitation and resentment entered in and grew with the passage of time.

For the peasant or humble citizen belief was probably complete. It would stretch from his own small magics, through the immemorial fertility rites that made the crops grow, the children be born, to the god who owned the city and the king who represented him with varying degrees of personal divinity. The tradition in which he had been reared gave him belief, but so too did the urge from his own psyche. We have seen in the twentieth century societies of simple people divinizing their rulers without, apparently, any initial encouragement from the wielder of power himself. The Ghanaians did it for Nkrumah, and this in an age when the last traditions of divine kingship are being eliminated one by one.

As for the élite, the priestly scribes, the high priests and the royal family itself who manipulated the temple and the divine offices, who in the name of their god led campaigns to secure trade routes, what was their state of mind? Perhaps it is foolish to ask. What is the state of mind of the Pope after his election, what of the Queen of England at her coronation or the Church of England parson when he prays for rain? Man keeps his innate capacity for a kind of holy make-believe, and how much easier this must have been in the days before the Greeks arrived at intellectual detachment. It must have been perfectly possible for a usurper to plot the overthrow or murder of a king, and yet himself to 'believe'—as well as putting out official propaganda—that the success of his plot meant that the gods had chosen him.

Certainly there came to be many cases of religious doubt and questioning, many prototypes of Job. These are well expressed in various works such as the dialogues of pessimism when men questioned how it could be that

> They walk on a lucky path who do not seek a god,
> Those who devoutly pray ... become poor and weak.

An ultimate expression of how such doubts could express themselves in social attitudes appears in the *Pessimistic Dialogue Between Master and Servant,* in which the hopeful impulse is always defeated by the despairing. In an early stanza the master intends to ride by chariot to the palace where the king will treat him graciously, then decides against it as after all it seems more likely that the king will send him to a foreign land and let him be captured. Towards the end the argument runs:

"Servant obey me." "Yes, my lord, yes." "I will do something helpful for my country." "Do, my lord, do. The man who does something helpful for his country, his deed is placed in the bowl of Marduk." "No, my servant, I will not do something helpful for my country." "Do it not, my lord, do it not. Climb the mounds of ancient ruins and walk about; look at the skulls of late and early men; who among them is an evil-doer, who a public benefactor?"

This, however, was a late composition of the last millennium B.C. when the vanities and pretense of this world were obvious to the citizens of an overripe civilization. There is no question whatever that in the third, and even the second, millennium each city-state individually, and the lands of Sumer and Akkad and of Babylonia also, were given force and cohesion by their loyalty to their gods and to the kingship that the gods had bestowed and that was accepted as an essential element of civilized living.

It must have been a fundamental belief of all society that each of the dozen or so city-states into which Sumeria was divided belonged to the presiding deity to whom it had been allotted when the world was made. In this sense there is no question that the state— the capital city with all its lands and lesser towns and villages—was the property of the god who dwelt in his great house, physically dominating the city. There is, however, deep disagreement among historians as to whether in practice the main temple, together with its subsidiaries, owned all the land and controlled the population of the state and its entire economy.

There is no serious difference of opinion concerning the organization of the temple estate itself. From evidence drawn mainly from tablets found in the temple of Girsu in the state of Lagash, and dating from the reign of Entemena to that of Urukagina, a very detailed and fairly coherent reconstruction has been made.

First of all the extent to which the convention of the divine ownership and management of the estate was insisted upon cannot be exaggerated and must not be pushed aside by the hard rationality of modern economic interpretations. The temple and its lands belonged to the god Ningirsu and his wife (Baba) and family. The children and entourage of the divine pair appear as lesser gods responsible for overseeing the entire establishment with its indoor and outdoor servants. One son, for example, is doorkeeper to his father's shrine, another is the head butler. To minor divinities are assigned all conceivable duties from those of bedmaker to charioteer, and from bailiff to gamekeeper. The seven daughters of Baba and Ningirsu serve as ladies-in-waiting at their court. It was only under all these divine overseers that their human subordinates did the actual work. In this way the fundamental Sumerian belief that men were created by gods to labour for them was grandly maintained.

Turning to the actual human executives, the overall picture is one of a complicated and heavily bureaucratic administration. There was evidently not only an ideal of careful orderliness, but also of minute documentation of that orderliness of a kind that from that day to this has been an essential part of bureaucratic method and bureaucratic peace of mind.

The temple was an enclosed, self-supporting unit in which the maintenance of the temple cult with its daily routine of sacrifices and its seasonal festivals was at the centre of a great economic organization involving agriculture and stock-keeping, fisheries, manufacture and commerce.

Farming and the storage of its produce was of course the basic activity of the temple community, providing rations, wages and special payments for all those employed. It also provided great numbers of sacrificial animals—which were in fact, it seems, largely eaten by the personnel of the sanctuary and perhaps by the *ensi* and his immediate circle.

The temple land, which was inalienable, was of three kinds. There was the *nigenna*-land, which was used directly for the support of the sanctuary; there was the *kurra*-land, some of which was assigned to farmers working the *nigenna*-land and some to craftsmen and administrators as payment for their work and services. This land was not heritable and could be taken from the cultivators if the administration so decided. The third category of land was the *urulal*, which was allotted to various individuals, much of it to temple personnel, as a boost to their income.

In addition to grain, vegetables were cultivated, cattle were kept, perhaps mainly for sacrifice (including milk offerings) and traction, and very large herds of sheep that served for food but, more importantly, provided wool for the temple weavers. There were, of course, bakeries and breweries to supply the whole community.

The fisheries owned by the temple seem to have been both sea and fresh water. One tablet from Girsu records, 'A total of twelve men who are seafishermen in the employ of Baba have gone to the sea with Lugal-sha-la-Tuk as their overseer.'

The temple workshops covered all the crafts. On a single tablet from Ur two supervisors list a year's output in eight temple workshops—the year being the twelfth of the reign of Ibbi-Sin. The craftsmen listed were a sculptor (in ivory and fine wood), a jeweller, a lapidary, a carpenter, a metalsmith working in gold and silver as well as bronze, a leather worker, a fuller and a basket-maker. The most important workshops of all (not included on this tablet) were those of the textile workers, in which women slaves did much of the work. The care and meticulous attention to detail with which the spinners and weavers themselves and their raw materials and products were organized has already been described.

Textiles would have been among the leading exports handled by the merchants who acquired foreign goods on behalf of the temples. The temples were responsible also for the necessary shipping.

The head of this whole organization, often mentioned in the Lagash tablets as receiving revenue from the god Ningirsu's estate, was the ensi, the ruler who was seen as Ningirsu's human steward. In the temple of the city goddess, Ningirsu's wife Baba, the ensi's wife played the corresponding role.

Produce raised and stored on the temple estate was used to provide rations for slaves and also for other dependents. Grain was issued monthly, women receiving only half as much as men and children variably less again; oil was a yearly issue, and here the share of men and women was equal, with children getting less than half as much. Wool for clothing was also supplied by the year, men receiving four pounds, women three and children from one to two. This payment by rations seems to have been dominant throughout Sumeria during the third millennium, but towards the end of the Third Dynasty of Ur it began to be largely displaced by wages paid to free workers or hirelings. This would seem to be part of a social change that went with the final Semitization of Sumer and Akkad.

This then is the approximately accepted account of the structure of a Sumerian temple estate. Where the disagreement begins concerns the relation between the temple and the city-state itself. For a long time most authorities believed that the two were virtually synonymous, an interpretation which meant that the whole state was managed on lines that amounted to a theocratic totalitarianism.

For the past decade this has been very commonly denied, largely as a result of the textual researches of the Russian historian Diakanoff. Those who follow him say that the idea that the city temple owned and controlled the state was due to an excessive dependence on the archives of the temples of Lagash. Temple records could not fail to be exclusively concerned with temple lands, but a calculation that the area of these lands corresponded with the area of the state of Lagash was entirely wrong. According to Diakanoff's estimate the temple lands represented something like an eighth of the whole. All the rest, according to this view, was largely in private hands and could be privately bought and sold. Much of it was taken up by large estates belonging to a 'nobility', partly as inherited family possessions, and partly as private property often bought from less fortunate citizens. These large properties were probably worked and managed on much the same lines as the temple estates.

The land-owning nobility comprised ruling princes and their families, palace officials and leading priests. Their large estates, however, still left a good share of land for an independent class of free commoners. 'Even the poor', writes Professor Kramer, 'managed to own farms and gardens, houses and cattle.' Much of the commoners' land, according to the post-Diakanoff view, had been held from the earliest times by patriarchal families or clans. It was, however, alienable, and could be sold by a representative of the family with the general consent of its members.

This picture of a predominantly free economy in landownership is supported, for those who accept it, by the recognition of private merchants thriving on inter-state and international trade conducted on their own account, and by ambitious artisans who sold their products in a free town market.

It will be seen that according to this view, Sumerian society was made up of nobles, commoners (presumably including most merchants), clients and slaves. If the 'clients' are looked at more closely they appear to divide into dependents of the temple, including administrators and superior craftsmen; the mass of the temple personnel; and thirdly, the dependents of the nobility.

While the free enterprise interpretation emanating from Moscow has received wide acceptance, particularly in the United States, some historians still resist it—at least in part. As represented by Otto Edzard, they reply that most of the documents relating to private sales of land in Early Dynastic times come from the north of the Plain in areas of Semitic (Akkadian) settlement and contain many Akkadian personal names. Very few land sale documents for this period come from the ancient Sumerian south, and those that do (from Girsu) are relatively late and concern purchases by the ruling house. The Shurrupak texts either refer to the military administration of the palace or to lands assigned to individuals for services rendered to the state—which could not be sold or inherited and are therefore irrelevant. It is not until the beginning of the second millennium, in the reign of Lipit-Ishtar of Isin, that documents for the private sale of land become at all frequent in the south.

Otto Edzard judges that the contrast in the documentary evidence between the Sumerian south and the Akkadian north is not likely to be a chance one. He would not say that private land-holding was prohibited (or, presumably, that merchants and artisans did not trade and work on their own account), but to him the evidence suggests that in the traditional Sumerian city-state the temple was the great proprietor of the arable soil. In short, 'It would appear that one of the chief differences between Sumerians and Semites in the Land of the Two Rivers, is the frequency of private property in land.'

These doubts about the distribution of ownership and power within the state are necessarily very much involved with authority of a more political kind—though by now it must have become obvious that the political cannot be separated from the religious function. This question of authority concerns the existence of an assembly of the people on the one hand and the supreme ruler of the state on the other. It will perhaps be easier to begin with the first—if only because so sadly little is really known about the subject.

The first direct documentary evidence for the existence of a popular assembly functioning in Mesopotamia dates from Old Babylonian times. There was a council of elders led by the town or precinct mayor. Large cities appear to have been divided into precincts, each administered from its own gate. There was also an assembly, called in Akkadian the *puhrum,* which appears to have consisted of a gathering of all free male citizens who cared to attend. It is unlikely, although not totally impossible, that women could take part. At this time the function of both bodies seems to have been entirely judicial, the mayor and elders judging minor cases, while the more important were referred to the *puhrum.*

This assembly was empowered to deal with civil pleas such as the ownership of houses and gardens and paternity cases, and also with criminal matters including seditious utterances and murder. While the king had supreme judicial power, he sometimes referred cases to the assembly. On one occasion, for example, a man who had been arrested for sedition by a royal official was sent before the *puhrum* for the charge to be proved before he was imprisoned.

Further evidence that some degree of judicial self-government was customary also among the Assyrians can be seen in the promptness with which it must have been instituted by the trading colony at Kanesh. There the expatriates set up what sounds like a bicameral body known as 'the *karum* young and old'.

It is reasonable to argue that as the second millennium was certainly a time of increasing autocracy, it is not likely that the *puhrum* of the Old Babylonian records was a new development or gaining in strength. The probabilities plainly lie in the opposite direction— that it was old and tending to lose its powers.

A single textual reference dating from the Akkadian age suggests that at that time the assembly was on occasion empowered to choose a king. 'In the common of Ereth, a field belonging to Esabad, the temple of Gula, Kish assembled and Iphurkish, a man of Kish, they raised to kingship.' Before that there are no historical records, but evidence of a kind comes first from epic and then from the myths of the gods.

The epic source is the poem known as *Gilgamesh and Agga,* a story unique among Sumerian epics in being entirely concerned with human beings and free from any divine interventions. Gilgamesh in fact appears in it, however unreliably, as the historical king of Uruk of Early Dynastic times. The relevance of the story here is that when Agga, king of Kish, sends envoys demanding the submission of Uruk, Gilgamesh first appeals to 'the convened assembly of the elders of his city' to be allowed 'to smite Kish with weapons'. When the elders are cautious and rule in favour of surrender, Gilgamesh turns to 'the men of his city'—taken as the assembly (in Sumerian *unken*) of the fighting males. The elders' decision is reversed, the men advising, 'Do not submit to the house of Kish, let us smite it with weapons.' The struggle then begins. The strong implication is that at the dawn of Early Dynastic times the *unken* controlled the greatest decision of the state: peace or war.

In order to follow this aspect of constitutional history back into the prehistoric age when the form of Sumerian civilization was first emerging, it has been held to be legitimate to draw upon the divine mythology. Although many of these stories of the gods have come down to us in much later versions—such as the Babylonian creation myth, the *Enuma elish*—they must embody the vision of the cosmos that was forming in men's minds even as they were bringing civilization into being. In them the cosmos appears as a state, and it can be assumed that this divine state was a projection of the order prevailing on earth. Jacobsen has interpreted the nature of the society revealed in the myths as representing a primitive democracy.

The prime source of authority, then, is the lofty sky god, Anu. The god of storm, Enlil, provides the force necessary for the will of authority to be imposed. Enlil can delegate this power to another god, just as the other god can delegate it to a human king, but it is so much his own that the kingship remains 'the Enlil function'.

This aspect of the divine hierarchy will be considered presently in connection with kingship itself; the significant fact here is that the authority and force of Anu and Enlil were not absolute; approval or disapproval rested with an assembly of all the gods.

This met in the enclosed space of the Ubshuukkinna (a name also given to the court of assembly in holy Nippur), where Anu might preside with Enlil at his side. The throng before them no doubt included such small fry and godlets as those who were overseers on the temple estates. The upper house, the equivalent of the elders, seems to have been composed of the fifty great gods or Anunnaki—the sons of Anu. Above even these great ones were the 'seven who decree fate'. In addition to Anu and Enlil themselves, the seven may have been made up by Enki, Ninhursag, Nanna, Utu and Inanna. It is the fact that there were probably two goddesses among fate decreers, and that Inanna undoubtedly spoke in the assembly and was admired for her wisdom, that has made it appear just possible that women once had their part in human assemblies.

On arriving in Ubshuukkinna (according to the *Enuma elish*) the deities greeted one another and then:

> *They smacked their tongues and sat down to feast;*
> *They ate and drank,*
> *Sweet drink dispelled their fears.*
> *They sang for joy, drinking strong wine.*
> *Carefree they grew, their hearts elated.*

This scene, which no doubt had its human counterpart, recalls Tacitus's account of how the Germans liked to make their decisions in a state of drunkenness.

The proposals having been introduced by Anu or Enlil, they were discussed in a manner described as 'asking one another'. The seven seem to have led the debates, which might become heated, but the purpose was to reach a consensus when all would cry, 'Let it be so.' The verdict could then be announced as 'the word of the assembly of the gods, the command of Anu and Enlil'.

In this sense the divine assembly was competent to choose kings and military leaders, to judge crimes (such as Enlil's raping of Ninlil) and to decide great issues (such as the fully understandable decision to destroy mankind by flood for making too much noise).

Taken together, the testimony of records, epic and mythological stories leave no doubt that the Sumerian city-states emerged into history with a dual assembling of elders and citizens. Their significance may, however, have been exaggerated by those historians who describe a democratic way of life that sounds more than somewhat like that of an American state of 1789. This conception of the original self-government of the Sumerian city-state is naturally most congenial to those who accept the idea of the dominance of private land ownership and enterprise in ancient Sumeria.

According to the very simple terms in which this interpretation is usually presented, the nobility formed the upper house of elders, while the land-owning commoners met in the popular assembly to make important decisions. Together they would have managed affairs of the state, appointing governors (*ensis*) and choosing kings (*lugals*) as temporary military commanders in times of crisis. There would then be an irresistible tendency, due to the increasing wealth and complexity of society on the one hand and personal ambition on the other, for these offices to become hereditary and to coalesce,

until an autocratic kingship was established and the traditional democracy lost most of its powers.

While any picture that makes the Sumerian city-state look like a
modern democracy is certainly misleading, Edzard goes rather far
in the opposite direction when he dismisses the Gilgamesh and Agga
episode as a 'literary convention for displaying the *hubris* of the
king' and the function of the assembly (as reflected in the myths)
as no more than a ventilation of public issues and the reception of
the ruler's pronouncements.

The best analogy would seem to be a magnification of the village
or tribal popular assembly where public opinion must be carried
along to some kind of 'So be it' consensus, but where the authority of
the head man and his most influential advisors is paramount. It is
in these terms that we can understand that revealing combination
in decision making implicit in 'the word of the assembly of the gods,
the command of Anu and Enlil'.

Although it is evidently true that the power and independence of
the rulers of the city-states increased during the third millennium
and that kingship became even more absolute under the Semites and
the Third Dynasty of Ur, the account of the early history of the
offices of *ensi* and *lugal* outlined above is unfortunately as much
over-simplified as that of self-governing democracy.

It has already been seen that the Sumerian titles *en*, *ensi* and *lugal*
were current by Protoliterate times. As they emerge into the light of
history their (no doubt changing and evolving) meanings can be
translated respectively as priestly lord, governor, and king—the
literal meaning of *lugal* being 'great man'. It may be, however, that
originally these titles did not imply distinct functions but were
simply terms selected by different city-states for their rulers—much
as, in England, through various historical chances, Oxford colleges
are headed by rectors, presidents, masters and deans, although their
duties are now all very much the same.

Certainly the title *en* had a special meaning for the city-state of
Uruk. During most of the Early Dynastic period there, and there
alone, it was used for the ruler in his secular, including military,
function. Elsewhere it was applied to high priests, and it was in this
sense that it survived into later times. That *en* was a holy and
ancient title is shown by the fact that it was incorporated in the
names of two of the oldest and greatest of the gods—Enlil and
Enki.

The derivation of the compound *ensi* is not understood. We have seen it applied to the man at the head of the temple estate, and after the separation of temple and palace it was still used by the supreme rulers of some city-states. The distinguished Gudea, for instance, remained the *ensi* of Lagash. It came, however, to have a much lower status than the other titles. It was used for vassal rulers under national kings, and imperial monarchs such as those of the Third Dynasty of Ur and the Sargonids appointed *ensis* as their official governors. Even at its highest it was not a title that was ever raised to cover the national kingship.

It was the title of *lugal* that came to represent true kingship. If it did originate in an elected war leader (which is doubtful) it was soon being applied to kings, including national kings. It is the word used in this sense throughout the *Sumerian King List*. Moreover, *lugal* came to be accepted as the equivalent of the Akkadian *sharrum*, the exaltedly royal title that was manifest, for instance, in the throne name of the first true imperial monarch, Sargon, or *sharrum-ken*. We have seen, too, how at least from the time of Mesalim the title King (*lugal*) of Kish was an honorific assumed by rulers who had won national dominion.

In the discussion of architectural history, it emerged that all Sumerian rulers, whatever their title, appear originally to have had their residence within the temple precincts. The separation of the palace from the temple building which took place in Early Dynastic times is, of course, the physical manifestation of the growing power of the throne and its at least partial independence of the temple. For many centuries from that time the city-states of Sumer and Akkad were to be dominated by two great organizations, the temple and the palace. Now the kings' house, like the gods' house, became a great self-maintained unit with its field and client farmers, its workshops and craftsmen, its trade and merchants, its many slaves—and, behind all activity, its hierarchy of officials, scribes and petty bureaucrats.

There were differences, obviously. Soldiers had to be housed in the palace. There may have been rather more opportunity for individual action, for personal success, in the palace than in the highly traditional temple. One of the developments that may have resulted from the need to rule an empire was the appointment of a grand vizier, a *sukkal-mah*, who was certainly an important palace figure under the Third Dynasty of Ur.

The exact nature of the relationship between these two organizations is obscure, and it is still more difficult to understand their relationship with the city itself. They may have evolved elaborate formalities and safeguards—of the kind that still persist between the City of London, the Palace and the Church. No doubt they varied widely with place and time, with rises and falls in prosperity.

Undoubtedly towards the end of Early Dynastic times, when the temples were still powerful but the kings were already tending to usurp that power, there could be rivalry amounting to antagonism between the two. This was a state of affairs that we shall find repeated in Egypt, and which was to become one of the frequent causes of trouble in European history.

Rivalry is exposed in the reform texts of Urukagina of Lagash. There is a clear tendency in this document for the temple to be identified with the popular interests—which is not surprising, as in later times there is evidence of the temple helping the poor in time of trouble with doles and shelter. The Urukagina text, in which the king first describes the evils that had overtaken society and then how he has set them right, is so revealing of how the rich and the bureaucracy could oppress the people that it demands attention even at the risk of delaying this account of authority in the Mesopotamian state.

That the times were so far out of joint can probably be attributed to the military ventures of Eanatum a century before, and the efforts of his successors to continue them, and also to the endless quarrel with Umma. Urukagina sounds very much like the leader of a popular revolt against the old royal house and the privileged establishment surrounding it. He claims that the city god Ningirsu, on behalf of Enlil, picked him out of 36,000 men (presumably all the free men of the city) and gave him the kingship of Lagash so that he should correct these abuses and restore the divine decrees of former days.

The greatest offence of the palace had been its annexation of temple lands, and also of its ploughing teams. So extensive had been the encroachment that the houses and fields of the *ensi* and of his harem and his family ('nursery') 'crowded each other side by side.' Moreover, 'the oxen of the gods ploughed the onion patches of the *ensi*, and the onion and cucumber fields of the *ensi* were located in the god's best fields.' Another offence against the temple was the seizure from the *sanga* (the chief administrator of the temple) on behalf of the *ensi* of many of his best donkeys, oxen and garments. There was also an unfair division of his barley. Other priests got short measure for their rations.

Similar seizures were made from ordinary folk, apparently by officials representing the *ensi*: not only sheep and donkeys were taken but also boats and fisheries—even fish from a poor man's fish-pond. In one instance, if the translation is correct, it appears to be the *sanga* who is at fault, having 'felled the trees in the garden of the poor mother and carried off the fruit.'

Another class of exactions from the relatively poor recalls the state of affairs in mediaeval Europe when peasants were obliged to take their grain to be ground in the mill of the lord of the manor and to pay through the nose for it. In Lagash shepherds and all kinds of sheep owners had to pay the palace in silver for the shearing of their sheep and lambs. The exorbitant charge of five shekels of silver had to be payed to the *ensi* (plus a sixth to an official) by a man seeking a divorce. Finally death had presented an obvious opportunity for such exactions. Evidently Lagash maintained two cemeteries where mourning families could bury their dear departed (one of them called Reeds of Enki, a name curiously similar to the more sentimental names of American gardens of rest). They were forced to pay for the privilege by odd but onerous fees to various officials. For each funeral, each 'citizen laid to rest among the reeds of Enki', seven pitchers of beer, 429 loaves, quantities of barley, a bed and a chair.

Yet another form of gross injustice often to be repeated in the future history of human greed was the forced sale. If an official of the *ensi* coveted a good young donkey and its humble owner named his price in the terms 'weigh out for me the silver pleasing to my heart', the official would take it by force on his own terms. In the same way a 'big man' wanting to extend his estate might coerce a humble neighbour into selling his house at an unfairly low price in barley.

The sense of a people despairing under so many state exactions is well expressed in a single sentence of the Urukagina text: 'From the borders of Ningirsu to the sea, there was the tax collector.'

The text also reveals signs of a general economic malaise: many people were in prison for debt, artisans were out of work and obliged to 'take the bread of supplication', while apprentices were reduced to 'food leavings at the great gate'—a phrase that seems to suggest that scraps were normally put out at the gate for beggars. (Even a poor man at the gate may eat the crumbs from his master's table.)

In the second half of his proclamation, Urukagina claims to have remedied all these abuses, to have remitted debts, provided help for the poorest and reformed certain laws. (It should be added that during the second millennium kings at the beginning of their reign seem regularly to have promoted 'justice' by the remission of debts.) Of most significance in the present context is Urukagina's reversal of the palace encroachment on temple lands. He says that he 'made Ningirsu king of the house of the *ensi* and of the fields of the *ensi*' and the same restitution to their divine owners was made of the harem and 'nursery' property. It appears, in fact, that Urukagina restored to the control of the temples the entire estates of the palace.

If this was so, and not merely a device of the king's to sweeten his illegitimacy, it was going against the general trend of Mesopotamian history. During the prosperous days of the Third Dynasty of Ur the temple and palace economy appear to have flourished side by side. The temples, however, were now letting lands to private tenants, and the absolute power of the Ur dynasty must have given the palace an ever great ascendancy. By the Old Babylonian period, presumably through Amorite influence, the swing was more or less complete. The palace still owned large estates and could still call up sections of the population to work on irrigations, fortifications, temple repairs and other royal responsibilities. At the same time (whatever may have been the situation before) there is now a large class of well-to-do free citizens, buying and selling private land and working it with hired or slave labour. Against this background of royal power coupled with what amounts to middle class free enterprise, the temples had sunk to being no more than one of many institutions within the state. Inevitably their priesthoods became involved in various ways with private interests. At the same time the palace now seems to have had unquestioned authority to use and even dispose of temple property. The king might draw upon it to meet immediate palace needs or even to invest in mercantile enterprises. All this was still not fully approved of. An omen text says, 'the king will take property of the house of the gods to the palace, but Shamash will see it.' As far as we can judge, Shamash might see, but could do very little.

From that time onwards the temples had slight authority. The position of the Assyrian kings as high priests of Assur must have changed the relationship of temple and palace—as it did physically. But it probably only made the royal authority closer and more complete. The temples had lost independence and authority, but could still be immensely rich. Successful imperial kings could serve their own glory by filling them with treasures—often the booty and tribute of war. One can leave the last phrases with Nebuchadnezzar: 'Under my government the great Lord Marduk held his entry into Babil with rejoicing. . . . The regular offerings of Esagila and of the gods of Babylon I established, the protectorship of Babil I retained. . . . I filled Esagila with silver and gold and precious stones, and made Ekua shining as the constellations of the sky.'

One other aspect of the theory and practice of Sumerian kingship demands attention. This is the meaning of the establishment of national kings. Such a system of shifting hegemonies was to recur elsewhere when circumstances were similar: that is to say when a land had a unified culture and sense of nationhood and yet was divided into small kingdoms. It probably existed in Mycenaean Greece and certainly in Anglo-Saxon England.

Part III has shown how among the cities of the Plain national kingship shifted with the chance rise of strong and ambitious kings. Yet although so much depended upon the personal fortunes of individual rulers, there is no question that high kingship was an accepted part of the Sumerian constitution. It was recognized as a *bala*, a term of office that could be bestowed on one city, then transferred to another, or sometimes allowed to go into abeyance. When Nanna, the moon god of Ur, complains bitterly to Enlil about the destined fall of his city (at the end of the third dynasty), Enlil tells him that from the earliest times the high kingship has always shifted and that its fate was irresistibly determined in advance by the gods themselves.

The national kingship had a special relationship with the cosmic state of the gods, quite distinct from that of the city-state—which a god simply held for his own livelihood, like a lord of the manor. The national kingship was determined by Anu and the assembly of gods, and the great god concerned, the owner of the dominant city-state, was an official of the cosmic state charged to exercise the Enlil-function. This meant that the human king of the state was also acting for the cosmic state. Nippur, which belonged to Enlil, was a holy city that never became a city-state. Presumably the god was regarded as residing there for the purpose of exercising his Enlil function over the national state, and that was why all aspiring national kings needed to claim possession of Nippur. Moreover, when a city first won the hegemony, its presiding deity had to go to Nippur to seek Enlil's acceptance of his or her human deputy in his office as supreme king. This would evidently have been impossible if Enlil's city had been in unfriendly hands.

The whole process of the chain of delegations of authority from Anu to the human *lugal* is eloquently expressed in the prologue to Hammurabi's laws. It will be remembered that Babylon and its god Marduk had been of little dignity before the conquests of Hammurabi raised them to national supremacy.

> *When lofty Anu, king of the Anunnaki, and Enlil,*
> *   lord of heaven and earth,*
> *who determine the destinies of the country,*
> *   appointed Marduk, the firstborn*
> *son of Enki, to execute the Enlil function over*
> *   the totality of the people*
> *made him great among the Igigi, called Babylon by*
> *   its exalted name, made it*
> *surpassingly great in the world, and firmly*
> *   established for him in its*
> *midst an enduring kingship whose foundations are*
> *   firmly grounded*
> *as those of heaven and earth—then did Anu and*
> *   Enlil call me to afford well-being for the people,*
> *me, Hammurabi, the obedient, god-fearing prince, to*
> *   cause righteousness to appear in the land,*
> *to destroy the evil and the wicked, that the strong*
> *   harm not the weak*
> *and that I arise like the sun over the black-headed*
> *   people, lighting up the land.*

The tenor of this inscription also shows how the old Sumerian forms of kingship and the underlying theological ideas were still being honoured by Hammurabi the Amorite at a time of much social change. To some extent they survived until the end, and that in both Assyria and Babylonia.

Before ending this discussion of authority and government in

Mesopotamia, a word should be spared for the condition of the venerable cities of the Plain in the days when power lay with the rulers of Assyria. As has already been hinted, the Assyrian kings generally sought to show their respect for their past by appointing local men as governors. They ruled with the assistance of elders, and when complaints came from this body they were attended to by the imperial palace. The Babylonian cities, in fact, had a far greater degree of autonomy than any other cities of the empire. Some Assyrian kings, and notably Sargon II, granted special privileges to city populations in both Assyria itself and in Babylonia. Assur and Harran, Babylon, Sippar and Nippur were among those fortunate places exempt from the corvée and military service and from paying certain taxes. They were also allowed freedom to trade.

ALTHOUGH MANY POINTS ABOUT THE STRUCTURE OF MESOPOTAMIAN SO-cieties have already emerged in connection with government, trade, crafts and other matters affecting the lives of the people, they need to be given more coherence. This is a subject much obscured by the difficulty of rendering Sumerian and Akkadian terms for social groups or of knowing whether they represent classes, age groups, occupational categories and so on.

While the classification set out on page 150 certainly has some validity, it must be made clear that the idea of a 'nobility' comes from the documentary evidence of large landholders, high officials and other notables, not from any distinct class recognized or named at the time. It has in the past been more usual to divide Sumerian and later Mesopotamian society into only three strata below the royal family—the free citizens, the 'clients', and the slaves. The middle class has proved particularly difficult to define, its members having been also referred to as serfs, 'semi-free' and landless freemen. It seems that these 'clients' could not own land but held fields allotted to them by temple or palace in return for services and dues. The Sumerian term *shub-lugala* means literally 'subjected to the king'.

In the laws of Hammurabi the three classes are clearly defined as *awilum*, a word which can mean simply 'man' but is here usually translated as 'gentleman' or 'seigneur'; *mushkenum;* and slave (*wardum*). The *mushkenum* again provides problems of translation, having sometimes been rendered as commoner, but also as 'depen-

dent tenant of the palace'. Nor is it known at all how large a proportion of the population is included. In the laws the *mushkenum* can
himself own slaves, but he has to pay only half as much as the
awilum for crimes of violence, and similarly is worth only half as
much in compensation.

The laws concerning soldiers make it clear that something very
close to feudal service existed in Babylon: the 'feudal dues' being
frequently mentioned in connection with their landholdings. Perhaps
this was a system that developed with semi-regular imperial armies
in which soldiers were called up for tours of duty when needed.

In Sumerian times the term *eren* was used for men who could be
called up either for the corvée to work on building and irrigation,
or for military service. There is no evidence to suggest that in this
period any class was formally exempt. When Gudea of Lagash described his mighty temple-building enterprise, he claimed to have
made the city labour 'as one man'. It is assumed, however, that the
'nobility' were not compelled to serve. Certainly by the age of
Hammurabi there were recognized exemptions, for a citizen wrote
to the king protesting at being illegally set to work and the king
set him free, ordering that a *corvéable* substitute should be found.
Perhaps these were special exemptions of the kind we have seen
granted to venerable cities.

Down at the level of the slaves we are on firm ground at last.
There were two sharply demarcated grades, natives and foreigners.
The native-born had various opportunities for manumission, the
others probably none, unless they were ransomed. As the Sumerian
words for male and female slaves were composed of the signs for
man and for woman plus 'foreign land', it seems that originally
slavery was for prisoners of war or destitute foreigners—but these
foreigners might come from no further than a neighbouring city-
state. In time, however, there were numbers of natives who had lost
their freedom. Most commonly this was due to indebtedness; from
Akkadian time parents could sell their children or in desperate
straits a man could consign himself and his entire family to a
creditor. In theory this debt slavery was temporary: 'Three years
shall they work in the house of their buyer and in the fourth year
he shall fix their liberty', states a law of Hammurabi. Enslavement
could also be a punishment for crime—including a curious series of
family offences such as the disowning of parents, kicking a mother
or striking an elder brother.

Slaves worked for the temple, the palace and, in small numbers, for well-to-do private citizens. The earliest record of the numbers of temple slaves comes from Girsu, where the temples of Baba and Nanshe, neither of them likely to own so many as the city temple of Ningirsu, had 188 and 180 female slaves respectively. Most of these girls would probably be employed at spinning, weaving and grinding flour. Probably the palace would have owned a large proportion of prisoners of war who could wear out their strength on such royal undertakings as canal building and fortification. Private citizens are likely to have used them about the house and garden. Female slaves often became concubines.

Slaves were property; the fact that their fathers' names were never recorded was a sign they had not full human status. Their heads could be shaved, their flesh branded with their master's mark, their ankles shackled; they could be sold for about the price of a good donkey. A slave who struck a gentleman could have his ear cut off, and a girl slave who cheeked her mistress have her mouth scoured with salt. Yet on the other hand they had legal rights, and there are many proofs of trust and affection existing between owners and slaves. A native-born male slave could buy his freedom for twice his purchase price, he could marry the daughter of a gentleman, and the children of either men or women slaves married to free persons were themselves free. Sometimes there was an agreement that slaves who had looked after their masters until death should be set free. If a gentleman had children by a slave, as they evidently very often did in Old Babylonian times, and he recognized them by calling them 'my children', on his death they had the right to share his property with his wife's family. At latest by the first millennium B.C., slaves were able to own property and engage in business—were in fact approaching the condition they enjoyed in the classical world.

A form of social grouping that must have been of great value to society and also a source of satisfaction and security to individuals was the associations of people in like trades and professions. The guild-like companies (*ugula*, Akkadian *aklu*) of skilled craftsmen such as weavers, smiths, brewers and carpenters had official palace or temple overseers, yet probably also had some independence outside these organizations. The traders and merchants also had their *ugula*, and their overseers might become rich and influential men. The musicians, on the other hand, were relatively few and poor.

Finally, one cannot leave the subject of Mesopotamian social groupings without giving a thought to that part of the population of Mesopotamia that did not lead a settled, law-abiding life in village, town or city. The historical chapter has left no uncertainty about the constant drifting in and periodic large-scale incursions of true desert nomads from the west, nor about the barbarians who descended on the valley from the mountains. Gutians, Amorites, Kassites and their successors became powerful enough to take over city-state and national thrones. At these times of crisis the life of the countryside could be largely disrupted by nomads and war bands. In addition to these outsiders, there were at some periods considerable numbers of natives living as best they could off the open country. Some might be ordinary country folk set adrift by deterioration of the soil, changes in the river's course, irrigation failures; others were perhaps political exiles, debtors, drop-outs of many kinds. Obviously, all such unattached peoples and outlaws made a threat to ordered society. Only powerful kings could deal with them by restoring old lands or reclaiming new land on the frontiers. Several royal inscriptions claim the 'ingathering' of the scattered peoples and their settlement on lands made available to them. Once in control, they could be made to cultivate and irrigate, pay taxes and become *corvéable*—in short to accept all the burdens of good citizenship which a few at least of them had sought to evade.

CORVÉE AND THE ARMY

TWO OF THE MOST ONEROUS RESPONSIBILITIES OF SUMERIAN KINGS were on the one hand to construct new canals and restore old ones and to build fortifications, temples and palaces, and on the other to create and lead the state or national army. It seems that the arrangements for calling up were the same for both and that the officials in charge of civilian and military service had similar titles. As we have seen, the term *eren* was probably applied to men who were liable either for corvée labour or for the army. In theory, at least, it probably comprised all free citizens. The crown could also command the services of a group known as the *aga-ush*, who might serve either as supervisors of public works or professionally in the army.

Judging principally from the pictorial evidence of the 'Vulture Stele' of Eanatum of Lagash, and the 'standard' of Ur, there was already a well-trained and probably professional element in the army in Early Dynastic times. On the stele the phalanx marching immediately behind the king, with their standardized helmets, overlapping shields and levelled spears, look like a royal guard of regulars. On the 'standard', the axe-carrying infantry appear to be in more open formation, but it seems unlikely that the chariot corps shown on the lower register could have been manned by temporarily conscripted men. The chariots are represented as they begin to advance at speed, the leading animals already at the gallop while the last are still moving only at a walk—an indication of the experienced skill and control that would have been necessary to manoeuvre these clumsy, solid-wheeled vehicles with their teams of four onagers. Each chariot had a driver and a soldier armed with a battle-axe and a quiver of spears, and were therefore almost certainly used for a direct frontal attack at medium and then close range. There was no possibility of using chariots as mobile, long-range firing platforms such as they were to become in the second millennium after the introduction of horses, spoked wheels and powerful bows.

The disciplined fighting power represented by the combination of phalanx and chariot corps must largely have accounted for the success of individual city-states and for the wider conquests of such kings as Eanatum. If, as has been assumed, they were composed of professional soldiers, they were, of course, supported in time of war by large numbers of *eren* when 'the king called up his army'. It is impossible to make any estimate of the total numbers involved in the Sumerian armies of Early Dynastic times.

With the rise of Sargon of Akkad and imperialist wars when 'he spread his terror-inspiring glamour over all the countries', the size and importance of the regular army must greatly have increased. There was also the adoption of a new mode of fighting to which Sargon may have owed much of his success. In place of the old Sumerian phalanx where soldiers fought with spears from behind a wall of shields, the Akkadians gave battle in a more open formation, relying on thrown javelins and above all on the tremendous penetrating power of arrows shot from composite bows. Sargon himself claimed to have 5400 soldiers who ate before him in his palace; presumably this would have represented his own crack troops of the royal guard, but his governors throughout the empire maintained their own forces. The state of Mari in the days of Jasmah-Adad had a standing army of about 10,000 divided into units of 200 men. Of these some 4000 were stationed in the capital, some of them in barracks within the palace itself. The palace courtyards were probably also used to store engines of war such as battering rams and siege towers.

In Mari men called to the army in times of crisis included tribesmen as well as settled citizens. The documents for the first time give us an idea of the troops as human beings. It will surprise no one to learn that men were often reluctant to be called to the standards, and the king's officers were prepared to use tough methods to bring them in. On one occasion when conscripts from a particular area failed to report, an officer wrote, 'If the king approves, let them kill one of the guilty men, cut off his head, and let them take it around among these towns . . . so that people may be afraid and will quickly assemble.' On another occasion, however, an officer was able to report that conscripts had arrived in good health and spirits, and 'there were no worries . . . only laughing and singing as though they were at home. Their morale is good.'

The Babylonian army from the first dynasty was well organized. Complete lists were kept in state registers. Just as today, however, individuals might be exempt on compassionate grounds—for example one of two conscripted brothers could win a release if he was needed as the family bread-winner—or because, like bakers and shepherds, they were engaged in essential work. All such exemptions had to be granted by the king, and sometimes he might demand a substitute. We learn from the Code of Hammurabi that the slipping in of substitutes without permission was a capital offence for both officers and men.

In the main the section of the Code dealing with military matters conveys the impression that soldiers, commissioned and uncommissioned, were privileged persons. By this time they were regularly rewarded with plots of inalienable land and livestock. They could not sell it, and it carried with it the feudal obligation to serve the king, but it was a sure foundation for the family's well-being. The laws are concerned to prevent soldiers from being deprived of this land by others. If a man is taken prisoner on the king's service his land must be restored on his return, and meanwhile it could be worked by his son or his wife and son together. If as a prisoner he has not enough currency to pay his ransom it is to be paid by his city god or by the state, 'since his own field, orchard and house may not be ceded for his ransom.' Finally, the common soldier is protected by law against exploitation by his officers: 'If either a sergeant or a captain has appropriated the household goods of a soldier, has wronged him, let him for hire, abandoned him to a superior in a lawsuit, has appropriated the grant which the king gave to him, that sergeant or captain shall be put to death.'

As a reminder that, like all kings before and after him, Hammurabi went to war in the name of his gods, and for a glimpse of the ceremonial of war, it is worth quoting an entry for the twenty-fourth year of his reign: 'He constructed the main emblem of reddish gold which is carried in front of the army, for the great gods, his helpers.'

Within a few centuries of Hammurabi's reign the employment of large numbers of horse chariots must have modified the tactics of battle and at the same time complicated the commissariat. Further changes came with the adoption of cavalry in the last millennium B.C. By this time military science was in the hands of the most martial people of the ancient world: the Assyrians. The armies of the great conquerors ran into hundreds of thousands of foot soldiers and many thousands of chariots and of cavalrymen. During campaigns in mountainous country, chariots were often taken apart and carried by soldiers or animals. The cavalry wore leather boots and sometimes chain mail; they included light skirmishers armed with bows. Most of the archers, however, were foot soldiers; and the success of the Assyrians in war was largely due to their extraordinary prowess. The king moved with his troops in a chariot large enough to carry an umbrella holder as well as a driver, and was followed by a bow-bearer and quiver-bearer.

The Assyrians have been called the Romans of the East. There is no question that in comparison with Sumerians and Babylonians they were a military people almost entirely devoted to war—and the looting and trade necessary to support it. Literature and the peaceful arts came to them at second hand. Their artists were largely concerned to show pitiless scenes of war and hunting. Were they in fact also exceptionally cruel in their military might?

It is true that their predecessors in Mesopotamia fought, massacred and levelled cities. It is true also that for a long time our view of them came to us through the hostile eyes of the authors of the Old Testament. True that in the intervals between imperial campaigns, rebellions and mass deportations, subject peoples were well ruled. Yet even those who have studied the Assyrians admit to their pitiless ferocity. The same spirit is manifest in the frightful mutilations prescribed in their laws. Because in the texts the kings were supposed to be informing Assur (the imperial god so often depicted hovering over their heads as they went to battle) of the victories he was winning over unbelievers, they may even have exaggerated the extent of their brutalities. Nevertheless there seems something new in horror in the way in which they boasted of what they did. Assurnasirpal, perhaps the most ruthless of all, proclaimed, 'I cut off their heads: I burned them with fire; a pile of living men as of heads I set up against the city gate; men I impaled on stakes; the city I destroyed, I turned it into mounds and ruins; the young men and maidens in the fire I burned.'

The impact of such words is reinforced by the palace reliefs. One scene shows Assurbanipal and his queen dining together *al fresco* with the severed head of the king of Elam dangling above them. Such things were not to be found in ancient Sumeria.

LAW

IT CAN BE ASSUMED THAT IN THE VILLAGES AND TOWNS OF PREHISTORIC Mesopotamia the relationships and dealings between people were controlled by an undifferentiated blend of personal government with social and religious custom. With the breakdown of kindred and small community ties, urban life demanded some degree of formalization—in fact the growth of custom into a legal system. Justice was, indeed, to become a major preoccupation of the Sumerians and their successors in Mesopotamia, their rulers leading the ancient world in publishing judicial formularies intended to 'bring justice to the land'.

Probably in the early days legal proceedings were conducted within the temple precincts or at its gate. There is disagreement on the subject, but it seems that in the later centuries of Early Dynastic times this was no longer the case, although the divine sanction on which justice rested was recognized by the litigants and their witnesses taking their oaths in the temple. Records of cases and other legal documents may also have been filed in the temple gate. There is one mention among documents from Ur of a 'judge of the House of Nanna', which could mean that special judges were appointed by temples, perhaps for ecclesiastical cases.

The *ensi* or *lugal* must from very early days have been responsible for the administration of justice, and it was as the palace became to some degree secularized and separated from the temple that the law followed a like trend. As in everything else, however, the *ensi* or *lugal* acted on behalf of divine authority. Urukagina proclaimed that his reforms were enjoined upon him by Ningirsu and that he kept closely to the god's instruction. A national king might act not only in the name of his city god but also in that of the god of justice, the sun god Utu (Shamash in Akkadian). Thus Ur-Nammu drew up his legal code 'by the might of Nanna, lord of the city of Ur, and in accordance with the word of Utu', and in so doing he was able to 'establish equity in the land, and he banished malediction, violence and strife.' At the top of the stone stele on which the laws of Hammurabi were cut, the king is shown standing reverently before Shamash, who holds the measuring rod and line, symbols of justice. In his epilogue Hammurabi says:

> *I am the king who is pre-eminent among kings;*
> *my words are choice, my ability has no equal.*
> *By the order of Shamash, the great judge of heaven and earth,*
> *may my justice prevail in the land;*
> *by the word of Marduk, my lord,*
> *may my statutes have no one to rescind them.*

Hammurabi's estimate of royal and divine power seems here to be nicely balanced.

The rulers of city-states were already promulgating a variety of legal regulations by the middle of the third millennium. Then with the tremendous increase in the complexities of trade and commerce and the ownership of property, together probably with a heightening of temptations in personal and family morality, the need to set such enactments down in some sort of order became very great. National kings, too, must have wanted to establish a standard of justice for all their subjects. Hence the drawing up of the more or less orderly collections of judgements and legal regulations usually referred to as codes. The earliest of these at present known to us is that of Ur-Nammu, founder of the Third Dynasty of Ur. It is followed by a code from the city of Eshnunna with no royal name attached, and a little later by that of Lipit-Ishtar of Isin (1934–24 B.C.) The Akkadian code which has made Hammurabi's name famous was in fact longer, better ordered and more authoritative in effect than any of its known predecessors. Yet in many ways it can be seen as no more than a revision and expansion of its Sumerian predecessors. Its excellence in our eyes also owes something to chance. All the royal codes were probably inscribed on a stele and exposed for public reading. The other examples, however, have come down to us only in the form of clay tablets, with gaps, uncertainties and whole sections missing. Hammurabi's handsome stone was carried off to Susa as war booty and was found there. The Elamites had made some excisions, but even these have been made good from clay copies.

From the centuries following Hammurabi the chief legal documents to survive are some Middle Assyrian laws, mainly concerned with women, dating from 1450–1250 B.C.

Although at least by the time of Ur-Nammu the national king was theoretically responsible for the rule of law throughout his land, it was of course in practice the *ensi* of each city-state who was responsible for the administration of justice. Under him, cases were actually heard by judges and other officials of the court. Yet the people were by no means entirely cut off from their king as the fountain-head, under the gods, of justice. The right of appeal to him was no fiction; there is evidence of kings interesting themselves in particular legal matters, and at some periods appeals and re-trials were frequent. One of the sections in the laws of Eshnunna concerned with physical injury says (if rightly translated), 'If it is capital murder, it is a matter for the king.'

Case records from the Third Dynasty of Ur give us an idea of court proceedings in late Sumerian times. The litigant initiating the action, perhaps involved in a row with his wife's family over her marriage contract, would present himself at court either with witnesses prepared to support his case under oath, or with a legal document or a statement from an expert or official. There, presumably, he would confront his opponent and they would go before the judges—usually three or four of them, but sometimes only one or two. If the litigant belonged to the professional class, he might know some of his judges, for the office was not a full-time one but, like a British magistracy, was held by men in any of the more esteemed professions. Many judges were from the upper levels of the temple administration, but others were merchants, scribes, augurs, archivists and so on. Even the *ensi* himself might sit as a judge.

Busying himself, perhaps fussing, about the court, the litigant would encounter the *maskim*, a kind of clerk of the court. He might already have had dealings with him, for the *maskim* seems to have been responsible for the preparation of cases as well as attending to the details of the procedure. He would come from much the same social background as the judges, but the litigants might have less respect for him, partly because he had no jurisdiction, but also because he was on occasion paid for his services.

At the appropriate moment the parties themselves, or the witnesses whose testimony was essential to the decision, would be conducted to the temple for the administration of the oath. Although there were people prepared to give false witness (they are provided against in the laws themselves) the invocation of the gods acted as a very real deterrent to perjury. An instance is known where the judge's order 'Go take the oath of the gods against the witnesses' was refused, and the case immediately lost.

There would probably have been a scribe present in the court throughout the session, taking notes on a tablet of soft clay that could be erased with a touch of the fingers or sweep of the palm. When the judges had announced their decision, in civil cases such as this one amounting to nothing worse than that the losing party should pay up, hand over the slave or distrained property or whatever it might be, a summary of the case and judgement, together with the names of all who had taken part, would be recorded on a tablet and filed in its chronological position.

A suggestion that during this period the judicial function was being more and more delegated from the head of state down to his representatives can be found in these records. The earliest of them were signed by the *ensi* and the judges, the latest by the judges alone. However, even in this last stage the *ensi's* name still appeared on the storage files.

These courts of the *ensis* with their many temple personnel probably represented the last stages of the former temple involvement in the administration of justice. There were already by the time of the Third Dynasty of Ur wholly secular provincial courts. These consisted of the mayor (*rabianum*) of the town sitting with elders or notables. The importance of the mayor continued to grow until by the time of Hammurabi civilian courts were in control of the administration of justice. Sometimes the judges sat with an assembly, perhaps serving as a jury of citizens. Appeals could be made to a higher court known as the Judges of Babylon, and above that (as always) to the king himself.

When we turn from the administration of the law to the laws themselves, three reactions of a general sort are almost inevitable.

One is the good sense and liberal moderation of their purposes, and another the contrasting ferocity of some of the punishments—at least by the time of Hammurabi. The third reaction is one of simple amusement at the extraordinary similarity they reveal between the human nature of that time and of this. In addition to crimes of passion and violence that could be assumed to be ancient if not eternal, it seems that every kind of fiddle, cheating, pilfering, debt, financial unscrupulousness and damaging incompetence or idleness familiar in the courts today already had its counterpart in the first civilization on earth.

There are two features found in all the codes, Sumerian and Akkadian, that are alien to the modern mind. Yet both existed in the Europe of earlier days—for example among the Anglo-Saxons.

One is the variation of punishment according to class. It would have seemed unquestionably right and proper in Bronze Age society for an assault on a gentleman to be a more heinous and therefore more expensive crime than one on a commoner or slave.

The other feature in question is trial by ordeal. If there was an irreconcilable conflict in sworn evidence, the judge could order the accused to jump into the river. If he had sworn falsely in the name of the gods they would see to it that he was drowned. This was not as hard on the accused as might appear, for if he survived then the accuser was liable to be put to death. It must have been a most potent discouragement to false testimony—and was probably a procedure seldom put into practice.

There has been much unrewarding dispute as to whether these legal formulations of Mesopotamian kings can properly be called laws, or be said to form codes. They are, some insist, less laws than listed precedents or ideal judgements, guides for the making of sound decisions. Certainly they are not 'Thou Shalt Not' type prohibitions. But does it really imply fundamental difference of intent to state 'If a man drives over seventy miles per hour on the motorway he shall pay a fine' rather than 'It is prohibited to drive over seventy miles on the motorway' plus a regulation that he shall pay a fine? As for the use of the word 'code', it implies no more than a systematic collection, and imperfect though the results were, a remarkable effort in that direction was certainly being made by Ur-Nammu, Lipit-Ishtar, Hammurabi and the legal draftsmen.

Their intentions are clear enough. Already Ur-Nammu claims that he has established 'equity in the land' according to the word of Utu, so that the orphan and widow are not delivered up to the rich and mighty, and 'the man of one shekel is not delivered up to the man of one mina'. Hammurabi is far more explicit. He states firmly in the epilogue to his laws that his statutes have been set up for the information of the ordinary man who seeks justice.

> *Let the oppressed man who has a cause*
> *come into the presence of the statue of me*
> *and then read carefully my inscribed stele*
> *and give heed to my precious words,*
> *and may my stele make the case clear to him;*
> *may he understand his case;*
> *may he set his mind at ease!*

While much from the Sumerian codes is incorporated in that of Hammurabi, and the series can be seen very much as a progressive bringing up to date of the inherited body of the law, there do appear to be certain consistent innovations that were of historical origin and great social significance.

They concern a striking increase in the severity of physical and capital punishment. Hammurabi's laws prescribe death for false witness, house-breaking, brigandage, rape, incest, adultery, abortion, killing by faulty building, black magic, kidnapping, aiding the escape of slaves, some forms of theft and the receiving of stolen goods. The methods of execution include drowning, burning, and impaling, and in addition various mutilations are prescribed. More precisely significant is the appearance of the principal of talion, an eye for an eye, so familiar to us from the Old Testament. Ur-Nammu had laid down money payments in cases of assault; so had the laws of Eshnunna. 'If a man bites a man's nose and severs it, he shall pay one mina of silver. For an eye one mina; for a tooth half a mina'; and so on down to ten shekels for a blow in the face. It has been proposed that these fines were all that got into the written law because it was taken for granted that they were in addition to a traditional physical punishment.

There is very little evidence for this, and a good deal to suggest that a relatively 'permissive' Sumerian system was being replaced by a much harsher one. This did not begin with Hammurabi, but is already showing itself in legal documents of a century before. Edzard is prepared to commit himself: 'Violent penalty clauses and talion are a trait of Old Babylonian law that is clearly contrary to Sumerian practice, and the Sumerian tradition in the Code of Lipit-Ishtar. We need have no cause to doubt the origin of those innovations. They are to be ascribed to the customs of the "Canaanites" [i.e., Amorites].' It need only be added that a still greater barbarity, in intention as well as enforcement, is obvious in the Middle Assyrian laws of several centuries later.

To read the laws of Hammurabi is to gain a wonderful insight into the life of ordinary people, well to do as well as poor, in ancient Babylonia. Mainly into the seamier side, it is true, but not entirely, for they also contain merciful clauses to help those ruined by flood, robbery and other blameless misfortunes. Also (like the Eshnunna laws) they include such simple economic provisions as rates of hire for men, vehicles and boats and the wages of labourers and crafts-men. (The government undoubtedly had a legally enforceable prices and wages policy, but trade contracts show that the fixed rates were not in fact maintained.)

Modern editors have divided the laws into 282 paragraphs. It is not possible here to do more than mention the main groups into which they fall. The most numerous category concerns the family— which it was the evident purpose of the law to protect in the interests of society. It covers questions of marriage, adultery, deser-tion, divorce, incest, adoption and inheritance. More will be said about some of these provisions in the next section. Women are in general quite fairly treated.

The second largest group is concerned with land tenure. Many items involve payments between owner and tenants, or trespass in the sense of damaging the neighbouring fields or pasturing with-out consent. Several relate to simple failure to cultivate land, a loss of precious food resources that was evidently intolerable to the community.

The next largest category deals with trade and commerce, includ-ing rates of interest, questions of debts and securities, defalcations of various kinds. After that, in about equal numbers, follow theft and other offences against property and bodily assaults. Several pro-visions concerning rewards and penalties for professional services include the execution of a builder whose faulty work has caused the death of the householder, and the cutting off of the hand of a surgeon who, operating with a bronze lancet, has caused the death of a gentleman. Particularly savage are the punishments to be meted out for all offences involving the harbouring and stealing of runaway slaves. It was evidently considered essential that they should remain absolutely bound to their legal owner's household.

Among a few provisions covering damage to hired oxen and also the keeping of dangerous beasts, one is worth quoting in full. It shows the good sense of many laws where evil intent was not held to be present, is one instance of the normal system of differential fines based on class, and also gives a glimpse of Babylonian life.

If an ox, as it went along the street, gored a man and so caused his death, there is no ground for claim in that case. If a man's ox is habitually given to goring, and the man's local authority has notified him [of the fact] and he has not protected its horns [nor] restrained his ox, and that ox has gored a man of the 'gentleman' class and caused his death, he shall pay half a mina of silver. If the man killed is a gentleman's slave he shall pay one third of a mina of silver.

Very properly, the first of Hammurabi's provisions are concerned with the administration of justice itself. They deal with false witness, and one with possible corruption among the judges. It reads:

If a judge gave a judgement, rendered a decision, deposited a sealed document but later altered his judgement, they shall prove that the judge altered the judgement which he gave and he shall pay twelvefold the claim which holds in that case; furthermore they shall expel him from the assembly from his seat of judgement and he shall never sit again with judges in a case.

With the divine and royal interest in justice so characteristic of Mesopotamia, and with the careful organization of the courts and provision for the dismissal of corrupt judges, men and women of all classes, even slaves, must have lived in some confidence that, whether sinned against or sinning, they would have a fair hearing under the law. If its enforcement tended to become increasingly harsh, that was one of the penalties they had to pay for wealth, conquest and imperial dominion.

MEN, WOMEN AND CHILDREN

PASSION, MARRIED LOVE OR AFFECTION, MARRIED HATRED, ADULTERY, incest, rape—all these features of the relationship between the sexes were as prevalent in Bronze Age Mesopotamia as in modern society. There is, however, no evidence in the laws or the literature of homosexuality. It seems unlikely that it did not exist, but possibly it was too rare, or alternatively too much taken for granted, to be the subject of concern or legislation.

Unlike the Egyptians, the Mesopotamians have left us no private love poems: the poetry of passion is all written in the name of the gods for the celebration of the *hieros gamos*, or sacred marriage, of the New Year festival. These marriages were in fact enacted by the king and a priestess filling the roles of the shepherd god, Dumuzi, and Inanna, goddess of love. There is no mistaking the intensity of human experience which they represent.

In the subsequent history of human sexual attitudes, there have been the most surprising swings between the view that women are essentially passive in love-making, that it is the man who demands and gets full sexual satisfaction, and the opposite opinion that woman's appetite is insatiable, that if allowed she would drain the manhood from her lovers. It is therefore not without interest to find that among the Sumerians, the first people to make some record of sexual passion, it is the second view that seems to prevail. In the sacred marriage texts it is Inanna who utters nearly all the expressions of love, and she who confesses to having sated Dumuzi in love-making. It is true that the goddess of love might be assigned exceptional feelings and prowess in 'the sweet bed', but the idea cannot have been alien to human experience. From *Inanna and the King*:

> The sun has gone to sleep, the day has passed,
> As in bed you gaze lovingly upon him. . . .
> She craves it, she craves it, she craves the bed,
> She craves the bed of the rejoicing heart, she craves the bed,
> She craves the bed of the sweet lap, she craves the bed . . .

In *Love in the Gipar*, Inanna's feelings are more tender:

> I will bring there my sweetheart . . .
> He will put his hand by my hand,
> He will put his heart by my heart,
> His putting of hand to hand—its sleep is so refreshing,
> His pressing of heart to heart—its pleasure is so sweet.

The use of nature analogies was, of course, appropriate to the fertility rite of the *hieros gamos*, yet verses that make use of them read very much like women's poetry of all ages. These songs are supposed to have been chanted by the priestesses who were to consummate the rite—did they in fact compose them? The second verse of the 'honey-man' has already been quoted; the first is even more telling:

He has sprouted, he has burgeoned, he is lettuce planted by the water,
My well-stocked garden of the plain, my favoured of the womb,
My grain luxuriant in the furrow—he is lettuce planted by the water,
My apple tree which bears fruit to its top—he is lettuce planted by the water.

In the song usually called *The Ecstasy of Love* Dumuzi is, exceptionally, allowed to speak about love—although it is between two utterances of the goddess. He has just told her how to mislead her mother as to where she is:

Thus deceitfully stand up to your mother,
While we by the moonlight indulge our passion,
I will prepare for you a bed pure, sweet and noble
Will while away the sweet time with you in joyful fulfilment.

Satiety is reached in *Set Me Free, Sister,* in which Inanna and Dumuzi address one another as brother and sister (the dots represent several obscure lines).

> *My beloved met me,*
> *Took his pleasure of me, rejoiced together with me,*
> *The brother brought me to his house*
> *Made me lie on its honey bed,*
> *My precious sweet, having lain by my heart,*
> *In unison, the 'tongue-making' in unison,*
> *My brother of fairest face made fifty times . . .*
> *My brother who . . . in his anger,*
> *My precious sweet is sated with me.*

Turning from passion expressed in terms of divinity towards everyday human marriage we are brought heavily down to earth. Sumerian proverbs reveal the same contradictory attitudes towards the institution that have continued to supply so much of the substance of popular humour—for example:

For his pleasure—marriage; on thinking it over—divorce.

Who has not supported a wife or child has not borne a leash.

My wife is at the outdoor shrine, my mother is down by the river, and here am I dying of hunger.

. . . the wife is a man's future; the son is a man's refuge; the daughter is a man's salvation; the daughter-in-law is a man's devil.

Feminists would not applaud the familiar image and implication of the Akkadian proverb 'A woman without a husband is like a field without cultivation.' Marriages were in fact normally arranged by fathers on behalf of their sons, and presumably quite often the young couples themselves had little say in the choice. On the other hand such social arrangements are often much more personal and wilful in practice than in theory. Another Sumerian proverb says, 'Marry a wife according to your choice, have a child as your heart desires!' Moreover, one of Hammurabi's laws lays down what shall be done if a betrothed revokes his contract *because he has fallen in love with another woman.*

Once the betrothal had been agreed upon the contract was drawn on a tablet and the groom-to-be or his father paid the bride money, and the dowry was set aside for the girl. It seems that the girl may then sometimes have continued to live at home for a considerable time before marriage—perhaps because she or her betrothed were too young to marry. Age is not mentioned until the Middle Assyrian laws, when ten years was laid down as the youngest age at which a boy could be betrothed.

It seems to have been the norm in Sumerian times for a man to have only one wife, but at least by the time Lipit-Ishtar's laws were drawn up a second 'preferred' wife was permissible. It may well have been that a second wife and regular relationships with concubines, slave girls and prostitutes became increasingly common from Akkadian times.

Edzard believes that a decline in the status of women in Akkadian times is shown in a difference between the Sumerian bride money, *ni-mi-usa*, which was originally given to the bride's father to cover the cost of the wedding feast, and the Akkadian *terhatum*, which was a bride price amounting to marriage by purchase. Nevertheless, woman's position under the law does not appear to deteriorate as between the late Sumerian laws of Ur-Nammu and Lipit-Ishtar and those of Hammurabi. The general impression given by the laws down to the time of Hammurabi is that a wife was not at all regarded as a possession, but as an individual with approximately equal, if different, rights from those of the man. The interests even of a slave girl were protected—at least if she had borne children to a free man.

Inevitably there was a double standard between husband and wife in sexual permissiveness. One of the surviving laws of Ur-Nammu declares, 'If the wife of a man, by employing her charms, followed another and he slept with her, the woman shall be put to death, the man go free.' This harsh provision certainly depends on emphasis being put on the woman's initiative 'by employing her charms'. To judge from later analogies, missing portions of these laws included a corresponding provision for a man who took a woman against her will to be put to death—if the victim was a betrothed virgin. Under Hammurabi, if a man had intercourse with his daughter both were exiled from their city; if a son took his widowed mother 'both were to burn'.

Under Hammurabi, if a gentleman's wife and her lover are caught *in flagrante delicto,* then both shall burn, unless the husband pardons the wife—in which case the king may also pardon the lover. Perhaps the worst part of the offence was in being caught. Another of Hammurabi's laws provides that if a woman who has been accused of infidelity swears by the god to her innocence, then she may return to her house. Malicious gossip was evidently much deprecated, for if a man slandered another's wife, he was liable to be taken to court and there have half his hair cut off.

While a wife was not legally allowed any extramarital sex—on pain of death—many of the codes assume that a man will have children by concubines and slave girls. Lipit-Ishtar twice refers to a second wife—in one case to a 'preferred' second wife, where it is said that the husband must continue to support his first partner so long as she remains in his house. Some consideration is shown for a wife's dignity or feelings: thus another Lipit-Ishtar law lays it down that if a man fails to have children by his wife but has them by 'a harlot from the square' he shall provide for the harlot and her family and make the children his heirs—but the woman may not occupy his house while the wife is alive.

Laws concerning various forms of separation of married couples are practical and mainly concerned to secure a living for the woman and her children. This is the spirit of several laws (Eshnunna and Hammurabi) providing for families left without a bread-winner because the husband and father has been held as a prisoner of war or otherwise detained abroad for a long period. If his family has sufficient to live on, then the wife is expected to remain faithful to her husband (or at least to remain in his house awaiting his return); if on the other hand they are destitute then the 'wife may enter the house of another, with that woman incurring no blame at all.' If the husband returns, then the wife shall go back to him, leaving any children she may have borne to her temporary mate in his keeping. (There is an interesting twist here that appears in both the Eshnunna and Hammurabi laws. If the husband is absent from his home not as a result of military service or any other socially approved reason but because he 'hates his town and his land and becomes a fugitive', then he has no right to claim his wife back.)

Separation through divorce appears to have been easy, and not infrequent; it was certainly legally equitable. If a man divorced his wife because she had no children, then he had to pay her a certain sum and also return her dowry. Distinct laws were for some reason necessary for men who were divorcing lay priestesses and temple slaves (*hierodules*): not only was the dowry to be returned, but half the man's property was to be handed over for the support of the children. If a wife fell ill of a fever (possibly preventing her from having children?) he could marry a second time without divorcing her, but must allow her to remain in his house and support her for the rest of her life. If, however, she preferred to leave, he had to restore her dowry.

One divorce procedure would certainly not be pleasing to feminists—but nevertheless discloses the possible independence of women. If a gentleman's wife 'has made up her mind to leave in order to engage in business, thus neglecting her house and humiliating her husband' and this state of affairs is proved against her, then the husband can divorce her without giving her anything.

On the woman's side, the laws of Hammurabi provide that 'If a woman so hated her husband that she has declared "you may not have me" her record shall be examined by her city council, and if she was careful and was not at fault, even though her husband has been going out and disparaging her greatly, that woman, without incurring any blame at all, may take her dowry and go off to her father's house.'

There are also provisions that appear to be intended to help a widow or divorced woman with money in one form or another so that she may settle down happily with 'a man of her heart'.

A later Sumerian marriage contract makes it clear that equitable provisions for divorce were not mere theoretical legal rights but were followed in practice. The contract is on the highest social level, the groom being a high priest of Enlil; the bride has brought a dowry of nineteen shekels of silver.

If Enlil-izzu ever says to Ama-sukkal his wife, 'You are no longer my wife', he shall return the nineteen shekels of silver and he shall also weigh out half a mina as her divorce settlement. On the other hand if Ama-sukkal ever says to Enlil-izzu, her husband, 'You are no longer my husband', she shall forfeit the nineteen shekels and she shall also weigh out half a mina of silver. In mutual agreement they have sworn this by the king.

Society evidently recognized the need to defend the possessions of widows, who enjoyed a life interest in their husband's estates, and of the children who would inherit them. A widow had the right to stay on in her old home. 'If her children keep plaguing her in order to make her leave the house' and the judges decide that her record is a good one she 'need never leave her husband's house'. If, on the other hand, she decides to quit, she can take her dowry 'in order that the man of her heart may marry her'. If a widowed mother of young children wanted to remarry, the judges would examine the husband's estate, and entrust it jointly to the widow and the man she was marrying on condition that they would deposit a tablet promising to rear the children and keep the estate in trust for them.

No one who is familiar with the legal rights of women in other and later societies can doubt that the Sumerian practice was relatively enlightened. The break in this good tradition did not, as we have seen, come in Old Babylonian times but with the Assyrians. Already in laws written down in the twelfth century B.C., but probably dating back some centuries earlier, not only is the implied attitude to women worse, but social assumptions in general appear to have been coarsened and even brutalized. A wife who has stolen goods from her husband is to be executed, while one who has stolen from a neighbour's house may either have her nose cut off by the neighbour or her ears cut off by her husband. Another law reads, 'If a woman has crushed a gentleman's testicle in a brawl, they shall cut off one finger of hers, and if the other testicle has become affected . . . or she has crushed the other testicle in a brawl, they shall tear out both her eyes.'

There are provisions against women acting as procuresses in their own homes, while if a woman friend gives shelter to a runaway wife without her own husband's knowledge, both women are liable to lose their ears.

Among various provisions that seem to suggest an increased pre-occupation with women's virginity is one which reveals how far in this Assyrian society a wife was regarded as her husband's chattel through whose person he could be punished: ". . . if a gentleman took the virgin by force and ravished her, either in the midst of the city or in the open country or at night in the street or in a granary or at a city festival' then the girl's father may take the rapist's wife to be ravished and never returned to her husband—while the de-flowered girl may, if her father wishes, be given to her ravisher in marriage.

The law on self-abortion was entirely brutal; whether the woman lived and was convicted of the crime or died in the course of it, 'they shall impale her on stakes without burying her'.

After a grim list of mutilations to be inflicted on women a further clause states that when she deserves it, a gentleman may pull out his wife's hair and mutilate or twist her ears 'with no penalty attach-ing to him'.

It is in general harmony with the social and psychological attitudes reflected in these laws that the wives, widows and daughters of gentlemen were forbidden to go out unveiled, while harlots, unwed temple prostitutes and slave girls were prohibited from veiling them-selves. If they broke this prohibition and covered their faces, not only were they to be flogged with staves, but any man who recog-nized the bright eyes of a harlot or slave girl and did not report her to the palace authorities was to be flogged, humiliatingly mutilated and made to do penal labour for the king.

Finally, the loss of women's rights is starkly evident in the Middle Assyrian law on divorce: 'If a gentleman wishes to divorce his wife, if it is his will, he may give her something; if it is not his will, he need not give her anything; she shall go out empty.'

It is obvious that to study marriage and sexual relationships through law tends to give an unduly gloomy picture of them. There is no need to doubt that, for Sumerian times at least, Kramer is justified in saying that the members of a normal family were 'knit closely by love, respect and mutual obligation'. As is usual in ancient societies, outwardly little attention was paid to children—they were very seldom portrayed in the visual arts or mentioned in literature, while the laws were only concerned to see that they were properly provided for materially. We know that sons of well-to-do parents went to scribal schools, rushing off with packed lunches in an effort not to be late and get a beating. Physical punishment was freely indulged in by the masters for anything from loitering in the street and having untidy clothes to bad writing. Masters were sometimes invited home and made much of—softened up—by the boys' parents.

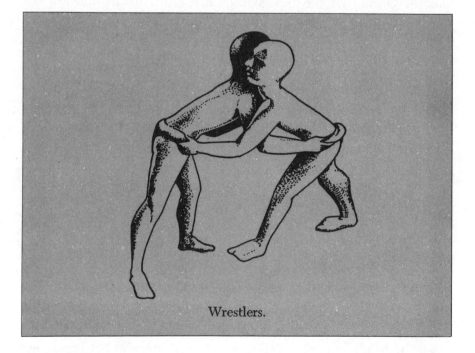

Wrestlers.

Children and young people were certainly in theory wholly subject to their parents and especially to the father—who, as we have seen, could even sell them into slavery when times were hard. Yet a single schoolboy letter, written in faulty Akkadian, is enough to show how far this picture could be from the reality. It is doubtful whether any supposedly disrespectful boy of today would write

so disagreeably to his mother as this son of a high official of Larsa.
After a hasty formal blessing, he plunges in:

Gentlemen's clothes improve year by year. By cheapening and scrimping
my clothes you have become rich. While wool was being consumed in
our house like bread, you were making my clothes cheaper. The son of
Adad-iddinam, whose father is only an underling of my father, has
received two new garments; you keep getting upset over just one garment
for me. Whereas you gave birth to me, his mother had him by adoption,
but whereas his mother loves him, you do not love me.

Wet nursing and adoption were, in fact, quite frequent. Fathers
were bound to keep the nurse in food, oil and wool, or alternatively
to pay her a lump sum at the end of three years. Adoption laws were
reasonably flexible: if a gentleman gave his adopted son his own
name the boy could never be reclaimed—and the same was true at a
humbler social level for an artisan who had taught a boy his craft.
In other circumstances, however, the blood parents might take their
child back.

Women had considerable opportunities in Sumerian society. They
could own estates and other property, qualify as witnesses and
engage in business. If, as the law quoted above shows, too many
outside interests might get them into trouble with their husbands,
they probably did not greatly care. There is a reference to a
woman as a scribe and to another as a physician. Although these
professional careers seem to have been rare, very many women were
engaged in the work of the temple—at any level from hierodule to
the supreme enship. The important office of en to the moon god
Nanna of Ur was always held by a woman, usually a daughter of the
national king of Sumer. It has been seen that for humbler women
making and selling beer and date wine was a recognized calling
and one that must have involved them actively in the talk and doings
of their communities.

In spite of all the strains to which family life was subject, and
the terrible penalties they could incur, there is no question of the
importance of blood-ties for the people of Mesopotamia. A Sumerian proverb runs, 'Friendship lasts a day; kinship endures for ever.'

3. THE MENTAL WORLD

RELIGION AND COSMOLOGY

RELIGION PERMEATED THE WHOLE OF SOCIAL AND PRIVATE LIFE IN
Bronze Age Mesopotamia. The Sumerians and their inheritors lived
in it as a fish lives in water: it flowed round them on all sides—and
it flowed through them, supplying the mental oxygen of their
inspiration. Not for them any division between the secular and the
religious, animate or inanimate, between man, nature and the divine.
All were part of a living and interacting whole.

This blending of concepts that have become categorized in our
minds is directly revealed in a remarkable product of Sumerian
thought, the list of *mes*, or divine laws, supposed to have maintained
the universe from its beginning. Out of a hundred of these *mes*
referring particularly to human affairs some sixty are more or less
comprehensible.

(1) kingship; (3) the exalted and enduring crown; (4) the throne of
kingship; (5) the exalted sceptre; (6) the royal insignia; (7) the exalted
shrine; (8) shepherdship (kingship); (10) lasting ladyship; (11) the
divine lady (the priestly office); (13) *lumah* (the priestly office) (14)
gutug (the priestly office); (15) truth; (16) descent into the nether
world; (17) ascent from the nether world; (18) *kurgarru* (the eunuch);
(19) *girbadara* (the eunuch); (20) *sagursag* (the eunuch); (21) the
battle standard; (22) the flood; (23) weapons (?); (24) sexual intercourse; (25) prostitution; (26) law (?); (27) libel (?); (28) art; (29)

the cult chamber; (30) 'hierodule of heaven'; (31) *gusilim* (the musical instrument); (32) music; (33) eldership; (34) heroship; (35) power; (36) enmity; (37) straightforwardness; (38) the destruction of cities; (39) lamentation; (40) rejoicing of the heart; (41) falsehood; (42) the rebel land; (43) goodness; (44) justice; (45) art of woodworking; (46) art of metal working; (47) scribeship; (48) crafts of the smith; (49) craft of the leatherworker; (50) craft of the builder; (51) craft of the basket-maker; (52) wisdom; (53) attention; (54) holy purification; (55) fear; (56) terror; (57) strife; (58) peace; (59) weariness; (60) victory; (61) council; (62) the troubled heart; (63) judgement; (64) decision; (65) *lilis* (the musical instrument); (66) *ub* (the musical instrument); (67) *mesi* (the musical instrument); (68) *ala* (the musical instrument).

This to us curious yet revealing list, in which each word seems to stand for an active, ordering entity within human society, also serves to show that although the Sumerians never produced a coherent philosophy of life, they did possess speculative thinkers who consciously sought to find answers to the problems that experience presented to them, particularly of the origin, sustenance and government of the universe as they saw it. Kramer may in fact be justified in referring to philosophers and theologians, and distinguishing them from the mythographers, although the boundary was certainly an open one.

In the great creative myths which, like the great Christian myth, led to so astounding an expenditure of psychic and physical energy in the arts and architecture and in ritual, we are confronted with so many elements that it is no wonder that their study has led to a theoretical babel. There is the purely historical element—for example the fact that in the formative period of the fourth and third millennia B.C. the prehistoric cult of the earth mother or Mother Goddess was still powerful, but was being overtaken by other cults more appropriate to an urban civilization. Even simpler examples are, of course, the identification, sometimes perhaps only partial, of Semitic with Sumerian divinities and additions to the pantheon such as Dagan. There is the other kind of historical element, the inclusion of great men of the past as gods or heroes—Gilgamesh and perhaps Dumuzi. Then there is the element in myth that was associated with ritual but which may either have preceded the rite or been derived from it—or have been involved in an interplay between the two. There is the immensely potent and often dominant element that seems to emanate from the human psyche, possibly from an unconscious inheriting archetypal forms from the remote past. Finally, as we have seen there is the element produced by rational speculation, the seeking for explanation on the basis of experience.

These theoretical problems cannot be further discussed here. They have already filled shelves with disagreement. What is, however, profoundly significant for social history is the fact that these myths were one of the most effective unifying forces in Mesopotamian life. They, and the pantheon of divinities who played the leading roles in them, united the city-states, and all parts of the Valley of the Twin Rivers, with shared traditions, rites and beliefs. And if they served to link various peoples over vast territories (and indeed affected most of the Bronze Age world) they also served to unite the centuries and millennia, joining most ancient Sumeria in understanding with the Neo-Babylonia of over two thousand years later. As a unifying force the myths and the pantheon proved more tenacious than language, and had a deeper significance than the cuneiform script.

Sumerian thinkers soon established their model for the physical structure of the universe. They called it *an-ki*, or heaven-earth, seeing the earth as a disk surmounted by the vault of heaven above, possibly made of tin (although the heavens are often likened to lapis lazuli) and with a corresponding realm below, but seemingly part of 'earth', that was the underworld. They recognized the presence of an 'air' substance between earth and the heavenly vault, and appear to have thought that sun, moon and stars were formed from it and then embued with luminosity. One view, and it seems very consistently held, was that the sun visited the underworld at night and that the moon went below once a month, on its 'day of rest'. There are some hints that the Sumerians entertained an idea like that prevalent in classical times of the heavenly bodies set in revolving spheres. If this notion did in fact occur to any thinkers, it had disappeared by the time that mathematical astronomy was being developed in the last millennium B.C.

As to how in 'natural' terms this structure of the universe came into being, the interpretation seems to be that the story began with an eternal and uncreated ocean, and that this primeval sea engendered a united *an-ki* presently to be separated by the expanding force of air. When the separation had been effected, it became possible for life to exist on earth. The Sumerians held the unusual view that the moon had the primacy among the heavenly bodies and gave birth to the sun.

If this was the Sumerian model of the universe and its history as set out in materialist terms, the kind of model which could in time become the object of a more scientific examination, it does not truly represent the universe as the Sumerians themselves conceived it. They saw all the phenomena of the world about them as being animated, sometimes as being imbued with will, and thus able to respond to their own being—person to person, as it were. So great was this sense of life and personality in all things, that it came to be experienced and expressed in terms of divinities, invisible beings that had human form but were immortal. From the complicated nature of things, there were bound to be thousands of such divinities, ranged within an hierarchical society according to the importance of the thing or phenomenon or force that they embodied.

From the point of view of the history of thought and perception, the humbler divine personalities can be the more interesting. The Sumerians were not, of course, so unlike ourselves as to think of each pinch of salt they took with their dinners, each reed they cut for a stylus, a pipe or a building unit, as a divine being, but rather that there was a quintessence of saltness, of reedness, that could be personified. Thus a sufferer from some trouble, a supposed bewitchment, might appeal to Salt as one who had been created by Enlil to savour the food of the gods, and cry, 'O Salt, break my enchantment . . . loose my spell . . . and as my Creator I shall praise thee.' As for the Reed, for which Sumerians had a very strong feeling, all the wonderful things that it gave them, including the music of the pipe, the words that could come from the stylus, found expression in the goddess Nidaba—who in this way became goddess of writing. Many hymns ended, 'O! Nidaba, praise!' It is tempting to see in such mental emanations a pre-philosophical version of the Platonic 'idea'.

Looking up now from these thousands of small divinities to the great ones of the pantheon, we find the Sumerians giving the supreme place to Anu (An), representing the vast and often awe-inspiring vault of the sky. The air that had separated heaven from earth was known as *lil*, a word that probably had much the meaning of *pneuma*, joining wind and breath with spirit. This power, which could be beneficent and yet also possessed the terror of the storm, was assigned to Enlil. In theory Enlil always remained second to

Anu in the hierarchy, yet in practice he was usually dominant in Sumerian myths, rites and prayers. Even in the earliest records he may be called 'father of the gods' and 'king of heaven and earth'. Ninhursag was the great Mother Goddess, bearer of all living things. She was also known as Ninnah, 'the exalted lady', and Nintu, 'the lady who gives birth'. Sumerian rulers often proclaimed that they were 'constantly nourished by Ninhursag with milk'. She may once have been Ki, 'Earth', and as such the consort of Anu and parent, with him, of all the gods. Certainly, in historical terms, it was she who inherited most from the great goddess who was probably the supreme deity of the prehistoric cultivators. To judge from the scenes of her worship shown on the Uruk vase and other reliefs, and from the frequent appearance of her symbol on early seals, her cult was still of very great importance during the third millennium.

The Sumerians were always aware of their two great rivers, of the waterways winding among reed beds and marshes and of the water that could everywhere be found by digging downwards into the disk of earth. Enki was lord of these waters presiding over the *abzu* or abyss (the one Sumerian word to have come down to us!). His waters fertilized the earth. *Enki and the World Order* says, 'He lifts the penis, ejaculates, fills the Tigris with sparkling waters.' In the same poem Enki himself speaks of 'the marshland, my favourite place' and of his swift boat 'ibex of the Abzu'. In many works of art he is portrayed with the Twin Rivers, filled with fish, flowing from his shoulders. Yet at the same time Enki is a wise and clever divinity, one who carried out the policies of Enlil for the ordering of the earth and the affairs of men. It is significant that he had special responsibilities for the management of the *mes*. The verse from the creation epic with which this book opens gives an idea of his practical part in making the elements of civilization. In all this Enki comes nearer to the role of the culture hero than any of his divine colleagues.

These three gods and one goddess had between them the authority, force, intelligence and fecundity to maintain the universe. Next to them came three divinities identified with heavenly luminaries: Nanna, or Sin, the moon·god and first born child of Enlil and Ninlil; his son Utu the sun god (who became Shamash in Akkadian); and Inanna, the proud, exigent goddess of love. Of these the sun god, having started in a lowly position in comparison with any of his opposite numbers in Egypt, seems to have risen in esteem, in his capacity of god of justice, as established law itself rose in social importance. Hammurabi exhorts, 'Through the order of Shamash, great judge of heaven and earth, may my justice prevail in the land.' Justice and the sun's all-seeing eye tended to involve Shamash also with morality, and with the banishment of demons bringing sickness and other ills to ordinary individuals. This last capacity gave him great popular appeal, for many an ill and demon-troubled man burnt incense and made offerings to the god, begging him, 'Judge my case, give a decision for me and lay your condemning curse on the evil thing.' Utu/Shamash provides one of the best examples of a divinity being tailored by society to fit its evolving needs and values.

As for his glorious sister Inanna, her being and her role, too, are more complex and elusive. Although she was a celestial divinity, identified (like her inheritors Ishtar and Venus) with the morning and evening star, she must have usurped some of the attributes and functions of the ancient Mother Goddess. If Ninhursag was indeed once spouse of Anu then Inanna took her place there, being seen in one of her aspects as queen of heaven and the supreme god's consort. She also presided not only over sexual love, but fertility and abundance as well. Perhaps as the traditions of the earth mother became too obviously gross and primitive, some part of the human emotion involved with her was transferred upwards to Inanna.

The goddess had prominent parts in many myths and tales, and those that gave her most prominence, and must have brought her closest to the people, were those in her role as the partner of Dumuzi. She also appeared in those myths that were involved with the sacred marriage and the New Year festival.

The position of these leading divinities, probably the 'seven who decree the fates', has already been discussed in relation to the Anunnaki and the assembly of the gods. So has the distinctive Sumerian concept of the gods presiding over a cosmic state involving the totality of things, which, in its structure, had many features in common with the national states of Mesopotamia. If this was an unusual way of interpreting the universe, so, too, was the relationship between the hierarchy of gods and the social and political structure of their human servitors. In this we return to the recognition of religion as one of the chief unifying influences in Sumerian and subsequent Mesopotamian societies.

The system of things by which each city-state belonged to its own supreme divinity while each divinity had an appointed place within a hierarchic national pantheon has already figured often in these pages. Many of the tutelary gods and goddesses dwelt in temples that had special names. *E*, it should be noted, was the word for house—in these instances the 'house' of the god. Among the most important were the Eanna of Inanna at Uruk, the Ekur of Enlil at Nippur (the national shrine), the Ekishnugal of Nanna at Ur, the Eninnu of Ningirsu in Lagash and the Esagila of Marduk at Babylon. A citizen of Ur, for example, lived all his life as a servant of Nanna, and looked with veneration towards the great Ekishnugal crowning the hill. Yet he also lived all his life knowing that Nanna ranked below Enki in neighbouring Eridu, and further below Anu and Inanna across the river in the rival city of Uruk. The inconsistency between the divisiveness of the city-state and the unity of the national pantheon was perhaps made more manageable by the institution of the neutral holy city of Nippur in the centre of the Plain, and the device whereby a king winning national hegemony could rule in Enlil's name—that is, transfer the Enlil function to his own city god and to himself as the god's servant.

Just how this state of affairs developed as a matter of historical fact is never likely to be reliably known. It has been suggested that the pantheon must already have been established and accepted by the early settlers of the Plain, that its leading deities were adopted by ruling families or tribes, and grew in power and importance as the settlements themselves grew into cities. All that can be said with reasonable certainty is that most if not all of the city gods must have been in possession of their city-states by the end of the fourth millennium B.C. Indeed, we have seen that Enki or his prototype was already established at Eridu far back in prehistory.

Although the tutelary divinity lived in the main temple of each city, many other gods and goddesses had shrines and minor temples devoted to their cult. In Ur the Ekishnugal of Nanna and his consort Ningal contained shrines and chapels dedicated to many minor gods who were part of their divine household. Outside the *temenos*, scattered through the purlieus of Ur, were numerous temples belonging to the great gods, usually founded by kings and maintained by the state. Thus Ur-Nammu built temples for Anu, Enlil, Ninsun, Ninezen and Enki—this last on the southern rampart facing across the Plain to Enki's own city of Eridu. It is known from the records that Inanna, Nirgal, Shamash, Dumuzi and several other divinities also came to have temples in Ur. The cost of maintaining all these establishments and their priests must have been a burden on the community. They do not seem to have had anything in the nature of a 'parish', but individuals who had reason to seek the favour of any particular god could bring a sacrificial animal or make a gift to the treasury. In addition to all such public sanctuaries, the residential streets of Ur had small chapels among their houses that were probably built and endowed by private citizens for their own immediate use.

Beyond that again, from the time of the Third Dynasty, each house had a burial vault and attached chapel where a family cult was probably conducted by the head of the household.

In their prohibition of graven images, the Hebrews were to recognize their power to attract worship to themselves. The simpler people of many ages and faiths have revered and perhaps worshipped the figures set up in their sanctuaries—especially if they are ancient. Buddha may have taught a way of life without a god, yet his images, often of enormous size, are everywhere brought offerings of food and flowers. There are many counterparts to the Black Madonna of Rocamadour, an archaic carving in blackened wood that still attracts hosts of pilgrims. We shall find in Egypt that Pharaohs of the New Kingdom developed cults of the 'living image' of themselves in which huge statues were the object of worship.

There seems no doubt that throughout Mesopotamia the image of the god that was kept in the *cella* of the temple was not only worshipped both immediately and from afar, but was served by the priests as a living being. Just as the king lived and was served in his palace, the divinity lived and was served in his own E. There was a divine wardrobe, with clothes changed at appointed times and for festivals. Two two-course meals were laid before the image, one in the morning and one at night; there were also lighter meals or divine snacks. This was the regime at Uruk in Seleucid times, and it was probably traditional. Before eating, the god's hands were washed. While the god was breakfasting or dining, curtains were probably drawn round him to screen so great a mystery from human gaze.

How near ordinary citizens were allowed to approach to the image is not known—and may have varied with time and place. It can be assumed that the *cella* was forbidden them. In some temples aligned doorways may have allowed a distant glimpse of the figure on its pedestal. Generally, however, it seems that the citizens had a clear sight of the images only when they were carried through the streets on the occasion of their festivals. They seem to have been fastened to beams that rested on the shoulders of bearers. This carrying of holy figures is still, of course, a familiar practice in many parts of the world, not least in Catholic lands where saints and madonnas are taken on such outings, borne shoulder high through great crowds of the faithful.

There was one other way in which ordinary citizens could approach the divine images—and indeed remain in their presence. This was by means of images of their own. In Early Dynastic times worshippers could arrange, by what system of observances and payments we do not know, to have sculptured stone figures of themselves in an attitude of devout prayer placed in the temple. The idea can be likened to a more ambitious form of the Christian worshipper placing a candle before the altar of his choice.

The physical tending of the god's image can be seen as the central purpose and justification of the whole programme and organization of the temple. The feeding is of special interest here from the point of view of the actual disposal of the meal. What happened behind the curtain? Probably the image was held to have consumed the dishes by looking at them. Perhaps not everyone would object to the comparison of the holy make-believe involved in this process to the enactment of a small girl solemnly eating the food of a dolls' tea-party. It seems that in fact some part at least of the god's food was transferred to the king's table, and that the eating of this blessed food was a symbolically telling royal prerogative. Considering the distance separating the palace from the temple *cella* it is a little difficult to understand how this was done—but there seems no doubt that it was. (Some Assyrian kings spoke of receiving the god's 'leftovers'.)

This feeding of the king with the 'divine jelly', as it were, is interesting as another link between the divinity and his royal executant and servant. The setting of the meal on the god's table was, however, at the centre of a vast system of temple sacrificial offerings of very substantial economic significance. Large numbers of beasts, most of all sheep, were brought daily to the temples to be offered across the sacrificial tables. Some idea of the scale of this carefully regulated inflow of flocks and herds is provided by the records, dating from the time of the Third Dynasty of Ur, that were kept at the town of Puzrishdagan, near Nippur. On the edge of the town was a huge depot where animals were brought from many regions of Sumer and Akkad to be sacrificed in the temples of Enlil and the other gods of sacred Nippur. Exact records were kept of their arrival and of their forwarding to all the various shrines. (Even the delivery of a dead sheep intended as dog food was entered on the tablets.)

The most important sacrificial beasts were bulls and rams—both milk and barley fed—the thigh being the prime cut usually specified for the god. Bullocks and lambs were also offered. The lists for daily offerings at Uruk (at a late period but probably traditional) included wild boar, ducks, cranes and other birds and ostrich eggs. Large numbers of loaves made from both wheat and barley flour were supplied, the miller being charged to utter a certain prayer while he ground the flour and the cook another when he kneaded the dough and when he took the loaves from the oven. Sweet concoctions were sometimes made from cream, honey and dates (sometimes specified as Dilmun dates) and there were innumerable libations of milk (reserved for the morning meal), prime beer and wine. These liquids were first presented in vessels—those for wine and beer usually of gold, and those for milk in alabaster. Large quantities of oil were also offered. The frescoes at Mari (where things may

Mural from palace of Mari; early second millennium B.C.

have been ordered differently) show the simultaneous presentation of a triple libation and a small burnt offering.

There were also a few prohibitions. Certain birds and animals were never to be offered to certain gods and goddesses. In connection with rituals for the repair of a temple, omens announce that the entry of a dog into a temple means misfortune for the people, while the entry of a rare beast of the desert into the city would mean their utter destruction.

The principles by which all this food and drink was transferred to the priests, craftsmen and others of the vast temple household are only partially known. With the king receiving at least part of the actual meal set before the chief god, it seems likely that the distribution was carried out on hierarchical lines, with humbler groups supplied from the humbler shrines within the *temenos*. Sometimes precise allocations were made for services rendered. Thus, in the preparations for the New Year festival at Babylon, craftsmen called in to make the costly effigies that were to be destroyed during the festival were to be supplied from the sheep offered before Marduk as follows: 'the tail to the metalworker, the breast to the goldsmith, the thigh to the woodworker, the ribs to the weaver'. Oppenheim points out that while in the earlier version of the kettle-drum ritual, that from Assur, the black bull was evidently to be eaten by priests, in the later, Uruk, version it was to be buried.

There must indeed have been a small wastage of sacrificial meats— rams were occasionally to be thrown in the river and heads and hearts to be burnt—but by far the greater part of the food that went into the temples every day left it only through the intestines of the human inmates.

As well as the service of the meals to the images, the offices of the priests by day and by night involved a round of exactly prescribed rites, including sacrifices accompanied by appropriate prayers and recitations. There were regular festivals for the new moon and on the last days of the month. Some idea of these priestly duties is conveyed by one of the Seleucid texts from Uruk concerning the rituals prescribed for the sixteenth and seventeenth days of one month.

The priest shall mix wine and good oil, and shall make a libation to Anu, Antu and all the gods. He shall smear some of it on the door sockets of the gate of the sanctuary and sacrifice a bull and a ram to Anu, Antu and all the gods. He shall spend the night [there]. The door shall not be shut.

He shall offer the meal to all the deities dwelling in the court. In the first watch of the night, on the roof of the topmost stage of the Resh temple . . . [the priest is to recite two prayers, the opening lines of which are given] You shall prepare a golden tray for the deities Anu and Antu of heaven. You shall present water for the hands of Anu and Antu of heaven, and then you shall set the tray, serving bull meat, ram meat and fowl . . .

So it goes on through the course of the two days. The document is late, it is true, but there is no reason to suppose that the temple offices had been greatly elaborated.

These details serve to give some idea of the ceaseless, ordered activity of the priesthoods in all their many grades from the *en* and the *sanga* (in Sumerian terms) down to the humblest hierodule. The names of different classes of priests are known in both Sumerian and Akkadian, but their functions remain uncertain. It is thought that the Sumerian *ishib* priest may have been in charge of libations and lustrations, while the *gala* may have been a poet and singer. The personnel undoubtedly included many singers and instrumentalists. The service of Inanna demanded exceptionally large numbers of eunuchs and hierodules.

The sweet smell of resins burning in the golden censer must always have drifted about the temple precincts, sometimes mingling with the stench of burning fat. All through the day and at intervals during the night, there would have been the sound of harps and the chanting of hymns, prayers, benisons and long incantations. In their outward manifestations, at least, religious observances do not vary so very much with time or faith.

The diurnal round of the temples was inturned and self-sufficient: the meals were in no sense mystical or concerned with a communion. Prayers and sacrifices were not directly on behalf of the people. Rather these services represented the temple carrying out on behalf of society its obligation to work for the gods, to supply them with their needs so that they themselves were freed from toil. It may have some meaning to say that this obligation brought about a kind of 'social contract' between gods and men; the temple, which by one means and another was supported by the entire community, saw to it that the contract was maintained.

There were, however, occasions when the temples opened their gates and looked outward to the people. As well as the monthly festival on the seventeenth and thirtieth days, there were a number of seasonal festivals, such apparently as the 'Eating of Barley' and the 'Eating of Gazelles'. No doubt the populace took part in these. At the height of the summer drought came the popular rites of lamentation for Dumuzi. But the really great occasion, the festival that brought the temples and their divine images, the king and the people all together in feeling and in acts, was the celebration of the New Year. This was essentially a celebration of revival, of the promise of fertility in the renewed cycles of the seasons. In some places, including Ur, it was celebrated twice, there being a repetition in the autumn at the parched death of late summer. But the principal celebration, and the one known to us from a well-preserved Neo-Babylonian text, took place at the beginning of spring and the month of Nisan, coinciding with the spring equinox. As the great, unifying event for all Mesopotamian society it is worth describing in some detail.

There seems no doubt that the original protagonist of the rites was Enlil, but in Babylon his place had inevitably been taken by Marduk. In the familiar version of the Akkadian creation epic, the *Enuma elish,* he was the young champion of the gods who finally defeated Tiamat, or primeval chaos, and created man from the flesh of her champion, Kingu. This drama formed the centre of the New Year enactments, and the *Enuma elish* itself was solemnly recited on the fourth day of the festival.

The first four days of Nisan were in fact largely given to preliminaries, including the necessary purifications, and culminating in the recitation of the epic in the temple. On the fifth, the king began to play his leading part. Within the shrine of Marduk, he was confronted by the high priest, who stripped him of his regalia and placed them before the god's image. The priest then struck his face, made him kneel and declare his innocence: 'I have not sinned, O Lord of the lands . . .' The priest addressed him on behalf of the god, announcing that his prayer was heard and that 'he will increase thy dominion, heighten thy royalty', then gave back the regalia and struck the king again. If the blow drew tears (fertilizing rain?), it was a good omen. In this curious rite, evidently, the ruler was purified and his reign renewed in preparation for the universal renewal in which he was to participate.

On this same day emotion began to grow in the streets. The god had disappeared, the power of death held him captive in the mountain; nature was lifeless, hung in suspense, chaos might be about to return. The crowds began to work themselves up, they ran hither and thither, wailing and lamenting; the people's eyes were turned towards the ziggurat—there was Marduk's 'tomb', there he was imprisoned in the dusty dark of the netherworld and needed the help of their mourning.

The next day, Nisan 6, was full of excitement. The crowds must have surged along the river banks to watch the arrival of the visiting god-images as they arrived at the quays in their sacred barges. They came from Nippur and Uruk, from Kutha and Kish. Most important of all, Marduk's own son, Nabu, who was resident at nearby Borsippa, came to Babylon as the saviour of his father. Possibly he led a triumphal procession of all the gods up from the river; the king was there and poured a libation. One can imagine the line of images, each standing on its 'cross beam' and showing above the heads of the crowd, swaying from side to side as the bearers struggled along.

Not so much is known of the actual 'liberation' which may have been enacted on the seventh day. In some manner Nabu led the gods against his father's foes and Marduk was set free from the mountain. Presumably his image appeared on some part of the ziggurat; in Sumerian seals illustrating this part of the myth, the god is shown cutting his way out of a real mountain with a saw. In some of these scenes a goddess is present, and it is very likely that a goddess took part in the Babylonian liberation. Ishtar, in the title of Beltiya, had been evoked by the high priest in the most flowery terms on the fourth and fifth days: 'Bright Beltiya, sublime and elevated, incomparable among the goddesses'.

Nisan 8 was a solemn day. All the divine images were assembled in the Ubshuukkinna, which here as elsewhere represented the place of assembly for the gods. They were ranged in order of precedence (this according to an Uruk text) and stood facing Marduk, on whom they were to bestow their united power, giving him 'a destiny beyond compare'. While the king, the priests and the images were occupied in this way within the walls of the Esagila, the populace were to remain hushed and peaceful, a day of calm between the lamentations and the outburst of rejoicing.

It was the ninth day that saw the great procession of gods and people from the Esagila to the Festival House (Bit Akitu) set in beautiful gardens outside the city. Evidently Ishtar went with Marduk and the king proclaimed the start:

. . . The Lord of Babylon goes forth, the lands kneel before him.
Sarpanitum [Ishtar] goes forth, aromatic herbs burn with fragrance.
By the side of Ishtar of Babylon, while her servants play the flute,
Goes all Babylon exultant!

This seems to have been the chief day for the visiting monarchs: Sargon II of Assur recorded, 'I grasped the hand of the great Lord Marduk, and made the pilgrimage to the Bit Akitu.' This pilgrimage, or march of the gods, accompanied by 'all Babylon exultant', represented the victorious host of the army led by Marduk to defeat Tiamat and her monsters. Sennacherib had the drama shown on the copper doors of the Bit Akitu at Assur—where of course Assur and not Marduk was the protagonist: 'A figure of Assur, going to battle against Tiamat . . . I engraved upon that gate, [also] the gods who marched in front and the gods who marched behind him, those who ride in chariots, and those who go on foot . . . [and] Tiamat and the creatures [that were] in her.' The battle and the subsequent creation of heaven, earth and mankind seem to have been expressed by symbolic acts. With chaos defeated and order triumphant once again, Marduk led the way back to Babylon through crowds roaring out their ritual cries of joy. This return may have taken place on the tenth of Nisan, after a grand banquet held in the Festival House.

If this ordering of the days is correct, then it was that night, either in the Esagila or in the chapel with the couch on the ziggurat, that the sacred marriage of Marduk and Ishtar, perhaps enacted by the king with the high priestess, was celebrated and the renewal of all nature secured.

On the eleventh day the gods had a second assembly for the determination of destinies comparable to that of the eighth. This time, however, it was the destiny of mankind that had to be settled. Just as in Genesis, the creation of man in the *Enuma elish* followed that of the natural world. This last solemn rite of the New Year festival seems in fact to celebrate the moment when Marduk and Ea (Enlil and Enki) killed Kingu 'and from his blood they formed mankind . . . Ea then imposed toil on man and set the gods free.' It was, in fact, a renewal of the 'social contract': mankind was engaged for the service of the gods through another cycle of the seasons.

The twelfth day of Nisan was the day of departures. The quays must have been thronged once more as all the visiting gods, and perhaps visiting royalty as well, set out on the waterway that would take them home. Now the king must return to his palace, the priests to the internal round of their temple, the people to home and work-shop, field and pasture.

If this was the one great occasion of the year when the ordinary private citizen saw the sacred images in action and participated with the religious establishments for the common good, the individual's everyday thoughts and observances were of a very different order.

Ur was certainly not unique in possessing little shrines built among private houses. These were open, facing the street, and anyone could slip in with a modest offering, and address a prayer to the image at close quarters—'face to face'. Probably all were minor divinities; the only one to be named in the Ur shrines was an ob-scure goddess able to protect desert travellers. It looks as though people living in the neighbourhood may have used these shrines for rather specialized pleas—but this might be as wrong an explanation as to assume that only travellers would worship in churches dedicated to St. Christopher.

These shrines were no doubt privately built and maintained, but they served a small community. The individual citizen may be said to have lived his own life within a yet more personal pantheon. There was, to begin with, his personal name. The great majority of these incorporated divine names, usually a god's for a man and a goddess's for a woman. On personal seals dating from the second millennium the owner is said to be the slave, or slave girl, of a particular divinity after whom he or she was named.

The significance of these god relationships is obscure. What is sure is that each individual from the king downwards had a personal deity on whose good offices he depended as an intercessor with the great fate-determining divinities of the national pantheon. There seemed to have been a particular need felt for these intermediaries among the Sumerians at the time of the Third Dynasty of Ur. Seal carvings and reliefs show the divinity grasping the protégé firmly by the wrist and presenting him to the high god. Very much more often than not the intermediary was a goddess—kings being able to seek the help of Inanna-Ishtar. The psychological promptings would seem to be the same as those that were to make the Virgin Mary the mediator for mankind.

The situation for the individual Mesopotamian was, of course, that he found the ways of the gods quite baffling. It was evident from the fact that he might suffer illness and ruin when he believed himself to have done no wrong, that there was much about the will of the gods that he could never know. He might seek the advice of a diviner and exorcist, but if these failed the right thing was to throw himself on the mercy of his personal deity, utter abject prayers and offerings—and hope for the best. His protector, if pleased, would not only turn aside 'the evil fate that had been decreed for him in accordance with his sentence', but also restore to him his good demon or guardian spirit. For this was the lowest tier of what has been called the personal pantheon: what appear to have been a male and a female spirit, and also a good and an evil demon, accompanied the individual throughout his life. The subject is far too subtle for discussion here—it can only be said that these presences were much involved with all the ideas of fate, luck and fortune which always dog the human mind.

The subject is illuminated by two literary works, a Sumerian poem that has been recognized as a forerunner of the Book of Job, and the Akkadian *I Will Praise the Lord of Wisdom*. In the Sumerian work the sufferer who was sick and abused by his former friends appealed to his personal god:

> *My god, you who are my father who begot me, lift up my face,*
> *Like an innocent cow, in pity . . .*
> *How long will you neglect me, leave me unprotected?*

He caused his mother, sister and wife to appeal for him, and also called in the help of an 'expert singer'. He was successful, 'his lamentation and wailing soothed the heart of his god', his 'pure and righteous' words also proved acceptable to his god. 'The encompassing sickness-demon, which had spread wide its wings, he swept away.' Finally the deity turned the supplicant's 'suffering into joy . . . Set by him the kindly spirit as a watch and guardian, gave him the genii of friendly mien.' This poem also contains the significant lines 'Never has a sinless child been born to its mother, a sinless youth has not existed from of old.'

In the *Lord of Wisdom* text, after moving praise of Marduk, 'whose rage is a devastating flood' but 'whose heart is merciful, whose mind forgiving . . . whose gentle hand sustains the dying', the sufferer goes on to say that both his god and his goddess have deserted him while 'the benevolent spirit who was beside me has departed, my protective spirit has flown away and seeks somebody else.' There follows a long account of how society has turned against him, how enemies will drive him from his job, his positions and his house, then he tells how no diviner or reader of dreams could explain what he had done wrong: 'Who can know the will of the gods in heaven? Who can understand the plans of the underworld gods? Where have humans learnt the way of a god? He who was alive yesterday is dead today.' Now comes a really horrific account of his many bodily afflictions, ending: 'I spent the night in my dung like an ox, and wallowed in my excrement like a sheep; my symptoms are beyond the exorcist, and my omens have confused the diviner.' The unhappy man's funeral was already prepared when he had a series of propitious dreams and learnt that Marduk would save him. The frightful afflictions are cured one by one, and the poem ends with the restored man pouring libations and making splendid sacrifices to the gods.

Demons, which are mentioned in both these compositions, were as important as the gods in the daily lives and thoughts of ordinary people. The *gallas* from the underworld already caused much trouble in Sumerian times, but the influence of demons probably increased with the passage of time. Some had been 'spawned' by Anu, some came from the netherworld, some were ghosts of the human dead. They lurked particularly in deserts, graveyards and ruins, and often worked their ill in gangs of seven. They were responsible for most of the sickness and misfortunes of mankind—though witchcraft (provided against in the laws) could also be responsible. The more powerful demons could even trouble the gods: they were, for instance, guilty of causing eclipses of the moon. One of the ways to make them end them was to beat the temple kettle-drum; this custom was kept alive even after the Babylonians had learnt the cause of eclipses and could predict them.

Magical devices for defeating hostile demons must have preoccupied all humble people in time of trouble. Sympathetic magic and the use of effigies were among them. For instance, dust might be gathered from various melancholy, demon-haunted places, moistened with bull's blood and modelled into a figure of the evil monster (demons were often in animal shape) and enclosed in a pot. Shamash would then be evoked to judge in favour of the sick man and against his foe and the pot buried in a desert place. Even these superstitious fringes of religion were not entirely removed from the higher forms of the temple. The evocation of Shamash just mentioned would be addressed to him in moving words as the bringer of light and warmth to the people and a source of justice to wronged men and women.

To a quite extraordinary extent the activities of the peoples of Mesopotamia came to be ordered by omens. This was true of all classes, and perhaps of the king most of all, for on his proper reading of these divine messages the fortune of the state or nation might depend. For peoples who believed that their fortunes and all events were in the control of divine powers this state of dependence was natural enough. If the gods knew what was going to happen they could be asked, or might freely decide to communicate, some information and guidance.

The Sumerians do not seem to have been so deeply addicted to omen-reading as their Semitic successors. They do, however, appear to have consulted the gods in this way over important appointments —such as that of the high priest. It was the Akkadians of the Old Babylonian period who began the systematization of the diviner's art, writing down a mass of observations for the guidance of future generations.

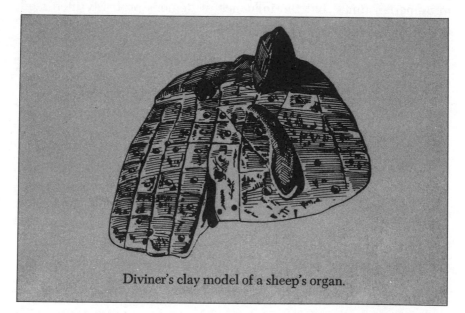

Diviner's clay model of a sheep's organ.

Omens could be either sought by men anxious for divine guidance or be vouchsafed by the divine good will. Of the first type the interpretation of the entrails of sacrificial animals, especially of the liver and lungs of sheep, was probably the earliest. It was never abandoned, but in later times it was surpassed by astrology. Models of sheep's organs were made in pottery and inscribed with interpretations very much like the ceramic heads of our phrenologists. A typical report sent to the king at Mari reads: ' . . . at the monthly sacrifice, I examined the omens. The left side of the "finger" was split, the middle "finger" of the lungs was over to the left. It is a sign of fame. Let my lord be happy.' Diviners showed an understandable desire for omens to be good; they might recast them again and again if the signs were depressing.

Other sought omens included the shapes assumed by oil poured in a bowl of water and the drift of smoke from a censer. Omens of one kind or another had to be taken before a king or any important person went on a journey or undertook any enterprise of serious import to the state. As for warfare, that uncertain business where reassurance is so much needed, it afforded professional employment to many diviners. They were attached to armies, and their findings were sometimes used even for local tactics.

The *Lord of Wisdom* text has already shown how normal it was for a private citizen to appeal to the diviner (and also to the interpreter of dreams and the exorcist). Sickness, as in this case, was a frequent reason for such consultations, but they might also concern having children, business ventures, or the choice of a wife.

Vouchsafed omens were also of many kinds. Some concerned the physical characteristics of the individual, especially hair colour, nail shape and the position of moles. The activities of birds and animals were of exact significance. More important were the births of monsters, either animal or human, for these, as in Rome, where they had to be reported to the Senate, could be portents affecting the fortune of the state.

Dream interpretation was a specialized branch of divination and had its own text books. There were even rites to prevent people from having dreams of ill omen. Dreaming could also give positive guidance, as in the case of Gudea's famous dream which provided him with instructions for the building of the great Eninnu temple. This literary dream, which included the display of an astrological tablet, was read for the *ensi* by the goddess Nanshe, dream interpreter for all the gods. (Women seem to have specialized in dream reading.)

It is difficult to judge how far this insatiable appetite for portents affected the actual doings of citizens or of government. Probably not very much; most people are likely to have carried out their desires and intentions even if they submitted to delays. There is, of course,

a curious inconsistency between the belief that the gods had determined the future and the notion that they would divulge it and
allow it to be altered. For ill omens did lead to avoiding action,
whether by ritual, magic or mere abstention. It is, however, an inconsistency that has remained with us ever since.

There is evidence that kings did not always accept the guidance
of their diviners, and that sometimes they tested their reliability one
against another. A legend of Naram-Sin of Akkad is of great additional interest in showing that the acceptance of omens was recognized as a part of the acceptance of civilized control in general. Good
citizens, it seems, must bow to these messages from their masters the
gods, while outlaws did not. The legend tells that Naram-Sin was
angry when the gods refused him any guidance and exclaimed, 'Has
a lion ever performed extirpacy, has a wolf ever consulted a female
dream interpreter? Like a robber I shall act according to my own
will!' Needless to say the story goes on to show that the king was
punished for his over-confidence.

Perhaps the most socially significant part of the whole tradition lay
in the diviners themselves. The authorized practitioners within their
various specializations were priests, and they belonged to a strongly
organized and apparently independent professional association. They
had undergone training and may even have had to pass examinations. Moreover, the profession was open only to the well-born and
physically perfect. It is reasonable to assume that, at least in periods
of good order, state policy gained from the king and his high officials
and generals submitting to what could amount to advice from a body
of highly educated and able priests.

We come at last, as come we must, to ideas of death and the afterlife. Mesopotamians' beliefs were certainly less hopeful than those
of the Egyptians, but they varied with time and place and were
probably always more or less inconsistent. Never, so far as the texts
reveal them, were they cheerful. The overall impression is of a Land
of No Return, darkness and dust. When Enkidu is allowed, by
divine intervention, to return to the living and Gilgamesh asks him
to describe what he has seen, he replies in anguish, 'If I tell you the
order of the Netherworld which I have seen, sit down and weep. My
body . . . vermin devour . . . is filled with dust.'

As we have seen, this land of the dead, which the Sumerians called
Kur, was envisaged as lying below the disk of earth. There was a
tradition that it could be entered through a gateway situated in the

city of Uruk. Already there was the notion that the dead had to
approach their land across a 'man-devouring river' (or sometimes a
sea) making use of the services of a ferryman. Inanna's sister, Ereshkigal, was queen of the netherworld and her husband Nergal its
king; their palace, it seems, had seven gates with seven gate-keepers.
Other divinities were in attendance on them and sometimes there
is a suggestion that dead kings had their shadowy thrones among
the dead. The deified Gilgamesh in particular (he who had rebelled
against death with what seems to be a typically Mesopotamian
bitterness) held high office there, seeing to it that the inmates obeyed
the many regulations.

There are a good many hints that men believed the dead were
envious of the living because of their own bloodless condition.
Thus, visitors to the netherworld were not to wear new clothes or
be anointed with good oil, be noisy or make love. In a later version
of a myth concerning Ereshkigal and Nergal, it is told that the queen,
then sole ruler of the land of the dead, felt sadly deprived because
she had not known 'the play of maidens, the frolic of young girls'.
Nergal, on being sent down to her, was warned to refuse bread,
meat and love-making. When he had denied himself in this way,
Ereshkigal showed her body to him and 'passionately they got into
bed.' The queen was so delighted by this erotic experience that in
the end she persuaded Anu to allow Nergal to remain with her as
consort.

One difficulty in the way of a clear understanding of Mesopotamian
concepts of death and an afterlife is a certain seeming incompatibility
between the archaeological evidence and the literary. There is in
the first place the tremendous, awe-inspiring evidence of the royal
tombs at Ur. Here a king and a queen had been accompanied to the
next world not only with all their most precious possessions, the
funerary vehicles and the draft animals harnessed to them, but
also by scores of richly attired ladies, by soldiers, servitors and
grooms. Ladies had been buried holding lyres, their fingers on the
strings. All these people of the court seem to have died readily,
peacefully, according to a well established practice. How inappropriate this splendid royal caravan appears if it were headed for
a dim underworld of dust and flittering ghosts!

An attempt has been made to find a literary reference to such an
immolation of a royal household in an epic fragment, known as *The
Death of Gilgamesh*. Here Gilgamesh is described as weighing out

Ur, the great death pit; Early Dynastic period.

gifts of bread for the underworld deities on behalf of his beloved wife, son, concubine, musician and other attendants. There are several objections to the identification. It is not made clear that his household was in fact in the underworld with Gilgamesh. At Ur, King A-bar-gi and Queen Shub-ad had not been buried at the same time, nor was there any sign of the interment of a son or other member of the family with either of them. More significant, the attendants at Ur had all been killed and buried solely to accompany their royal master and mistress: they were not given burial in their own right, but for the same reason as the oxen, asses and all the treasure. This is not a picture that fits at all with the idea of gifts being offered to the deities in their name.

It is certainly true to say that these were royal burials, and that kings and queens, because of their relationship with the gods, were expected to enjoy a more substantial afterlife than any of their subjects. So far as is known, human beings were killed only to accompany royal persons, and this practice seems in itself to have been abandoned after the period of the Ur tombs (representing some two generations) about the middle of the third millennium B.C.

On the other hand large numbers of commoners' graves in the Ur cemeteries and elsewhere were richly furnished with worldly goods of all kinds, and would seem to represent hopes for a well heeled afterlife similar to those entertained by royalty—even though of a more modest kind. Woolley saw the great change in burial rites as coming during or at the end of the Third Dynasty of Ur when the dead were no longer carried to public cemeteries but instead were laid in a family vault at the rear of the house. Here they were not provided with furniture or offerings of any kind. Woolley's interpretation of this change is that the dead now remained with their family in the house and therefore had no need of other possessions. The divinity worshipped in the adjacent domestic chapel he sees as

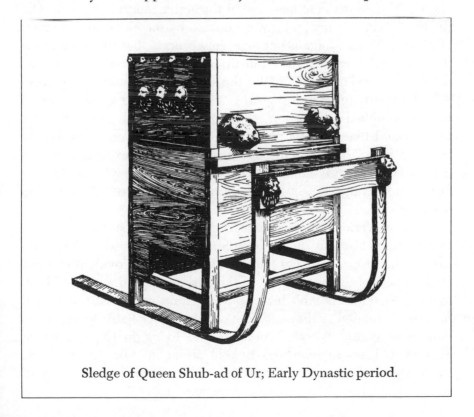

Sledge of Queen Shub-ad of Ur; Early Dynastic period.

representing the family in all its generations—a kind of Mesopotamian Lar.

It seems possible, then, that throughout most of the Early Dynastic
period Sumerian funerary practice and ideas of the afterlife were
closer to what we shall find in Egypt—that is to say that there was
a general belief that at least the important dead would enter a
world not unlike the one they had left—and needed to be equipped
accordingly. The change to a more sad and ghostly netherworld
could then be attributed to Semitic influence. It is true that a Land
of No Return is not consistent with the idea of having the run
of their old homes—but then ideas of life after death have never been
wholly consistent.

This view of the Early Dynastic approach to death may conceiv-
ably find support in two Sumerian funeral songs or dirges recently
discovered. The texts were written down in Nippur as late as 1700 B.C.,
but can be assumed to have had much earlier origins. These, supposedly composed by a citizen of Nippur for his father and his wife,
are interesting for the picture they give of the frantic grief of the
widow (the elegist's mother) and of the active mourning not only by
the dead man's family and slaves but also by the elders and matrons
of Nippur. What is significant here, however, is that these Sumerian
dirges contain the only known mention of the sun and moon visiting
the netherworld and also of Utu, the sun god, as a judge of the dead
—both ideas familiar in Egypt. It is also suggested that the deceased
will be supplied with water, that the underworld gods will pray
for him and that his own personal and city gods can be evoked to
befriend him. Altogether the picture given of the expectations of a
private citizen seems unlike that netherworld where 'ghosts like bats
flutter their wings . . . on the gate and the gateposts the dust lies
undisturbed.'

However various and inconsistent their ideas about an afterlife,
there is no doubt that the civilized Sumerians believed in the necessity for the proper burial of their dead. Failure to provide it was one
of the marks of the uncivilized, of the barbarians and nomads. Moreover, those citizens who for one misfortune or another were not
interred or tended as they should have been were liable to appear as
dangerous ghosts, working harm on the living in the manner of
demons. Gilgamesh questions Enkidu about his visit to the dead:
'Him whose corpse was cast out upon the steppe hast thou seen?'

And his friend replies, 'I have seen his spirit finds no rest in the netherworld.'

The single mention of Utu judging the dead is not enough to build a theory that the Sumerians believed that good or evil in this world would be rewarded or punished in the next. The judgement theme does not appear in any funerary iconography and it most certainly had nothing like the importance that it was given in Egypt. Probably the reference in the dirge would be a natural development from the appeal to the sun god to judge in favour of the supplicant that so often accompanied the use of magic against demons.

The ethos and moral values of the Mesopotamian peoples was in fact very much involved with the pervading Sumerian concern for justice. Enough has already been quoted in this book to make it obvious that there was an official concern to help the 'orphan and the widow', to protect the poor and helpless against the rich and strong that found expression in more than pious platitudes. Even refugees were sometimes included among the weak who needed protection. There was no thought on the lines of the meek inheriting the earth. On the contrary, proverbs and other literature may belittle the poor, as for example:

> How lowly is the poor man; the edge of the oven is his mill.
> His ripped garment stays unmended; what he has lost
>   remains unsought for.

It was a question of social conscience demanding that they should be to some extent protected.

Goodness in individuals, ideals of truth, honest dealing and wisdom were fully recognized. There was also a strong sense that the good should flourish—and this was where the difficulty with the equally strong sense of justice came in. In a society that accepted the divine control of all things, it was hard indeed to understand why right conduct and goodness were not always rewarded. In the *Lord of Wisdom* text the supplicant clearly states, 'What is good in one's sight is evil for a god. What is bad in one's own mind is good for his god.'

Thus, in a land where disasters of all kind were so frequent, there was a pervading feeling of 'unfairness' which is often revealed in the literature—even in the "Job" literature where absolute acceptance of this apparent lack of divine justice is being recommended. Inevitably it extends also to death. When demons brought illness it was a punishment for some offence against the gods, known or unknown, and might be averted by their appeasement through supplications and sacrifices. When, therefore, the demons brought death, it had to appear as a kind of final punishment. The emotions thus involved seem to lie behind the view of death as an outrage that finds such powerful expression in the greatest theme of the Gilgamesh epic.

Another inevitable effect was that 'sin' had to include not only recognized evil and wrong-doing, but also all kinds of completely non-moral failure in religious observances. There is, for example, an Assyrian prayer which contains such beautiful lines and sentiments as:

> The sin which I have done turn to goodness;
> The transgressions which I have committed,
>   let the wind carry away;
> My many misdeeds strip off like a garment . . .

but which also makes the nature of some of the transgressions clear:

> In ignorance I have eaten that forbidden by my god;
> In ignorance I have set foot on that prohibited
>   by my goddess . . .

In another incantation the exorcist asks a number of questions relating to moral failings on strikingly different levels:

> Has he sinned against a god,
> Is his guilt against a goddess,
> Is it a wrongful deed against his master
> Hatred towards his elder brother,
> Has he despised father or mother . . .
> Has he used false weights . . .
> Has he fixed a false boundary . . .
> Has he possessed himself of a neighbour's wife,
> Has he shed the blood of a neighbour . . .

and then continues with a number of sins that are purely ceremonial. Obviously his beliefs encouraged the citizen to goodness and social morality and perhaps even more to correctness in the minutiae of ritual observance, but at the same time (so often was he punished without knowing why) to magical devices and to ever reiterated protest that men could not know the will of the gods, that 'he who was alive yesterday is dead today.'

As for the gods themselves, they were not themselves righteous (had not even the great Enlil raped Ninlil?), but it was accepted, it seems without theological debate, that they had created the elements of evil with the good. This is at once apparent in the *mes* that included falsehood and goodness, and placed fear, terror and strife beside peace. There is, however, nothing to disprove that Utu-Shamash, whose responsibility for justice involved him with morality, was not himself just and virtuous.

There was probably a development in moral ideals, particularly, perhaps, in the Babylonia of the last millennium B.C. This is, however, very difficult to establish while the original date of composition of many late textual copies is unknown. It seems that the concept of the supreme deity as one merciful of heart 'whose gentle hand sustains the dying' would not have come to the Sumerians. A Babylonian Wisdom tablet, composed by 700 B.C. but how long before is not known, has something of the Sermon on the Mount:

> *Unto your opponent do no evil;*
> *Your evildoer recompense with good;*
> *Unto your enemy let justice be done. . . .*
> *Let not your heart be induced to do evil.*

It continues:

> *The one begging for alms, honour, clothe:*
> *Over this his god rejoices,*
> *This is pleasing to Shamash, he rewards it with good . . .*

A few lines further on, it is worth noting, we are back to very worldly wisdom: 'Do not marry a harlot whose husbands are six thousand.'

Finally, it is important to try to understand how far all morality was embedded in the social. A Sumerian hymn to Enlil shows the city as the guardian of its people's morality:

> *It grants not long days to the braggart,*
> *Allows no ill word against the divine judgement.*

Hypocrisy, distortion,
Abuse, malice, unseemliness,
Insolence, enmity, oppression,
Envy, force, libelous speech,
Arrogance . . . breach of contract, abuse of legal verdict,
All these evils the city does not tolerate.

It is true that this was holy Nippur so that its virtue may have had a particular symbolic meaning, yet it is an idea that would have been acceptable to all citizens. Prone to violence, ambitious, libidinous though the Mesopotamians were (perhaps more so after the Semitic ascendancy), the ideal of the good life was, as Jacobsen has insisted, identical with the obedient life. The individual owed obedience up and up through the hierarchy of authority: to the elder brother and elder sister, to the parents, the overseer, the judge, the king, and to the personal god on the way to the great gods and the lord of heaven. This was citizenship, this was civilization, this was what the good and wise man had to accept: if he did not, he was no better than the outlaw or wanderer.

INTELLECTUAL LIFE

EDUCATION AND LEARNING

LITERACY, AND THEREFORE THE INTELLECTUAL LIFE OF THE SUMERIANS and their inheritors, was rooted in the *edubba* or 'tablet house'. These most remarkable institutions are usually referred to simply as schools —for the good reason that children began to attend them in 'early youth', which probably means before ten years old. On the other hand, as students remained into early manhood, while the staff engaged in a wide range of learned studies and in literary composition, they could also qualify as universities.

In a quite extensive literature referring to schools, there is no mention of a girl pupil. Again, there is only one known reference to a woman scribe and one to a woman doctor. Yet it would seem that the high priestesses would have had to be literate. Possibly a few clever and ambitious girls had private tutors.

Already by about 3000 B.C., when writing was still pictographic, word lists for study and practice were being used by the budding

profession of scribes. Writing being at this time wholly in the service
of the temple administration, no doubt these early studies took place
within the temple. Progress at this pioneer phase was not very fast,
yet by the middle of the third millennium there were *edubbas*
established throughout Sumer where writing was being formally
taught. They appear by now to have been quite distinct from the
temples. There is plenty of evidence that Sumerian schoolboys could
be very rowdy indeed, so it is understandable if the priesthoods did
not want them rushing into or exploding out of their orderly precincts.

The timetable was a heavy one. Pupils normally lived at home,
attending class from sunrise to sunset. (In later times there were
boarding schools.) They had six days off per (lunar) month, as a
tablet written by a student at an *edubba* in Ur makes plain.

> *The reckoning of my monthly stay in the tablet house is:*
> *My days of freedom are three per month.*
> *Its festivals are three days per month.*
> *Within it, twenty-four days per month. . . .*
> *They are long days.*

Mari has produced the only specially furnished *edubba*—two rooms
with monotonous rows of low benches in fired brick. One would like
to think that this kind of classroom was used for young pupils and
that the seniors had a more academic type of accommodation.
Nippur, as a great religious centre, was inevitably a centre of learning, and here there seems to have been a scribal quarter where it is
possible that learned men took students into their own homes. Very
many of the surviving Sumerian literary texts were found in this
quarter.

The staffing of the schools was based on the typically Sumerian
hierarchy of authority and paternalism. The headmaster was in fact
called 'school father'—although he was also an *ummia*, or professor.
He was assisted by masters whose title can properly be translated as
'big brother'. They appear to have done such scholastic chores as
preparing tablets for the boys to copy (which they did either below
a line or on the back), correcting the copies and hearing memorized
lessons. There were also subject masters, the man in charge of
Sumerian, mathematics, drawing and so forth. The pupils were
called 'school sons'. The severity of the discipline, the determination

that learning and good behaviour could be beaten into them, has already been mentioned. Yet we know that Sumerian schoolboys, like all the hundreds of millions who have followed in their footsteps, were sometimes unpunctual, untidy, careless and lazy. Indeed, as they became older and less apprehensive, some of them behaved so rowdily towards their big brothers that an appeal had to be made to the school father.

One can guess that those graduates who stayed on as big brothers may have tended to be poorer and of humbler origin than most of their pupils and that this was one cause of the insubordination. Certainly most of the boys who could afford to enter on the long scribal training came from the upper professional class of the cities. From tablets dated to about 2000 B.C. we know that the fathers of professional scribes included governors and city elders, ambassadors, army officers and sea captains, priests and temple administrators, high tax officials, supervisors—and, of course, professional scribes. It is known that scribes put pressure on their sons to join their profession even though it does not seem to have been held in quite such high esteem as it was in Egypt. Even princes might attend school; Ur-Nammu's son Shulgi boasted of having attended the *edubba* in his youth and mastered the scribal art.

As for the incomes of the teachers, they depended on contributions made by the pupils. In the revealing and amusing essay *Schooldays*

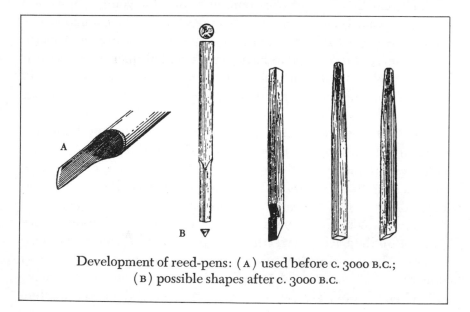

Development of reed-pens: (A) used before c. 3000 B.C.; (B) possible shapes after c. 3000 B.C.

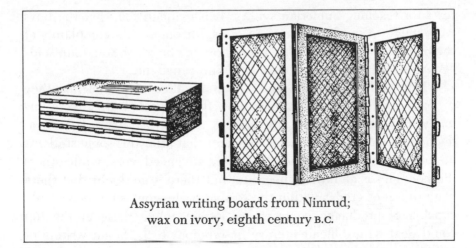

Assyrian writing boards from Nimrud;
wax on ivory, eighth century B.C.

(again written in about 2000 B.C.) a boy who had done badly at
school and been so much beaten that he began to hate and neglect
'the scribal art' saved the situation by asking his professor home,
where his well-to-do father and their house servants could oil him
both literally and metaphorically, and arrange to 'dress him in a
garment, give him some extra salary, put a ring on his hand.' The
relationship between masters in this position and their richer, snob-
bier and more arrogant pupils can be easily imagined.

The basic purpose of the school education was to attain perfection
in the difficult and highly specialized skills of writing Sumerian in
cuneiform and understanding its grammar. Hundreds of surviving
exercise tablets have made it possible to see just how these skills
developed from the new boy's shaky attempts when the big brother
would 'guide his hand on the clay' up to the already virtually
professional standards of the senior students. The finest cuneiform
calligraphy shows such delicacy and control, such mastery of
arrangement on the tablet, that it must arouse wonder and admiration. Although the scribe could never enjoy the pure aesthetic expression of Chinese and other Asian calligraphers, for sheer
command of a preposterously difficult medium, no one has ever surpassed the finest of the cuneiform writers of Mesopotamia.

From Sargonid times onwards more and more of the students
would have spoken Akkadian and had to learn Sumerian as an academic language. For this purpose bilingual lists of words and phrases
were prepared—the first time that anything approaching a lexicon
had ever been devised. There were also quite advanced grammatical

texts for teaching Sumerian syntax. It is evident, too, that the boys were made to speak Sumerian in class, for one of the complaints of the boy in *Schooldays* reads, 'The fellow in charge of Sumerian said: "Why did not you speak Sumerian?" and caned me.'

When students had reached a certain stage of proficiency they probably had to take an examination. If they passed, they were formally told that they were now scribes and warned against the academic man's danger of conceit. It seems that after this some students might remain with the *edubba* for more advanced work, while others did not. This is all rather uncertain, but there is no doubt that there were different grades within the scribal profession, some being only capable of producing contracts or letters, while those at the top could deal with difficult literary or religious texts. Some writers of religious texts, indeed, indulged in the use of rare ideograms and words, or an abstruse style—so much so that their writings have partially defeated our modern translators. The specialist's love of devising a language incomprehensible to the uninitiated is evidently no new failing. This may be an appropriate point to mention an amusing identification recently made. It appears that the American word 'sophomore' derives from the Greek *sophos-moros*, meaning 'clever/fool', which in turn finds an exact counterpart in a Sumerian term of abuse, *galam-haru*.

The graduate of the *edubba* became an alumnus, or old boy, under the title 'school son of days past'. After his long grind and disciplinary suffering he was ready to indulge in the nostalgia of old boys everywhere.

There were, of course, many callings open to him. Here we encounter a very real confusion in the meaning of the term 'scribe'. Where reading and writing were quite rare accomplishments, this name could be given to anyone who was literate. In this sense many of those who controlled society from high office and the professions were scribes—governors, priests, administrators, doctors and scholars of various kinds. In addition to all these who were, like the proud Shulgi, 'masters of the scribal art', there were professional scribes in the sense implied by the use of the name in the list of scribal parentage given above. Even in this specialized usage of the name, which can best be rendered as 'secretary', the profession had a wide range of activities. The main openings were in commerce and the service of the temple, the palace and the law courts. Every important official had a personal secretary on whom he depended at least as much as his counterpart does today. Scribes also accompanied all military expeditions, writing despatches, listing prisoners and booty, working in the quartermaster's office. Very many, perhaps of the less academic kind, became what might be called estate managers and accountants for well-to-do landowners. There is an essay describing an interview between an estate superintendent and a (probably young) *edubba* graduate who is serving under him. The senior, having congratulated himself on the virtuousness of his own school days, ends up by telling his underling that he must 'be courteous to man, supervisor and owner, must make their heart content.' The graduate's reply, a rudely expressed defence of his own proficiency, makes it plain how many purely practical duties such a scribe was expected to undertake both indoors and out. He speaks of seeing to it that the household slaves and slavegirls worked properly and supervising their food and clothing, and also of making the field workers toil under difficulties and managing the draft oxen. He seems at times to have had to dance attendance on the landowner, and he said daily prayers—perhaps for the protection of the estates and its livestock.

Yet at the same time many of the mathematical problems set in the *edubba* and tables drawn up for the calculation of field areas and the like show that this type of expertise was also needed by those who went from school to estate management.

It is in the relationship between *edubba* graduates and the priesthood that the use of the name of scribe becomes most difficult. Presumably all priests must have had training in the scribal art, but had then to go on to their own even more rigorous education. Some of the most highly placed, including those initiated into the writing and use of the obscure sacred texts already mentioned, are held to have been leaders in the scribal profession. On the other hand not all scribes could become priests of standing. Some might not be capable of qualifying for the upper categories with the priesthood, while some were disqualified from holding office in the temples by physical imperfections.

One of the most remarkable facts about the *edubbas* is their independence of the temples—already established in Sumerian times. The essays and other texts concerning these schools are secular in tone and content, and the fact that they were financed from students' fees must have made their independence complete. It is probably fair to attribute to this state of affairs not only the high standards maintained over an immensely long period of time but also their considerable progressiveness and ability to advance in several branches of learning and intellectual study.

All this does not mean, of course, that the scribes were not devout individuals accepting without question the divine inspiration and control of human affairs. They were devoted to Nidaba, the reed divinity who had grown to be goddess of writing. At the end of the *Schooldays* essay, the headmaster (softened by flattering attentions and gifts) tells the boy that his father's god will pray to Nidaba on his behalf, and ends, 'You have exalted Nidaba, the queen of learning.' Many hymns and other texts were ended with the words 'O Nidaba, praise!' Owing to their adherence the goddess attained a high place in the pantheon. In the Old Babylonian *Curse of Agade* she appears with Sin, Enki, Inanna, Utu and three others among the great gods of Sumer. When in later times her patronage was taken over by Nabu of Borsippa, his standing as son of Marduk was already an exalted one. In his temple, the Ezida, it was a custom for scribes to offer up the finest specimens of their works as votives.

Among the subjects developed by the scribes first place must go to writing itself. Rendered into wedge impressions, the pictograms of the first Uruk tablets of about 3000 B.C. had become stylized almost beyond recognition five hundred years later. At about this time, too, their appearance was further changed when the scribes found it more convenient to turn the signs over 90° to the left and start writing at the top left hand, in place of the right hand, corner. At the same time the change had been made from simple ideograms or word signs that were good enough for the temple accounts to the free use of syllabic signs based on sound. One of the earliest stimuli that hastened this use of the phonetic syllable came from the need to write the proper names of those many individuals who figured in the accounts. Sometimes these (like Hawkes and Plumb) could be rendered by ideograms, but more often they had to be divided into syllables and rendered by the word signs with the same sounds. For instance, if 'Bar-clay' had been listed in this fashion, the sign which had once meant only a bar could be used for the beginning of 'barbarian', and that meaning 'clay' for the beginning of 'claymore'.

In time a much stronger impetus began to speed up the all-important adoption of phonetic syllables. This was the need to adapt them to write another language—Akkadian. Already by 2400 B.C. simple Akkadian forms were being written, and after another century long Akkadian inscriptions appeared in this syllabic cuneiform. In Old Babylonian times it was being used for literary and all other advanced forms of text. In the second millennium, too, Akkadian cuneiform had the distinction of becoming the world's first international diplomatic language. It was widely used in the Bronze Age world for letters and despatches—as is particularly well shown in the El-Amarna correspondence. The foreign scribes often wrote it very ill, but it eased the correspondence of princes.

The reading and writing of Sumerian and Akkadian was always to remain so very difficult as to demand long years of scribal training, because although phonetic syllables were adopted the ideograms from which they were taken remained in use. The resulting complexities meant that although Mesopotamian civilization was in a sense highly literate—all the way from its endless administrative records to its splendid literature—most people remained unable to read or write. Not only ordinary folk, but generals, highly placed officials and presumably many royal persons as well had not passed through the *edubba* and could make nothing of a cuneiform tablet. No idle scribblings, no amorous or comical graffiti, have come down to us from ancient Mesopotamia (or for much the same reasons from Egypt either). Popular literacy had to wait on the development of alphabets.

It was also in part due to the extreme difficulty of teaching the scribal art that a curious kind of document was produced that started as a pedagogic exercise but developed into something much more. We have seen how word lists were being drawn up for study purposes in the earliest days of writing. By the middle of the third millennium these had developed into teaching texts of carefully listed gods, animals, categories of artifacts, as well as assorted words and phrases. Looking more closely at categories representing the natural world, we find domestic animals; wild animals including birds and some flying insects; fishes; trees; plants; vegetables; minerals.

The long lists of items within these categories prepared for use in the *edubba* consisted of no more than names. Yet students may have been taught more about them from a topical rather than language point of view, as some more literary texts contain descriptions such as:

The shepherd bird says ri-di-ik, ri-di-id,
The shepherd bird has a variegated neck like the dar bird,
He has a crest upon his head.

It is amusing to see the Sumerians making the same vain attempts to verbalize the notes of birds that are still printed in our modern ornithological handbooks. In case this instance should give the impression that the subject list went with regular glosses of a 'scientific' descriptive kind, it should be made clear that often they were poetical and metaphorical. There is the *mur*, probably a sting ray, of which the head is said to be a hoe, the teeth a comb, 'its bones a tall fir tree . . . its slender tail the whip of the fisherman . . . the sting serves as a nail.'

When Akkadian took over from Sumerian as the spoken language, these Sumerian lists were inevitably developed into bilingual texts —still arranged according to Sumerian classifying words since their primary purpose was the study of the ancient tongue. By the end of Old Babylonian times the categories had become further elaborated. Groups of artifacts contain great numbers of classified items. For instance, under wooden objects were included more than fifteen hundred ranging from pieces of wood to boats and chariots. There were similar classes for objects made of reed, skin, metal, ceramic —also for clothes, foodstuffs and drinks. There was an additional list of place names covering lands, cities, hamlets, rivers, canals and fields. Yet other of these bilinguals are of a more sociological kind giving lists of officials, craftsmen, social classes—and human deformities. (The documents have not as yet been made to yield any considerable part of the information they contain for us.)

While it is wrong to see in these schoolmen's texts the beginnings of botany, zoology, mineralogy, geography, anatomy and sociology, it would surely be unjust to the able men involved with drawing them up, and perhaps expounding them, to treat them simply as linguistic lessons on a par with the syllabaries and phrase books that were in contemporary use. Many of them demanded some degree of exact observation, and some thought about the division into categories. It would imply a greater change in human mentality than can be shown to be justified if some of the teachers and learned men of the *edubba* did not become interested in the subject matter of these lists and make themselves to some extent expert in them. Neither does it seem too fanciful to suppose that their pupils may sometimes have been encouraged to bring in specimens, at least botanical and mineralogical, by way of illustrating the lists. This would be in harmony with the collecting of foreign specimens that we shall find being undertaken by Queen Hatshepsut's expedition in sixteenth-century Egypt and the botanical and zoological gardens later to be established in Assyrian Kalah.

However, the Sumerian world view obviously did not lead to the pursuit of secular knowledge for its own sake that came into the world with the Ionian Greeks. Therefore, as most of the interests represented by the lists had no practical outcome for Bronze Age life, they were not much developed. Yet there were a few non-linguistic subjects within the *edubba* curriculum which had immediate practical application and in these good progress was made. They were mathematics, astronomy-cum-astrology and medicine.

MATHEMATICS AND ASTRONOMY

THE ACCOUNT-KEEPING ORIGINS OF WRITING MADE IT ALMOST INEVIT-able that the Sumerians should begin to devise a means of numeration no later than they began to made word signs. From the first the dominant counting system was sexagesimal (based on sixty). How this came to pass is uncertain, but one explanation is that it was due to the fact that within the order of weights and money the *mina* 'happened' to be sixty times the shekel. For ordinary purposes, however, this sexagesimal system was combined with a decimal one, the factor of 10 being combined with that of 6: 1, 10, 60, 600, 3600, 36,000. When mathematics developed as a subject and true mathematical texts were written, they were exclusively sexagesimal, with a place value system based on the step 60—a system that we retain in our writing of time and degrees. The devising of place value, by which the position of a number symbol determines its value, was of the greatest importance for the advancement of mathematical ability.

As for the writing of numbers, after the pictographic phase it became wholly cuneiform. Small numbers were represented by appropriate numbers of vertical wedges arranged in standard groupings; there were distinct symbols for 10, 100 and 1000 and certain fractions such as half and quarter and third had their own signs. The use of zero was not developed in the first flowering of Mesopotamian mathematics, but had appeared by Seleucid times.

More even than in other fields, our knowledge of the history of mathematical studies in Mesopotamia is limited by the chances of discovery. The subject is represented almost entirely by the two types of text: problems and tables. Some Sumerian tables have survived—one, for instance, written in about 2500 B.C., was intended for calculating the area of square fields. By far the greater part of the mathematical tablets come from Nippur and other cities of the Plain and date from the Old Babylonian period between about 1800 and 1500 B.C., or from the Seleucid period after 300 B.C. Most of the Old Babylonian problem texts were written in Akkadian, but a few were in Sumerian and all make use of Sumerian technical terms. It is reasonably sure, therefore, that although mathematics reached its brilliant flowering only in Old Babylonian times it was firmly rooted in the Sumerian past. After this age of high achievement it seems to have stagnated, entering another progressive phase only about a thousand years later, when it responded to the challenges presented by the astronomers.

Primarily the table texts served practical needs. One group list measures used for the conversion of larger units to smaller—or the reverse. Another consisted of tables for sexagesimal multiplication and division and lists of figures for the calculation of compound interest. But the Old Babylonian mathematicians carried their preparation beyond what was ordinarily needed. They made tables for squares and cubes, for the sums of squares and cubes, for square roots and cube roots and so forth.

It seems clear that these advanced tables were intended mainly for working out the mathematical problems that form the second type of text. These were exercises designed for use in the *edubba*; sometimes only the problem was stated but often the solution was also indicated. Here again the problems were often set out in practical terms—the equivalent to the running taps, the trains and motor cars of more recent school text books. There are problems concerning the number of workmen, their wages and food, about the making and carrying of bricks (of which there were at least seven standard types) and, as would be expected, a very large number relating to irrigation works. These include the difference between light surface

work on the canals and digging at greater depths, the labour necessary to construct both cylindrical and prismatic wells and the area
to be flooded by water released from a cistern of a given volume.
Others again involve weaving, sheep, grain volumes, value ratios
of precious metal and the division of fields between inheritors.
Already, too, the practice had begun of devising problems in con-
crete terms that were also quite unrealistic—as for example one
concerning a city with an exactly circular wall and a trapezoidal
section.

The majority of these problems with their practical casting were
essentially algebraic exercises to be solved as linear or quadratic
equations, and as such they formed the core of the teaching in
Babylonian schools. This consistency of purpose is most strikingly
known by the fact that many hundreds of such problems were set
out in a connected series covering some fourteen tablets.

Although algebraic methods dominated, numerical ones were used
where appropriate and geometry was well advanced. Geometric relations such as the theorem of Pythagoras and the triangle inscribed
in a semi-circle were understood, and the value of *pi* was well taken
as $3\frac{1}{8}$. Tablets dealing with the area of geometric figures show the
figures neatly drawn in boxes with the texts below each one. Such
studies were carried as far as the determination of the areas of
regular polygons.

Bertrand Russell dismissed Babylonian algebra and geometry as
rules of thumb and said that the Greeks 'invented mathematics'. This
opinion could no longer be accepted. First challenged by the practical questions that their highly organized civilization forced upon
them, the Sumerians and Babylonians went far beyond those challenges and became interested in mathematics for its own sake.
Absolute pioneers, they invented numerical methods that were
capable of infinite development, and gropingly but knowingly they
established general rules of procedure. In these matters they left the
Egyptians far behind and made the Greeks their debtors. In fact
we have here in mental form that human prodigality of effort that
has been discussed in relation to craftsmanship. In thought as in
skill these innovators loved to work on immeasurably beyond what
was demanded of them for survival in their environment. They were
slaves of the gods, perhaps, but did even Enki expect mathematics?

Astronomy is the study most obviously related to mathematics,
and it might be expected that the mathematicians of the Old Baby-

lonian schools would have turned their attention to the movements of the heavenly bodies and produced at least the beginnings of an exact, mathematical astronomy at that time. Perhaps the identification of the moon, sun and other bodies with divinities and their relation to omens and the control of fates may have made a mental obstacle to such a theoretical application. As it was, the step from a utilitarian to a theoretical and creative phase of study which the mathematicians took in the first half of the second millennium B.C. was not taken by the astronomers for another thousand years. Yet even utilitarian and divinatory study of the heavens produced a very considerable body of knowledge for the use of the Bronze Age world.

From the point of view of the practical organization of society the most important purpose was for the measurement of time. For simple farming communities the passage of time is apt to appear as an endless series of cycles rather than a linear progression divided into sections of various lengths. Fixed points within the cycle necessary for the agricultural year and its festivals are then marked by such things as the movements of migratory birds, the appearance of plants or flowers—and also the rising and setting of the heavenly bodies. Both earthly and heavenly signs may be used by the same people. Thus Hesiod (writing about 800 B.C.) stated both 'The cry of the migrating cranes shows the time of ploughing and sowing' and also 'when the Pleiades, Atlas' daughters, rise it is time for harvest—and for sowing when they go down again.'

The moon was, of course, the most obvious indicator of a more regular division of the annual cycle and therefore the most likely inspiration of a calendar. On the other hand the great complication of lunar motion and hence of the exact length of the lunar month, together with the fact that these months did not coincide with the solar year, was to cause men endless trouble in their efforts to regulate an exact calendar. It was not in fact until the age of mathematical astronomy in the second half of the last millennium B.C. that Babylonian astronomers learnt how to predict the exact lengths of lunar months.

Originally the Sumerian calendar, like the Egyptian, was a purely lunar one. This meant that it was regulated by actual observation of the moon, each new month beginning with the evening of the reappearing crescent—from which it followed that the calendarial day began at sunset. (This arrangement was reversed in Egypt.)

Like the Christian Easter, many religious festivals were linked with
the lunar calendar and gave it a deep and lasting religious significance. In the creation epic it is recorded of Marduk:

The Moon he caused to shine, the night to him entrusting.
He appointed him a creature of the night to signify the days:
Monthly, without cease from designs with a crown.
At the month's very start, rising over the land,
Thou shalt have luminous horns to signify six days,
On the seventh day reaching half crown.
At full moon, in mid month, stand opposite the sun.
When the sun overtakes thee at the base of heaven,
Diminish thy crown and retrogress in light.

Supullu, the Akkadian full moon, was a day like the Sabbath when
all activity was forbidden.

The twelve lunar months, sometimes of twenty-nine, sometimes of
thirty days, the Sumerians named after agricultural time marks such
as the barley harvest, or after the festival days of gods. Not only did
these names vary from state to state, but so for a very long time did the
calendars themselves. This state of affairs, which must have caused
citizens some inconvenience and uncertainty, was brought about by
the need to keep the lunar year roughly in cycle with the sun and
the agricultural seasons. Plainly a barley harvest month could not
be allowed to fall at midwinter or sowing time. A thirteenth intercalary month was therefore added whenever the lunar-solar years
became obviously too far out of step. Neighbouring cities might
make the decision at different times, and it was only as centralized
government became stronger that a national lunar calendar could
be established. This was perhaps facilitated by checking against the
heliacal rising of certain conspicuous stars and constellations, three
to each lunar month. These signs had probably long been used by
the farmers (in the manner of Hesiod), and when the calendar was
regularized the month names were related to 'the rising of the stars'.
The Assyrians, for much of their history, kept consistently to the
year of twelve lunar months—as do most Islamic nations today.

Meanwhile, however, secular urban life and widespread commerce
had demanded a more regular system unaffected by the still unpredictable length of lunar months or erratic intercalations. A civil
calendar of twelve months of thirty days was therefore instituted

and used for commercial and other economic purposes. The payment of interest on loans, for example, was based on this calendar—which in this and other ways must have facilitated interstate and international relations. Yet in spite of their much greater commercial interests, it was the peoples of Mesopotamia and not the Egyptians who clung more tenaciously to the traditional moon calendar with its religious associations.

Urban life, and perhaps most of all the service of the temples, called also for shorter graduations of time—that is, for fixed divisions of the day. The day was divided into twelve. One of the devices for telling these 'double hours' was the gnomon or shadow clock, forerunner of the sundial. Herodotus recorded that 'the Greeks learned the gnomon and the twelve parts of the day from the Babylonians', a statement which is supported by the three-tablet compilation known as the *Mul Apin*. This text, as well as star lists, contains tables showing the times of day through the seasons at which the shadow length is equal to the pointer length (i.e. when the sun is at 45°). The *Mul Apin* probably derives mainly from the later second millennium, but the use of the shadow clock is thought to have begun in Sumerian times.

This is true also of another time-measuring device described in the *Mul Apin*: the water-clock or clepsydra. Measurement depended upon the rate of water running out through a hole in the base of a container. In Mesopotamia this is said to have been cylindrical or prismatic, but the only ancient specimen found, from the Egypt of about 1400 B.C., is an alabaster bowl narrowing towards the base, a shape which would give a fairly constant rate of outflow, reduction of volume compensating for reduction of pressure.

The fascination and social significance of the use of the Mesopotamian clepsydra, however, lies in the fact that it seems to have been associated with an unbroken watch maintained through all the divisions of daylight and darkness. Day and night each had three watches, but the actual length of these had to change with the relative duration of light and darkness. In Babylonia the ratio of longest to shortest days and nights is about three to two, and with the vertical-sided vessel (in which the last part of the column ran out more slowly than the first) this ratio was secured by a two-to-one ratio by weight of water. Thus at midsummer each day watch might have four pounds of water in its cylinder, while each night had only two. Thereafter the night watch added one sixth of a pound

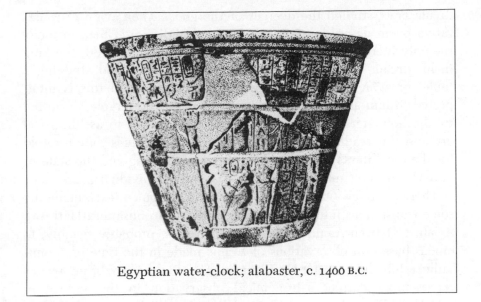

Egyptian water-clock; alabaster, c. 1400 B.C.

every month while the day removed the same amount; at the equinox they were, of course, equal at three pounds each and by the winter solstice the midsummer ratio was reversed. There is some evidence that wages, too, came to be adjusted so that the best pay went to those serving through the long, cold nights and the long, hot days.

It is fascinating to think of those guardians of the hours and their endless watch over the heavens. Where were they stationed and what did they do besides tending the clepsydra? One would like to think of them having their post on the ziggurat, and observing the risings and setting of the heavenly bodies—especially of certain planets and fixed stars that were of particular concern to king and people.

In the opinion of the Mesopotamians themselves, another practical application of celestial observation was for the reading of omens. As such astrological law was generally inseparable from accumulated knowledge qualifying as primitive astronomy, the two have to be treated together. Sumerian word lists already include stars— some twenty-five being named. Although there are no direct records, astrology was evidently already a powerful influence in Sumerian times. It will be remembered how in the myth of the gardener and Inanna, Shukalitude 'gazed at the auspicious inscribed heaven, from the inscribed heaven learnt the omens, saw there how to carry out the divine laws, studied the decrees of the gods.' Then again in a narrative poem describing Gudea's temple-building at Girsu, virtually the only literary work of the Third Dynasty of Ur period, the king in his dream sees a woman holding a gold stylus and studying a tablet on which the starry heaven is inscribed—and this is interpreted to him as Nidaba telling him to build the temple according to 'the holy stars'. Astrology is sometimes referred to as 'the royal art' and this reading of the heavens and the destinies they foretold for the inhabitants of the earth referred to the king and the state or nation and not (until much later) to private individuals.

There are a few Old Babylonian astrological omen texts, including some translations into Elamite and Hittite from Susa and Hattusas. A late text from Assurbanipal's library refers, probably reliably, to omens based on observations of Venus made in the time of Ammisaduqa, fourth king after Hammurabi. These tablets are of interest as representing correct astronomical observation in the service of astrology. They show that the Old Babylonians had already recognized the identity of the morning and the evening star—an achievement to be claimed by the Greeks. The movements of the planet are divided into periods, covering the first and last appearances of the morning and the evening star, giving a total period of 584 days.

Another type of text that can be assumed to have dated back to Old Babylonian times was the star lists relating to spatial positions. They consist of the thirty-six month stars and constellations already mentioned. The earliest form of arrangement may have been in three concentric circles named after great gods. On the *Mul Apin* another arrangement is followed: three parallel roads across the heavens.

The great age for both astrology and astronomy in Mesopotamia was in the last millennium B.C. Astrology was particularly patronized by the Assyrian monarchs, and large numbers of tablets, dealing with the moon, the sun, the planets and fixed stars, found their place in Assurbanipal's library. There were also texts marking a new departure—personal horoscopes with the birth or conception day of the subject, a star reading and prediction for the child's future. These date from the fifth century B.C.

Babylonian astrology spread vigorously westward, infecting Egypt, Greece and Rome and building up the long-lasting fame of the Chaldean seers. This growth of astrology did not impede the simultaneous remarkably vigorous growth of a true astronomy. During the century or so after 500 B.C. the Babylonians appear to have made two great advances. One was the use of the sun's ecliptic as a fixed base for measurement, making possible numerical computation. The second was the recognition of periodic cycles, particularly the nineteen-year cycle, that came to be named after the Greek Meton, regularizing the intercalation of the calendrical months (seven years with thirteen months, the rest with twelve) and the *saros* or 223 lunations (eighteen years and ten or eleven days) after which eclipses of the sun and moon recur. These advances led on to a brilliant flowering of mathematical astronomy in Seleucid times, when its spread to the Hellenistic Greeks, especially of Alexandria, was as inevitable as it was valuable for Western science.

No doubt by this time astronomy and astrology were pursued in distinct intellectual circles. Apparently the predictability of eclipses did not check their significance as omens any more than it prevented the beating of the temple drum to drive away sun-and-moon-devouring monsters. It was an inconsistency that can surprise no one living in modern scientific societies where horoscopes are still cast and papers and magazines carry columns of zodiacal omens.

MEDICINE

ANOTHER PROFESSION IN WHICH STUDENTS OF THE SCRIBAL ART COULD specialize was that of medicine. It was one of the subjects in which Mesopotamians lagged behind Egyptians—possibly because they had less hope or care for their bodies after death. Yet it would be wrong to dismiss it as entirely a branch of divination or of magical hocus-pocus and concoctions. Some of the drugs and treatments could certainly be efficacious, and doctors may have developed many manipulative and other skills unrecorded on the tablets. There were, besides, all those opportunities to cure psycho-somatic illnesses through impressive appeals to the gods and magico-religious rites and spells. That people expected cures from doctors is shown in an inverted form by one of Hammurabi's curses against anyone who abused his laws.

May Ninkarrak . . . inflict upon him in his body a grievous malady,
an evil disease, a serious injury which never heals,
whose nature no physician knows,
which he cannot allay with bandages,
which like a deadly bite cannot be rooted out . . .

(Ninkarrak was a goddess normally concerned with healing whose cult centre was at Isin. This city probably had a well-known medical school. We shall find a medical impostor claiming to come from there.)

Large numbers of texts concerned with medical practices have been found. Most of them are written in Akkadian and come from Assur and Assurbanipal's library at Nineveh. It is evident, however, that they represent a tradition deriving from the Old Babylonian period, which probably saw the greatest developments in medicine as it did also in mathematics. Yet the Sumerians had made a strong beginning. As it happens, only one substantial medical text and a fragment of another have come to light from Sumerian times, but they are enough to prove that there were already a well established *materia medica* and methods of treatment.

As various quotations have already shown, illness was generally attributed to divine displeasure or to possession by demons and ghosts. As such, the causes were seen as sins and mistakes in religious observances committed knowingly or in ignorance, and the cures consisted in pacifying the gods and driving away the evil visitors and securing the return of protective spirits. On the other hand the practical side of man's thinking suggested that something could be done to treat the actual physical symptoms of the sufferer. To meet these two quite different demands for the curing of illness, two distinct types of medical practitioner had their places in society.

There was the divining and omen-interpreting physician, the *asipu*, who foretold the patient's fate from signs, and the practical doctor, the *asu*, who worked with a handbook listing symptoms for every part of the body and appropriate doses and treatments for their cure.

The division is not so intellectually simple as might be supposed. It was the *asipu* who seems to have observed the patient's symptoms most objectively and individually—concerning himself with his pulse (though not understanding what made it), his temperature, the colour of his blood. It is in fact from the *asipu*'s texts that we have learnt most anatomical and physiological terms. Yet the *symptoms* were studied as *omens* on a par with such particulars as the time of day and the date. At the same time, while, as we shall see, the *asu* used a number of effective drugs among his 'simples', their working may very well have been regarded as in a sense magical, not to be distinguished from the supposed potency of ingredients similar to those used by Macbeth's witches or from the prescriptions and actions based on sympathetic magic. Akkadian medical omen texts of the type appropriate to the *asipu* circulated in large classified collections. The items, of which there were many hundreds, usually began, 'When the exorcist goes to the house of a sick man'— the chief exception being the few concerned with gynaecology. Although some of the maladies are ascribed to such natural causes as cold and dust, the majority are caused by supernatural interventions. The usual way to signify these sickness omens was to say 'Hand of' a god great or small, of a demon or human ghost. A typical example is: 'If the penis and epigastrum of a man are hot, if he has a fever, if the lower part of his body pains him and his belly is tempestuous . . . this man is suffering from a venereal disease. Hand of Ishtar.'

The treatments undertaken or recommended by the *asipu* are not precisely known. They probably included conjurations and magic rituals. Presumably if these things failed grosser forms of magic, such as the use of demon images, might be resorted to, or, on a higher mental, and perhaps social, plane, to religious supplications on Job-like lines.

In contrast the treatments of the *asu* might be called cut-and-dried—if they were not in fact often very damp and messy. The scores of items in his handbook might be arranged according to the parts of the body affected or to the symptoms. The majority of individual items had three parts: the symptoms, the *materia medica* and the method of treatment.

The Sumerian tablet from Nippur, dated to the last quarter of the third millennium B.C. and therefore the oldest known pharmacopoeia in the world, omits the symptoms. It contains fifteen prescriptions, five of them with the directions 'fasten as a poultice', three in which the simples are to be infused in beer and drunk, and four that include washing the affected part with an elaborately prepared solution, sometimes rubbing with oil and covering with ashes or other dry stuff. One of this last category gives a good idea of the blending of chemistry and fancy:

Prescription No. 13. Pour water over a dried and powdered water snake, the *amamashumkaspal*-plant, roots of thorn plant, powdered *naga* [a plant yielding alkali], powdered fir turpentine, faeces of bat, after having heated, with this liquid wash [the affected spot] and after having washed with the liquid rub with oil and cover with *shaki*.

One of the most interesting things about this Sumerian tablet—which applies also to the single prescription on the broken specimen—is that in spite of the use of such ingredients as powdered water snakes, it was essentially rational, without any mention of intervening gods and demons. Although the evidence is insufficient, it looks very much as though the Sumerian *asu*, whose calling as we have seen went back to very early dynastic times, developed the practical tradition of the treatment of symptoms, and that the tradition of the *asipu*, together with the whole omen-reading obsession, was largely due to Akkadian and Amorite influence.

As for the very numerous later tripartite *asu* texts, often referred to as the *Summa Amelu* books because each item begins with these words meaning 'When a man' (is suffering from . . .), some are rational in the same sense as the Sumerian specimens. The following compressed example refers to a lung complaint—possibly pneumonia:

When a man is being devoured by pain in his breast, his epigastrum and his belly, he is ill in his lungs. If he is hot and coughs, has sputum, spittle . . . and water stand in his breast . . . the breath of his mouth is difficult. When a man's epigastrum burns and the saliva of his mouth pricks [?], when his spittle has blood he has reached the crisis.

The man with the lung disease should have mustard, emmer grains and malt ground and mixed with oil spread on a skin and bound on his chest and abdomen. He will get better. [After naming several more herbs for further treatment the prescription ends, 'He shall drink fine beer and will become healthy.']

Other handbook prescriptions may contain magical elements, though they were never dominant.

The *asu's materia medica* was very largely of vegetable origin; indeed the same word, *sammu*, was sometimes used for both plant and medicine. Many of the plants were therapeutic and have remained in use until today. The *asu's* bag contained such narcotics as opium, hemp, belladonna, mandragore and the potent water-hemlock. He might also give camomile for stomach upsets, mustard water as an emetic, and mustard seed as a laxative. He also used the versatile but dangerous hellebore—for what purposes we do not know. All this is enough to show that the practitioners inherited a pharmacopoeia based on generations of empirical observation. On the other hand it was used uncritically; many different ingredients were put together and it would be a rare doctor who knew which caused a reaction, which could never be more than placebos. As well as vegetable, there were animal ingredients, the majority of which we should consider non-effective or magical—such as the powdered watersnake already encountered, powdered tortoiseshell and the like. The minerals employed were mostly of the same sort—such as powdered copper and lapis lazuli—but also included salt and bitumen oil. The liquids that often served as vehicles for the other ingredients may have had more effect on the patient's health and spirits than the 'drugs' themselves: milk and honey were nourishing, while the beer and wine so often recommended made for a sense of well-being and gratitude.

Treatments, too, must have been quite helpful: especially the poulticing, bandaging and rubbing with oil. Practitioners were able to give oil enemas as well as emetics.

Medical texts hardly refer to surgery. Yet the laws of Hammurabi decree payments for successful surgery and punishment, cutting off a hand, for causing death or the loss of an eye. The laws mention 'major operations' and opening up the eye socket, all to be done with a bronze lancet, also the setting of bones and the healing of sprained tendons. The inclusion of these items in the national laws suggests that surgery was not so unusual as the dearth of texts might suggest. Archaeologically a lancet probably could not be distinguished from barbers' or other knives. Today there is a tradition that surgeons are less couth than physicians. It is just conceivable that there were specialist surgeons in Mesopotamia who had not attended the *edubba,* or at least were not far advanced in the scribal art. It is surprising that there is no mention of military surgeons in a land where war wounds must have been common.

Childbirth was largely a matter for midwives and no doubt involved a mixture of experienced skill and magic. Well-to-do women might consult the medical diviners, and the medical omen texts already quoted do in fact end with a section dealing with pregnant women and new-born babies. They include some delightful literary lines—'The child must fall out and see the light; this is the storm; may the ship be sound, may the ship be well guided . . . the ship at the Quay of Life'. There is also a spell to be recited concerning the childbirth of one Enzuma, who was to bear a child begotten by the moon god and was visited by two goddesses bearing oil and water 'to prevent the pains'. They stroked her forehead with oil and sprayed her whole body with water, and 'the boy fell like a young gazelle to the ground'. The spell ends, 'As this maid Enzuma bore her child normally, so may this maid in labour bear her child.' The woman herself was, of course, sprayed and rubbed with oil—and in the oil were various things that could fall readily, and also pot-sherds—because 'her waters should not remain, as it does not in a broken vessel.' In a difficult birth the mother was to fast and drink beer infused with herbs—probably solanum and houndstongue—'She will give birth rapidly.'

These texts do not conform with either the medical omens or the *asu*'s handbooks. Is it possible that they originated among women practitioners of midwifery? There is a single record of a woman doctor. She was attached to a court in Old Babylonian times.

The social position and way of life of doctors probably varied much as they do today. It is doubtful whether they or their calling were ever held in such high esteem as they were in Egypt or in Greece. The most ambitious would seek for places at court. We have the personal seal and votive inscriptions of an *asu* of Lagash who held an important position under Gudea's son. Letters contain many references to court physicians, but from later Assyrian times they were never called *asu* but *asipu* or other titles for diviner or exorcist. It has been suggested that the *asu* lost status after Babylonian times, and this would be in harmony with the idea that his tradition was Sumerian, the *asipu*'s Semitic. Perhaps it was simply that the old name was dropped. We do not know enough to judge.

The court physicians not only attended the king, his family and harem, but were often sent off by their royal master to tend sick officials and send back reports on their health. Occasionally they were even sent to foreign courts where there was sickness—missions that must have added to their own prestige, as well as that of their king and country.

Other doctors had, of course, to be content with less exalted patients. The laws of Hammurabi decree a range of fees for the gentleman, the 'member of the commonalty' and the gentleman's slave. The gentleman was in fact to pay his surgeon ten shekels for operating on him himself, five shekels for bone-setting and tendon healing and two shekels for any of these services performed for his slave. The commoner's fees were five and three shekels in place of the gentleman's ten and five. There is no way of telling whether the same individual might attend on all three levels—but the social likelihoods of all ages point against it. (Hammurabi's laws also make one of the rare mentions of a vet or 'ox and ass doctor'. His fee was by far the lowest, and so too, no doubt, was his social standing.)

As for medical etiquette, we have seen that the *asipu* invariably went to the home of his patients, and there is no reason to doubt that the *asu* did also. When the protagonist of *The Poor Man of Nippur* wanted to disguise himself as a doctor from Isin, he shaved his head and armed himself with a libation jar and censer. If it were not that the pretended treatment was for cuts and bruises, this equipment would seem to prove he was playing the part of an *asipu*. As it is, it looks as though the *asu* also sought to please the gods. The *asu* is known to have carried a bag for his herbs, bandages and other remedies. Presumably the contents of his handbooks he carried in his head.

MUSIC, LITERATURE AND HISTORY

ALTHOUGH IT WAS ONCE THE CUSTOM TO WRITE HISTORY LARGELY in terms of kings, battles and politics, for which economics and social affairs have now been substituted, most of us in fact think of past civilizations in terms of their art and architecture, their music and literature. They provide us with our inner image, our composite mental portrait, of each culture and civilization. The reason is, of course, that while facts, however remarkable, appeal only to the intellect and are devoid of life, the arts stir our imaginative feelings and are conjured up instantly for the inner eye and ear. Their profound importance must not be forgotten even in a book of this kind where little space can be given to them.

Probably the art which meant most in the everyday life of men and women of all classes was music. That it was considered important by thinkers must surely be proved by the places allotted to it among the *mes*. Court patronage from early times is reflected in the lavishness of the instruments at Ur and their burial with the royal dead. We know from several literary references that there was music and dancing as a regular feature of the public square. Perhaps they were performed partly by local professionals, partly by visiting groups, as happens, for example, in the famous market place at Moroccan Marrakesh. It seems more than likely, though we have no direct evidence for it, that there was plenty of singing, strum-

ming, piping in the ale and wine houses. Both singing and instrumental music were an important part of the temple services,
including a musical accompaniment to the divine meals. This temple
usage of music while you dine was a reflection of a custom that
must have begun in wealthy circles in Sumeria and lasted ever
since. On the so-called 'standard' of Ur, itself almost certainly the
sounding box of a stringed instrument, the king and his entourage
are drinking while a man plays the lyre and a woman sings. Nearly
two thousand years later the strings are still being plucked as
Assurbanipal and his queen dine together in the palace gardens at
Nineveh. Martial music does not seem to have been so usual as
might be expected, but trumpets were in use by the army.

A wide range of instruments had already been devised in Sumerian
times. Percussion was represented by drums of many types and
sizes up to the huge temple kettle-drums that might measure five
feet across. These were often played by two men with drum sticks,
and their note was likened to the bellowing of bulls. Timbrels were
also used for temple music as an accompaniment to hymns and
liturgies. The sistrum was known in the Early Dynastic period, but
does not seem to have maintained the popularity that it always had
in Egypt and the Mediterranean. Wind instruments included three-
holed reed flutes held vertically and blown across the top. They
were considered to make joyful music for either secular or religious
occasions: Gudea told a temple director of music 'to cultivate flute-
playing with diligence and to fill the forecourt of Eninnu with joy.'
It was also sounded with love songs, yet no one seems to have
accused the performers of arousing lasciviousness as the angel was
to blame the flute-players of Sodom. Pipes single and then double
were also being played in very early days. They were four-holed,
made of reed, wood or metal and blown with the vibrating reed
between the lips. Curved trumpets, of actual bull's horn or metal,
were very much temple instruments and must have helped to make
an awe-inspiring roar when played together with the kettle-drum to
produce 'full music'. The straight military trumpet may have been
of foreign origin and introduced only in the second millennium.

Anyone thinking of Sumerian music is likely to give first place to
the harp and lyre. The exquisite specimens that Leonard Woolley
extricated with appropriate delicacy from the Royal Cemetery of Ur
make an unforgettable impression with their rich colouring and
strongly imaginative design. Two main forms of harp were popular,

one bow-shaped, of primitive origin, but often splendidly elaborated, and another more rectangular. The largest harp found at Ur was of the 'bow' form, stood three feet six inches high, and had eleven strings and a sound-box embellished with a calf's head in gold. (The invention of the harp was attributed to the god Enlil, and his instrument, too, bore the head of a golden calf.) This harp must have been heard in palatial rooms at Ur. Two of a commoner sort are shown on small ceramic plaques of the early second millennium —one held horizontally by a standing player, the other vertically by a man sitting on a folding stool. Each has seven strings, and this was a common number; four, five, eleven (as at Ur) and twenty-one are also known from actual specimens.

The true lyre, with two arms, crossbar and strings stretched over a bridge on the sound box, was a much-loved instrument, being often used as an accompaniment to the human voice. Known ex amples had seven, eight or eleven strings but some in pictures have fewer. Lyres in popular use were quite small, but the Ur cemetery revealed how large and splendid those could be that were played at court or in the mansions of the great. In one of the most splendid the sound-box ended in a bull's head in gold and lapis lazuli. Among the scenes inlaid in shell on the ends of the box is one with a donkey playing on a gigantic lyre, while a jackal performs with sistrum and timbrel. A quite different, and musically more interesting, rela-tionship between instruments and animals was revealed in the death pit at Ur where three ladies had been buried, or sat down to die, their fingers on the strings of their lyres. One of the lyres re-presented a bull, another a heifer and the third a stag. In a number of texts the sound of the lyre is again likened to the bellowing of a bull, and this makes it appear very probable indeed that these lyres, evidently played together, were of different tones. Whether this implies any theoretical understanding of harmony it is impossible to tell.

Apart from the animal musicians, there are few early representa-tions of different instruments being played together, but they surely were on both jolly and solemn occasions. There are various Assyrian reliefs showing groups of court musicians, including one in which four men are playing the harp, the lyre and two double pipes.

Attempts to read part of an eighth century hymn tablet from Assur as musical notation have led to nothing but ludicrously contra-dictory interpretations of the nature of Mesopotamian music. On the other hand the evidence of the instruments themselves is enough to suggest that the Mesopotamians used their knowledge of mathematics to create a more subtle system of notes than anything achieved by the Egyptians. Leonard Woolley wrote:

It was the Mesopotamians . . . who decided on a geometric progression whereby in music the distances of stopping are increased proportionately. Having observed that stopping at ½, ⅓ and ¼ of the entire length resulted respectively in the three principal intervals they logically went a step further and accepted the stopping at ⅕ as producing the major third and that at ⅙ as producing the minor third. It was the divisive principle, which would not have occurred to the Egyptians.

It is impossible, for the present, to go further; we cannot conjure sounds from the dust. Was it perhaps because lyres so often sounded together with words that the finest were decorated with mythological scenes and (if the 'standard' is indeed the sound-box of one of them) with heroic subjects of war, victory and peace? Perhaps, and this leads at once to an important question concerning the formative stages of Sumerian literature.

In the Sumeria of the third millennium B.C. the art of written literature was born. No doubt for very long before that man's image-making mind had been creating stories of the gods or god-like heroes and perhaps also of more local chiefs and war leaders. As time went by the bards who must have been mainly responsible for passing on such tales probably gave greater formality alike to the episodes and to their use of rhythm, word music and poetic imagery. But while all had depended on memory, tongue, ear and vibrations in the intervening air, creative shaping could not go far and much might be lost through the destruction of communities and the deaths of individuals. Now at last there were letters to pin down the sound of words, and oral tradition could become literature.

The question raised by the lyre is how far the *nar*, the Sumerian bard or minstrel, contributed to this literature, and in particular whether he provided elements that were incorporated in the Gilgamesh and other epic works. Professor Kramer, who has taken so heavy a share in the immense labour of identifying, assembling, and translating the precious tablets by which the world's first great literature survives, has no doubt that the *nar* was 'a key figure in the growth and development' of the literary tradition of Sumeria.

Although there has been some opposition to this idea, it seems inherently probable. Several Sumerian Gilgamesh episodes were certainly woven into the long and magnificent poem written in Akkadian and preserved at Nineveh which is what people generally have in mind when they refer to the *Epic of Gilgamesh*. These Sumerian poems, the finest and most substantial called *Gilgamesh in the Land of the Living*, are known only from texts dating from the first half of the second millennium, yet they have far older origins. The same is true of the other Sumerian epic tales concerning the heroes Enmerkar and Lugalbanda, both of them (according to the *King List*) predecessors of Gilgamesh as kings of the first dynasty of Uruk. There must have been some living tradition to link the written epics with the lives and reigns of the royal heroes. What is more likely than that *nars*, finding patronage at the courts, transmitted the tales until the time that they could begin to be written down, woven together and given literary style?

It is true that the obvious parallel with the bards of Mycenaean Greece and the composition of the Homeric epics should not be pushed too far. Sumerian courts, set in cities and in early days dominated by the temples and strongly theocratic beliefs, differed considerably from the humbler, more secular royal houses of Bronze Age Greece, where the northern barbarian tradition of the warlord and his band of followers must still have counted for much and a religious hierarchy for very little. Yet there was also much in common: the small kingdoms, the courts that must have been in touch with one another, the rival kings who loved to go to war. It seems probable that the Sumerian rulers, like the Greek, loved to have their deeds and those of their half-forgotten ancestors celebrated by bards who sang or recited to the lyre while they themselves ate and drank at leisure.

In style the Sumerian epics have much in common with the Greek: fixed epithets, long repetitions, detailed descriptions and reported speeches. In content there is the same concentration on the fortunes of individual heroes, but there are also fundamental differences. Not only do they have far less individual characterization, but they lack the essential rationality and humanity of the Homeric tradition, the heroes seem not quite human and their adventures are more profoundly affected by mythical forms—descents to a weird underworld, symbolic dreams, battles with monsters, mystic birds, the flood, the visit to the Dilmun 'paradise' and so forth. These distinctions would seem to be appropriate to the social differences already defined, and most directly to the greater dominance both of religious organization and of mythico-religious modes of thought. To put it another way, it could be said that the Sumerian epics are far more deeply permeated by elements rising from the unconscious mind and therefore closer to the myths where these elements are supreme.

One of the greatest difficulties in the way of studying the literature of Mesopotamia is that so much of it comes to us from late copies and redactions. Again and again in the course of this book some such phrase as 'but must be of far earlier origin' has followed a textual reference. The greater part of the five thousand or so literary tablets so far discovered either date from the opening centuries of the second millennium or had been copied for Assurbanipal's library. It is impossible to know when many of the works were first composed or written down, or how much they had been modified in the course of time. On the whole, however, research has tended to push back their origins and to emphasize the remarkable conservatism of a tradition that persisted through all the upheavals of Mesopotamian history. Although fluency and style might be improved in the second millennium, an astonishing proportion of the forms and content of the literature sprang from the creative energy of the Sumerians.

It is thought that cuneiform was sufficiently advanced for the first literary works to have been written down by 2500 B.C., but the earliest to have been found is a myth of Enlil and Ninhursag dating from about a century later; a second, fragmentary, myth concerning Enlil's son lost in the underworld was written about a century later again. Although neither can be fully read, they come close enough to later myths in style and construction to show that the conservative tradition of Mesopotamian literature went back to the beginning of expressive writing.

There is every reason to suppose that there was an increased output of Sumerian literary works during the last centuries of the third millennium when the *edubbas* were many and flourishing. At present the only substantial literary text surviving from this period is the long hymnal poem celebrating Gudea's building of the Eninnu temple of Lagash. It was probably composed by an Eninnu poet during the Third Dynasty of Ur. We can hope that more tablets inscribed at this time will one day be unearthed. We know that after the fall of the Third Dynasty the scribal schools were zealous in copying and revising the old texts, a scholarly activity that continued in Old Babylonian times. Although by now, of course, Akkadian had become the spoken language of the country, the scribes not only copied the old compositions in Sumerian but wrote more of their own. At the same time Akkadian literature was being created. The *Epic of Gilgamesh*, which, in spite of its incorporation of Sumerian episodes, was virtually a new and far finer creation, was probably first composed quite early in the second millennium. Among other major works the creation epic, *Enuma elish*, may not have been very much later. Indeed it seems that the Mesopotamians had already written most of their outstanding literature by the end of the Old Babylonian period. There were, of course, some later compositions, probably including the unique popular story known as *The Poor Man of Nippur*, *The Lord of Wisdom* poem and the *Pessimistic Dialogue Between Master and Servant*. Assyrian kings, too, left accounts of their campaigns and victories that had literary merit.

The main groupings of Sumerian and Akkadian literature were the myths of the gods; the epic tales where kings and other heroes mingled with their divinities; hymns, mostly addressed to gods and their temples but also to kings during the divinizing Third Dynasty of Ur and the succeeding period of Isin; lamentations and elegies of a more or less historical kind; the wisdom literature consisting mainly of collections of precepts and proverbs but also including the disputations and the 'Job' type compositions. Most of these works were composed in poetic form. Rhyme, alliteration and regular metre were not used, but the rhythmic structure of the line, with its well marked caesura, was carefully controlled and sometimes, as in the *Gilgamesh* epic, there was a division into stanzas. The poetic effect was heightened by such devices as the balance of opposites—say that of heaven against earth—refrains, and by a use of similes that were sometimes of brilliance and beauty. These were the arts of the poet, but much of the poetic quality emanates from the universal sense that all living and being were animated by the divine. It seems that it was only in the late period of such works as *The Poor Man of Nippur* and the *Pessimistic Dialogue* that Mesopotamian authors could be prosaic.

Enough has already been quoted from almost all these literary categories to give as much idea of their character as the obstacles of decipherment and translation allow. It is unfortunately far more difficult to relate them to the societies among which they were composed, written down, read, recited and listened to. Extraordinarily little is known about their authorship or how or where they were enjoyed.

Of one thing we can be reasonably sure: this was not a private literature. Although it would be rash to say that such a scene was impossible, we need hardly picture professional men or others adept in the scribal art reclining on their couches with tablets from their own libraries piled on the table beside them silently reading some work of national literature. Both in its composition and its reception Sumerian and Akkadian literature was a social undertaking.

The problem of how much the bard contributed to its origins has already been discussed. If anything was known about the relationship between the *nar* and the *edubba* this problem might be solved, for such evidence as there is points to the scribal schools as becoming the centres of literary creation as well as copying and study. Most of the texts other than those from Assurbanipal's national collection have come to light in what appear to be scribal quarters and not in the temples or palaces. Kramer has suggested: '. . . some of the graduates of the *edubba* specialized in religious compositions and went into the service of the temple to teach its singers and musicians and supervise and conduct the cult liturgies, while others, specializing in myths and epic tales, went into the service of the palace to train and instruct the court singers and entertainers.'

On the question of the occasions when any of the more important works were to be heard, the only certain information we have is that in later times at least the creation epic was recited during the New Year festival. It is not implausible that some of the other myths were similarly related to the religious calendar. Hymns must, of course, have been intended for temple services and perhaps the lamentations also. What one would most like to know was whether a predominantly secular masterpiece such as the Akkadian *Gilgamesh* was ever recited to popular audiences in the cities or whether it was heard only in courts and princely houses. The Gilgamesh story certainly had a wide appeal, for copies taken from it have been found as far apart as Hattusas, Ugarit and Megiddo.

Many authorities speak of the *reading* of the myths and epics, yet is it not unlikely that any performer actually read aloud from cuneiform tablets? It seems far more reasonable to think that even if they had a text before them, priests, court poets and entertainers had really memorized their lines and were reciting them after the manner of actors who perform 'readings' today. It is tempting to guess that the *Dispute,* that peculiar Sumerian device that was maintained, though with less enthusiasm, by the Akkadian writers, may have been dramatically performed by two individuals representing the protagonists—silver and copper, pick axe and plough, cattle and grain, the two graduates and the rest.

Obviously of popular origin as well as popular appeal were the proverbs, of which there were at least a thousand already extant in Sumerian times. The scribes collected them and made them into anthologies—and they provided a favourite exercise for pupils to copy. Yet like our own proverbial sayings they certainly came from the 'wisdom' of ordinary experience. In addition to those quoted there are many with this flavour:

Let what's mine stay unused, but let me use what is yours—this will not endear a man to his friend's household.

Into an open mouth, a fly enters.

The traveller from distant places is an everlasting liar.

A loving heart builds the home; a hating heart destroys the home.

Has she become pregnant without intercourse? Has she become fat without eating?

We can be grateful to the scribes who saved these sayings to remind us of some of the unchanging commonplaces of human affairs. No doubt there were all kinds of fables and stories of the *Poor Man* kind, as well as the songs, mostly love songs, that never got into the scribal canon.

The scribes and scholars of the Sumerian *edubbas* and the schools that followed them were marvellous conservationists, keeping a dead language and its literature current through two millennia. This long-drawn effort represents an exceptional reverence for ancient traditions which is manifest also in most aspects of Mesopotamian culture. Did this go with anything that could be called historical writing or any other expressions of an historian's approach to the past?

Certainly not in the sense of an evolutionary view of what had gone before, or detached observations and speculations of the kind that came with the Greeks and returned with the Renaissance. The

Sumerians' intuition about origins had embued them with a faith in man's creation by and for the gods, and so there could be no need to conceive an historical development of the 'black-headed people'. Against an eternal background of field and canal, of flocks, herds and the turning of the agricultural year, attention was focussed on the doings of kings and the flashes of glory or disaster.

It was principally great rulers and great disasters that inspired writings about the past. One of the earliest is the short account of the sack of Lagash by Lugalzagesi the Ummaite. It may have been written soon after the event at the behest of Urukagina—who seems to have survived his overthrow. More interesting is the powerful poem now known as *The Curse of Agade* on the fall of Akkad before the Gutians. It was composed by a Sumerian poet several centuries after the invasion and is exceptional in seeking an explanation for an historical event—although the cause was inevitably recognized in religious sacrilege. Beside this *Curse* might be set the relatively prosaic account of Utuhengal's defeat of the Gutians. Then there are the lamentations for the fall of Ur and of Nippur, but these are literary works almost devoid of historical purpose. Outstanding among the writings about great men were the largely legendary tales woven by later bards and poets round the name of Sargon the Great.

There are two other large and loosely defined groups of documents that reveal the Mesopotamians' concern for historical events, if not for the reconstruction of the past. One might be said to be derived from the scribes' fondness for lists and ordering, the other from the kings' sense of the importance of their acts—a conviction which was shared by their educated subjects. This latter group represents an interest in posterity rather than in the past, yet a desire to be known to posterity implies a certain kind of historical susceptibility.

First among the scribal compilations must come the famous *Sumerian King List*. It is believed that all versions of this derive from one written in the time of Utuhengal, but the list was extended down to about 1950 B.C. This document shows an unmistakable interest in chronology and chronological order, but for us a curious attitude to time. How could scholars compose a chronicle the greater part of which sets out historical reigns more or less correctly, but which merges into a pre-Flood dream world where eight reigns span a quarter of a million years? Merely to ask the question presumes a critical attitude hardly appropriate to the age in any circumstances,

and certainly not to thoughts about the days when 'kingship descended from heaven'. While the *Sumerian King List* was mainly
concerned with a supposed sequence of reigns and included only a
few scattered references to historical and mythical happenings, some
of its successors, such as the *Sargon Chronicle*, gave more space to
memorable events. Between them the Babylonian and Assyrian king
lists cover their ages almost completely. One provides a synchronous
tabulation setting out Babylonian kings and their Assyrian contemporaries side by side. Here and there it even enters the names of
viziers beside those of their royal masters.

Another scribal involvement with chronology began as an aid to
practical administration but came to have historical meaning. The
necessity of identifying calendar years has always arisen within
literate civilizations and has been met in various ways. This was the
first time it had been felt, and the Sumerians and Babylonians met
it by the rather clumsy device of naming years after political and
religious events. The king's public works and votive offerings, his
campaigns and victories, inevitably predominate, but such things as
rebellions and invasions might find a place. To enable themselves to
refer back over extended periods, the scribes drew up long lists of
year names, in this way creating brief annals of a limited kind. The
Assyrian system was different. Instead of events they named their
years after important state officials.

A unique Sumerian document can be mentioned here because it,
too, exemplifies the scribal concern for chronological order. Extending from well back in the Early Dynastic period down to the reign of
Ishbi-Erra, it records the names of kings who built and repeatedly
restored the Tummal sanctuary of Ninlil at Nippur. It is proving to
be of value to modern historians, but the purposes of the compiler
are obscure.

The scribes were, of course, great archivists, but a more lively
understanding of matters of historical moment may be manifest in
the fact that significant letters exchanged between kings and their
officials were taken into the scribal canon and copied in the *edubbas*.
Though some is earlier, the most important part of this royal correspondence dates from the Third Dynasty of Ur.

Coming now to the second group of documents, we are confronted
by a vast range of royal inscriptions. They are of the most various
lengths and written on the most various objects. They appear on
vessels of pottery or precious metals, on door sockets, maceheads,

bricks, clay prisms, cones and 'nails' as well as on tablets, statues in both stone and metal, steles and native rock. Many of them were dedicatory texts supposed to be addressed by the ruler to his god telling him of his achievements and asking long life and prosperity in reward. Very many of the actual inscriptions that have come down to us were never intended for human eyes but were hidden in walls and below foundations of the dedicated temples and palaces. (Some of these hidden inscriptions, however, were expressly intended to be read by future kings engaged in rebuilding. Nabonidas, as we know, did in fact read such texts at Ur.) Yet the writings on these dedicatory cones, bricks and other carriers were in no consistent way different from those on steles and statues intended to be exposed to view. For example, Entemena's informative account of the war between Umma and Lagash and Urukagina's detailed proclamation of his reforms were alike inscribed on hidden cones. Except that they are rather shorter, these can well be set beside the Lagash-Umma treaty carved on Eanatum's famous 'Vulture Stele'.

Is it not, in fact, very likely that many of the important hidden inscriptions were counterparts of monumental inscriptions which have been destroyed? Whether or not the writings on steles and statues were intended to be generally read, they were certainly intended not only to secure the goodwill of the god but also to proclaim the king's name, his victories, buildings and other achievements to posterity. In a sense one can say that the dedicator was there-in-himself, a living presence in stone and word. It was for these reasons that victors who had conquered a city liked to carry off or destroy the monuments of the vanquished. The 'Vulture Stele' expressly refers to the 'whipping out' of stele, and we know from an extraordinary catalogue that a number of royal monuments set up at Nippur have almost certainly disappeared. This is an urge that has been overcome only among the most civilized. How many statues of Queen Victoria have been toppled or smashed throughout the former territories of the British Empire?

The catalogue just mentioned appears to be an expression of antiquarian interest. On a large tablet with fourteen columns on each side a scribe had copied the inscriptions from statues and victory steles set up in Enlil's Ekur temple by Lugalzagesi, Sargon, and two of Sargon's sons. This unknown epigrapher, who was probably at work just after the end of the Sargonid dynasty, noted whether the words appeared on the statue or the pedestal and even that 'the pedestal is uninscribed'. Did he do it from sheer scholarly interest or because he feared the monuments were in danger? Excavations have suggested that they were in fact to be shattered or removed.

All these various types of text and monument, then, show that while the Sumerians, Akkadians and Old Babylonians produced no historians in the modern sense, they were not uninterested in ideas of man in time. Scribes were devoted to chronological ordering and the preservation of archives, including letters and inscriptions; literary men liked to weave historical traditions and the names of past national heroes into their works; kings and other rulers greatly wished to record their achievements for the gods and for human posterity. Although these preoccupations, like all history until recent times, were almost entirely concentrated on kings and wars, some literary texts show a real awareness of the nationhood of the 'blackheaded people' and their involvement in good times and bad.

In later Assyrian and Neo-Babylonian days these historiographical interests advanced a little further towards history. The chronicles and annals of Assyria's monarchs, usually written in the first person, were more formal, often fuller, and less heavily encrusted with religious matter than early records had been. These developments are already on their way in the account of the twelfth century Tiglath-Pileser's campaign in the Levant, but they are more fully established from the ninth century onwards. The story of Assurnasirpal's campaign against Carchemish and Palestine from inscribed slabs at Kalah gives details of all his movements as well as the lists of tribute and booty which became a favourite form of royal boasting. It was immediately followed by the annals of Shalmaneser III, Tiglath-Pileser II and other empire-builders down to Assurbanipal's very long and full record of his wars against Egypt, Syria and Palestine. It would be ungrateful to leave this last great Assyrian king without recalling that, whatever the quality of the historiography of his time, he performed the immense service to modern historians of commissioning agents to collect and copy texts from all over Mesopotamia and to form in his finely decorated palace at Nineveh the first great library of the ancient world. The Neo-Babylonian kings maintained the tradition of the Assyrian chronicles, but on a lower rather than a higher level. They were still being written round about the Esagila and the Ezida when Herodotus came as a visitor to Babylon.

VISUAL ARTS

IN BROAD TERMS IT CAN BE SAID THAT MESOPOTAMIAN ART WAS PRE-
dominantly religious, élitist, anonymous and traditional. This traditionalism is as striking as it is in literature, but here, happily, there
is much less uncertainty about chronology. Compared with Egypt,
rather few works of art have survived, but we know when they were
made.

The upshot is that in this field it can be said with absolute confidence that the spirit, styles and leading art forms were all created
by the Sumerians and maintained by their inheritors. Akkadians and
Babylonians clearly affected the tradition, but there was nothing like
a transformation. The arts developed rapidly in Protoliterate and
Early Dynastic times, perhaps reached their highest point under the
Sargonids, remained on a plateau for several centuries and then
entered a slow decline when too much respect for tradition produced
some stale and imitative work. The imperial age of Assyria saw an
artistic revival. While the vast array of bas-reliefs from the palaces
generally kept to the old subjects, they made a sharper break in
style and technique than anything that had gone before.

While this insistence on continuity of tradition is justified, it is
also true that Mesopotamian art, particularly that of the third
millennium, is more variable within its tradition than is that of Egypt.
There is a wide range in quality and proficiency, while the appearance of odd, unexpected works suggests a greater freedom to
experiment.

The spirit of the original Sumerian art is most of all distinguished
by strength and controlled energy. The human figures, muscular and
sturdy, are shown in a state of arrested movement, yet they convey
an impression of energetic movement waiting release very different
from the graceful passivity of much Egyptian art. The figures on the
Ur 'standard' are pedestrian, but even they are sturdy. When it
comes to the naked priests on the big vase from Uruk, the slightly
later lion hunt from the same city and the Early Dynastic 'Vulture
Stele', the bodily force is palpable. It finds complete expression in
that first great Mesopotamian monster, the lion-headed man now in
the Brooklyn Museum. The way that the sombrely ferocious head is
sunk between shoulders muscled like a Japanese wrestler's, and the

power of the huge arms, are really awe-inspiring. In the beasts carved in high relief on certain stone cups all restraint has been abandoned in a surge of demonic energy.

Nearly all important works of art were made either for the temples or the palaces—and at least in Sumerian times the royal art was as much inspired by religious ideas as was that of the temples themselves. Parrot has said that from prehistoric times 'we shall very rarely find in Mesopotamia a work of art that is not, more or less, a cultic object.' This is true, yet at the same time in expressing a religious vision of life in which the divinities were in human form and divine and everyday human affairs were wholly interpenetrating, artists were able to portray many subjects that were in themselves quite simply secular. There was also the animal art in which from the earliest to their latest days the Mesopotamians excelled.

Like the writers and musicians, the artists worked in anonymity. Very little is known of their conditions, but clearly they enjoyed none of the privilege and institutional backing that the *edubbas* provided for literary and scholastic men. In Sumerian times their status was similar to that of other artisans or craftsmen. They had their guild-like groupings and their workshops in temple and palace. We have seen how in the temple organization at Ur, 'chisel-cutters', jewellers and lapidaries were classified along with carpenters and basket-makers.

In stoneless Sumeria the sculptors could never have had the numbers, status or individual recognition that they attained in Egypt. It does seem likely, however, that as the monarchs became increasingly worldly and given to self-glorification, they would have employed favourite artists, personally known to them and their circle, to carve monumental statues and steles.

The media in which most of the work of Mesopotamian artists has come down to us are shell and ivory inlays, intaglio seals, reliefs and sculptures in the round in stone, bronze and ivory. Painting, before the last millennium B.C., has to be judged almost entirely from the palace of Mari although there were murals, including both animal and human figures, in the Protoliterate temple at Tell Uqair.

The best of the 'cut-outs' proves the remarkable draftsmanship of the Early Dynastic artists. The 'standard' of Ur, though a most interesting approach to narrative art, is relatively uninspired in its drawing, but the animal scenes on the lyre have tremendous charm and style, while some of the little figures from Mari show a brilliant control of line and even a comic sense of characterization. These works would be worthy of first class book illustration in any age, and it is remarkable that such a finished style should have been achieved so early in the history of civilized art. Known specimens come from court contexts, but although these inlays with their lapis and other precious materials were luxuries, it seems likely that any well-to-do citizens might have commanded such possessions.

The miniature art of the seal cutter is of peculiar social as well as aesthetic interest. The idea of making personal identity marks by impressing intaglios on clay sealings began, as we have seen, in Protoliterate times and was later extended to tablets. Seals were thus from the first associated with commerce and quite soon, if not from the first, with private ownership. This association with trade is proclaimed not only by their use in Mesopotamia itself but by the appearance of specimens in Egypt, the Indus and then, in the second millennium, in Mycenaean Greece and the Aegean. Possibly Mesopotamian merchants sometimes entrusted them to their agents in these distant lands. A personal seal remained an essential possession down to the later days of Babylon: Herodotus said of the Babylonians of his day, 'everyone owns a seal'.

As works of art the cylinder seals are full of surprises. It is in the first place surprising that the world's first seal makers should have had the idea of laboriously excising their designs rather than the much easier method of carving them in relief. Then again it is most unexpected that they should have devised the cylinder form rather than the simple stamp that was to be preferred by most other peoples, ancient and modern. The positive impression was, of course, potentially far more beautiful, while the rolled cylinder was well adapted to clay surfaces and could produce the frieze form of picture pleasing to the Sumerians.

Another unexpected feature of the glyptic art is its excellence. The Protoliterate subjects were mostly domestic cattle and wild animals, often heraldically confronted, and simple ritual scenes. Although the human figures are quaint to our eyes, the animals, and particularly the wild deer and goats, are small masterpieces, perfectly modelled, and sometimes full of life and movement. That a perfect contrast of horn and of muscle, an exact rendering of a leaping form, could be scooped out of lapis and other hard material with only bronze tools and without the aid of a magnifying glass appears almost miraculous. Yet it was a seeming miracle that was to be repeated. We shall find that within the Indus civilization the seal cutters were pre-eminent, while in Minoan Crete and Mycenaean Greece they again produced masterpieces. It seems that the challenging difficulty of the medium tended to provoke a most effective response.

The liveliness and naturalism of the earlier Protoliterate seals was followed at the end of the period by a curious disintegration of the realistic animal and human figures into abstract patterns, usually of no great virtue. This decadence has been speculatively identified with cultural upheaval caused by Semitic settlements. By middle Early Dynastic times representation was again in favour, but the free movement of some of the old animal studies was largely replaced by what can best be described as formalized struggle. Bulls, lions, rams, men and combinations of the four engage in standing combat or trials of strength. Often a man stands between two upreared animals apparently subduing them by sheer force of command—in fact the prototype of the 'master of animals' so familiar in Crete and Greece.

The glyptic art reached its height in Sargonid times when intricate scenes of the gods were successfully carved in so small a space. It has been said that they represent the first appearance in history of the dramatic rendering of myth. Cuneiform inscriptions, often including the name of the seal owner, were now added to the design. Towards the end of the third millennium simple presentation scenes in which his personal god is leading the worshipper (presumably the owner) to the divine presence eclipsed all others in popularity. Old Babylonian seals, though often overcrowded, were still fine, but thereafter glyptic art along with the other arts tended to lapse into a stale traditionalism. The Assyrians brought it fresh life and even a return to secular scenes of wild animals and hunting. As for those seals that Herodotus observed every Babylonian to possess, they would mostly have shown religious motifs in the ancient tradition, now often rather tamely conventionalized.

It may be significant that in spite of the worldly purposes for which the seals were used, such a large proportion of them depicted cultic subjects. The same thing is even more conspicuously true of Minoan Crete and Mycenaean Greece, where so much of the other art was secular. Perhaps a man's seal was also his personal amulet, one that he wore perpetually, much as today many Roman Catholics wear holy medals.

While some sculpture, and especially statuary, went into the royal palaces, most of it, in all its many forms, was destined for the temples. It might take the form of architectural embellishment, of movable furnishings, votives, sanctuary 'worshippers' and foundation figurines. Presumably much of the finest work must have gone into the main cult images of the holy of holies, but no single example has survived. The royal monumental steles also seem usually to have stood in the temple precincts, but, like the images, were very liable to be smashed or carried off by conquerors.

The worshipper figures are of interest here because while many were of royalty, high officials and priests, others introduce us to citizens of the middling sort. They have been called portraits, but although they were certainly intended as stand-ins for the individuals who placed them in the sanctuaries, it is very improbable that they were meant to be likenesses.

Attempts have been made to establish an evolutionary sequence of these figures from a highly formalized style to one far more naturalistic. This may to some extent hold good for the Diyala region, but it certainly does not everywhere. It seems rather that the stiff and uncouth sculptures are introducing us to the work of the provincial, journeyman carvers patronized by ordinary citizens, work that does not compare with that done by sculptors attached to a major temple or palace. This is obvious enough in the case of the comically crude Khafajah worshippers, but it can also be recognized in the famous assorted dozen from Tell Asmar. It is true that they have an appeal to our own primitivizing age, and that these men and women with their huge eyes turned up to heaven have a worshipful power. Yet the fact that one among them, a kneeling priest or king, is a work of polished and successful naturalism is surely enough to show that the style of the other owes more to the background of the sculptor than to period.

Among the more naturalistic worshippers, these from the Diyala region and Mari tend to have more sensuousness and vitality than those from the southern cities. The women in particular have the full-blooded brilliance so often to be seen in young Semitic women everywhere. One from the Diyala region with her eager smile and her small breasts just covered by her robe is enchanting, while the blue-eyed singer from the Ishtar temple at Mari—who must have been a dancer too, to judge from her cross-legged posture and short pantaloons—combines great strength with a rare poetic quality.

It is tempting to see in this greater brilliance and vitality in the northern areas the particular Semitic contribution to the high flights of Mesopotamian art in Sargonid times. One of the most remarkable of all these unique and unexpected works that star the traditional course is the bronze head, believed to be that of Sargon himself, found at Nineveh. The complete mastery of technique as well as the creative power of the portraiture make this so exceptional a work of art that critics could not at first believe that it had been made in the twenty-fourth century B.C. This head shows the acceptance of Sumerian cultural tradition in the elaborate chignon hair style that we have seen as far back as Protoliterate days, but there is something in the sensuality and vital immediacy of the face that was not native to Sumerian art.

The complexity of the situation is shown by the fact that Sargon's victory stele, of which only fragments survive, is completely Sumerian in style, subject and composition. Among these steles the change begins with the conqueror's son, Rimush. His monument, though divided into friezes in the old manner, shows a new freedom and fleshy naturalism in its figures, especially those of the naked and helpless foe. This development is completed in the famous stele of Sargon's grandson, Naram-Sin, probably the most widely known piece of Mesopotamian sculpture. The great Akkadian king is portrayed leading his men up a steep, tree-grown mountain slope and routing the enemy, the Lulubi, at the edge of a precipice.

This scene is significant here not only for its freedom and movement and new dramatic sense, the marvellous contrast between the hard, upright, advancing victors and the soft, falling, beseeching vanquished, but also because this at last is a true historical picture. It is an actual battle, the man falling headlong from the cliff suggests even a particular moment in an actual battle, seen in humanist terms. Divine intervention is ignored—or is manifest only in two benign stars, perhaps Shamash and Ishtar, shining above the mountain peak.

If the city of Akkad is found much more may be learnt of this climax in Mesopotamian art. Meanwhile it is satisfactory to see how fully the political revival of Sumeria that followed the fall of the Sargonid dynasty was reflected in the art. Gudea made Lagash the centre of tremendous cultural activity, and the art of his court, as expressed in the thirty known statues of the good *ensi*, is again essentially Sumerian. Something had been taken from Akkad, certainly—some softening in the portrayal of the human face, more individuality and humanity. There was also an improvement in technique that could be fully shown off by the fine-grained dolerite imported for the sculptors.

A superficial yet effective difference was due to changes in men's prevailing fashions in dress. Gone now for good were the short tufted skirts (*kaunakes*), and Gudea was one of the last rulers to be shown clean-shaven. From this time the over-all form of statues was to be monotonously conical, with the long beard leading down to the long robe. But here again is the old sturdiness, austere control, complete arrest of movement. The Sumerian spirit was, of course, maintained when political power returned for the last time to Ur. The huge stele of Ur-Nammu is full of it.

The Old Babylonian period, so distinguished in learning, saw no great changes in the visual arts of the élite. The blended tradition continued to produce decent but uninspired work—such for example as the presentation relief on Hammurabi's own stele of the laws. Some of the best pieces come from Mari. There the palace had given standing room to numbers of sober and even sombre governors and princes. Yet among this traditional stuff, Mari can still spring surprises. There is the snarling fury of the bronze lions guarding the temple of Dagan, and the magnificence of the 'goddess with the flowing vase'. This lady, who combines nobility with voluptuousness, and seems to proclaim a continuance of Semitic vitality, had been provided with a tanked supply so that real fertilizing waters could stream down her skirt from her firmly held vase.

It is known that foreign princes sought to come to Mari for the educational benefits the palace could provide. Its great parade of courts and of statue-set and brightly frescoed rooms must have been immensely impressive. The one large mural to have survived is stiff in its ritual scenes and symbolic beasts, but the huge trees that flank them are highly decorative and professional. Moreover, a fragmented painting of an ox-sacrifice is far more powerful. It seems, then, that by the second millennium the work of the brush-wielders may have equalled that of the chisel-cutters.

Where there was a significant change in Old Babylonian art was in the appearance, appropriate to a more secular society, of popular subjects of work and play modelled on small clay plaques. Here in a friendly, relaxed style the artists showed musicians, entertainers

Mural from palace of Mari; early second millennium B.C.

with monkeys, boxers, carpenters and in one instance a peasant riding on a zebu ox.

No bold artistic innovation could be expected from the recently barbarian Kassites who were doing their best to maintain the cultural traditions of the civilization they had conquered. Animal art remained at a high level, but perhaps their greatest service to art and architecture was the invention, usually attributed to them, of reliefs in moulded brick. In this technique a small part of the relief subject was moulded on one face of each brick, so that the whole could be fitted together as the wall was built. It was to have its finest display, the brick faces now coloured and glazed, in the bulls and dragons of the Ishtar gate at Babylon.

All that can be said here of the revival of monumental sculpture under the Assyrians was that it was all that would be expected of an imperialist age and that its greatest development was that of a fully narrative art. From the days of Assurnasirpal by way of Sargon at Sharrukin and Kalah down to Assurbanipal at Nineveh the subject of this palace art was the vaunting of royal might through warfare, big game hunting, rites and ceremonies and palace building. Warfare is overwhelmingly predominant, with countless scenes of marches, river crossings, sieges, sackings, battles, the trampling of enemies and the impalement, mutilation and torture of prisoners.

Although a few are in repoussé on bronze doors, nearly all these scenes appear in low relief on huge slabs of 'alabaster' and were originally completely over-painted. The main palace gateways were protected from evil visitors by vast decorous monsters assorted of man, lion, bull and bird. It seems that the Assyrians took over both the guardians and the slab-linings not directly from their Mesopotamian inheritance but from the Hittites whom they had met for so long in both trade and war. The amount of labour involved in cutting and carrying the stone as well as in the sculpture itself was of course immense and probably could only have been undertaken by a power able to employ thousands of enslaved prisoners of war. In a scene in Sennacherib's palace at Nineveh, Phoenician and Lachisite slave gangs are shown hauling one of the colossi destined for a gateway of that same palace. The king looks on from above and taskmasters brandish their rods.

This is a narrative art in the sense that scene follows scene exactly as in a strip cartoon. In the ninth century each episode tended to occupy its own slab, but in later works they spread freely into extensive landscapes with human activity set against a lifelike background of city, mountain or marsh. The sculptor would often add familiar details—such as the *shaduf* user in the scene of the colossus. In this way, and because the actual servants and victims of the kings of Assyria were immensely various, these products of military imperialism have left us with more vivid pictures of human life than anything that had gone before.

Something must be said concerning the famous lion hunt from Nineveh. It is an experience to compare this highly accomplished product of the last centuries of Mesopotamian power with the earliest rendering of the subject on the Uruk stele of two thousand years before. The kings with their drawn bows have not changed very much, but whereas the old ruler confronted wild beasts, Assurbanipal's are captive, released from cages for his pleasure. Consciously or unconsciously the sculptor had been so much moved by the sights of the hunt, by these battling, wounded and slaughtered animals, that it was to them he lent his sympathy, to them he imparted a royal greatness. Assurbanipal and his minions look insignificant. Then, as at most times, society allowed artists little wealth, position or name, but these masters of the undying image were not without power.

In the brightly decorated Assyrian palaces, courtiers could rest on chairs, couches and beds ivory-pale or overlaid with gold. These exquisite ivories demand attention partly because they prove the consistent luxury of the palaces, but more for the contrast they present to the sculpture in stone. The palace reliefs were violently chauvinistic, the palace furniture was light-heartedly eclectic, the work of artists happy to play with the styles and motifs of various cultures. Though some of them may have been natives, others were Syrians and Phoenicians who either sold their products to the Assyrian courts or themselves went to work there. These Levantines particularly liked to work in the Egyptian mode, though with a subtle feminizing of its forms. Carved on this furniture from the banks of the Tigris (most surviving specimens come from Kalah) are Egyptian gods and goddesses, falcons, sphinxes, lotus designs and even curious hieroglyphs. Here, against a martial background, were the overripe but still delicious fruits of 'fin de siècle' civilization.

The Babylonian kings in their last century of glory do not seem to have been much affected by Assyrian palace styles. There were sculptured lions at the gates of Babylon, but Nebuchadnezzar's throne room, like the Ishtar gate and processional way, was enriched with animal friezes in moulded and glazed brick. The colours were clear and the intention purely decorative. Astonishingly little is known of contemporary works of art or of the style of the priceless treasure in precious stones and metals that filled palace and temples.

In the open courts of his palace Nebuchadnezzar set up a collection of foreign and ancient sculpture. There were some Hittite carving, Assyrian bas-reliefs and steles, and many fine statues from Mari, mostly dating from the early second millennium. Many of these pieces were war booty and put on display partly for that reason. Nevertheless, the collection seems to have been formed with something of the museum spirit behind it. Patriotic pride in the Babylonian past must have encouraged traditionalism; as it did also the restoration of the architectural inheritance of the southern cities which the kings of Babylon undertook with enthusiasm. There was a deliberately archaizing school of art. A good example is the stele commemorating the restoration of the temple of Shamash at

Sippar by the seventh century king Nabu-apalidina. This presentation scene imitated old forms so painstakingly and so nearly successfully that Hammurabi himself would have found it only a little odd.

PART V

THE INDUS CIVILIZATION

AT ITS GREATEST EXTENT THE CULTURE REPRESENTING THE INDUS
civilization prevailed over a far larger area than the states of Mesopotamia or the Kingdom of Egypt. This culture, often referred to as
the Harappan, is so coherently organized and so nearly uniform in
all its elements that it has always appeared right to assume that the
area covered was in fact a state controlled by a centralized government. This was certainly true of the two main areas surrounding
Harappa and Mohenjo-daro. It would also appear to be true of the
north-western area extending coastwise through the Makran where
Harappan sites now some distance inland were probably ports involved with the trade along the Persian Gulf. On the other hand the
south-western area, the Saurashtran, extending down to the south
side of the Gulf of Cambay, may well be largely a secondary extension from the north always containing an admixture of other
cultural elements, and possibly—though this can be no more than
a guess—not so strictly controlled by central government. Yet even
here the port of Lothal at the head of the Gulf of Cambay was in
every way a typical Harappan town, and if its huge burnt-brick
enclosure was indeed a dock for shipping, it too must have played
an important part in the maritime trade.

It is a striking fact that while so much is known about the life
and the history of the peoples of Mesopotamia and Egypt that
twenty volumes would still only summarize it, a single lean book

can tell all that is known of the vast Indus civilization beyond historically and humanly insignificant archaeological detail. The first reason for this contrast is, quite simply, that far less digging has been done at Indus sites. This being so, it must be remembered that anything claimed today may be contradicted by new finds tomorrow. The second reason is lack of contact with the minds of the creators of the civilization through the written word, and the slightness of contact with their imaginations through the visual arts. All that has been discovered of both together would go into a few boxes and a crate. Even should the script come to be deciphered, on present evidence it seems unlikely that it would tell us much. Known writing is limited to short inscriptions—no one of more than seventeen signs—on seals, pottery and small copper objects that look like amulets.

Any account of the Indus civilization, then, has to rely almost entirely on the dryer type of archaeological evidence. To remind us of its human creators it may be helpful to begin with an impression of their physical appearance. The skeletal evidence, the best of which comes from a cemetery used by the ordinary citizens of Harappa, suggests that two distinct types prevailed. The majority had fairly long heads, low foreheads and strongly marked brow ridges; they were tallish for the period—5 feet 8-9 inches. This racial stock can be called 'Caucasic' or proto-Australoid. A substantial minority were even more dolichocephalic, with higher, smoother foreheads, narrow noses and generally neat features. These people, who were also of slighter build than the others, can best be identified as of 'Mediterranean' racial stock. It has been supposed that it was these Mediterraneans who were largely responsible for creating the Indus civilization, yet the well-known figurine from Mohenjo-daro has an extraordinarily low forehead with marked ridges. This sculpture respresents some kind of grandee, and it seems unlikely that his head form was due only to an artistic convention.

It is of interest that among the citizens of Mohenjo-daro who had been slaughtered in the street during the last assault was one pure Mongol—possibly a trader from Turkestan or even China.

In their dress and hair styles the Indus people seem to show definite similarities with the Sumerians. The men wore trimmed beards but shaved their upper lips; their hair was rolled into a bun at the back and held by a fillet. A light robe left the right shoulder bare. As far as can be judged from crude 'mother goddess' figurines, the

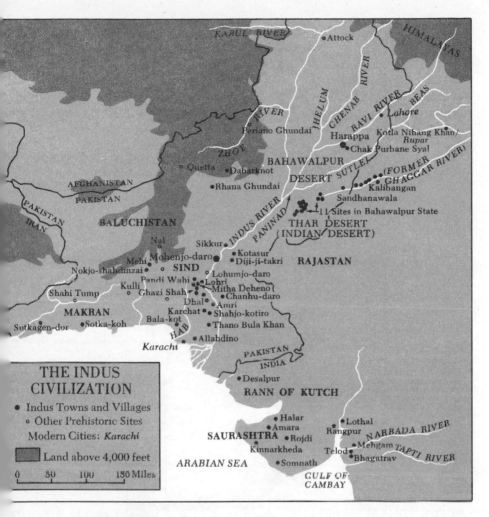

THE INDUS
CIVILIZATION

- Indus Towns and Villages
- Other Prehistoric Sites

Modern Cities: *Karachi*

Land above 4,000 feet

0   50   100   150 Miles

women (like those of the villages) went in for quantities of necklaces and huge headdresses; for the rest they wore mini-skirts and ornamental belts round the hips.

Of all the uncertainties concerning the Indus civilization, our ignorance of its origins is the most damaging. At present there is no sign of any direct connection between the earliest Indus traditions and those of the village cultures of the region. Deep soundings recently made at Mohenjo-daro have shown occupation still continuing at great depths in the flood silt. It is possible that evidence for origins is hidden here below the present water table, but the hints are of the vaguest. Much other evidence suggests the very sudden emergence, or arrival, of a truly urban civilization built on substantial social and economic foundations. Sir Mortimer Wheeler has been inclined to believe that this can best be explained by the

Harappa, the citadel and
cemeteries. Plan.

creative influence of a spreading 'idea' of high civilization. By the middle of the third millennium, when the Indus cities are thought to have been founded, civilization had five centuries or more behind it and might be said to be 'in the air' from Egypt to Iran. We know that from quite early in their history the Indus people were in trading contact with their neighbours to the west. There was already a considerable settled population in north-west India, and it is only necessary to suppose that somewhere in the region there were ambitious chiefs with able followers, to make the notion of a seed of civilization falling into fertile soil and quickly sprouting an acceptable possibility.

Some theorists have not liked Wheeler's point of view, preferring to deal in more material concepts. For the moment there is nothing better to put in its place, and it is fair to say that it must contain at least an element of truth.

Just as in the other two river valleys, the foundations of Indus prosperity were an agriculture based on irrigation and a fertility maintained by silt-bearing floods. The cereal crops were also similar—wheat and barley. Two varieties of wheat were grown, club and an Indian dwarf form (*Triticum sphaerococcum*), while the barley was of the six-row kind (*Hordeum vulgare* and a subspecies of it). It seems that rice was already cultivated on the west coast: it has been found at Lothal and Rangpur.

For vegetables only the field pea is known to have been raised, and for oil crops sesame and mustard. For fruit the Indus people certainly grew melons and dates. It is interesting to find that cotton was already being grown in India (*Gossypium* species). It seems to have been extensively spun and woven for garments, taking the place of linen among the Egyptians.

The importance of the zebu or humped cattle among Indus livestock has already been emphasized; there was also a variety of humpless, horned cattle, apparently rather close to the wild aurochs in general character. It has been claimed, doubtfully, that like the zebu, and perhaps the water buffalo (*Bubalus bubalis*), the Indus sheep and pig were also domesticated from local wild species. We have seen that the camel, and even the horse, may occasionally have been used for transport, while portrayals of elephants, with man-made objects standing in front of them, encourage the belief that these beasts were already domesticated and serving men in at least some of the ways so familiar in the India of later days. Cats and dogs were kept as pets, and it can be certain that some of the cats earned their keep by catching vermin in the public granaries that were such a conspicuous feature of the towns. Presumably a very large part of every farmer's crop had to be paid into these granaries, and we can picture the deliveries. At Mohenjo-daro there was a high loading platform set above a recess evidently intended for waiting carts. It can be assumed, then, that when the threshing was done, a farmer would load his small ox cart with its two solid wooden wheels (so exactly like those still used in Sind today) and go creaking along country tracks and the road in the shadow of the city wall until he could draw in and hand up his wheat or barley to the unloaders at the granary. In Harappa, on the other hand, grain seems to have been brought in by boat along the Ravi.

Fish were both netted and caught by barbed hook and line, but whether fishing was a sideline or a full-time calling it is impossible to say. The wild animals—elephant, tiger, rhinoceros, buffalo, antelope and gharial—that were such favourite subjects with the seal-cutters must presumably have been hunted along the jungly fringes of the valley. It is a reasonable guess that tigers here took the place of lions in providing the sport of princes. One seal shows a Gilgamesh-like figure standing between two upreared tigers, and another a man tackling a buffalo with a barbed spear.

The Indus metalsmiths do not win much admiration for either their artistry or their technical skills. Many of their products were of copper or contained only the small amounts of tin that may occur as accidental impurity. Although the advantages of adding tin came to be understood (or may have been from the first), it never seems to have been very accurately controlled. Spears, knives and other bladed implements were poorly shaped and thin, while the smiths continued to turn out primitive flat axes long after the Sumerians had perfected the far superior shaft-hole variety. That their products were not only poor but also costly is suggested by the fact that for most domestic purposes Indus householders made do with neatly flaked chert blades.

Metalsmiths on the whole achieved rather higher standards on the less utilitarian side of their trade. Shapely bowls and vases were made in bronze, and silver was used for both vessels and ornaments. Goldsmiths produced a variety of beads and other ornaments (Egyptian contemporaries would certainly have sneered at their craftsmanship). As beads were so much worn, it is appropriate that a beadworker's shop should have been found at Chanhu-daro. Various semi-precious stones were skilfully cut, and beads made from a ground steatite paste were delicately inlaid.

Among lesser craftsmen, the potters were relatively far more competent, using the wheel to turn out quite pleasing if standardized shapes, usually in a pinkish ware and often most attractively painted. There was even a period in the early days of the civilization when they experimented with a vitreous glaze.

Faience was also manufactured. Although this craft was of Mesopotamian origin, it was by now so widely diffused that it cannot be said to mean any direct contact between the two countries. The Indus faience workers attempted nothing large, but made pretty little goods such as miniature vessels, beads, buttons, rings and inlays. Tiny models of animals—sheep, monkeys, dogs—are so good that in a land of artistic scarcity they qualify as works of art.

Weavers were probably mainly engaged in making cotton cloth. Whether they can be credited with its invention or whether the spinning of cotton fibre had already occurred to earlier village communities there is no means of telling. Nor is it known whether there was any kind of centralized cloth industry on Mesopotamian lines, though it seems quite probable.

To judge from the later history of Indian crafts, more has probably been lost in the handiwork of Indus carvers and carpenters than in any other class of perishable things. A single large coffin made from the local sweet-smelling rosewood is almost all that has been identified. Yet to judge from the faience inlays there must have been some decorative furniture made—or at least fine chests and caskets. More important, when the apparent monotony of the brick architecture comes to be considered, it should be remembered that in courtyards and interiors this bareness may have been transformed by more or less ornate woodwork.

Some of these crafts involved the import of raw materials, and of these the most important were, of course, metal ores. Copper may have come from Baluchistan and Rajastan within the Indus area of influence, or from Afghanistan, but it seems very probable indeed that most was Makan copper shipped across from Oman. Once again, as in Mesopotamia and Egypt, the source of tin is unknown. Gold may have come from southern India, and silver, perhaps extracted from lead ores, from near at home in Rajastan or from the Persian-Afghanistan highlands. The ladies' fondness for beads might be largely satisfied by home produced carnelian, steatite paste and faience, but a more luxurious demand brought in lapis lazuli from Afghanistan, turquoise, probably from Persia, and jade from the Pamirs or even Burma.

Long distance trade in small luxury goods for the privileged has always been so normal to human societies that it is of no great significance here. Yet one way and another there are a number of strong hints that foreign trade was of substantial importance for the Indus civilization. It is suggested on the home front by the very large number of seals found in the cities, most of them with inscriptions that are likely to represent personal names. It looks, then, as though in spite of the totalitarian cast usually assigned to the Indus state, trade may have been largely in the hands of private merchants. Much of their trade would have been within the Indus territories, but enough has already been said to prove that a number had foreign interests. There is evidence for overland caravan routes south of the Elburz linking north-west India with Mesopotamia, but far more important must have been the sea route along the Persian Gulf. We have seen that some ships may have sailed from as far south as Lothal and that there were ports north of the Indus delta, but the weight of evidence, both archaeological and textual, centres on Bahrein Island—which we are accepting as having been the port of Dilmun. The large walled town which flourished there at the end of the third millennium had its own culture, but the fact that the Indus system of weights prevailed there, and had to be translated into their own system by the traders of Sumer and Akkad, seems quite strongly to suggest that the influence of Indus merchants was paramount at the port of Dilmun. This is further supported by the number of Indus type seals found there. We have seen that Indus merchants or their agents were probably resident at Ur and other Mesopotamian cities.

If it were quite certain that the name Meluhha did in fact refer to the Indus state or some part of it, then this maritime trade would appear even more substantial. We know that ships from Meluhha often tied up at quays of Sumer and Akkad in Sargonid times. There is even a record of an official translator of the Meluhhan language resident in the Akkadian empire.

What goods were carried in the high-prowed single-masted Indus boats? Perhaps rare woods were important (there is also a mention of Meluhha tables); also such luxuries as carnelian, pearls, ivory, and, probably, pet monkeys. But surely there must have been some more solid base to the traffic? It is tempting to suggest cotton textiles, surely welcome in the heat of the Sumerian Plain, but there is no evidence for their sale. Or again, Indus merchants could have acted as brokers for Makan copper.

While trade from India had probably existed from the time of the Kulli venturers, it certainly reached its peak in Sargonid times at the end of the third millennium. These were the days when the entrepôt of Dilmun was most thriving and when, as we shall see, the whole Indus civilization was at its height. Thereafter trade declined, owing mainly to declining prosperity at home, but also to political change in Mesopotamia. By about 1700 B.C. it was at an end.

Almost all that can be known or guessed of the character and institutions of Indus society has to be derived from the remains of its towns and cities. Of these the two capital cities of Mohenjo-daro and Harappa are by far the most important, although information about the nature of smaller towns is now forthcoming from Kali-bangan, situated beside the long dried-up Ghaggar river, and also from Chanhu-daro, south of Mohenjo-daro. Of towns in the southern, Saurashtran, extension of Indus territory the port of Lothal has special importance.

The early excavations at the two capitals were poorly executed and recorded. The ruins of Harappa were dug away for railway ballast, while a part of the citadel at Mohenjo-daro is still occupied by a Buddhist stupa. The attempt that has to be made to reconstruct Indus life from its material remains meets with many frustrations.

There are two most significant facts about the towns and cities just mentioned, and presumably also about those that have not as yet been explored. One is the exceptional regularity with which each is laid out, the other the no less exceptional uniformity between them all.

Indus cities were built on a regular grid plan of straight streets, the first known appearance of this kind of city planning in the history of civilization. At Mohenjo-daro three thirty-foot-wide streets running north and south, and two crossing them at right angles, made twelve blocks measuring 1200 by 800 feet. These very large blocks were subdivided by alleys up to ten feet wide on to which many of the houses opened. The streets and alleys were not paved and may have been dusty, but there were plenty of public wells and, as we

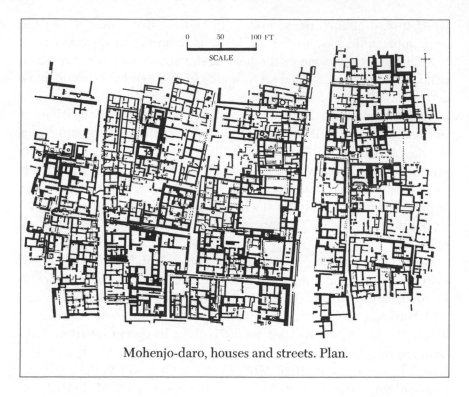

Mohenjo-daro, houses and streets. Plan.

shall see, a complete drainage system. At street corners single room dwellings probably housed watchmen who patrolled the streets by night.

The central western block at Mohenjo-daro was occupied by the citadel, sited in relation to the lower town very much in the manner of Assyrian citadels. It was raised to a height of at least forty feet on an artificial mound of mud-brick with fired brick revetments. The foot had been further protected against floods by massive embankments. The mound with its buildings was strongly fortified with towers and walls built on a distinctive rhomboidal plan. The periphery of the lower town was not preserved, but to judge from Kalibangan it was probably walled. Each side of the square city must have measured about one mile.

The same general layout, with the long axis of the blocks running north and south and the rhomboidal citadel on the west side, was repeated at Harappa and Kalibangan. Chanhu-daro (where many workshops were found) and Lothal had the same street plan and drainage system. Lothal was distinguished by an enclosure of burnt-brick measuring no less than 730 by 120 feet. It is thought to have been a dock that would have been accessible to shipping sailing up the Gulf of Cambay.

The regular planning of the Indus towns and cities can only mean that each was built as a whole by an authority with absolute control. Their uniformity over so wide an area makes it almost as certain that the entire Indus territory was a unified state. The existence of two capitals of equal size linked only by the thoroughfare of the river presents a problem. Both must have been administrative and commercial centres, but it seems unlikely that there were two rulers. More probably Harappa and Mohenjo-daro can be likened to the Thebes and Memphis of the Middle and New Kingdoms. If there was a duality within the Indus state, then, like the Two Lands of Egypt, it was probably merged in the far more significant unity of a single realm. What kind of rulers were they who maintained that unity? For direct evidence we have to turn first to the citadel, but the clues are both unreliable and incomplete.

One thing is sure, massive walls, bastions and towers had to have soldiers to defend them, so it can safely be assumed that the overlords had a military force of some size and one that probably included archers. All buildings inside the citadel at Harappa were destroyed, but at the Sind capital several could be identified. One of these, surprisingly, is a bath or artificial pool, nearly forty feet long and waterproofed with bitumen. Broad flights of steps leading into the water at either end make it plain that it was designed for bathing, and considering the prevalence in India of sacred tanks there seems little doubt that this bath, too, was used for religious purification.

So far, then, the citadels suggest the presence of a combined military and religious ruling power of the kind to be expected from the analogies of almost all primary civilizations. Unfortunately the other buildings do little to clarify this vague image of a priestly lord with power at his back. A very long building next to the Great Bath and extending well beyond it has a courtyard with verandas and a row of cell-like rooms. The excavator of long ago ventured to recognize it as 'the residence of a very high official, possibly the high priest himself, or perhaps a college of priests'. The only virtue in these suggestions is that they do imply a certain apparent lack of focus in this building that might make it inappropriate for a full-blown royal palace. There seems to be no throne room or audience hall. At some distance, towards the southern end of the citadel, there is a pillared

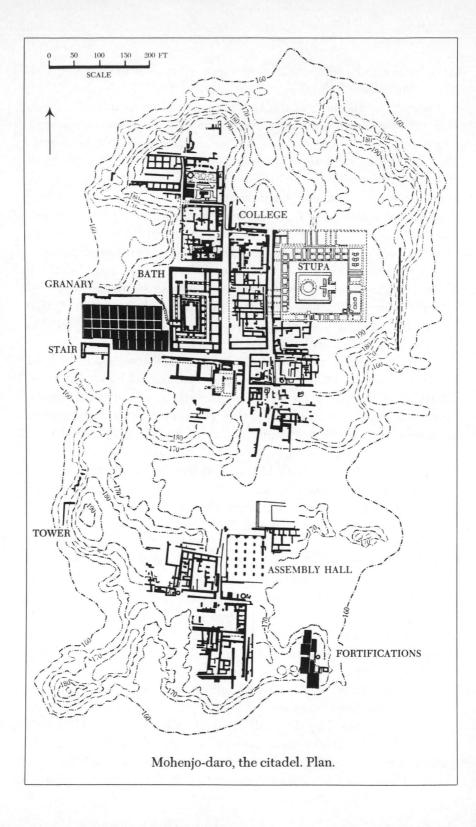

0   50   100   150   200 FT

COLLEGE

STUPA

GRANARY

BATH

STAIR

TOWER

ASSEMBLY HALL

FORTIFICATIONS

Mohenjo-daro, the citadel. Plan.

assembly hall of some kind, but this also lacks a throne room or any other marks of royal dignity.

As it is unlikely indeed that the Indus state had decided to prefer 'collective rule' a princely ruler may be assumed, but it does look as though, in spite of his apparent authoritarian regime and wide lands, he dispensed with the tremendous pomp of Pharaoh. More will be known if royal tombs are ever found.

One other large building within the Mohenjo-daro citadel is both comprehensible and socially significant. This is the huge granary, set on the containing wall in such a way that the grain carts could approach it from outside. It was a heavy timber building 150 feet long by 75 feet wide and supported on a massive podium of burnt-brick divided by a grid of passages that ventilated the store over-head. It was essentially a single building, although there must have been internal subdivisions; in this it differs from the Harappan granary, which is in twelve quite distinct sections, though the total storage area is about the same. Another difference is that the granary at Harappa was not inside the citadel walls, but, as we have seen, stood some two hundred yards beyond them close by the river bank.

As Wheeler has said, in a Bronze Age economy city granaries of this kind were the equivalent of a state bank or treasury, with the level of the grain representing the level of public credit. State and temple grain stores were important in Mesopotamia and Egypt, yet there is something about the size and architectural assertiveness of these Indus granaries, and about the concern for security implicit in setting the Mohenjo-daro building inside the citadel, that seems to suggest that they were of extraordinary importance in the national life. Groping for social meaning, we may be justified to claim that the Indus government paid out wage-rations to very large contingents of servile labour in its direct employ.

This can be supported by the rows of little, standardized two room dwellings that had evidently been built to order at both the capitals. Those at Harappa were associated with an establishment thought to be a city flour mill, where grain was pounded in numbers of wooden mortars. The 'coolie lines' (as they have been called) of Mohenjo-daro were in the heart of the lower city and the employ-ment of their inmates cannot even be guessed. There is no question, however, that these places resemble the Egyptian cantonments and are likely to have housed a specialized labour force.

It would be misleading to give the impression that coolie lines

were a major feature of urban housing—on the contrary, most of
the city blocks were well filled by substantial brick houses of various
sizes but all with an air of middle class bourgeois comfort. If this
kind of density persisted over the whole of the lower towns, Indus
urbanization must have been remarkably successful. As in Roman
Britain (or at Akhetaten), deliberately founded and planned towns
often fail to fill up, with lots and even entire blocks remaining un-
developed.

Private houses were of at least two storeys. In Oriental fashion
they turned blank walls to the outside world, giving streets and
alleys a deadly blank monotony of brick. Once past the door and
porter's lodge, the court with rooms all round it and possibly over-
hung with wooden balconies would have been agreeable enough
and busy with domestic life. Each had a well and a brick staircase
leading to the upper floors and the roof. It is an archaeological failing
to deal too lovingly with drains, but here in the Indus cities they
really were remarkable. Wheeler has said that the urban drainage
system was 'unparalleled in pre-classical times and unapproached
in the non-westernized Orient of today.' Every house had its bathroom and its privy, often a seated privy: earthenware pipes carried
the waste, from upper as well as ground floors, into public drains
running below the centre of the streets. These were very neatly and
methodically constructed of brick and had inspection holes, and there
is material proof that sanitary inspectors and their men used them
to clear out accumulated rubbish and muck. There is no question
of the unusual cleanliness of the Indus citizen or of the efficiency
with which the city authority served his needs.

Nothing has as yet been said about temples, and on present
evidence it appears that they did not dominate the scene to anything like the same extent as in Mesopotamia and Egypt. It is true
that one may have stood in the Mohenjo-daro citadel on the site
now occupied by the stupa, but there is no proof of it and it would
not have been very large. A probable temple in the lower town has
some architectural distinction but would not have stood out more
than a modest church in an Italian street. It had housed some small
works of sculpture.

Turning now to the question of Indus art, the situation is a puz-
zling one. So very little has come to light, and yet among that small
collection the standard is high and the style sophisticated. The
famous, seven-inch figurine of the 'priest-king' or divinity or noble-

man has now looked superciliously from under his lids on so many pages and book covers that he is as well known—and deservedly— as some life-size Greek masterpiece. The head (from the temple just mentioned) is less lordly, less stylized too, and more sensitive. As for the diminutive bronze of the dancing girl, naked except for an arm of bangles, her cheeky, almost defiant stance has been quite marvellously caught by the artist.

Among the pitifully few other examples of stone sculpture are some crude squatting human figures with hands on knees, of interest only in showing what may have been a religious attitude, but of real aesthetic interest are two four-inch male torsos, one of them a dancer's. With their finely modelled strongly marked muscles and complete naturalism they have a superficial look of Greek and Roman work and have been suspected of being later intrusions. Yet it is more likely than not that they were carved by Harappan artists, who show a corresponding naturalistic skill in some of their animal figures, to say nothing of the dancing girl, whose naked body is well modelled.

The Harappans certainly had great talent for animal art. Little models in faience or terracotta of monkeys and other creatures are sometimes masterly and full of life and character. Even finer, and far more numerous, are the intaglio carvings of sacred animals of the steatite seals. These, and particularly the bulls, could hardly be surpassed. As a background to such élitist works, themselves so few and on so small a scale, there is only the popular art of the Mother Goddess figures, some amusing grotesques and innumerable crude little animal figurines.

All in all the art of the Indus civilization (especially if the torsos do in fact belong to it) is curiously unsettled in style and distinguished by an almost complete break between a few highly accomplished and presumably aristocratic works and the rest— which is on no higher level than that of the surrounding village cultures. The most likely explanation seems to be a wood-carving tradition, the products of which have been entirely lost to us. Yet even allowing for this possibility, there seems no doubt that the Indus civilization produced no monumental or large-scale decorative art. Among all other primary civilizations of the world of a comparable size and power only that of the Inca Empire shows equal poverty.

This poverty in the visual arts reduced also what is usually the best source of information about religious ideas and practices. The figurines of a mother goddess, sometimes pregnant, sometimes carrying a child, so similar in symbolism if not in style to those found in prehistoric Mesopotamia and Egypt and indeed throughout much of the Old World, suggest that this cult was a persistent popular substratum for Indus religion. Probably many of them stood in little domestic shrines bringing their hope of family and prosperity. There may have been a sacred tree growing in the temple in the lower town of Mohenjo-daro, and there are a few other signs of a cult that may have been linked with the Mesopotamian Tree of Life. Columnar and perforated stones have been identified with the *linga* and *yoni* of later times and evidently manifest a phallic cult among the Harappans. The seated Siva-like figure about to be described appears to be ithyphallic; unfortunately it is impossible to be sure that the object in question is not a pendant belt-fastener.

One aspect of the worship of the ruling élite is known to us through a divinity carved on a few seals. The most striking of these shows the god with three faces and a huge horned headdress, seated on a low stool, the soles of his feet together and his elegant hands resting lightly on his outspread knees. He has in attendance a tiger, elephant, rhinoceros, buffalo and two deer or goats, all animals that are shown on other seals and evidently venerated. His headdress probably associates the god himself more directly with the bull.

This divinity has been recognized as a prototype of Siva in his aspect as Pasupati, Lord of Beasts, and Wheeler sees him as 'replete with the brooding, minatory power of the great god of historic India'. If, as seems probable, this figure was sometimes carved on a much larger scale, it could have made a truly awe-inspiring image for Indus temples.

Finally there is no doubt that the religious practices of the ruling élite involved ritual lustration and a related devotion to personal cleanliness through bathing. This cult probably spread through the whole society; citizens who could not afford baths and running water in their houses no doubt made use of the river.

It is a remarkable fact, though one with many parallels, that when all other elements of the Harappan culture disappeared almost without trace, so many religious forms survived to play a great part in the worship of historic times. Religious bathing, the phallic cult and, much more significant, the Siva-god with his bull, all had a long and much-honoured future before them.

The original name of the god may well be made known to us if the Indus script ever comes to be read. Its baffling pictographic signs appear on these seals as on almost all others. For the present there is not very much that can be said about it. The known signs number a few less than four hundred, about half the number of the earlier Sumerian pictographic script. This is still far too many for an alphabet, so that the script must be basically syllabic, the pronunciation modified by the use of accents. It seems to have been written from right to left and then back again in the boustrophedon manner. It appears that no cursive writing was ever developed, for even signs scratched on potsherds are in the exact pictographic form.

The entire known corpus of inscriptions from seals, pottery and copper 'amulets' shows no development; the signs appear fully formed, accents and all, and do not change. In this the Indus writing may be said to serve as a model for the entire Indus civilization. So far as present knowledge goes the highly standardized Harappan culture remains the same, except for the addition of one new pot form, from its beginning until it falls into decline. Yet before that it may have flourished for six or seven centuries. More even than the notoriously conservative Egyptian tradition, it seems to have become ossified.

The evidence provided by contacts with Sumer and Akkad harmonizes well enough with that provided by Carbon 14 analysis to give a credible if rough chronological frame. The Indus cities were established by 2400 B.C. and should probably be allowed a margin of another hundred years before that. Their time of greatest prosperity, as of greatest foreign trade, coincided with that of the empire which Sargon the Great founded in about 2340 B.C. and probably lasted through the Third Dynasty of Ur. After that social and cultural life may have begun to decline, and by about 1600 B.C. we can picture all the towns and cities from furthest east to furthest west falling into heaps of dust and brick. Only in the south, in Saurashtra, something of the Indus cultural tradition seems to have persisted long enough to merge with the developing cultures of central and southern India. It may indeed have been from this southern extension and not from the Indus heartlands that ancient forms of worship and belief were renewed in Hinduism.

What caused the collapse of the Indus civilization over the rest of its vast extent? From the upper levels of Mohenjo-daro we know that there was a melancholy period of civic impoverishment and disintegration. Mean houses shoddily built, sometimes of old, broken bricks, began to displace the neat bourgeois residences. Courtyards of these old houses were partitioned to make living room for more families. Accumulations of rubbishy buildings were allowed to engulf the base of the public granary. The city which had been governed with such meticulous care was turning into a slum. We can suppose that municipal workers no longer cleared the drains and that the watchmen's shelters had become poor men's sleeping places.

There may have been many reasons for such civic decay. Perhaps, as in Sumer, the soil lost its fertility, perhaps men bred too fast and exhausted their natural resources, or revolted against a too harsh authority. The prime cause, however, may have had nothing to do with human folly or error. There are signs that the coastal lands were rising in relation to the sea level, with the inevitable result that water ponded up in the lower Indus valley. In these conditions exceptionally heavy spring floods could easily cause disaster. Mohenjo-daro was certainly more than once choked with flood silt, and such repeated damage to homes and fields may have weakened both the economy and the will to recovery.

This flooding would have affected Sind much more than the Punjab area, and it is quite likely that Harappa and surrounding towns would have been relatively little impoverished. In any case there is a tendency in our scientific age to over-stress natural forces as the destroyers of cultures: usually they have proved to be no more than secondary causes.

At Harappa and in many other parts of Indus territory there is archaeological evidence that foreign peoples arrived after the cities had fallen, non-urban peoples whose cultural affinities were with Iran and the north-west generally. In the latest occupation levels of Mohenjo-daro, in alleys, houses, and by a public well, groups of skeletons of men, women and children were found, representing in all several dozen unburied corpses, some with marks of sudden and violent death. In spite of some chronological difficulties, there is no sufficient reason to resist the strong historic promptings that tell us that an ailing Indus civilization was brought to an end by the invading Indo-European peoples whose thrust eastward we have seen probably coincided with the Kassite invasion of the Tigris-Euphrates valley.

In the hymns of the *Rigveda* which preserve memories of these first incursions into north-west India, the divine hero, Indra, with his chariot-driving warriors, is described as conquering dark-faced people, despicable, of course, yet rich in gold and living in fortified strongholds. Indra is explicitly and often referred to as a fort-destroyer, one who 'rends forts as age consumes a garment'. The dates are about right, and what other opponents could possibly have existed at that time who would fit the descriptions in the *Rigveda*? It must surely have been the Indus peoples and their citadels whom the barbaric invaders overthrew.

That they had not the strength to resist or to recover after a period of Aryan rule may very well have been due to the fact that their culture had already become ossified and their social and economic life enfeebled. Certainly their civilization disappeared, leaving only a religious inheritance to its successors. So, while Mesopotamia still had a long history of change and revival ahead of her, and before Egypt had even attained the height of her imperial splendour, the youngest of the three river valley civilizations died and was forgotten for three and a half millennia.

PART VI

THE KINGDOM
OF THE
TWO LANDS

THE RISE, RULE AND DECLINE
OF THE PHARAOHS

BEGINNINGS
AND THE OLD KINGDOM

THROUGH MOST OF THE FOURTH MILLENNIUM B.C. EGYPT HAD LINGERED well behind Sumeria in the progress towards civilization. While she remained a land of villages and small towns with a largely tribal society, Sumeria had in Uruk, Eridu and other centres well-ordered cities already creating a monumental architecture. Yet by the end of the millennium Egypt had shot ahead, at least in several elements of that progress. The reason appears to lie in Egyptian kingship. Once the Nile lands north of the First Cataract had been unified under a central monarchy, Egypt had a concentration of political power and wealth, and hence a potential for grandiose cultural achievement, beyond anything yet possible to the city-states of contemporary Sumeria.

Unification was to be a dominant theme in Egyptian history from Late Predynastic times, through the Archaic period of the first two dynasties, to the beginning of the Old Kingdom. Indeed, it was never altogether left behind, for whenever pharaonic rule was seriously weakened the kingdom split up and unification was once again the goal of the contenders.

We have already seen that there are alternative explanations of the rise of Egyptian kingship and civilization. One is that it was an internal affair, kingship growing from chieftainship with no more than some cultural stimulus from Asia. The alternative view sees a vigorous dynastic race, the Followers of Horus, entering the Nile valley from Asia and providing the royal houses of both Upper and Lower Egypt—the Two Lands that were finally to be unified under the Upper Egyptian house.

Historical records for the early kings of Egypt are more useful than the legendary opening of the *Sumerian King List*. Yet they have suffered tragic damage. What would have been by far the most valuable document for the beginning of Egyptian history is generally referred to as the Palermo Stone. The stone now in the Palermo museum is in fact the largest of five fragments which are all that survives of a huge slab of black diorite inscribed with royal annals. Its find-place is unrecorded, so that no search can be made for the missing parts. The annals were inscribed as early as the fifth dynasty, and not only gave the names, regnal years and principal acts of the Pharaohs of the five dynasties, but even went back before the Unification to kings ruling separately over Upper and Lower Egypt.

There are also two king lists inscribed on temple walls in New Kingdom times and extending back to Menes, the *Abydos Table* and the *Karnak Table*. A version from Lower Egypt, the *Table of Sakkara*, is known from an inscription in the tomb of a royal official dating from about 1250 B.C.

The *Turin Papyrus* is a temple document in hieratic script, said to have been taken from a tomb in almost perfect condition. Acquired by the King of Sardinia, it was sent to Turin so ill-packed that it arrived in small pieces. Immense labours have failed to restore it at all completely. Beginning with dynasties of gods, it originally purported to list every king from Menes down to the nineteenth dynasty, when it was compiled. The *Papyrus* gives the length of each reign in years, month and days, and (unlike the *Tables*) groups them into dynasties.

Finally we come to Manetho, an Egyptian priest of the third century B.C. who compiled his *Aegyptiaca* from the pharaonic records. This work might have made all losses good had it not burnt with the library of Alexandria. It is now known only from extracts, fortunately including the king list, made by later historians. Manetho's Greek versions of proper names have been widely adopted in Egyptology and his thirty-one dynasties universally so.

In addition to these six principal sources, there are of course countless other inscriptions, and all the testimony of archaeology. For an approach to absolute dates there are the calculations based on the

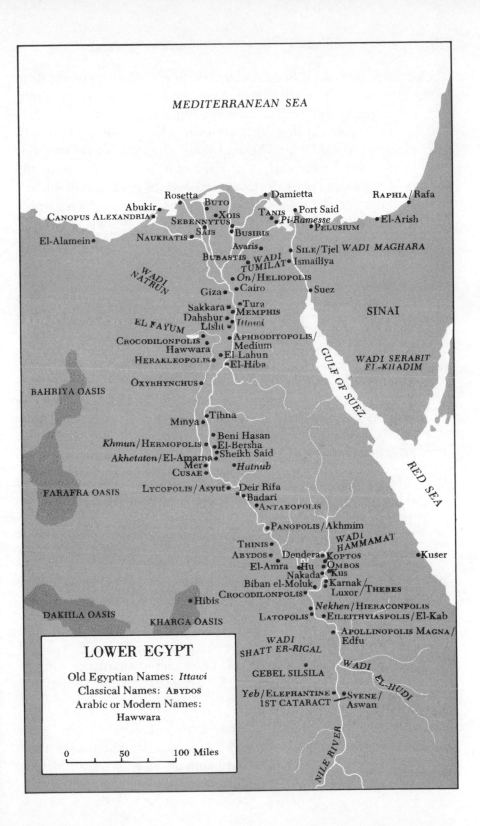

MEDITERRANEAN SEA

Rosetta • • Damietta
Abukir • BUTO • TANIS • Port Said
CANOPUS ALEXANDRIA • XOIS • Pi-Ramesse
SEBENNYTUS • El-Arish
NAUKRATIS • SAIS • BUSIRIS • PELUSIUM
El-Alamein •
Avaris • SILE/Tjel WADI MAGHARA
BUBASTIS • WADI • Ismailiya
WADI TUMILAT
NATRUN On/HELIOPOLIS
Giza • Cairo
Suez
Sakkara • Tura
Dahshur • MEMPHIS SINAI
EL FAYUM Lisht • Ittawi
CROCODILONPOLIS • APHRODITOPOLIS/ WADI SERABIT
Hawwara Medium EL-KHADIM
HERAKLEOPOLIS • El-Lahun
El-Hiba
BAHRIYA OASIS OXYRHYNCHUS •
GULF OF SUEZ
Minya • Tihna
Beni Hasan
Khmun/HERMOPOLIS • El-Bersha RED SEA
Akhetaten/El-Amarna • Sheikh Said
Mer • Hatnub
CUSAE •
FARAFRA OASIS LYCOPOLIS/Asyut • Deir Rifa
Badari
ANTAEOPOLIS
PANOPOLIS/Akhmim
WADI
THINIS • HAMMAMAT
ABYDOS • Dendera • KOPTOS • Kuser
El-Amra • Hu • OMBOS
Nakada • Kus
Biban el-Moluk • Karnak
CROCODILONPOLIS • Luxor/THEBES
DAKHLA OASIS • Hibis Nekhen/HIERACONPOLIS
KHARGA OASIS LATOPOLIS • EILEITHYIASPOLIS/El-Kab
APOLLINOPOLIS MAGNA/
WADI Edfu
SHATT ER-RIGAL
WADI
GEBEL SILSILA EL-HUDI
Yeb/ELEPHANTINE • Syene/
1ST CATARACT Aswan

NILE RIVER

LOWER EGYPT

Old Egyptian Names: *Ittawi*
Classical Names: ABYDOS
Arabic or Modern Names:
Hawwara

0   50   100 Miles

Sothic cycle and the civil calendar, which provide an earliest fixed point at 1872 B.C. For still earlier dates corrected Carbon 14 results agree reasonably well with historical estimates.

It might be thought that with so much evidence the dynastic history of Egypt would be firmly established. The main reason why it is not, at any rate for the early periods, lies in the complexity of the system of names and titles devised to express the royal and divine nature of Pharaoh. As these are conspicuous in many hieroglyphic inscriptions and throw light on Egyptian kingship, it is worth describing the system of the royal titulary.

When this was fully developed in Old Kingdom times, the king had five 'great names', the first normally written within a rectangular *serekh* representing the palace facade, and the two last, the sacred prenomen and the secular nomen, within oval 'cartouches'. They can best be expounded by taking the titulary of an individual ruler, that of the great conqueror Thutmose III. The regular titles are italicized.

I.   *Life to the Horus:* Strong bull arisen in Thebes. This was the supreme name of the king as the divine Horus, the dynastic god of all Egypt. The falcon symbol of this deity was usually shown perched on the *serekh*.

II.   *The Two Ladies:* Enduring in kingship like Re in Heaven. This *nebti* name signified that the king was under the protection of the vulture goddess Nekhbet of Upper Egypt and the cobra goddess Wadjet of Lower Egypt, and that he is the force uniting the two.

III.   *The Horus of Gold:* Powerful of strength, holy of appearance. A further divine Horus name.

IV.   *He Who Belongs to the Sedge and the Bee:* Menheperre. This *Nesu-bit* title with the sign of the sedge for Upper Egypt and the bee for Lower Egypt can be rendered simply as King of Upper and Lower Egypt. The associated name is the prenomen.

V.   *The Son of Re:* Thutmose ruler of truth. This title refers to the King of all Egypt as son of the sun god, Re. The nomen itself (Thutmose) was the personal name of the prince by which he was already known before his accession.

Unhappily for historians, a different choice from the range of names was favoured at different times. The early rulers generally used the Horus name for their monuments and their inscriptions; the *nesu* prenomen was preferred by the New Kingdom compilers of the Abydos, Karnak and Sakkara king lists, while Manetho most often employed a Greek version of the personal nomen. Egyptologists have therefore had to play a most difficult game of identification with results that cannot always be certain—especially for those intermediate periods when the royal power was weak.

Returning now to the facts of the Unification, it has been seen that almost all sources attribute this crucial success to King Menes. Archaeology has introduced two southern kings, one known from the pictographic sign for his name as King Scorpion, the other named Narmer. Scorpion had victories in the north probably over both native delta-dwellers and neighbouring peoples, and is once shown wearing the northern Red Crown. Narmer also celebrated victories in Lower Egypt, and on his palette he wears the southern White Crown on one side and the Red on the other, evidently claiming to be ruler of the Two Lands.

The evidence of the palette convinces many people that Narmer was Menes. Others, however, believe that while King Scorpion began the conquest of Lower Egypt and Narmer perhaps completed the military subjection, it was Narmer's son, Hor-aha, who can be identified with Menes and recognized as the first king of the first dynasty.

This problem of the name behind Menes is of no great moment here. What is far more significant is to find him establishing a new capital. The site he chose, about twenty miles up river from the apex of the Delta, is near the natural frontier between Upper and Lower Egypt. There, after modifying the course of the Nile, he built an entirely new foundation, White Walls, later Memphis. What is so remarkable is to see a victorious southern king thinking in terms of immediate reconciliation and a national state. White Walls was to be the neutral capital of the federation, reconciling the rival claims of the old capitals of north and south. In myth the divine antagonists, Horus and Seth, fought nearby and were reconciled; Memphis was known as 'balance of the Two Lands'. Further moves to secure the union appear in southern kings marrying northern princesses and also founding temples for northern deities.

The image of the Two Lands never faded and must have had deep psychological roots. It was linked with belief in a duality created when 'one god' separated heaven and earth and distinguished the sexes. The persistence of the idea of two in one is manifest in the royal titles, while in practice there were always to be northern and southern centres of administrative government. The concept had one particularly strange effect on the funerary rites of the first two dynasties. It was the custom for the king to be buried not far from his residence, yet royal graves at Abydos duplicate others at Sakkara, the necropolis for Memphis. As the jewelled corpses were stolen long ago, it has usually been impossible to tell where the bodies were in fact buried. Some have assumed that the Abydos tombs were merely cenotaphs built to satisfy the claims of Upper Egypt. Yet the discovery at Abydos of an arm bone richly encrusted with jewels suggests a more complicated story.

Although some authorities would make it later, the Unification under Menes and the beginning of dynastic times is now most usually dated to about 3200 B.C. The first and second dynasties are known as Thinite, as according to Manetho their families came from Thinis (near Abydos). Together they make what can be called either the Early Dynastic or the Archaic period.

Almost from the first the political history of the kingdom shows a sketch of patterns that were to be firmly drawn in later times. Already there was campaigning in the south against the Nubians and the establishment of some kind of military ascendancy as far up river as the Second Cataract. Already, too, there was campaigning against the Libyans (as we will prematurely call them) of the western deserts and against the Bedouin peoples to the east. These tribesmen, like their counterparts by Tigris and Euphrates, were always ready to infiltrate and to take what they could of the riches of the settled folk. Moreover, in the east it was essential for Egypt to protect her sources of gold and the routes leading to the copper and turquoise mines of Sinai.

The kings of the second dynasty seem to have had less opportunity for foreign adventures since the unity of the kingdom itself was threatened. Those Egyptologists who believe in the Asian origins of the Followers of Horus see the disturbances as at least partly due to pressure by the indigenous Egyptians against their alien rulers. On the whole, however, it seems more probable that the main source of trouble was renewed tension between the Two Lands, and that once again a southern king subdued the north. The struggle seems to

EGYPT

Carved ivory handle of a flint knife;
Gebel el-Arak, Predynastic period.

LEFT: Votive slate pallet (26 inches long)
of King Narmer, the pharaoh wearing the White Crown;
Hieraconpolis, c. 3200 B.C.
ABOVE: Unity of the Two Lands symbolized
by Horus and Seth and various other emblems; relief
on the throne of Sen-Wosret I at Lisht.

BELOW: Amenhotep, son of Hapu, as a scribe, in black granite; Karnak, c. 1370 B.C.
RIGHT: Menkaure and his queen, in dark slate; Giza, c. 2500 B.C.

LEFT: Large statue of Ramesses II;
in the temple of Amun, Luxor.
ABOVE: Miniature portrait head,
almost certainly of Sen-Wosret III;
twelfth dynasty.

LEFT ABOVE: Egyptian spearmen;
painted wooden model
from the tomb of Mesehti
at Asyut, c. 2100 B.C.
LEFT BELOW: Two fishing boats
with trawl net;
painted wooden model,
Middle Kingdom.
ABOVE: Jewelled pectoral
of a twelfth dynasty princess;
Kahun (El-Lahun), c. 1885 B.C.
RIGHT: Pectoral of Tutankhamun,
with semiprecious
stones and glass;
c. 1350 B.C.

ABOVE: Procession
of prisoners; relief from
the tomb of Horemhab
at Sakkara,
mid-fourteenth century B.C.
RIGHT: General Horemhab is
awarded gold collars
by Tutankhamun;
from the tomb
of Horemhab at Sakkara.
FAR RIGHT: Girl entertainers
at a party; painting
from the tomb of Nakht
at Thebes, c. 1425 B.C.

BELOW: Tutankhamun and his wife;
scene in gold,
silver and blue faience
from the back of a throne,
C. 1350 B.C.
RIGHT ABOVE: Blind harp player;
from the tomb of Pa-aten-em-heb
near Sakkara,
eighteenth dynasty.
RIGHT BELOW: Seneb the Dwarf
and his wife; painted limestone,
Giza, sixth dynasty.

LEFT: The temple of Amun,
with an obelisk in the foreground;
Luxor.
BELOW: Cowherd carrying a calf
across water; painted relief
from the tomb of Ti, c. 2500 B.C.

ABOVE: Funeral procession and mourners;
painting from the tomb of Ramose
at Thebes, c. 1370 B.C.
BELOW: Weighing the heart of Hunefer;
from a facsimile of papyrus
of a *Book of the Dead*, Thebes,
c. 1300 B.C.

have lasted three generations and to have been settled in the fourth under the last king of the second dynasty. The two factions had been identified with the divine enemies Seth and Horus, and this ruler, one of whose names means 'The two Gods in Him are at Peace', was unique in having his *serekh* crowned by both the Seth animal and the Horus falcon—the deadly foes symbolically brought together. In the reign of this peace-maker, the kingdom was not only made whole but restored to full prosperity.

Egypt was now ready for the flowering of the age known as the Old Kingdom, in many ways the greatest in her history. We shall find that the Archaic period brought notable advances in art, architecture and all the technical skills, and in medicine, administration and the art of writing. Yet these achievements are over-shadowed by the concentrated power of a society that could build the pyramids of Giza.

The beginning of the Old Kingdom is usually dated to 2700 B.C. or a little later. Curiously enough the historical records of the age that left the most enduring, mortality-defying monuments in the history of the world are scanty and confused. The little wooden or ivory labels tied to grave goods in the royal tombs of the first dynasty have told us far more about the monarchs concerned than gigantic piles entombing their successors of the third and fourth dynasties. Records of the lengths of the reigns, the number and names of the Pharaohs are all alike confused or contradictory in the king lists and other sources. (The title of Pharaoh will now be adopted, though with a lack of logic, since the word itself, He of the Great House, did not come into use until New Kingdom times.)

The glory that shines from the obscurity of the third dynasty was generated by the Pharaoh Djoser and his famous official Imhotep. The oldest of all the pyramids, the Step Pyramid of Sakkara with the wonderful group of temples and courts surrounding it, was traditionally their creation. While still strongly influenced by mud-brick building in general and Sumerian architecture in particular, it shows the Egyptians suddenly making splendid use of the abundance of building stone easily available to them in the Nile valley. This was, indeed, the first monumental architecture in hewn stone. Manetho is therefore probably justified in attributing the invention of such building to Imhotep. Later generations of Egyptians venerated this great man as magician, astronomer and father of medicine, as well as architect. In the end he was worshipped as the son of Ptah, and the Greeks identified him with their god of medicine, Asklepios. In spite of all such accretions Imhotep stands firmly in history as the first genius whose name we know. His position already manifests an element in Egyptian civilization distinguishing it from the Sumerian and Babylonian. The valley of the Nile seems to have given just a little more shelter than that of the Tigris-Euphrates for the recognition and honour of individuals and of the achievements of men and women of peace.

As well as his great undertakings at home, Djoser seems to have done some campaigning in Nubia and to have sent expeditions to Sinai, but after him the third dynasty tails away in obscurity. The new line opens vigorously with the reign of Snefru, builder of the first true pyramid (at Dahshur). He fought in the south, looked after the eastern mining interests and also developed the long-established timber trade with Byblos. There is a record of an argosy of no less than forty vessels bringing back cedar of Lebanon for the ships and buildings of Snefru.

This reign, with its firmly established pattern of campaigns and expeditions for raw materials, and with its surplus wealth made evident in pyramid building, was typical of the prosperous and confident days of the fourth dynasty. Pharaoh, the 'good god', 'son of Re', towered over his kingdom in his divine nature and human power. He was not only a divinity, shown on equal terms with the great ones of the pantheon, the infallible intermediary between the Egyptian people and their gods and hence with the forces of nature, but also supreme head of the administration and of judicial and military affairs.

Snefru had the assistance of a vizier—an office which now if not before displaced that of the chancellor, the chief administrator in Early Dynastic times. He seems to have been Snefru's own brother. Indeed, most of the élite gathered round the throne were royal kinsmen, dependents who on their death did well to be buried in modest graves near the royal tomb, hoping perhaps to share in the immortality of Pharaoh. Some of these courtiers and officials had ancient titles such as 'Unique Companion' and 'King's Acquaintance', while others devised honorifics that suggest they suffered from the same vanity of exclusiveness that besets modern civil servants. There was a 'Master of Secrets' and a 'Master of the Secrets of the Things that only One Man Sees'. No one is likely to have foreseen that all these royal servitors and kinsmen would outgrow their dependence and threaten the throne itself.

The wealth of the kingdom and the omnipotence of Pharaoh must have reached their summit with Snefru's son Khufu (Greek Cheops) and his son Khaefre (Cephren), builders of the two great pyramids at Giza that are still the most massive monuments ever raised by man. Khaefre also commissioned the ever wonderful Sphinx.

While historically the kings of the fourth dynasty appear as faint ghosts against the solid mass of their monuments, they have left us some fine portraits. In particular the sculpture showing Khaefre's son, Menkaure (Mycerinus), tenderly held by his sister-wife, Khamere-nebti, is touchingly personal. Yet the vigour and confidence with which this stalwart young couple face the world expresses the spirit of the Old Kingdom in its greatest days.

Evidently Menkaure did not feel able to command such vast resources as his ancestors, for the pyramid that he started to build at Giza is very much the smallest of the three. He died before it was finished, and after him the line fell into such rapid decline that his successor could only complete Menkaure's pyramid in brick and build himself a much more modest tomb at Sakkara. The dynasty seems to have ended in actual confusion, for a legitimate heir failed to reach the throne.

More is known of the relatively modest Pharaohs of the fifth dynasty than of the mighty pyramid builders of the earlier house. Their nine reigns stretched from about 2480 down to 2340 B.C.—a final date that approximately coincides with the accession of Sargon the Great at Akkad. The kingdom remained prosperous and well ordered through most of this period, with the usual activities beyond the frontiers—including now expeditions to Pwene (Punt), the source of incense and spices. What declined was, apparently, the status of Pharaoh as a figure in the divine hierarchy. Although this demotion presumably also affected his worldly power to some extent, its origin seems to have been religious, due to a rise in the influence of the priesthood of Heliopolis (Egyptian On) and its sun god, Re.

The Pharaohs' attitude to the gods became less that of equals and more of suppliants. They prayed to be accepted at the oar of the solar boat or to serve as Re's scribe. At the same time, instead of lavishing the national wealth on their own tombs, these fifth dynasty Pharaohs built temples where Re could be worshipped under the open sky. Their names usually incorporated Re, and they made many pious gifts to the god, his daughter, Hathor, and the Souls of On. They themselves were (or had to be) satisfied with little pyramid tombs that were to collapse with time instead of standing to become wonders of the world.

If the revolutionary change in the interpretation of the kingship was more or less clearly willed—perhaps the first instance of an idea altering the government of a civilized state—another and greater social change was developing in the fifth dynasty without any intention behind it. This is the growth in the power and independence of the nobles. It may perhaps have been connected with the weakening of the divine autocracy of Pharaoh, but it certainly had its own momentum. For centuries kings had been granting their kinsfolk and other favourites substantial grants of land, remission of taxes and many privileges. These endowments came to be inherited as a matter of right. Now the dependent position of this élite, so well symbolized by their little mastaba tombs hardly to be noticed at the foot of the royal pyramids, was giving way to higher ambitions. The elegant tomb of Unas, last king of the fifth dynasty, though distinguished by the royal pyramid, was not much larger than that of some of the great officials.

It seems to have been the judgement of posterity that an epoch of Egyptian history ended with the reign of Unas, for it is at this point that the king lists of the *Turin Papyrus* are marked by the adding up of all the years from the time of Menes. If this was so, then the break was mainly concerned with an acceleration in the rise of the nobility. By now it involved not only those gathered about the king, but also those who ruled the provinces in the king's name. This represented a genuine regionalism, a decentralization of political power. At many towns in Upper Egypt there were hereditary princes, usually provincial governors or nomarchs, with their own circle of high officials, who enjoyed considerable local independence.

In spite of the growing weakness of their position, several kings of the sixth, Memphite, dynasty were themselves strong and active rulers. Such were Piopi (Pepi) I (who significantly married not a divine sister but, one after the other, two daughters of a provincial prince) and his son Piopi II. This king probably had the longest reign in all history, for Manetho's claim that he came to the throne at six and lived to be a centenarian appears to be a true one.

With the sixth dynasty the effort to write history with little more

than king lists, tombs and pictures of Pharaohs smiting their neighbours to east, south and west is suddenly inspired by some living
words. It may have been an attempt to control the provincial nobles
that led the crown to create the office of Governor of the South,
responsible for the collection of taxes, and probably the general
supervision of the nomarchs, throughout Upper Egypt.

One of the first holders of this office was Weni (or Uni), whose
own rags to riches story is enough to show that the society of the
Old Kingdom was open to the talents. Having won a foothold at court
in the previous reign, Weni rose rapidly under Piopi I, becoming
a Sole Friend and a magistrate. In his judicial office it fell to him to
investigate a conspiracy in the royal harem.

When there was litigation in private in the king's harem against the
Queen, His Majesty caused me to go to hear the matter alone, without
there being any vizier or any official there, only myself alone. . . . It
was I who put it in writing alone with one magistrate, though my rank
was that of Overseer of the Tenants of the Palace [he had displaced four
other such Overseers]. Never before had the like of me heard a secret
matter in the King's harem, but His Majesty caused me to hear it because
I was excellent in the heart of His Majesty beyond any official of his, beyond any noble of his, beyond any servant of his.

Weni was advanced from these domestic successes to lead an army
against the 'Sand-Dwellers' or Bedouin of the eastern deserts. The
troops came from all over the country and Weni was put in charge
'because I was well suited to prevent one from quarrelling with his
fellow, to prevent any one of them from taking a loin cloth from any
village . . . bread or sandals from a wayfarer . . . any goat from any
people.'

This determination to prevent the pillage of civilians en route is
interesting; there was no tenderness for the troublesome Asiatics
themselves, for Weni next breaks into verse, describing how the land
of the Sand-Dwellers was harried, razed, its walled settlements over-
thrown and:

> This army returned in peace, it had cut down
>   its figs and vines.
> This army returned in peace, it had cast fire
>   into all its princely houses.

This army returned in peace, it had slain troops
in many tens of thousands.
This army returned in peace, it had carried away
many troops as prisoners.
And His Majesty praised me on account of it
more than anything.

After this Weni had further military triumphs and was awarded with the governorship. Even in his advancing years the labours of Weni on behalf of Pharaoh continued. He went far into Nubia for the king's sarcophagus and pyramidion, to Elephantine for red granite door frames and to Hatnub for a gigantic alabaster offering table. Always he attributed his successes to the greatness of His Majesty.

This autobiography comes from a tomb at Abydos; others almost equally fascinating can be read in the tombs of princes of Elephantine near Aswan. These men, who may have been part Nubians, also went on missions for their royal masters, sometimes to Byblos or Punt, more often up the Nile. The most interesting of these personal histories concerns Harkhuf, a prince of the generation after Weni.

The policy was evidently still in force of holding the frontier at the First Cataract, while pushing further south for trade, for visits to friendly chieftains and perhaps occasionally to punish troublesome tribesmen. The third of Harkhuf's Nubian expeditions was made under the young Piopi II. He records, 'I returned with three hundred asses laden with incense, ebony, oil, leopard skins, elephant tusks . . . and all goodly products.' He also acquired a living pygmy, one of the Deng. When a despatch brought the king news of this, he wrote an excited reply which Harkhuf luckily had inscribed in his tomb. After praising the prince and promising him rich rewards, the boy went on:

Come north to the Residence at once. Hurry and bring with you this Deng. . . . If he goes with you into the ship, get strong men who shall be round him on the deck; take care that he does not fall into the water. Also get strong men to surround his tent at night, and make inspections ten times in the night. My Majesty desires to see this Deng more than all the tribute of Mine-Land and of Punt.

Ebony, leopard skins, elephant tusks and a pygmy: here indeed was the eternal African being brought into the consciousness of Egypt.

As Piopi II advanced towards old age, his government was increasingly threatened by the nomarchs. Dynastic troubles followed his death, and the sixth dynasty seems to have ended with a number of ephemeral rulers. One was a Queen Nitokerti (Greek Nitocris), whom Manetho calls 'the noblest and loveliest woman of her time'. According to legend, she was put on the throne by murderers of her brother, and herself committed suicide after avenging his death.

So, after five hundred years when prosperity and stable government prevailed, Egypt slid back into a condition of rival and often warring states that has been likened to the era before the Unification. This end of the Old Kingdom can be dated to 2180 B.C. or rather earlier.

It was the first time that a fully organized national state had disintegrated. Probably it happened gradually enough for no one generation to have a clearer picture of what was happening than we have of our Western civilization of today. Yet there is no question that a people shaped by the confident superiority of the Old Kingdom days suffered a profound psychological shock as kingship, and with it the social structure, collapsed and they were exposed to the worst horrors of famine and riot. We shall find this anguished change of old assumptions reflected in the literature written both during and after the period of upheaval.

This time, usually known as the First Intermediate period, when there was no effective central government, covers the seventh to tenth dynasties and the beginning of the eleventh. The opening phase, when rule was still being attempted from Memphis, is historically obscure, but one most remarkable document throws a shaft of light on the actual conditions of the time.

These *Admonitions* of the sage Ipuwer deal, in a confused fashion, with three aspects of the general turmoil: government and administration, relations with foreigners and social revolution involving class war. Ipuwer's remarks about the crown itself are ambiguous, for while he says, 'The king has been removed by the populace . . . a handful of lawless men have succeeded in stripping the land of royalty', his own *Admonitions* are addressed to a ruling king. On the other hand, the collapse of the administration is sharply summarized: 'The hall of judgement, its archives are carried off, the public offices are violated, and the census lists torn up . . . the officials are murdered and their papers seized.' As for foreign relations, Ipuwer describes both the infiltration and violent settlement of the Delta by Asian nomads, and the end of Egypt's ability to send expeditions abroad: 'No one raises sail for Byblos today: what shall we do to replace the cedars for our dead? Gold is lacking.'

By far the most vivid passages from the *Admonitions* concern the social revolution; they are as interesting for what they reveal about the old order as they are about its overthrow.

The wrongdoer is everywhere. There is no man of yesterday. A man takes his shield when he goes to plough. A man smites his brother, his mother's son. Men sit in the bushes until the benighted traveller comes, in order to plunder his load. The robber has riches. Boxes of ebony are smashed. Precious acacia wood is cleft asunder.

The upset of the class structure appears equally appalling:

He who possessed no property is now a man of wealth. The poor man is full of joy. Every town says: let us suppress the powerful among us. He who had no yoke of oxen is now possessor of a herd. The owners of robes are now in rags. Gold and lapis lazuli, silver and turquoise are fastened on the necks of female slaves. All female slaves are free with their tongues. When the mistress speaks it is irksome to the servants. The children of princes are dashed against the walls.

With the ninth dynasty the main centre of power shifted from Memphis up to Herakleopolis, its founder assuming the title of King of Upper and Lower Egypt. He seems in fact to have established some kind of authority over Upper Egypt, leaving the Delta in the hands of the Asian infiltrators. After this, fighting between the nomes was resumed, but with the tenth dynasty, again ruling from Herakleopolis, another vigorous prince began the restoration of Egyptian unity and independence. This was Akhtoy III, perhaps best known as the probable author of the *Instruction for Merikare*, a political testimony addressed to his son.

While tendering much worldly-wise political advice, Akhtoy makes it plain that he had driven the foreigners from Lower Egypt. He says that he pacified the Libyan west, then continues:

In the east, too, everything was going badly . . . the authority that should have been in the hands of one only was in the hands of tens. But now these same lands bring their taxes, tribute is paid and you [Merikare] receive the products of the Delta. On the frontier . . . cities have been established and filled with inhabitants from the best of the land, to be able to repel the Asiatics . . . you need worry no more about an Asiatic . . . he can still raid a single post, he can do nothing now against cities.

This early use of holding a frontier by settlement is very interesting and is proof of Akhtoy's authority. Yet so far as his own lineage was concerned his successful policy was to be in vain.

One of his father's injunctions to Merikare was to 'be on good terms with the South', and this referred to the growing power of Thebes. In Old Kingdom days Wise (the Egyptian name of Thebes) had been a small town of the fourth Upper Egyptian nome, with the warlike Mont as its presiding deity. Not very long before Akhtoy III began his rule, a Theban prince established a line that was to be recognized as the eleventh dynasty and began the aggrandisement of a city that was to become the richest in the world. The name of the god Amun first appeared there at much the same time. Thebes and Amun were to grow great together.

As Thebes won control of the southern nomes, independent Egypt was divided between two opposed confederations, under the tenth dynasty at Herakleopolis and the eleventh dynasty at Thebes. In the early part of his reign Akhtoy had battled with Thebes for the supremacy, but later evidently determined to come to terms with the south and devote his energies to the expulsion of the Asiatics and the settlement of his north-east frontier.

Merikare may have had little chance to obey his father's behest, for about ten years after his accession Menthuhotep, a most ambitious Theban prince, claimed the White Crown of Upper Egypt and must have set out to unify the kingdom. Herakleopolis was crushed, and Menthuhotep changed his Horus name to one meaning 'Uniter of the Two Lands'. This reunification is dated to about 2040 B.C., and with it there began the Middle Kingdom, recognized as a second Golden Age of Egypt.

THE MIDDLE KINGDOM

MENTHUHOTEP ENJOYED THE FRUITS OF HIS RIVAL'S STRONG ASIAN POLIcies, winning the double crown of a kingdom that was once again whole, independent and secure. The relief of the people of Egypt must have been immense. During the struggles of the past century they had suffered terribly. It was not only the perpetual fighting. Upper Egypt in particular had known famines so extreme that it was said men had resorted to cannibalism. Probably, like the intellectuals, they could never recover the innocent optimism of the Old Kingdom, but now at least they could put their hope in the renewed efficiency of the divine kingship.

The kings themselves must have been deeply affected by the changed psychological climate. It is not in the least fanciful to recognize the change in the sculptured portraits of the greatest monarchs of the age. These faces show a combination of physical and moral strength, with the marks of personal suffering or disillusion. A bitter spirit is expressed also in words attributed to the great Amenemhet I: 'Do not trust even your brother; have no friends, no confidants . . . when you sleep, guard your own heart, for on the day of misfortune no man has true followers.'

Menthuhotep kept his capital at Thebes, embellishing the west bank with his fine and original temple tomb. Indeed his long reign and the short span covered by his two successors in the eleventh dynasty saw a swift revival of art and of temple building (much of it concentrated in Upper Egypt) as a part of the general return of prosperity. Expeditions to Punt and for fine stones were resumed and the Wadi Hammamat road to the Red Sea provided with wells. One mission despatched to the Wadi by the third Menthuhotep to obtain stone for his sarcophagus deserves mention because of the man who led it. This was one Amenemhet, 'Hereditary Prince, the Count, Governor of Thebes and Vizier; Chief of all nobles, Inspector of all that heaven gives, earth creates and the Nile brings. Inspector of everything in this entire land.' The expedition was not only perfectly successful, returning without having lost so much as a donkey, but was also accompanied by a fall of rain in the desert, and other miraculous portents.

Only a few years later, when Menthuhotep III's reign had apparently ended in dynastic troubles, an Amenemhet who can surely be identified with the vizier is found on the throne of Egypt as the founder of its twelfth dynasty. He was a southerner and not of royal stock. His father seems to have been called Sen-Wosret (Greek Sesostris), and this name was to alternate with that of Amenemhet (Greek Ammenemes) throughout the twelfth dynasty.

The first concern of the new ruler was to reorganize the administration, control the princely nomarchs and secure the frontiers. He wisely moved his capital northward to a site some twenty miles south of Memphis, near modern Lisht. This Ittawi was not only well placed to command the Two Lands, but had easy access to the Fayum, a

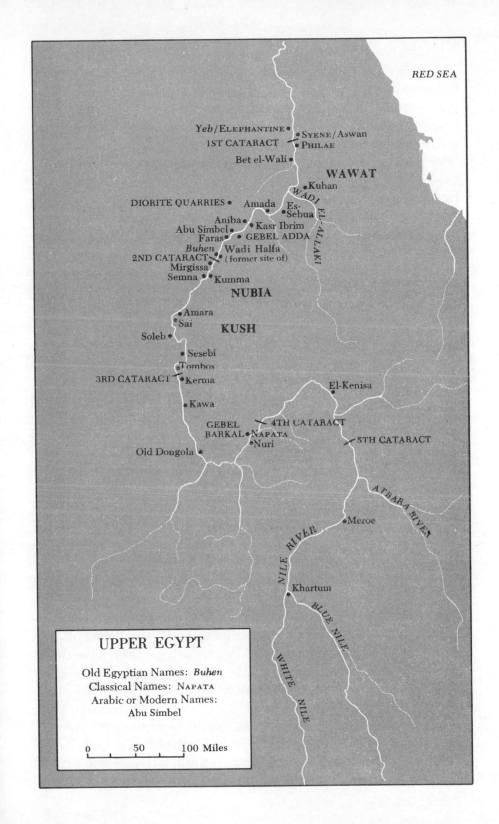

RED SEA

Yeb/ELEPHANTINE •
1ST CATARACT
• SYENE/Aswan
• Philae

Bet el-Wali •

WAWAT

• Kuban

WADI EL-ALLAKI

DIORITE QUARRIES • • Amada
• Es-Sebua
Aniba •
Abu Simbel • • Kasr Ibrim
Faras • • GEBEL ADDA
Buhen • Wadi Halfa
2ND CATARACT (former site of)
Mirgissa •
Semna • • Kumma

NUBIA

• Amara
• Sai
KUSH
Soleb •

• Sesebi
• Tombos
3RD CATARACT • Kerma

• El-Kenisa
• Kawa

GEBEL
BARKAL • 4TH CATARACT
• NAPATA
• Nuri 5TH CATARACT
Old Dongola •

ATHARA RIVER

NILE RIVER

• Meroe

• Khartum

BLUE NILE

WHITE NILE

UPPER EGYPT

Old Egyptian Names: *Buhen*
Classical Names: NAPATA
Arabic or Modern Names:
Abu Simbel

0   50   100 Miles

region that was to be immensely enriched by the efforts of twelfth dynasty kings.

Amenemhet I was not powerful enough to end the rule of the nomarchs, but he saw to it that the limits of their territories were firmly defined ('he caused one city to know its frontiers with another') and also that they recognized their allegiance to Pharaoh. A good instance is provided by the rulers of the Oryx nome of Upper Egypt. Their tomb paintings show them as potentates indeed, with their court officials, army captains and even their receipt of foreign tribute. Yet the inscriptions proclaim their loyalty to the national throne. One of these Oryx princes described how he gave royal overseers thousands of oxen 'and was praised on account of it in the King's House in every census year . . . there was no shortage against me in any bureau of his.'

This text in fact illustrates the method by which the king worked. It was largely through his treasury. While it was centrally controlled by high court officials, he appointed trustworthy inspectors throughout the nomes to assess taxes and supervise their collection. In this way an independent royal bureaucracy combined control of the provinces with the provision of adequate wealth to maintain the power of the crown. In the opinion of Alan Gardiner, 'A balance had been struck between royal power and princely pride, and at this moment Egypt was a feudal state more completely than ever before or after.'

Amenemhet's foreign policy was on the whole defensive. He built a fort to contain the Libyans, and a line of strongholds, known as the Walls of the Ruler, to check incursions from Asia. In the south, however, he may have initiated the more forward policy that was to be developed by his successors. During the troubled times of the First Intermediate period, the Nubians had become more warlike and aggressive. This was probably due to their re-inforcement by a cattle-raising people whose arrival is conspicuous in the archaeological record. Certainly the Pharaohs of the twelfth dynasty were determined to subdue them, while at the same time recruiting soldiers and slaves and securing Nubia's abundant resources of gold. Amenemhet claimed to have subdued Wawat, and his son Sen-Wosret I, at a time when the two were ruling jointly, built the massive mud-brick white-painted fortress at Buhen and took prisoners even further south. They included a contingent from Kush, a territory now heard of for the first time. It stretched southward from the Second Cataract, corresponding roughly to what was to be the Ethiopia of the Greeks.

During the co-regency, Sen-Wosret I was also active on the desert frontiers, and had in fact just completed a successful campaign in Libya when word reached him that his father had been murdered in an attempted palace revolution. This drama stands out in Egyptian history because it is described with extraordinary intensity in the *Instruction of Amenemhet* and is briefly seen from another point of view in the *Story of Sinuhe*. So the man who had done so much to order and stabilize the kingdom himself died violently. The assassination probably took place in the year 1962 B.C.

The capable Sen-Wosret did not fail to secure the throne, and lived to enjoy the rewards of his early campaigning. He was on cordial terms with his neighbours, and the small kingdoms of Palestine and Syria were wooed with royal gifts and trade. Peace allowed Egypt to enter on a period of prosperity at home. The kings ruled through powerful but not too powerful viziers, and the nomarchs remained rich but loyal. There were all the usual signs of national well-being: a new port on the Red Sea and expeditions to Punt, a big development of mineral extraction in Sinai and much building activity. The wealth and cultural revival of the time are well represented by the superb jewellery of the ladies of the court.

Sen-Wosret III came to the throne in 1878 B.C. and was, therefore, an approximate contemporary of Hammurabi of Babylon. Those who judge the Middle Kingdom to have reached its peak under this Pharaoh are showing a preference for toughness and action: with him the era of peace at home and abroad came to an end. His was the main contribution to the composite hero, Sesostris, to be created by Greek historians, and so great was his traditional reputation as a soldier that they credited him with having conquered to the frontiers of India.

In fact Sen-Wosret did himself lead an army into Palestine, probably penetrating as far as Sechem in the Samarian hills. The *Execration Texts*, intended for the destruction of enemies through sympathetic magic, include the names of various Asian peoples and rulers. His most vigorous efforts, however, were directed to the south, perhaps in response to some positive threat from the Nubians. It is true that his four campaigns did not altogether crush them. He called them cowards, 'people not worthy of respect', because, with a Nubian, 'when one rages against him he shows his back; when one retreats he starts to rage.' It looks as though the people of Wawat adopted good guerrilla tactics against the royal armies. Yet he did hold them down by restoring and building forts and establishing a strong frontier at Semna and Kumma. Here a keen watch was maintained and no Nubians other than traders were allowed to pass further north.

At home, too, Sen-Wosret III reversed the cautious policy of his predecessors. They had allowed the provincial nomarchs to live in almost kingly state so long as they remained loyal subjects. He felt strong enough to suppress them. Soon the very title of nomarch was to disappear. Instead the kingdom was controlled from the Palace, rather as it had been in the Old Kingdom but with a more regular bureaucracy. These changes at the social summit encouraged the emergence of a new middle class of moderately well-off officials, small landowners and artisans.

The long reign of Sen-Wosret's son, Amenemhet III, seems to have shown a reversion to peaceable policies and economic development. Above all he must be credited with bringing to full fruition the plans of his house for the reclamation of the Fayum. He built the main system of barrages and canals for controlling the flow of water from the river into this potentially most fertile depression. In this way he added thousands of acres to the precious cultivable soil of his kingdom. Amenemhet also undertook less practical construction, notably his funerary temple and pyramid at Hawwara. This Labyrinth, as the Greeks called it, was declared by Herodotus to be more wonderful than the Great Pyramids themselves. Hardly anything remains of it today, but we have impressive sculptures of this king, including massive sphinxes, in which his high-cheekboned, earnest face is framed by a lion's mane and ears. No representation could appear a surer embodiment of unshakable power. Yet within a decade of the death of Amenemhet, in about 1797 B.C., the twelfth dynasty was collapsing and with it almost all that it had done to renew the greatness of Egypt. His son seems to have been followed by a daughter, Queen Sebekneferu. The rule of this lady seems to have heralded the end of the Middle Kingdom, rather as did that of Nitocris the end of the Old Kingdom.

Sebekneferu died in 1786 B.C. and the New Kingdom can be said to have been established by 1570 B.C. The years between, those of the Second Intermediate period, are as obscure to us as they were confused for those who lived through them. All least 217 kings ruled in

Egypt, a number that can probably be explained by a combination of frequent *coups d'état* with dynasties ruling simultaneously in different parts of a divided land.

RECENT PLUMBINGS INTO THESE OBSCURITIES HAVE BROUGHT UP SCRAPS of information that have considerably modified Manetho's story that the collapse was caused by a single violent invasion from the east by the 'Hyksos'. It seems rather that the thirteenth dynasty kings, of Theban origin, continued to rule from Ittawi for a considerable time, being recognized as the true Pharaohs but gradually losing control over Lower Egypt. Asians had always drifted into the Delta and settled when they could, and now with no vigorous authority to repel them, the trickle of individuals became an infiltration of tribal communities. These people were mostly Semites, and bore names already familiar among Egypt's Asiatic neighbours from Middle and even Old Kingdom times. They were probably on the move because of pressure from Indo-European peoples further north—indeed they seem to have included a few Hurrians. The name 'Hyksos', which should be translated as 'chieftain of a foreign hill country', applied only to the rulers and was indeed a term which had long been used for Bedouin sheikhs. It is very likely that the story of Joseph, brought to Egypt by Semitic slavers, represents the kind of thing that was happening at this time.

The Hyksos seized Avaris (the later Tanis or near it), but it took them nearly another half century to take Memphis. They now had good reason to regard themselves as the true rulers of Egypt, and their kings in fact won recognition as Manetho's fifteenth dynasty. There seem to have been six of them who ruled for just over a century, using Egyptian names and hieroglyphs, employing Egyptian officials and becoming increasingly Egyptianized in all their ways.

The political map during the fifteenth dynasty was a curious one. The Hyksos Pharaohs ruled directly over a kingdom that may have extended to southern Palestine and certainly southward as far as Cusae. The Nile valley from there up to Elephantine was governed by a princely house at Thebes, but was a subject province probably paying tribute to the Hyksos. The Theban rulers formed the eighteenth dynasty, which was to launch the war of liberation. Southward again from Elephantine there had grown up an independent kingdom seemingly ruled from Kerma above the Third Cataract. These princes of Kush were allies, though sometimes unreliable allies, of the Hyksos Pharaohs.

With the war of liberation the historical record emerges from the darkness with a text concerning a campaign led by Kamose, last king of the seventeenth dynasty. The struggle had been begun by his father, Sekenre the Brave, who is known to have been on bad terms with the Hyksos. His mummy shows ghastly head wounds, so it is tempting to guess that he died fighting them. Kamose first appears resisting the cautious advice of his councillors—a familiar literary device. 'I should like to know what is the use of my strength when a chieftain is in Avaris and another in Kush, and I sit with an Asiatic and a Nubian, each man in possession of his slice of Egypt.' He cannot pass as far as Memphis, he complains, and all are being despoiled through their servitude to foreigners. 'My desire is to deliver Egypt and smite the Asiatics.' His text then describes how, ignoring his council's suggestion that conditions were quite good as they stood, Kamose launched a water-borne attack down the Nile against the Hyksos ruler, Apophis.

His force included Medjay mercenaries from Nubia who served as scouts and look-outs. Evidently he reached the very walls of Avaris, for he captured Hyksos treasure ships and was able to see the women-folk of his enemy peering down at him from the battlements. Indeed, he seems to be claiming to have taken Avaris, but if so it was no more than a raid, for he lacked the strength to hold the north and probably withdrew to a frontier a little south of Memphis.

One of the most historically significant facts emerging from this narrative is that both on the way north and during his return Kamose wiped out numbers of Egyptian 'collaborators' including one who had made his town 'a nest of Asiatics'. Of all those who have willingly paid tribute to Apophis he proclaims that he will 'reduce their homes to red mounds because of the damage that they did to Egypt when they put themselves at the service of the Asiatics, forsaking Egypt, their mistress.' Evidently, then, Hyksos rule had not been so hateful as the Thebans claimed; many Egyptians had been content to accept it. Like later liberation movements, this one had an element of civil war.

Of equal interest is Kamose's reproduction of a message he intercepted on its way from Apophis to his ally the prince of Kush. The

Hyksos king implicitly reproaches the Nubian for not acting in spite of Kamose's unprovoked attack, and urges him to come north at once while he keeps the Theban engaged; 'Then we shall divide the cities of Egypt between us and our two lands will exult.' If this message was genuine, and it reads as though it were, then it proves how real was the threat from the south and helps to explain the determination with which the New Kingdom Pharaohs set about re-establishing their authority there.

The Hyksos and their people were not to be finally expelled by Kamose but by his successor Ahmose (Amosis), probably a younger brother. The capture of Avaris proved arduous, and even after the Egyptians had pursued their retreating enemies into Canaan they were involved with a long siege of the remnant in Sharuhen.

So ended the only period in full pharaonic times when Egypt was ruled by foreigners. We have seen that the presence of the Hyksos had been accepted by many Egyptians. We shall find that they helped to advance Egyptian culture in various fields from music to armaments. Nevertheless, the unity of the kingdom does appear to have imbued its people with a stronger sense of nationality than could be found in multi-racial Mesopotamia. It was a spirit that found forceful expression in Kamose's condemnation of the collaborators, for 'forsaking Egypt, their mistress'. So it is not a sign of being blinded by Theban propaganda to suppose that the expulsion of the 'base Asiatics' was received throughout the country with rejoicing and a resurgence of national pride.

THE NEW KINGDOM

THE AGE OF THE NEW KINGDOM THAT BEGAN WHEN AHMOSE FOUNDED the eighteenth dynasty was to be characterized by nationalism, strong central government and, in relation to the outside world, a policy that can properly be called imperialistic. For here was the fundamental change of New Kingdom times. Even in the Middle Kingdom the importance of Pharaoh's role as a leader of troops had increased, but now Egypt's rulers were no longer content to secure their frontiers and dominate Nubia, but became outward-looking, concerned fully to conquer and exploit the south and to assert their power over their Asian neighbours.

It was a change partly due to the Thebans' experience of being held between the Hyksos and the rulers of Kush. It may have been initiated by the successful pursuit of the Hyksos forces into Asia. Yet the change was also forced upon Egypt by outside events, by the rise of expansionist powers such as the Mitannian, Hittite and Assyrian, whose imperialism in Syria and Palestine stimulated an almost inevitable Egyptian response.

The eighteenth dynasty Pharaohs did not move their capital nearer to the point of balance between the Two Lands but kept their residence at Thebes. It may have been decided that it was now of paramount importance to remain close to Wawat and Kush and the whole catchment area of African resources in men and wealth. There is no doubt that Nubian soldiers were as necessary for the Pharaohs' armies and garrisons as Nubian gold was for their diplomacy by royal gift. The import of other raw materials was not unimportant. There was also, of course, the absolute necessity of a secure African frontier if they were to indulge imperialist ambitions in Asia.

The frontier was in fact advanced stage by stage. Amenhotep (Amenophis) I restored it to the Middle Kingdom line; his son Thutmose (Thothmosis) I broke through to the Dongola Plain and also fortified the old trading station of Kerma, calling himself 'he who opens the valleys which his forebears did not know'. Finally the all-conquering Thutmose III reached Napata at Gebel Barkal and established the frontier just short of the wild, unprofitable reaches of the Fourth Cataract.

The Egyptian presence in these expanding territories beyond Elephantine was more substantial than formerly. From the first they were put under the control of a military viceroy known as the King's Son of Kush. At the same time new cities were founded and great temples built, until the lands of Wawat and Kush were very largely Egyptianized. Although tribal risings had to be crushed from time to time, and although the Pharaohs exploited southern gold and manpower, their occupation brought prosperity, and their rule a sense of ordered government that was to enable kings of Kush to assert themselves when Egypt herself was disintegrating.

Egypt, then, had a secure back door through which plenty of goods were delivered to support the Asian ambitions of the royal house. The political situation was propitious. The Hurrians were disturbing the Levant, Hittite power was in recession, and the kingdom of Mitanni, although strong, was not yet at its most aggressive. The conquests made in the wake of the Hyksos had evidently given Egypt a wide 'sphere of influence', for when Thutmose I came to the throne he claimed that his kingdom extended to the Euphrates. He soon set out to make this a reality. Crossing the great river, he defeated the Mitannian forces in their land of Nahrin. On the stele he then raised by the Euphrates he claimed that Egypt extended 'as far as the circuit of the sun'. Presumably he established some kind of control through garrisons and local governors. Leading his victorious troops homeward, he broke the march in Syria to hunt elephant in the region of Niy, an act of prestigious sportsmanship that was to be exactly repeated by his grandson.

Thutmose I was the first Pharaoh to have his tomb cut in the rocks of the Biban el-Moluk—the Valley of the Kings. The dynastic events that followed his death are of such intrinsic interest that they demand more attention than their historical importance could justify. He had left as issue by his Queen only the heiress, Princess Hatshepsut, and by a secondary wife a son, Thutmose, who was duly married to his half sister and inherited the crown as Thutmose II. When he died the position was much as it had been at his own accession; he left a daughter by Hatshepsut and a little son, another Thutmose, by a concubine named Isis. They were betrothed, but as the boy was far too young to rule, his half-aunt, mother-in-law and dowager queen, Hatshepsut, assumed the regency.

This, for a woman of character and ability, was quite in order; she had the support of a man who combined the powerful offices of vizier and high priest of Amun, and also apparently of officials and soldiers surviving from her father's court. Yet surely it must have been a resolution of her own, startling to these men, when after a few years she proclaimed herself king, taking all the titles except (understandably) that of Mighty Bull. As she herself was to have it written: 'Came forth the king of the gods, Amun-Re, from his temple saying, "Welcome my sweet daughter, my favourite, the King of Upper and Lower Egypt, Maatkare, Hatshepsut. Thou art the king, taking possession of the Two Lands."'

It is proof, later to be repeated more forcefully by Akhenaten, that an extraordinary character could break through the heavy constraints of Egyptian tradition and attract all eyes to the stage of history. It is true that there had been two other queens on the throne of Egypt, but they had ruled briefly in times of upheaval and neither claimed to be king or dressed as one.

Hatshepsut's revolutionary acts were not, like Akhenaten's, inspired by ideas, but apparently by a sheer will to power. In this she
succeeded so well that she ruled supreme for at least twenty years.
As one old court official put it, 'She governed the land and the Two
Lands were under her control; people worked for her and Egypt
bowed the head.'

Hatshepsut's reign was peaceful and prosperous, wealth was accumulated and distant voyages undertaken. Her court was brilliant
and inevitably sycophantic; she heaped offices and favours on a
gifted man assumed to have been her lover. This was Senmut, who
appears to have been responsible for designing her a funerary
temple that many judge to be the finest work of architecture in all
ancient Egypt.

During these years Thutmose III was her co-regent. He appears
in reliefs in her funerary temple as an adolescent, welcoming the
return of the Punt expedition, but also as a handsome young man.
At Karnak he is shown as the secondary monarch until their twentieth regnal year, when he and Hatshepsut are portrayed as equals.
The interpretation almost always put on this unusual situation is that
the young king lived in a state of passionate but helpless resentment
against his auntly mother-in-law, and that on her death it was he
who had her cartouches hacked from her monuments and his own
or those of his paternal forebears substituted. Yet in human terms
it is a most unlikely story. An able and ambitious prince, legitimate,
energetic and popular with the army, unable for years to topple so
ambiguous a figure as Hatshepsut? Alternative explanations have
so far proved even less satisfactory, but perhaps some altogether
new answer will be brought to light.

Almost as soon as he was ruling alone, Thutmose III had to meet
trouble in his Asian territories. At the back of them may have been
the growing influence of the kings of Mitanni, but the immediate
threat came from the always restless petty states of Palestine and
Syria. A large confederation was being led in rebellion by the prince
of Kadesh. Pharaoh marched his army against them in what was
to be the first of seventeen Asian campaigns fought by this inde-
fatigable conqueror.

The high point of the expedition was the battle of Megiddo, a
victory that Thutmose seems to have regarded as the most important
of his career. A lively description is included in the record of his
deeds which, when his campaigning days were over, he had in-

scribed on the temple walls of Karnak. It is renowned as the earliest detailed account of an historic battle. The 'vile enemy of Kadesh' had based his confederate forces on Megiddo, an ancient walled city on the Plain of Esdraelon. Pharaoh displayed his ex officio superior tactical skill in insisting that the town should be approached by a difficult and therefore unexpected route. Later he himself commanded the attack against the armies which were massed outside the walls. They were routed and 'fled headlong to Megiddo with faces of fear. They abandoned their horses and their gold and silver chariots . . .' Meanwhile the townsfolk had shut the city gates, and all they could, or would, do for the fleeing soldiery was to 'let down garments to hoist them up into the town'. The place might have fallen there and then instead of after a long siege had the Egyptians not been too busy collecting booty.

By far the most spectacular of Thutmose III's expeditions was the eighth, which he led some ten years after Megiddo. He crossed the great bend of the Euphrates, trounced the Mitanni and went plundering their land of Nahrin. He had the satisfaction of setting up a victory stele side by side with the one left by his grandfather. It was also on the return from this campaign that he followed Thutmose I in hunting the elephants of Niy. He claimed to have shown unique valour in fighting a herd of 120 beasts. This is confirmed in the tomb of one of his soldiers who tells how, when the king was threatened by the largest of all the beasts, he came to the rescue by cutting off its trunk (which he calls its 'hand').

Thutmose was not satisfied merely to win campaigns through the superior organization of his army: he was determined to consolidate his gains. After Megiddo he appointed his own nominees to govern the city-states, while bringing back their sons or other relatives to serve as civil hostages in Thebes. Some of these might later be sent back as ruling princes duly anointed by Pharaoh. He probably extended the garrison system and gave the occupying forces land to cultivate; he provisioned northern ports such as Byblos and Ugarit. No wonder that he received presents from Assyrian, Babylonian and Hittite kings or that much of this Asian dominion was held without serious trouble for a century.

Two results of conquest and empire are of particular significance here. One is that large numbers of Egyptians came to know foreign lands and large numbers of foreigners came to know Egypt. The other is that great quantities of loot in the shape of men, livestock, battle gear, gold, silver and treasure of all kinds poured back to enrich Thebes—presumably to be followed by regular tribute.

It is difficult to judge just how securely Thutmose's northern conquests were held, but although there was some fighting in Syria during his son's reign, when his grandson, Amenhotep III, acceded in 1405 B.C., the kingdom was immensely rich and he could still at least claim to rule from Napata to Nahrin. There were many foreign princesses in his harem, yet for his 'Great Wife' Amenhotep chose an Egyptian commoner, the remarkable Queen Tiy, and these two ruled from their new palace in West Thebes over an opulent, cosmopolitan society. Although he is usually painted in crude colours as hedonist and voluptuary, this Pharaoh was sufficiently a man of culture to show high favour to Amenhotep, son of Hapu, a man of modest origins and fine endowments.

Amenhotep III was certainly no leader of armies, but preferred to maintain his imperial interests through diplomatic alliances cemented by royal gifts and marriages. The shift in foreign policy to the support of the old enemy, Mitanni, against the now renascent Hittites is reflected by the presence in his harem of the Mitannian princess Gilukhipa, and later by the arrival of her niece.

A detailed if confused picture of international politics as they were developing towards the middle of the fourteenth century B.C. is to be found in the unique diplomatic correspondence unearthed at El-Amarna. This covers the later years of Amenhotep III and a part of the reign of his famous son, who was crowned as Amenhotep and became Akhenaten. The Pharaohs were exchanging letters both with their 'brothers' the Mitannian, Babylonian, Hittite and Assyrian monarchs and with the petty princes, most of them at least in theory their own regents, of the small states in Palestine and Syria.

El-Amarna, where this archive had been stored, was, of course, the site of Akhenaten's new capital and holy city of Akhetaten. Although it may often have been exaggerated, it must be largely true that Amenhotep III's unwarlike tastes and his son's preoccupation with his religious and artistic revolution led to a neglect of Palestine and Syria. Rebellion was the inevitable result. With the court at Akhetaten the situation seems to have worsened. Pitiful appeals for help came from Egyptian regents, particularly from Ribaddi, who held the important entry port of Byblos. An Amorite king and his family led this revolt in Syria in alliance with tough nomads, the Apiru or Habiru. Many cities that had been loyal to Egypt either fell or were forced to change sides. Behind these troubles were Hittite intrigues. King Suppiluliuma wrote Akhenaten a cordial letter on his accession, but it has already been seen from the Asian angle how he was to crush Mitanni, reducing her to a mere buffer state between himself and the Assyrians. This defeat, and the death of the Mitannian king (who was Gilukhipa's brother) took place not long before the end of Akhenaten's reign.

Akhenaten's cultural revolution failed and the court returned to Thebes and to religious orthodoxy. This retreat must have been managed by Ay, once close to Akhenaten but now first the power behind Tutankhamun's throne and then for a short time its occupant. Ay seems to have been content to begin the restoration of the temples and the placating of their gods with gifts of treasure. His successor, Horemhab, had also served under Akhenaten as army commander and probably as his viceroy in Lower Egypt. Throughout his life he remained very much the old soldier. He found the people suffering many abuses and attempted to set them right by the threat of terrible punishments. At the same time he may have improved their chances of getting justice by setting up courts of law in the principal towns and assigning temple priests and mayors to serve as judges. It is noticeable that many of the men he appointed to important priesthoods belonged to his own army élite.

Horemhab evidently never lost his faith in the military virtues. Having no son, he chose to succeed him an elderly general of similar background. While Horemhab himself appears to hover between two dynasties, on his accession in about 1308 B.C. this Ramesses I was quite surely founding the nineteenth dynasty. It was a line which now, with hindsight, is judged to have presided over a New Kingdom in decline, but which nevertheless made a great effort to maintain Egypt's power abroad and grandeur at home.

In naming old Ramesses, Horemhab may have had an eye on his capable son, who in fact soon came to the throne as Seti I. He immediately set out to restore Egypt's position in Asia, now more than ever assailed by a Hittite empire that was dominating all northern Syria. At first he had to deal with rebellious city-states as far south as Galilee, but by the end he was able to enter Kadesh. The return of a large army led by Pharaoh in person must in itself have done much for both prestige and the realities of power.

However, Seti's gains were not held, and when Ramesses II, a man eager for military and every other kind of glory, succeeded his father he had to fight over much the same ground. Once again the Egyptian army won its way step by step up to Kadesh, now reoccupied by the Hittites and their very numerous allies. Here, in 1286 B.C., the great battle was to be fought.

The account of the battle of Kadesh that Ramesses had inscribed in several temples has made it possible to reconstruct its every move and clash—it is in fact fuller and more flowery than the record of Megiddo. The interest here, however, is not so much in the course of the fighting itself as in the accounts of it known from both sides and in the events that followed. There is no other passage in the history of the Bronze Age world that tells us more clearly how little human conduct has changed, even when it is the conduct of public affairs.

According to the Egyptian story the battle was going badly when Pharaoh turned the tables by taking on single-handed, without so much as a charioteer or shield-bearer, 2500 Hittite and confederate chariots. With the help of some newly arrived troops he drove them into the Orontes. Many well-known Hittites, including the king's brother, were trampled to death or drowned and the king afterward sued for peace. This record of Kadesh as a resounding victory for Egypt and a triumph of valour for Ramesses was generally accepted by Egyptologists—with due allowance for the puffing up of the royal reputation. Then a brief version was found on tablets from the Hittite capital of Hattusas. There Kadesh was treated as an Egyptian defeat.

There is a good deal to suggest that the Hittite version was nearer the truth. On the other hand, unless his records are total lies, Ramesses was not prevented from further campaigns and is even heard of fighting as far north as Aleppo. Again, the Hittites would hardly have been ready to accept the reasonable peace treaty that was to end the story if Egypt had not been negotiating from a position of some strength.

This treaty was drawn up some sixteen years after Kadesh, by which time there had been a change of kings at Hattusas. What makes the documentation unique and a pride to archaeology is that one complete version can be read in hieroglyphics at Karnak, while the virtually identical Hittite text, written in cuneiform, was found in remote Hattusas, one thousand miles distant from Thebes.

The terms were statesmanlike and even humane. Each great power agreed to refrain from attacking the other and to come to the other's assistance in the event of external aggression or revolt. There were also carefully worded extradition clauses by which both promised to return fugitive subjects of the other on condition that they were not slain or mutilated or their families harassed. No line of demarcation between the two states was laid down in the treaty itself. Probably in practice the Egyptian sphere of interest extended about as far north as Byblos.

In the thirty-fourth year of the reign of Ramesses II the grand alliance was strengthened by a splendid dynastic marriage. The Hittite king sent his richly dowered eldest daughter to Egypt with a vast and sumptuous cortege, and Pharaoh sent troops to his furthest frontier to escort them back. He even contrived with divine help to secure them good weather. The nuptials were celebrated with tremendous enthusiasm; Hittites and Egyptians 'ate and drank together, they were as harmonious as brothers'. Pharaoh found the princess 'beautiful of face as a goddess', gave her an Egyptian name, and raised her to the dignity of Great Wife.

Egypt flourished under Ramesses II. To the south Kush was by now virtually an Egyptian province, so that to meet the needs of his Asian policies the king felt free to create a new capital in the eastern Delta. This was Pi-Ramesse, alternately with Memphis the chief royal residence for the nineteenth and twentieth dynasties. It was on or near the site of the Hyksos stronghold of Avaris, and can probably also be identified with the city known to the Greeks as Tanis and in the Old Testament as Zoan. Ramesses, notoriously, was an extravagant builder both here and throughout his realm. A great part of the titanic Hypostyle Hall at Karnak, the Ramesseum in western Thebes and the rock-cut Nubian temples of Abu Simbel are only the most showy of his many monuments.

The number of this Pharaoh's monumental statues was rivalled by the number of his offspring. By concubines, wives and several Great Wives he had over 150 sons and daughters, so that when his sixty-seven years of rule came to an end there was no shortage of male heirs. He was in fact succeeded by Merenptah, thirteenth in the list of progeny proudly posted in the Ramesseum.

A new age was now stealing in upon Egypt and her Asian neighbours. The main agency were those 'People of the Sea' already briefly mentioned. Early in Ramesses II's reign there had been an attack by Sherden pirates, but they were repulsed and a number pressed into the king's guard. Now migratory pressures from further north were forcing the peoples of the Mediterranean coasts and islands to take to their ships. Soon the whole eastern Mediterranean was violently disturbed.

The attack on Merenptah's Egypt was led by the king of a Berber tribe that now for the first time introduces the actual name of Libu (Libyans). He was reinforced by five groups of Sea People who probably included Achaeans and Lycians, possibly also Etruscans and Sicilians. It was not a mere military raid but a true migration. The hordes that advanced from Cyrenaica, overran the Egyptian frontier forts and reached the Canopic branch of the Nile Delta included wives and children, cattle and household belongings. Moreover, it was recorded that they had 'come to the land of Egypt to fill their bellies'. The Egyptian army was still strong enough to defeat them utterly and many were slaughtered with the customary barbarities. The sense of danger had evidently been very great, and Merenptah rejoiced not only over such great things as that Libya was 'destroyed', Palestine and Syria subject and the Hittites peaceful, but also in an Egypt now secure. 'Pleasant indeed it is when one sits and chats. One can walk freely on the road without any fear in the hearts of men.'

Although the times seemed propitious and Pharaoh's success had saved Egypt from anything worse than minor Libyan raids for half a century ahead, his dynasty was to sink into a quick decline. There were usurpations, and it is a reflection of the growing influence of foreigners in Egyptian society that for a time a Syrian king-maker seems to have been in real control of the country. Once again one of the last to rule in a collapsing royal house was a woman, Twosre, who secured herself burial in the Valley of the Kings.

It was the task of the twentieth dynasty to restore order and the authority of the double crown. Fortunately the second in the line, who ascended the throne as Ramesses III, was a vigorous and able man who had evidently made up his mind to emulate the style and achievements of Ramesses II. In large measure he was successful, but the forces of external aggression and internal decay were too strong to be more than checked.

Ramesses III built a huge funerary temple-cum-palace in western Thebes, now known as Medinet Habu. Its walls were inscribed with a great number of turgid texts, and contrastingly vivid reliefs, that provide an illustrated historical glorification of his reign. Yet the very form of the building may represent the internal insecurity of the realm, for it was thought desirable to enclose its buildings within stout defensive walls. Not only did it have the appearance of a fortified citadel but can be said to have served as one, for it came to house the courts of justice, and sometimes the office of the vizier and other administrative offices.

Merenptah had been confronted by a joint onslaught of Libyans and Peoples of the Sea; now some half century later they were to attack Egypt again, but this time separately. In the fifth year of his reign, that is to say in about 1174 B.C., Ramesses III repulsed an attack from the west led by the Libu and Meshwesh tribes. In spite of this success it proves that six years later Meshwesh Libyans were occupying much of the western Delta down to Memphis. Again they were defeated and enslaved or expelled, yet many seem to have been able to remain or return as mercenaries—later to become a power in the land and even to form dynasties.

Meanwhile, between these two Libyan wars, Ramesses had to meet a far more dangerous threat on his Asian front. A vast and presumably loose confederacy of Peoples of the Sea and others were sweeping through the lands of the eastern Mediterranean, effectively changing the ethnographic map. The already enfeebled Hittite empire collapsed and the armed migration thrust southward from Syria, the families of the warrior bands travelling in ox-carts.

They attacked Egypt by both sea and land. The land forces seem to have been repulsed at some distance beyond the Egyptian frontier, but their fleet, in which ships of the Peleset, or Philistines, played a large part, was allowed to sail as far as the Delta. Here a skilful trap had been set for them: as it says at Medinet Habu, 'A net was prepared to ensnare them, those who entered into the river mouths being confined and fallen within it, pinioned in their places, butchered and their corpses hacked up.' It was a famous victory, but as soon as Egypt passed into feebler hands the Philistines were to begin their settlement of the southern coasts of Palestine.

As though in imitation of the days of Ramesses II, this reign, too, seems to have ended in peace abroad and outward prosperity at home. The king felt able to make large benefactions to the temples; expeditions were mounted not only to Sinai but also to Punt. A woman, it was proclaimed, could 'walk freely wherever she would unmolested', while the soldiers and chariotry could sit idle, and even the mercenaries could 'lie at night full length without dread'.

Yet below the surface there were already signs that all was not well—particularly in the economic life of the kingdom. The wealth that had gone to the temples might better have been used to provide the rations of such workers as the Theban tomb-builders, whom we shall find striking from lack of rations. Ramesses III's own life was to end in turmoil. There was a widespread conspiracy concerning the succession hatched within the harem. It may or may not have accomplished the murder of the divine Pharaoh himself, but it certainly helped to weaken central government. The royal line was to continue through another eight kings; all hopefully assumed the names of Ramesses, but succeeded only in diluting its greatness.

Egypt became increasingly confined and inward-facing. Not only did she relinquish her Asian territories but such foreign enterprises as the time-honoured expeditions to the mines of Sinai came to an end. None is recorded after the reign of Ramesses VI. Efforts were still made to bring timber from Lebanon, but it was done on the cheap. In the *Story of Wenamum,* dating from the days of the last Ramessid (XI), the hero, almost an anti-hero, has to go to fetch wood for the bark of Amun without gold and silver to give in exchange and without as much as a ship of his own. The prince of Byblos and others treated him with contempt, and spoke disparagingly of Pharaoh.

During the long tailing away of the Ramessid, there are records of theft and corruption in high places, of troubles caused by Libyan and other foreigners living in Egypt, and above all of a great outbreak of tomb-robbery in Thebes that was at least in part due to poverty and the failure to pay workmen. Probably the greatest source of weakness in home affairs was the conflict for power between Palace and Temple. Just as in Babylonia, the kings added to their own difficulties by heaping riches and privileges on the temples and therefore their priesthoods. The gods did nothing to avert the inevitable results. In particular the temple of Amun at Thebes held a huge part of the national wealth, and when its high priests made their office hereditary they appeared as powerful secular princes. Indeed it seems that the Pharaohs, ruling from Pi-Ramesses, more and more confined their own active control to Lower Egypt, leaving the management of the south to the religious hierarchy of Thebes.

THE LATE PERIOD

WITH THE END OF THE RAMESSIDS, THE LAST FULLY 'PHARAONIC' AGE of Egypt was over. The succeeding centuries, during which Egypt was to suffer a variety of divisions and foreign conquests, but also to enjoy interludes of relative well-being, are usually known as the Late period. In archaeological terms the ancient world was now well into the Iron Age, and iron-smelting did in fact begin in Egypt, rather belatedly, under the twenty-first dynasty that opened the Late period.

This dynasty saw Egypt at a low ebb at home and abroad. It is characteristic that all hope of maintaining the Theban tombs of the Pharaohs was abandoned and their pathetic mummies, stripped of all their gorgeous apparel, were docketed and crammed into two secret caches like neglected specimens in a museum store.

It was now, in about 950 B.C., that the Libyan settlers and mercenaries, whose influence had been growing, produced a leader capable of seizing supreme power. This was Shoshenk, better known as that Shishak of the Book of Kings who took Jerusalem and carried off the treasures of the Temple. Undoubtedly Shoshenk's Palestinian campaign was the most spectacular, and by far the most profitable, of the sporadic interventions that Egypt made in her old Asian territories during the Late Period. Her feeble politicking among the small states there, and the weakness of the support that she gave to her allies, earned her Sennacherib's scornful condemnation as 'a broken reed'.

The twenty-second dynasty ruled in Egypt for a century and a half, but it was beset by factious disputes, and before the end one branch of the family had established the rival twenty-third dynasty at Thebes. This could not fail to cause such a further weakening of government that the old problem emerged of ambitious provincial nobles and soldiers ruling as petty princes. This squalid scene of Egypt given over to alien rulers and upstarts provoked a reaction from the deep south that is of extraordinary social and cultural interest.

Since the time of the Ramessids the southern province had assumed increasing independence, until the role of King's Son of Kush had become virtually that of a monarch. The upper level of society maintained an essentially Egyptian culture, speaking and writing the language correctly and glorifying the greatness of Amun from his leading temple at Napata. Now, in about 730 B.C., a Kushite ruler named Piankhi, probably seeing himself as a saviour of the old order at Thebes, led a host down river to take control of the situation. Hermopolis, Herakleopolis and then Memphis fell before him, and all the rulers great and small made their submission.

Piankhi's ethnic origins are unknown but were probably mixed. Perhaps he resembled most present-day Nubians in being very dark but without pronounced negroid features. The wonderfully lively account of his conquest inscribed on a stele at Napata makes it clear that he was essentially a devout and virtuous man, always fulfilling religious observances, and refusing the proffered services of the women of the harem at Hermopolis. He also naively trusted in the promises of obedience made to him by the defeated Egyptian rulers —promptly broken when he himself returned to Napata.

The rule of the Nubian twenty-fifth dynasty had its ups and downs, and is perhaps most notable for its evident veneration of the past and a desire for its regeneration. Temples were restored throughout Egypt, and we shall find works of art of the period looking back to the Old and Middle Kingdoms for their inspiration.

Under the third of Piankhi's sons, Taharka, there was a moment of hopeful unity when he was ruling a kingdom from the junction of the White and Blue Niles to the Mediterranean. However, Egypt's opposition to Assyria in Palestine could hardly fail to provoke reprisals. Esarhaddon's and Assurbanipal's brief annexation of the kingdom has been described: it virtually ended the strange interlude of the Kushite rule of Egypt after it had lasted some seventy years.

Egypt was deeply humiliated by the Assyrian conquest, yet surprisingly she still had the reserves of energy to produce a nationalist revival. This took place under the twenty-sixth dynasty, established in 663 B.C. by Psammetichus, a member of the princely house of Sais. With the help of Lydian troops, he drove out the Assyrians, pursuing them far into Palestine as though he were the reincarnation of Ahmose expelling the Hyksos. Egypt was now again embroiled in Asia, and even dreamt of a restoration of imperial power. We have seen how, with Assyria tottering, Egypt patched up an alliance with her against the Babylonians and Medes. A son of Psammetichus led a victorious army as far as Carchemish, probably the first Pharaoh to reach the Euphrates since the time of Thutmose III. Here, however, in 605 B.C. he and the Assyrians were routed and he had to flee back to the Nile.

At home the rule of the twenty-sixth dynasty brought the Egyptians their last spell of quite prosperous independence. These kings were more and more involved with commerce, and through commerce and their army with the Greeks. There was, indeed, a curious contrast in Egyptian life. On the one hand great numbers of foreigners were coming in. There were Ionians, Carians and Lydians in her armies, a concessionary port for Miletians at Naukratis and many other Greeks throughout the kingdom. There was a refugee Jewish settlement on the old southern frontier at Elephantine. Yet side by side with this alien penetration, which was loathed by the Egyptian people, the Saite kings greatly developed the Kushite fashion for venerating and imitating the past.

It was, of course, the Persians who were to end this pleasant evening hour of Egyptian freedom. When Cambyses invaded in 525 B.C., Psammetichus III put up a stout but vain resistance at Pelusium; Memphis was captured and Egypt made a satrapy within the well-organized Persian empire.

The Persian rulers seem usually to have shown suitable reverence for Egyptian traditions, assuming the full titulary and symbols of Pharaoh. Archaeology has proved that even Cambyses himself, accused by Herodotus of impious acts, had Apis bulls dedicated in his name. He also pleased the Egyptians by cleansing the temple of Neith at Sais of foreigners, restoring its revenues and seeing to it that festivals and processions 'should be made as they were aforetime'. Darius went further, building temples for native deities and ordering all Egyptian laws to be written down.

The dynasty of Persian kings ended with Darius II near the close of the fifth century B.C. The last three dynasties of Manetho (the first two very short-lived) were again native Egyptian, and although the Persians persisted in regarding Egypt as a rebellious province, their consistent purpose was to assert their independence. Generally a pro-Hellenic policy was followed, and two Persian attempts to reoccupy the country were frustrated.

Then, after the middle of the century, the Persian empire, which had seemed to be collapsing, had a last resurgence under Artaxerxes

III (Ochus). This king recognized the renewed strength of Egypt by leading a huge force against her, and was then able to secure piecemeal surrender by offering clemency. Diodorus records:

Artaxerxes, after taking over all Egypt and demolishing the walls of the most important cities, by plundering the shrines amassed a vast quantity of silver and gold and carried off the inscribed records from the ancient temples, which later on [were] returned to the Egyptian priests on the payment of vast sums.

When, a decade later, in 332 B.C., Alexander the Great was ready to take Egypt, he was faced by a Persian satrap, who surrendered his province without resistance. The Macedonian entered Memphis, sacrificed to her gods and was accepted as Pharaoh. He was indeed welcomed by the high priest of Ptah as a deliverer from Persian tyranny. He spent the winter in Egypt and it was then, early in 331, that he crossed the Libyan desert to consult the oracle of Amun at Siwa oasis. As the accepted Pharaoh, it followed that the priest of the oracle would hail him as the divine son of Amun. Whether or not this had any influence on his vision of himself as world conqueror cannot be known, but it has been recognized as a solemn moment in his life.

Of far greater significance, however, was his marking of the site for his new foundation of Alexandria—the first port to be established on the open sea coast of Egypt. Here, behind rocky Pharos, an Egypt that still looked back to so much of her ancient traditions was to support the most brilliant intellectual light of the forward-looking Hellenistic world.

PART VII

LIFE
IN THE
NILE VALLEY

1. THE MATERIAL WORLD

AGRICULTURE

THERE ARE TWO REASONS WHY IT IS MUCH EASIER TO IMAGINE THE LIFE
of the ancient Egyptian peasant than that of his Mesopotamian contemporary. One is that whereas Sumeria is now largely waste with
the map of its ancient waterways and settlements no more than
marks on the dusty soil, life by the Nile remained almost unchanged
until the building of the great dams. Even now in some regions it
still maintains much of its simple, immemorial ways. The other reason is that the Egyptians' love of portraying the everyday activities
of ordinary folk on the walls of tombs and temples has provided a
marvellous pictorial record, detailed and touchingly realistic. For
example, among the many enchanting reliefs in the late Old Kingdom tomb of Ti at Sakkara, there is one in which a naked drover,
leading cattle through a deep ford, carries a calf astride his back.
The young creature has turned its head and is straining towards its
anxious mother—which is lowing and reaching out towards it from
behind. The scene is so much alive, so sympathetic, that one not only
sees men and beasts but imagines that one can hear and smell them
as well.

The Nile valley offered agricultural conditions decidedly different
from those prevailing by the Tigris and Euphrates. They were in
general very much easier. Although there were some large canals,

such as the one that led up to Heliopolis, irrigation of the narrow
strips of fertile alluvium lining the river did not normally demand
them. The valley was gently concave in section and the annual
flood could be expected to cover the greater part of the cultivable
soil. Moreover, the fall of the river was twice that of the lower Euphrates, making the drainage of surplus water less difficult: Egyptian
fields were not ruined by salinization, nor did the waterways suffer
from rapid silting.

As well as the first distinction between the black land of the alluvium (associated with Osiris) and the red land of the desert (associated with Seth) the ancient Egyptians distinguished between
'lowland' and 'upland' cultivation. The upland, it seems, consisted
of the fields furthest from the river which might not be cultivable
when the flood failed to reach its normal level. Sometimes, however,
the term seems to have been used for artificially irrigated land. Thus
a feudal benefactor of the First Intermediate period boasts, 'I brought

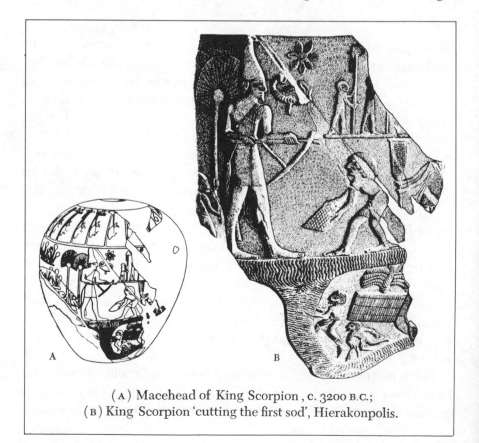

(A) Macehead of King Scorpion, c. 3200 B.C.;
(B) King Scorpion 'cutting the first sod', Hierakonpolis.

the Nile to the upland in your fields so that plots were watered that had never known water before.'

One of the oldest administrative titles given to the local governor was that of the *adj-mer* or 'canal digger'. In Predynastic times each village was able to design and manage its own simple irrigation, but after the unification of the kingdom the central government began to have some responsibilities for water control. It is a most striking fact that on the famous archaic macehead of King Scorpion the king is shown wielding a hoe for the ritual opening of a channel. Yet it is probably true to say that owing to the smaller scale of the hydraulic system, canal construction was not nearly such a highly esteemed royal activity in Egypt as it was in Mesopotamia. The pride taken by the Pharaohs of the twelfth dynasty in their irrigation of the Fayum was exceptional.

The method of crop watering that was best adapted to both the geographical and seasonal condition of the Nile valley was also different from the perennial irrigation of Sumer and Akkad. This was the basin system. The area of cultivation was divided by massive banks into compartments, or basins, extending to as much as 40,000 acres (though often smaller). When the river was at a high level or in flood, water was led from upstream by canal into the basin, where smaller channels distributed it throughout the area. When the soil was thoroughly soaked the surplus water could be let into another basin or downstream back into the river.

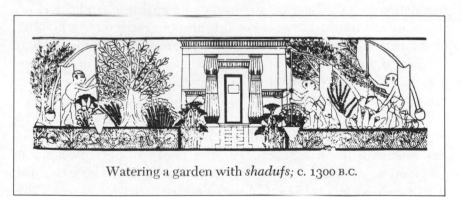

Watering a garden with *shadufs;* c. 1300 B.C.

Gardens and orchards needed perennial irrigation. Perhaps in early days this was maintained by hand-lifting of water, but by the New Kingdom the *shaduf* or swipe, lifting by means of a bucket and counter-weighted pole, had become a feature of the Nile banks. This device, by which a man can raise some six hundred gallons in a day, had long been known in Asia and may have been introduced by the Hyksos.

Although the Egyptians did not have the frequent struggles against sudden and violent floods familiar on the Tigris and Euphrates, they had to work to keep water out as well as to retain it. At the height of the floods in September the water might spread from desert's edge to desert's edge, but its shining face would be scattered with island villages where the peasants' huts and gardens were protected by carefully maintained dykes. Low floods were probably commoner and more harmful, but exceptionally the inundation might be excessive, threatening towns and villages. In these emergencies dykes were patrolled and if they showed signs of collapsing every man was called out to strengthen them. A mark on the inner wall at Luxor shows where an abnormal flood during the twenty-second dynasty had risen to two feet above the paving. The inscription states, "The entire valley was like the sea; there was no dyke that could stand its fury. All people were as water birds or swimmers in a torrent . . . all the temples of Thebes were like marshes.' When Herodotus visited Egypt a huge dam protected the Memphis district from flood water. According to tradition it had been built by King Menes.

The central government had a specialized water administration, the *per mu*. One of its obligations was to measure the height of the inundation as it rose and try to estimate its final level and therefore the prospects for the harvest. For this purpose there were a number of 'nilometers' along the course of the river, usually with the graduations cut in the stone of quays or riverside temples. Two of the more important were at Elephantine and (perhaps the oldest of all) at the House of Inundation on the island of Roda near Old Cairo.

The agricultural seasons, and therefore the dominant rhythm of life in the Nile valley, were determined by the so nearly regular movements of the inundation. The rise began to be noticeable at Elephantine in June, but it would take up to another two weeks for it to reach Memphis. The Coptic calendar dated to June 18 the 'night of the drops' when a tear let fall by Isis caused the Nile to rise. This brought it close to June 23 in the Gregorian calendar, the theoretical New Year's Day of the Sothic calendar. The season of inundation (*Akhet*), then, was the first in the farmer's year. The waters rose rapidly in July and August, reached their height in September (or in the north in early October), then began to subside, the Nile being back between its banks by November. Now began *Peret*, the sowing season. The soil of the great basins had been thoroughly soaked and enriched by the fresh silt, and the grain grew splendidly in the mild winter sunshine. After four or five months the harvest began, occupying much of the third season, *Shemu*. It was completed by early May, when the river was dropping to its lowest and the fields beginning to parch and crack open. This was the lifeless time so far as the fields were concerned, when farmers could only wait for Isis to shed her next tear.

Although the conditions and seasons of the Nile differed so considerably from those prevailing by the Twin Rivers, the food crops produced in the two valleys were basically much the same. A great variety of cereal crops have been claimed for ancient Egypt, but most of these claims do not stand up to archaeological and other forms of scrutiny. For pharaonic times the only grains quite reliably identified are barley and emmer wheat (*Triticum dicocum*), though a single identification suggests that a little millet may have been grown. Durum or macaroni wheat was probably introduced during the Late period. Barley, mainly of the four- and six-rowed varieties, seems to have been the more important crop for the Old and Middle Kingdoms, but with the New Kingdom emmer wheat went ahead and became the staple of the Egyptian diet. This generally beneficial reversal of the cereal history of Sumer and Akkad was made possible by freedom from salinization.

It seems that the vitamin-rich sprouted barley was used for food in Egypt as in Mesopotamia, and was also employed for brewing.

Perhaps because cultivation was easy, the Egyptian farmers were conservative rather than inventive in their design of implements. So far as is known, ploughs were not in use during the Archaic period. Instead, when the sowing season came around the wet soil was turned either with the primitive forked stick or with the slightly more advanced type of wooden hoe shown in the hands of King Scorpion. A hoe with a thin metal blade seems already to have been in occasional use at this time. The plough, which was adopted early in the Old Kingdom, was little more than an enlarged hoe with a second handle and shaft added. Ploughs of this kind are represented in early hieroglyphs. They were drawn by a pair of oxen or donkeys,

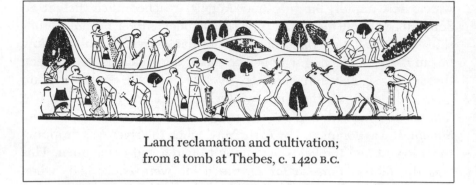

Land reclamation and cultivation;
from a tomb at Thebes, c. 1420 B.C.

the ploughman holding the handles and driving the point into the ground. By the New Kingdom the plough had become more substantial, often with a metal share and the handles secured by several crosspieces.

The Egyptians seem never to have thought it worth while to attach a drill as the Sumerians did. The sower carried the seed grain in a handled bag and scattered it; in some pictures he appears to be walking in front of the ploughing oxen as though it were intended that they should help to trample it in. The main work of treading in the seed, however, was undoubtedly performed by flocks of sheep driven across the field after the sowing.

By the earliest dynastic times the straight reaping knife of the

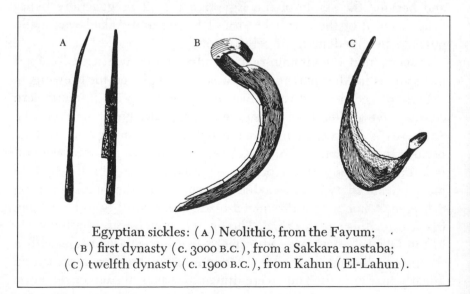

Egyptian sickles: (A) Neolithic, from the Fayum;
(B) first dynasty (c. 3000 B.C.), from a Sakkara mastaba;
(C) twelfth dynasty (c. 1900 B.C.), from Kahun (El-Lahun).

prehistoric past had been replaced by a crescentic form, but the cutting edge was still provided by serrated flint bladelets set in a groove. With these sickles the corn was cut some distance down the stalk, then bundled and carried on donkey-back to the threshing floor. In the New Kingdom a strongly curved metal sickle was

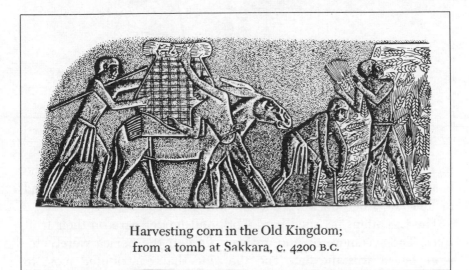

Harvesting corn in the Old Kingdom;
from a tomb at Sakkara, c. 4200 B.C.

adopted. With it there seems to have gone a change in the method of reaping, the ears now being cut off quite short, leaving a longer stubble. The ears could be tossed into a net or basket and be carried on poles for threshing. The grain was trodden out by oxen or other farm animals and winnowed by being tossed into the air with wooden shovels; one tomb scene dating from New Kingdom times shows eight men winnowing together, watched by their master. Finally the grain was measured and stored in brick-built granaries, which might be either cylindrical or with rows of rectangular compartments.

Abundance of vegetables and fruit was produced by means of the perennial irrigation of gardens and orchards. Leeks and onions were much eaten by peasants and workmen as they still are today. Cucumber, garlic and lettuce were also grown—the last being thought to be the aphrodisiac of the phallic god Min, an association for the lettuce that may explain its popularity in Sumerian love songs. Radishes as well as onions and garlic were supplied to labourers on the Great Pyramid. Vegetable protein was forthcoming for the poor

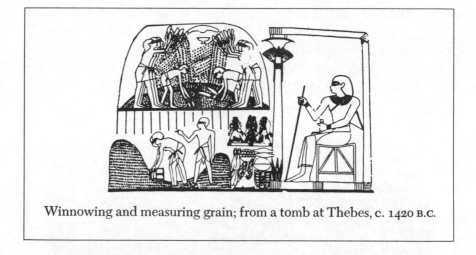

Winnowing and measuring grain; from a tomb at Thebes, c. 1420 B.C.

in the shape of beans, at least by the time of Ramesses II, who boasts of providing them in quantity for his workmen. Gourds and melons flourished between hot sun and moist soil.

The Egyptians lavished hard work and tender care on their fruit trees. The sycamore fig and ordinary fig and the persea were common, but it was the date and the vine that contributed most to wealth, health and happiness. Date palms might be grown on the river bank, scattered through the fields or round villages. Sometimes each tree stood in an artificial basin of mud which could be watered with the aid of a *shaduf*. Just as in Mesopotamia, dates were used for making fermented drinks as well as for food.

It was probably the vine that received most attention of all—as is suggested by the compounding of the hieroglyphic sign for the vine in the words for gardener and orchard. From Archaic times there were royal vineyards, and later Pharaohs took pride in having wine from the best vineyards in their cellars. The leading centres of viticulture were in the western oases such as Khara, Dakhla and Fayum and round the fringes of the Delta, particularly round Pelusium and Tanis and on the west at Mareotis and along the Canopic

Storing the harvest; from a tomb at Beni Hasan, c. 1900 B.C.

Picking figs; from a tomb at Beni Hasan, c. 1900 B.C.

branch of the Nile. Wine jars with seals showing that they came from these Canopic vineyards were found both in Amenhotep III's Theban palace and that of his son at Akhetaten. The vineyards of Tanis were evidently maintained by the Hyksos rulers, for Kamose threatened Apophis, 'See, I shall drink of the wine of your vineyard, which the Asiatics of my own capturing shall press out for me.'

The olive was never extensively grown in Egypt—although this certainly was not from lack of appreciation, as the very earliest

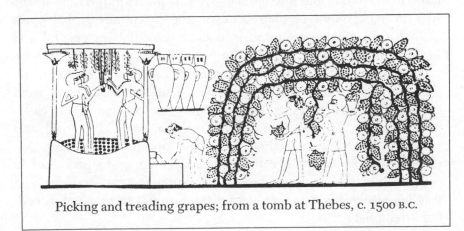

Picking and treading grapes; from a tomb at Thebes, c. 1500 B.C.

record of its cultivation anywhere refers to the Egyptian importation of olive oil from Palestine and Syria during the fourth dynasty. Olives seldom appear in the records, yet may be depicted in garden scenes in New Kingdom times. Perhaps they were mainly cultivated in small numbers as domestic garden trees. They do, however, appear to have been planted on a larger scale in the Fayum. At first the commonest home-grown oil came from the castor-oil plant, and the moringa tree, but at least from the New Kingdom sesame was also grown. Oil was certainly enjoyed by Egyptians in their food (as well as being used for lamps and cosmetics). Just as in Mesopotamia it was a regular part of the rations issued to workmen.

Flax, the one important field crop which has not yet been mentioned, can find a place here, since it may originally have been cultivated for the oil pressed from its seeds. Although this practice continued, from the earliest dynasties onwards it was being grown primarily for the manufacture of the superb Egyptian linens. Unlike corn, flax was sown carefully along the line of the furrow. This method made it easier to harvest, for flax was not cut, but uprooted in large clumps before being bound into sheaves.

Among plants that made no contribution to the diet but were of economic importance the papyrus sedge is outstanding. It was used for boats, ropes, mats and sandals, as well as for papyrus. The cultivation of flowers—which the Egyptians loved with a wholly aesthetic passion—will be discussed in connection with their houses, their parties and their festivals.

Although bread, onions and other vegetable foods must have supplied the principal nourishment for humble peasants and workmen, large numbers of domestic animals were kept. Appropriately to the African background of their country, the Egyptians probably attached even greater importance to cattle-breeding in general and to bulls in particular than did the Sumerians and their successors.

There seem to have been two African breeds frequently to be seen in Egypt from Old Kingdom times. One (the *iwz*) came from up river, perhaps from the Dongola region and beyond. These cattle had wide-spreading horns (sometimes deliberately distorted) and were short-legged, fat-bodied and generally thick-set. Once imported, they seem to have been kept tethered or in paddocks in order to be fattened. These beasts were intended for sacrifices, and it is doubtful whether cows were often brought in or much breeding attempted.

The second breed (written *ng*) was native to the Delta and the hills edging the valley. These animals, too, had spreading horns but were much leaner, higher on their legs and altogether more rangy than the southern cattle. They presumably formed the bulk of the herds and were also used for traction.

The cattle country *par excellence* was the Delta, where there was always good pasture even in summer. For this reason the king and the great landowners of Upper Egypt kept big herds there. Astonishingly, this practice did not end even when the Hyksos were ruling Lower Egypt. When his counsellors are trying to persuade Kamose not to attack the Hyksos king they beg him to leave well alone, for 'The finest of their fields are ploughed for us, our oxen are in the Delta. Emmer is sent for our pigs, our oxen are not taken away.' It continued in the Ramessid age; Ramesses III himself boasted that he had given five Delta herds to the temple of Amun at Karnak. They did not all come from the same area: at least one herd was on the western, Canopic Nile and another on the eastern, Damietta branch. These arrangements enhance the picture of the economic and administrative unity of the kingdom.

In any attempt to estimate the size of the herds, the numbers given in various inscriptions, especially those concerned with war booty, have to be treated with reasoned scepticism. However, the document known as the *Harris Papyrus*, listing in meticulous detail Ramesses III's benefaction to temples throughout the land, is certainly reliable. To the Theban temples he gave 421,362 cattle large and small (including sheep) and 297 bulls; to those in Heliopolis he gave 45,544 various cattle, to those in Memphis 10,047 and to other temples 13,433.

Such figures give some ideas of the scale of stock-breeding in New Kingdom Egypt, and of the huge numbers of beasts that, as it were, passed over the sacrificial tables. Hermann Kees must be justified in saying that although the 'sacrifices ultimately served as food for the priests and for the vast crowds attending the festivals', offerings on this scale were nevertheless 'a very heavy burden on agriculture for the benefit of certain privileged classes'.

Of sheep there seem again to have been two main varieties. During the Old Kingdom, the usual breed was *Ovis longipes*, the Egyptian fleeceless sheep. These creatures had curious, goat-like horns, conspicuously twisted and spread horizontally, almost parallel with the ground. This was the breed of the ram sacred to the god Khnum.

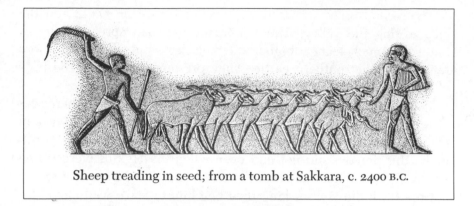

Sheep treading in seed; from a tomb at Sakkara, c. 2400 B.C.

During the Middle Kingdom the fat-tailed, woolly sheep, with down-curved horns, *Ovis platyra,* was introduced, the older variety persisting for a time but becoming extinct by early New Kingdom times. When this happened the fat-tailed sheep had to be used as incarnation animals for Khnum, and it is fascinating to discover from their mummies that these were fitted with a gilded wooden crown bearing the horizontal, twisted horns of *Ovis longipes.*

Herodotus recorded that the tails of *Ovis platyra* became so large and heavy and therefore liable to sores that shepherds supported them on little wheeled trolleys. This is not, as it sounds, an example of the great historian's credulity. In a part of the Delta fat-tails could be still seen trundling their tails behind them until quite recent times.

As sheep and goats can do without rich pasture, flocks could be led over the poor lands bordering the desert in Upper Egypt. Probably even larger numbers were grazed in the Libyan frontier districts of Lower Egypt. Very large flocks (even allowing for the exaggeration of military counts) were captured from time to time in the Libyan wars. These would have been kept in the Delta area, probably still in the care of Libyan shepherds.

The goat was as always the best stand-by of the poor. It may have been a sign of the economic hard times of the Second Intermediate period to find the Theban scribe recording as a good deed towards his own salvation that 'I gave a goat to him who had none.' By ritual decree the he-goat was prohibited as a sacrificial animal because of its identification with Seth. The ritual law, however, was based on aristocratic tradition, and there is no doubt that goats were in fact offered by middle-class worshippers. The attitude towards pigs was even more anomalous. They, too, were identified with Horus's deadly enemy, Seth. Since prehistoric times they had been freely eaten in the Delta, but it seems that when at the Unification Lower Egypt was conquered from the south, the Horus kings of Upper Egypt were shocked to find people eating pork, and laid it down that pigs should neither be eaten nor offered in sacrifice because they were 'abhorrent to Horus'. Swineherds, too, shared the guilt of their beasts and were to be excluded from religious occasions. Once more, however, practice differed from precept. Pigs were in fact kept not only in Lower but also in Upper Egypt—and even at the temple of Osiris at Abydos. Pork was certainly eaten by the tomb workers' fraternity in West Thebes. In short, the ritual prohibition was probably only observed by the royal and noble and by priests. Much the same situation prevailed over eating Nile fish—a most valuable food for the humbler Egyptians. Here there was the further complication that in some myths and in some places the fish was held sacred. There is no question that large quantities were eaten, but again they may have been avoided by the religious élite.

From very early times flocks of geese were kept for their flesh, eggs and fat. Sometimes, perhaps particularly for sacrificial purposes, they were forcibly fed. So, too, were cranes, and in Old Kingdom times a stuffed crane was considered a delicacy. Duck, and in New Kingdom times hens, were also among the fully domesticated table birds. In addition to these, however, in autumn and winter the Egyptians netted thousands of migrant birds, including many kinds of wild duck and goose, and kept them in fattening pens. Both barnyard birds and these wild captives were offered for sacrifice at the temples in enormous numbers.

The meticulous pictorial record left by Egyptian artists has exposed an interesting fact about the domestication of animals that might well have been overlooked. This is that during Archaic and Old Kingdom times efforts to domesticate a wide range of birds and animals were made. Presumably they proved unrewarding and the Old Kingdom Egyptians fell back on the standard farmyard animals of the Old World. Among birds the crane is a case in point. Among the native wild animals shown tethered or in paddocks together with *iwz* bulls are ibex, oryx, addax, gazelle and hyaena. The other animals were probably fattened for both the sacrificial and ordinary domestic table, but the hyaenas' case is hard to explain. They are depicted being held on their backs and very forcibly fed, yet they

Domestication of animals in the Old Kingdom;
from a tomb at Sakkara, c. 2500 B.C.

nowhere appear as offerings or items of diet. There are signs of their being used in the hunt, but this cannot explain the fattening.

Such practices as the capture and fattening of wild creatures and attempts at the domestication of wild species resistant to the process rather confuse the question of hunting as a means of adding to the larder and its variety. In addition to the partially ritual royal hunting of lions and hippopotamuses, the nobles certainly hunted antelope, gazelle and other animals of the wadis and desert fringes. Presumably they ate the game they had killed. Well-to-do people (such as the important official Menna in the days of Amenhotep II) were pictured as going into the papyrus swamps to capture wild duck and spear fish. It can surely be assumed that poorer folk did likewise. There are records of the regular collection of the eggs of water-fowl.

Among the most numerous of all animals in both town and country were the donkeys, originally native of North Africa, that were employed for every kind of transport. Horses were introduced by the Hyksos a little later than their first significant appearance in Mesopotamia. In Egypt, too, the fast war chariots that came with them

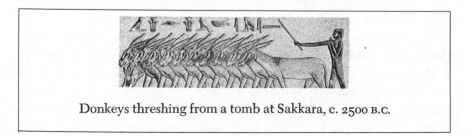

Donkeys threshing from a tomb at Sakkara, c. 2500 B.C.

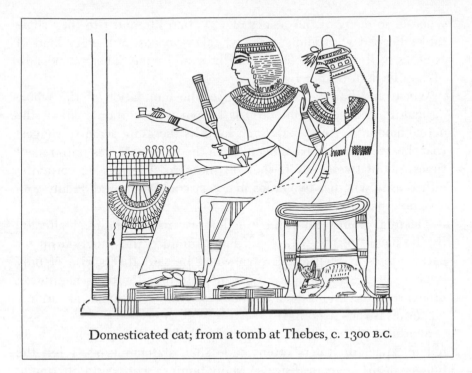

Domesticated cat; from a tomb at Thebes, c. 1300 B.C.

revolutionized military strategy. The introduction was not without its effect on art, for the colossal figure of Pharaoh driving his splendidly decked chariot horses over the bodies of his enemies became the leading image of Egyptian imperialism.

In addition to all their food and draft animals and their birds, the Egyptians loved to keep household pets, particularly cats, dogs and monkeys. Ornamental aviaries probably featured in more Egyptian gardens than those of Akhenaten. Yet by far the most remarkable aspect of the Egyptians' exceptional preoccupation with birds and animals was, of course, manifest in their religious practice. The relationships between gods and beasts were as intimate as they were ancient, and all kinds of creatures both wild and domestic were kept in temples for cult purposes. So, too, thousands upon thousands of carefully embalmed bodies of all these cultic species from cats to crocodiles went into vast animal cemeteries. If one is looking for ways in which peoples differ from one another zoomania can be recognized as an Egyptian peculiarity.

Here, then, were the main resources and products which in normally prosperous times supplied the Egyptians with an abundance of food. Egyptian artists seem to be proclaiming this abundance when in so many of the scenes of Egyptian life and rite they show tables heaped with joints, poultry, cakes, loaves and every kind of fruit, as well as vessels filled with beer and wine. There is no mistaking the flesh pots of Egypt.

Wheat and barley were, of course, the foundation of the whole agricultural economy, but little is known with certainty about the actual amount of the yield. Such hints as there are seem to suggest that the average may have been much the same as it was until recent times: about twenty-six bushels to the acre. There is no certainty, either, as to whether two crops in a year could be raised on any considerable part of the land.

The total grain yield of the kingdom was inevitably much affected by the height of the Nile flood. Pliny summed the situation up for earlier times as well as his own when he said that a rise of only twelve ells meant hunger, thirteen suffering, fourteen happiness, fifteen security, and sixteen abundance. (Above eighteen, he added, meant disastrous flooding.)

Shortages of food among the poor, probably often quite local, were not unexpected. Rulers often made such statements as 'I fed the hungry in the years of distress.' Many famines were certainly due to low Niles. The well-known inscription from the island of Sehel near Elephantine which purports to record how King Djoser (of the Step Pyramid) was sorrowing because of a seven-year famine caused by failures of the inundation, dates in fact from Ptolemaic times yet probably represents some genuine tradition of a series of low Niles.

No less often, however, shortages and famine must have resulted from the collapses of central government that led to failures in overall water control, local abuses, lawless disturbances and civil wars that disrupted agriculture. Thus there are repeated mentions of famine during the bad times of the First Intermediate period. One nomarch of Upper Egypt in those days was surely piling on the horrors in order to increase his own goodness in mitigating them when he declared, 'The entire south died of hunger, every man devouring his own children.' There is only one pictorial record of famine, a terrible scene of emaciated peasants carved in the causeway of the pyramid tomb of King Unas, last king of the fifth dynasty. No explanation is given, so we cannot tell whether their bone-thin limbs, protruding ribs and fainting weakness should be blamed upon human failure or the failure of the Nile.

Grain shortages due to political weakness seem to have recurred in the days of pharaonic decline, during the twelfth century B.C. At the very end of the thirteenth century the late nineteenth dynasty Pharaoh Merenptah was able to send grain to relieve a famine in the land of the Hittites—surely the earliest case of overseas, international aid. Yet only seventy-five years later the cost of wheat shot up on the Theban market as a result, it seems, of excessive taxation and neglected farming. It must have caused hardship equivalent to that which the English suffered before the repeal of the corn laws.

Yet although, looking back across the records, references to food shortage and even famine seem quite frequent, as seen from the perspective of most men's lives they would have appeared exceptional disasters. Moreover, the easy transport offered by the Nile made relief quite feasible. In times of shortage, grain, and especially seed grain, could be supplied from the granaries of each nome. The system by which many landowners in Upper Egypt had herds and other possessions in the Delta enabled them to transfer rations from one to the other according to need. The relief of hunger among his subjects was also a responsibility of Pharaoh himself, and at any rate during New Kingdom times aid was sent from the royal stores.

During all the centuries of strong central government comprised in the Old, Middle and New Kingdoms, country life in Egypt was not generally hard. The impression that the people were wretchedly exploited left to us by Herodotus and his dragoman's tales of the building of the pyramids and by the inevitably bitter biblical accounts of Israelite enslavement, is certainly misleading. It may be that the scenes in the tombs of the great or well-to-do showing these privileged ones sharing in the life of the countryside with wealth and beauty flowing from cornfields and pasture, gardens and vine-yards may be idealized, but it is not false. Even the taxman, who so often figures in them, was advised by precept to remit two-thirds of his exactions if the peasants were in difficulties. The dry season and the months of the inundation left them with little to do but feed the cattle if they were not involved in the corvée; there was plenty of beer and sometimes wine to drink; festivals to provide both solemnity and jollity. The Egyptians had songs to go with the different rhythms of work then as they do today. Probably the setting of the story of the *Two Brothers* gives a fair picture of the humble farmer's life. The two young men took pleasure in their ploughing and seeding, in leading the cattle to the best pasture, and in bringing home the plentiful produce of their fields in the evening. Work over, the elder brother liked to sit with his wife, perhaps on the bench outside their house, while the west still glowed and the rest of the heavens filled with the calm brightness of Egyptian stars.

The Egyptian kingdom depended for its wealth upon the lives of country folk like the Two Brothers in a way that was not true of Sumer and Akkad or Babylonia. This was because it was not truly urbanized before Greek times. Essentially it remained a land of farms and villages and country towns. Peasants took their small surpluses into town to exchange them, often by simple barter, for the products of humble craftsmen and shopkeepers. The *Eloquent Peasant* went down to the valley from his home in a distant wadi to fetch food for his children, probably from the markets of Herakleopolis. Provisioned by his wife with bread and beer, he loaded his donkeys with local specialities, especially salt and natron, which he intended to proffer in exchange. The Two Brothers, when they ran out of seed corn in the middle of their sowing, went into the village for more. Such were the small affairs that made up a large part of the dealings between farm, village and market town.

ARCHITECTURE AND THE CITIES

THE CHIEF TOWNS OF THE NOMES CERTAINLY MADE CENTRES OF MORE cultivated life within the rural world. In the times of the nomarchs their provincial courts must have attracted artists and craftsmen as well as courtiers, officials and soldiers. Even after the suppression of the nomarchy they remained centres of local government managed by an educated élite. They also, of course, at all times had their temples and temple personnel. Yet so far as we know none of these towns, nor even the royal capitals, were true cities in the Sumerian sense. They were not compact centres of manufacture where specialist craftsmen worked in their own crowded quarters and souks, nor had they any equivalent of the city quarters of merchants, native and foreign, of sea captains and business men of all kinds with their private offices and their *karum* or exchange—such as those at Ur.

Information about Egyptian houses is very patchy and about the layout of towns even more incomplete. Thinking of the countryside first, what kind of house would the Two Brothers have returned to at nightfall? It has been seen how by the earliest dynastic times the reed and matting huts of the prehistoric villages had given way to mud-brick. Presumably even the humblest peasant houses would have been built of it and would have followed a rectangular plan with a foot-puddled flat roof. Egyptians of all degrees seem to have made use of the roofs of their houses for relaxation and perhaps for sleeping in the hottest weather. It is usually assumed that peasants shared a part of their house with their livestock—particularly during the inundation when cattle large and small were hand-fed. A regular feature of every house was the simple saddle quern where the housewife spent many hours on her knees grinding flour. In the kitchen was the clay oven where she baked her bread.

A rather more advanced type of house such as might have been the home of a minor official or of a family with a moderate country estate is represented by rough models from twelfth dynasty tombs at Rifeh. These houses were approached through a courtyard furnished with a pond, and perhaps a stand of water jars, beyond which, in the usual single-storeyed type, there was a columned veranda with three living rooms behind. Some of the Rifeh houses were on two floors, and in these the veranda was on the upper storey where it would be cooler and more private. The grander country house that would have adorned large country estates in New Kingdom times was probably very much like the finer residences at Akhetaten described below.

A distinctive type of development, which might be likened to the modern industrial estate, provides a more consistent picture of the kind of housing designed for artisans and skilled labourers. The great undertakings of the crown, from monumental building and tomb-cutting to mining, often necessitated the building of cantonments or special 'villages' for the workers. The earliest known example was established at Kahun (El-Lahun) near Herakleopolis for the people engaged on the building of the pyramid for the twelfth dynasty Pharaoh Sen-Wosret II. This Pyramid City was enclosed within a rectangular compound measuring as much as 985 by 1310 feet. It was designed to house rich and poor—but they were separated by an internal wall. On the east side there were well over two hundred tiny houses, on the west a range of much larger ones, and to the north five mansions with about seventy rooms, including business offices and quarters for servants. Little streets were laid out on a grid plan and had stone drains running down the centre.

Another cantonment, usually referred to as a 'model village', was built to the east of the capital of Akhetaten, probably to house workers engaged in cutting and decorating tombs in the neighbouring cliffs. Here the compound wall was square and except for a warden's house near the entrance all the seventy-four dwellings were quite small, with an entrance hall, living room, bedroom and kitchen. They were laid out in dead straight terrace blocks with narrow alleys in between. If they were cramped and monotonous, these skilled workers' houses were sound enough, and have been judged more comfortable than the average home of the modern Egyptian *fellah*. They were certainly greatly superior to the wretched accommodation provided for conscripted manual labourers working the famous alabaster quarries at Hatnub, some fifteen miles away. There the quarrymen, who in New Kingdom times are known to have been mainly convicts and prisoners of war, had to live in tiny, cave-like stone huts ranged along the road or above the cuttings.

There had been little change in the standard of workers' houses during the five centuries separating Akhetaten from Kahun, and there was to be little again between Akhetaten and a third cantonment, occupied down to late Ramessid times, at Deir el-Medinah in western Thebes. It was a settlement for tomb-cutters and craftsmen employed in the nearby necropolis consisting of seventy little houses in two terraces with a street between.

For the houses of the well-to-do, Akhetaten again provides the best examples. Although they ranged in grandeur according to the social pretensions of owners who included a high priest and a vizier on the one hand and relatively modest professional men on the other, all followed much the same design. The whole rectangular property, garden and buildings together, was enclosed within a wall. As a visitor entered through a large doorway with the gatekeeper's room beside it, he would see the garden shrine in front of him, but would turn off to pass through a courtyard and up a few steps to the porch. He would now enter the house itself, passing through a vestibule into a cool, northward-facing hall (with a loggia above) where he might be received by the owner. If he were more than a casual caller or petitioner he would be led into the main reception room, a formally proportioned chamber lit by clerestory windows and with its ceiling supported on four stuccoed wooden columns. The walls might be white, painted with garlands of flowers. This room formed the structural centre of the house. Round it were the women's quarters, guest chambers, and the imposing master bedroom with a raised niche for the bed and adjoining well-fitted lavatory, bathroom and unguent room.

The servants had quite separate accommodation with their own entrance leading through the granary court, set near the kitchens and bake house in the corner of the compound.

The remainder of the enclosure was taken up by an irrigated garden with flowers, trees and an ornamental pool and kiosk. Upper class Egyptians had always loved gardens, and here in the holy city of the Aten such a love had its religious significance greatly magnified.

An establishment of this kind was both civilized and comfortable— rather more so, surely, than its equivalent in the residential quarters of Mesopotamian cities. Yet the two standards are not strictly comparable, for the Akhetaten houses did not represent a true urban architecture: they were reduced versions of the houses in which the nobility lived on their estates. Indeed, even the royal palaces were yet further magnified versions of the same plan.

From the first realization of the possibilities of stone architecture in the third dynasty, to quarry and to build were royal prerogatives. With this went the limitation of stone architecture to temples, shrines and tombs. Even the stone itself, with its evocation of the Egyptian idea of 'eternity', had a religious meaning.

Although masonry was being used in small ways during Archaic times, and masons may have been learning the elements of their craft, true architecture seems to arrive with extraordinary suddenness in the Step Pyramid complex of the third dynasty. Earlier buildings may have been lost, yet there is much in Imhotep's creation to make it reasonable to think that his individual genius played a great part in this sudden advance. To begin with the pyramid itself, the fact that it was built up in two attempts from a traditional mastaba suggests that somebody was dissatisfied by the old form and groped his way towards a monumental style that would proclaim Pharaoh's celestial godhead near and far. As for the associated temples and courts, their imitation of forms proper to the old mud-brick and wooden construction suggests a single decision to change to the new medium. The size and shape of mud-bricks was reproduced in stone. Masons were evidently directed to imitate columns of plastered reed, palm-log ceilings, picket fences, beam ends and rolled matting blinds. The faience tiles in the tombs are meticulous copies of coloured mats. Strangest of all, a hinged wooden gate thrown open at an angle to the wall has been reproduced in stone.

It is easy to suppose that a man of powerful imagination, inspired by what he knew of the grandeur of Mesopotamian architecture, determined to wave the wand of his genius over the traditional forms to magnify them and turn them into the substance of eternity.

Whether or not this unique and graceful creation at Sakkara owes so much to one man's genius, it ranks with Palaeolithic art, and far above Stonehenge, among the glorious improbabilities of human history.

Imhotep used fine-grained limestone from the Tura quarries across the river for his masterpiece. Limestone, which occurs abundantly along the Nile valley to as far south as Esna, was to remain the most popular building stone until well into eighteenth dynasty times. Most often it was quarried locally, but for special purposes finer qualities, such as that from Tura, might be transported—as was the case with the outer skin of the great pyramids of Giza.

South of Esna, sandstone displaces limestone as the prevailing rock, and from about the reign of Thutmose III architects came to prefer it, probably because its greater tensile strength enabled much longer blocks to be cut for roofing spans. It has been used for most later buildings other than the temples of Seti I and his son at Abydos. The best quarry for sandstone was at Silsila, some forty miles north of Elephantine. There, as in all the other important quarries, the exercise of the royal monopoly in stone was recorded by inscriptions cut into the rock face.

Granite was the third stone frequently used by Egyptian builders —virtually all of it coming from the great ridge that crossed the Nile near Elephantine, forming the First Cataract. The exceptional hardness of granite which has defied the erosive might of the Nile appealed to the Egyptians just as it appeals to the makers of Christian tombstones. It spite of the immense labour of working it, this stone 'of a million years' was used for flooring a tomb as early as the first dynasty, then for the burial chambers of the step and Giza pyramids among other tombs, and very widely for door frames. Only one entire granite building is known—the beautiful valley temple of Khaefre. It was the ideal material for the magnificent obelisks that were such a striking addition to Egyptian architecture—and which are now scattered about the capitals of the world as the fruits

of martial and cultural looting. There is no sight in the whole kingdom that better conveys a sense of the toil that the Egyptians were
eager to devote to the most impractical ends than the huge rough-cut
obelisk that still lies attached to the native rock at Aswan. The
granite cracked through before the grim task of undercutting had
been completed.

The small blocks used by Imhotep in imitation of mud-bricks were
soon superseded, for large ones reduced quarrying time. The Great
Pyramid of Giza contained about 2,300,000 blocks with an average
weight of 2½ tons. Some, however, were as much as 15 tons, and the
granite slabs roofing the King's Chamber 50 tons.

For their unsurpassed feats of building the Egyptians characteristically neglected technical aids. They never devised capstans,
pulleys or scaffolding, and did not even employ wheeled carts before
New Kingdom times. Instead they relied on plentiful and well-
directed human muscle power. The very inundation which made it
possible to transport stone by raft to the edge of the desert also
left many strong peasants idle and free for corvée. For transport on
land, log rollers or wooden sleds could be used. In a famous scene
from the tomb of a Middle Kingdom nobleman, a colossal statue
is being drawn on a sled, a foreman directing from his perch on
the knees of the figure and a man pouring water from the front of
the sled to ease its passage. The colossus probably weighed about 60
tons and there are 172 men pulling on the ropes. It is easy to exaggerate the manpower needed to shift large objects; what is rarer
and can hardly be exaggerated is the degree of will-power and political power needed to impel it.

Stone masons at work; from a tomb at Thebes, c. 1450 B.C.

Massive building blocks were brought from the quarries roughly squared out; the jointing faces may then have been trimmed before they were pulled up earthen ramps into position. The exposed faces of walls and columns, and presumably the polished facets of pyramids, were then finished off, working from the top downwards as the ramps were gradually removed. The greater part of the stone-working both in the quarry and at the building site seems to have been done with stone implements, and an utterly simple equipment of square, plumb line, and boning rods was good enough to control the erection of gigantic buildings that were to stand for thousands of years. A host of men skilled in stone-working and building became a feature of Egyptian society without parallel in Mesopotamia.

As for the architects and designers who must have directed this great labour force after the deified Imhotep, we can only name Senmut, who probably created Hatshepsut's beautiful Deir el-Bahri temple, and the humbly born Amenhotep son of Hapu who built Amenhotep III's funerary temple in West Thebes and transported the two sixty-eight-foot-high 'colossi of Memnon' from quarries near Heliopolis to sit before it. Egyptian architecture is easily called conservative, yet there was constant evolution—first that of the true pyramid, one great achievement of the Old Kingdom, then the planning of a great variety of temple forms in harmony with changing religious concepts. There was the remarkable creation of an architecture cut from the native rock. In detail there are such achievements as the development of the free-standing column and of the closed- and open-bud papyrus capitals, the palm tree and tent pole capitals, all of which clothed their symbolic meanings in grandeur if not in grace. Certainly there was a decline in taste and even in building standards in the late New Kingdom, and the men who worked for Ramesses II were subject to his megalomania. Even so there are few modern visitors who are not awed, even reluctantly, by the titanic size and sheer effectiveness of the Karnak Hypostyle Hall and Ramesseum at Thebes. It must not be forgotten either that every step of this evolution of a civilized stone architecture was pioneering, for no other people entered the field until after the end of the Old Kingdom, and none ever had power to influence Egyptian builders.

Stone architecture was created in the service of the gods, including that god incarnate, the divine Pharaoh. It was therefore used almost exclusively for temples and shrines of the many deities and for funerary temples and shrines of the kings. The temples of local deities in ordinary nome capitals were architecturally unpretentious, and any attempt to picture the great stone buildings in their contemporary settings must inevitably be focussed on the principal religious centres and the royal capitals. To make this attempt, then, will bring us back to a brief consideration of the true nature of Egyptian cities by another way.

Among the sacred towns of which anything substantial is known, Heliopolis was one of the most important. It had a ship canal running up from the Nile with a harbour at the entrance guarded by an old fortress. A processional way also led up from the harbour district to the city itself with its temples of Atum and of Re. There must have been worthy accommodation for the large and powerful priesthood of Re, and accommodation of a sort for the pilgrims who crowded there—mostly from the Delta. Possibly, too, the position of Heliopolis near the starting point of routes into Sinai and Asia may at various times have added settlements involved in the handling of goods or other forms of eastern traffic—though most of this would probably have gone to Memphis, only some twenty miles to the south.

Abydos came to be the first of the sacred cities of Egypt once it was established as possessing the tomb of Osiris. From the start of the Middle Kingdom everybody who was anybody wanted either to be buried there or to raise a cenotaph. The temples, rich and splendid though they came to be, must have been dominated by the vast City of the Dead through which ran the processional way of Osiris. People flocked there from up and down the river for the festivals of the god. Abydos must, therefore, have housed large numbers of priests and humbler folk tending the necropolis, many artisans and masons turning out funerary monuments, and all kinds of hangers-on offering refreshments and religious knick-knacks to the pilgrim throngs. Nothing is known of where or how they lived.

Another place with a distinctive character was Elephantine, centred on the miniature Manhattan of the island crowned by the temple of Khnum. Here the houses were crowded almost in the oriental manner, but the area so covered was very small. At this important bottleneck of the Nile valley there would have been facilities for handling African traders and trade goods, frontier and customs posts (before the New Kingdom) and fluctuating colonies of quarrymen, masons and shippers involved in the supply of granite to the north. Elephantine was the capital of its nome, so somewhere it sheltered the residence of the nomarchs (whose tombs

were in the western cliffs) and of their more official and bureaucratic successors.

Among the three royal capitals that demand attention it is most
helpful to return first to Akhetaten, because short-lived and atypical
though it was, the plan is at least known in its entirety. We have seen
that the individual houses were essentially non-urban, and the same
can be said of the place as a whole. Unwalled, without any suggestion of an inner citadel, it lay sprawled along about five miles
of the Nile bank, its two irregular main streets running parallel with
the river. There was, it is true, a magnificent architectural focus at
the centre, formed by the vast stone-built Aten temple, the principal
royal palace, the Record Office, Hall of Foreign Tribute, the university, and other royal and ministerial buildings. A considerable distance to the north and south two other royal establishments with
pleasure gardens were quite casually sited.

As for the houses of the courtiers and those who served the courtiers in one way or another, they were scattered in an almost haphazard fashion. The grander ones stood in their gardens facing the
main streets, while the more humble were usually on the side streets.
An unplanned suburb developed to the north. Some small houses
seem to have belonged to clerks working in the ministries, and only
these showed anything like urban density. Hermann Kees has
commented of Akhetaten: 'Its character in general was more that
of a sprawling provincial town inhabited by prosperous gentlemen
farmers than of an ancient oriental city in which houses were
crowded together for protection.'

Akhetaten cannot, of course, be accepted as a fully representative
Egyptian capital. In being unwalled and without a citadel it was
normal. Egyptian towns did not expect to go to war with one
another or to be attacked from without. The fact that it was built
all at once on virgin soils and had an unusually high proportion of
well-to-do dependents of a court devoted to the beauties of nature,
may well have led to exceptionally low-density building. Nevertheless it is improbable that the Akhetaten town house with its spacious
garden and out-buildings was a complete innovation. Much the
same kind of dwelling might be expected in provincial capitals and
perhaps in the national capitals as well.

It is with Memphis and Thebes that our lack of solid information
has brought the most serious historical deprivation. Memphis, the
royal capital of the Old Kingdom and always to remain the adminis-

trative headquarters of Lower Egypt, can hardly be imagined in isolation but as part of a fluctuating complex of settlements and religious establishments. Like Heliopolis, the town was served by a ship canal from the Nile, and probably was in fact bounded by canals on its east and west sides. The harbour must have been a busy one, and somewhere in the neighbourhood was the royal estate of Perunefer with its big shipyards. The main town seems to have extended for about 1½ miles north and south, with a width of less than a mile. It had grown up round the original Early Dynastic foundation of White Walls, a white-painted fortress-like building with recessed mud-brick walls which probably stood on the same site as a later palace. To the south was the architecturally dominating feature of the temple of Ptah; a sacred lake and gardens may have occupied the hollow in between. Presumably the priesthood of Ptah, in Old Kingdom days strong rivals of Heliopolis, would have had a college and other premises. There may also have been a temple of Ptah's great daughter, Hathor, in the town—as there certainly was a few miles out at Dahshur. Memphis must also have possessed many administrative buildings such as those named at Akhetaten.

What again remains maddeningly unknown is the nature of the residential and trading quarters of this northern capital. What remained of their mud-brick has long ago gone to fertilize the fields. There were certainly plenty of artists, craftsmen and skilled artisans in Memphis and there must also have been an exceptionally large class of administrators. Altogether if there was anywhere in Egypt with a sizeable area of crowded houses in the oriental manner, it seems most likely to have been in Memphis.

Outside the central city, we have to picture the landscape dominated from the edge of the western desert by the line of pyramids and sun temples, often with causeways running down to waterside temples, all the way from Dahshur to as far north as Heliopolis. In the pyramid age itself these foundations would have their pyramid cities built on the plateau and probably broadly similar to the one described at Kahun, with their populations of priests and workers raising their own food on the adjacent edge of the cultivable land. The western plateau also supported the sanctuaries of many other divinities in addition to Hathor, and from the eighteenth dynasty there began the extraordinary ceremonial of the entombment of the Apis bull at Sakkara in the vast catacombs that finally became the Serepeum. Across the river on either side of the Mokattam Mountains were many famous quarries. If any Egyptologist could wish himself a single visit to the past, he would surely choose to see those historically crowded miles from Memphis to Heliopolis.

If Memphis knew its greatest glory in the vigorous, pure-hearted, creative age of the Old Kingdom, Thebes of the 'hundred gates' was essentially an imperialist capital, the creation of an élite passing from ripeness to overripeness. At Memphis the greatest architectural monuments were outside, standing guard along the desert plateau: at Thebes, both east and west, they dominated the town, a vast stage set for high-pitched ceremonial. In this it might be likened to Delhi, although its fanes and processional ways were essentially designed for religious rather than military or state ceremonies. Still, the deliberately tent-like temple built by Thutmose III to commemorate his life under canvas and his victories and the marvellous pictorial records of his campaigns on the walls of the main sanctuary introduce something· of the spirit of an imperial *arc de triomphe.*

Homer's epithet of the 'hundred gates' has caused many to picture Thebes as a walled city. This it never was. The gates were enormous, chunky pylons built at the entry to temples and to their inner courts. Thebes of the east bank (Karnak and Luxor) was devoted to divinities other than Pharaoh and principally of course to Amun (Amen-Re). Thebes of the west bank, presided over by el-Qurn, 'the western mountain peak' of the ancients, was devoted to the Pharaohs, to their tremendous funerary temples, palaces and (hidden away in the wadis running up toward el-Qurn) their tombs.

The vast temple of Amun at Karnak records in its stones most of the history of the New Kingdom with many addenda carrying it down to our own era. Pharaohs built, added, demolished, rebuilt again and again, took over their predecessors' buildings, carved their historical reliefs and inscriptions. As well as the main temple buildings of Amun and the sacred lake, the enormous walled precinct contained a temple for Amun's son, the divine child, Khonsu. Outside, but linked by a sphinx avenue, was the temple of the third member of the family, Amun's consort, Mut. To the passing public this gigantic accumulation of buildings revealed little more than the tops of pylons and obelisks showing above the severe ashlar of the sanctuary wall. On occasion, however, the people of Thebes were admitted to be awed by the superhuman size of the Hypostyle Hall. At the greatest festival of the Theban year, the festival of Opet, the pylon gates opened and the images of Amun, Mut and Khonsu were conveyed in their sacred barques 1½ miles south to the second great temple of eastern Thebes at what is now Luxor. This temple, belonging to the divine family itself, was largely built by Amenhotep III at the height of Theban prosperity. It was a noble work of architecture, grand but not suffering from gigantism. Its papyrus columns are well proportioned and all the stone work of the finest. Standing close to the Nile, it must have impinged on the notice of the citizen more than the much larger temple complex of Karnak. So, too, must the long avenue lined by ram-headed sphinxes that led from one to the other.

The main city of Thebes can be presumed to have stood on this eastern bank, occupying the area between or to the east of present-day Karnak and Luxor. But the intentions of the ancient Egyptians have been fulfilled: the houses of the gods have largely endured while those of men have vanished. Hardly anything is known of the residential quarters of Thebes, whether of the rich or of the poor. Probably the building density was greater than that of Akhetaten —there were certainly two-storeyed houses. One is tempted to guess it was less than that of Memphis. Possibly the housing tended to be divided into separate quarters and suburbs, some assigned to foreigners: there was certainly plenty of space—but we simply do not know.

At all times and seasons there was traffic crossing the Nile from one side of Thebes to the other. On the west side a raised causeway led through the broad strip of farmland, past the funerary temple of Amenhotep III with its colossi, still on cultivable land, to the desert edge with its line of funerary temples and necropoli stretching all the way from the fortress-like foundation of Ramesses III (Medinet Habu) in the south to that of Seti I at Gournah to the north-east. Set further back into the cliffs were the lovely terraces of Hatshepsut's creation adjoining the one great Theban survival of the Middle Kingdom, the pyramid-temple of Menthuhotep.

On this side of the river we know only residences representing social extremes, the palace built by Amenhotep III and Queen Tiy, of mud-brick like all dwellings but large and richly adorned, and the tomb-workers' settlement already described. There must of course have been much accommodation for priests and workers employed at the funerary temples, and those supplying food and other necessities for all the rest. There is no question, however, that West Thebes was just as much a secondary suburb of the main town as the extension across the Euphrates was of Babylon.

Shockingly inadequate though our information is, this look at the fabric of some leading Egyptian centres seems to confirm the judgement that the kingdom was never fully urbanized in the Mesopotamian sense. It could be said that in this aspect of her social and economic life Egypt had more in common with New World civilizations than with that of her Asian neighbours. More than anything else her cities were ceremonial centres, their populations relatively small and very largely devoted to the service of the royal and religious establishments.

CRAFTS AND FASHIONS

THIS SURVEY OF THE COUNTRY LIFE OF EGYPT AND OF ITS RELATION to the cities has included an account of the work of stone masons and architects so essential to the setting of the scene. It is now necessary to say something of other Egyptian crafts and skills, but as these have many similarities with those already described for Mesopotamia, it will as far as possible be limited to what was distinctively Egyptian. Once again, as in the practice of agriculture, temples and tombs provide illustrations of the Egyptians at work that are detailed, lively and accurate. No words could possibly give as vivid an idea of just how the men and women of the Nile valley set about their tasks of baking, brewing and wine-making, of spinning, weaving and tanning, of potting, carpentry and metal working of all kinds as these sculptured and painted scenes. Indeed, some record particulars of far more specialized techniques such as the production of cosmetics— and of chariots.

In addition to this wonderful pictorial record, there are the wooden models from the tombs that enable us to see some of these activities in all their dimensions. Finally, of course, there is the survival of actual furniture, textiles and other perishable goods that have been lost in most other lands. Tutankhamun's tomb alone yielded more such things than all of ancient Asia.

Most of these scenes and models relate to the premises of the

well-to-do or of the temple establishments where large numbers
of servants and craftsmen worked together—as in the castles, great
country houses or monasteries of Europe. How far some of the skills
percolated down to the much more modest establishments of
farmers or of the artisans themselves can only be surmised.

In the Egyptian kitchens the long-burning fuels were such things
as the dried roots of papyrus or mimosa and tamarisk wood. Chaff,
datestones and dung were also burnt. In many scenes from the Old
Kingdom onwards geese are being roasted on hand-held spits or
boiled in large stew-pans. In the New Kingdom, after about 1500
B.C., the roasting of beef is more often shown.

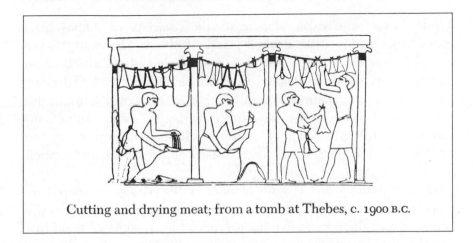

Cutting and drying meat; from a tomb at Thebes, c. 1900 B.C.

As for the cereal foods which formed a large part of the diet of
the ordinary people, they included a good range of bread and cakes.
Until New Kingdom times the preparation of wheat and barley
flour seems to have been carried out by each establishment, large
or small, for itself. By about 1500 B.C. there are records of a miller
working on a commercial scale. The usual method seems to have
been to husk the grain in mortars, then grind it on a sloping quern.
One of the many technical devices that Egypt was slow to adopt
was the rotary quern, or hand-mill. They were not saving labour for
housewives and millers before Hellenistic times. Among the Egyptian peculiarities described by Herodotus was the fact that they
kneaded clay with their hands and dough with their feet. This
is a fantasy so far as pharaonic Egypt is concerned, for several
scenes show male bakers vigorously working the dough with their

Making unleavened bread; from a tomb at Thebes, c. 1900 B.C.

hands. Loaves and cakes were made in a variety of shapes from cones to large thin disks cooked griddle-fashion. These must have resembled the bread still enjoyed in Arab lands and often to be seen on the tables of archaeological expeditions. Other types of baking seem to have been done on stones laid horizontally over a bright fire —until the closed oven was introduced in about 2000 B.C. In peasant homes no doubt grinding and baking would have been done by the woman, but in the large households usually depicted men and women servants are shown working together.

The Egyptians were as fond of beer as the Mesopotamians, and in many ways their methods of brewing were similar. Already in the Old Kingdom there were five main types of beer, some of them distinguished as being extra strong; it is thought that an alcoholic content of as much as 12 percent could be obtained, especially if sugary substances were added. The Egyptians trod the mash in huge pottery vats. A quaint Predynastic ceramic model shows a woman up to her waist in such a vat. One hieroglyphic sign, on the other hand, represents a man trampling in a still larger vessel. It appears that in fact brewing was first done by women but later largely taken

Preparing and cooking meat and poultry; Giza, c. 2500 B.C.

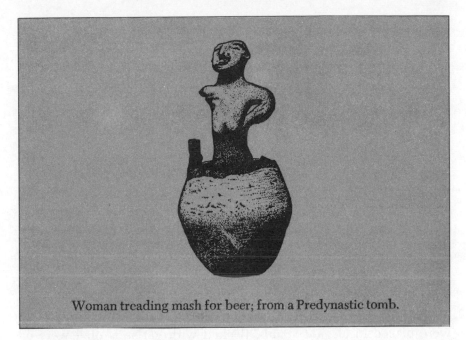

Woman treading mash for beer; from a Predynastic tomb.

over by men working more professionally. There is no evidence for the existence of the woman brewer and inn-keeper who was such a well-known figure in the Mesopotamian world.

Egyptians recognized the virtues of intoxication in giving their beers such distinguishing names as 'the joy-bringer', 'the beautiful-good' and the 'heavenly'. While the Greeks found Mesopotamian beer rather sour, Diodorus Siculus praised the Egyptian as 'very little inferior to wine'. Probably this was because beer jars were always carefully stoppered before the second fermentation could begin.

Date wine must have been widely drunk in Egypt, but perhaps was never quite so popular as it became in Babylonia. Palm wine made by tapping the trunks was tried, but may have been abandoned because of the damage inevitably done to the tree. As we have seen, viticulture was made much of in Egypt and many scenes show the gathering of the grapes and the preparation and enjoyment of the wine.

The vintage itself was celebrated with music, and there was music, too, when the grapes were trodden in large vats. A method for squeezing out the juice by twisting the fruit in a linen bag slung between posts had been invented as early as Old Kingdom times, but the finest wines were always held to result from the use of human

Bag-press for wine or oil; from a tomb at Beni Hasan, c. 1500 B.C.

feet. Fermentation took place in a cellar or dark room—where the workers might grow faint from carbon dioxide fumes. The fermented liquor was then strained through linen into pointed-bottomed jars like the amphorae of classical and modern times. Some were used immediately, some sealed and stood in the cellar, supported by sand or by rings of straw. For the choicest wines the seals were marked with the name of the vineyard and its head gardener and the year of growth. When these jars were brought out for festivities they were placed in elegant stands, decked with garlands of flowers or trailing vine branches, sometimes with bunches of grapes still attached. The spirit of Bacchus was evidently already present in the Egypt of the New Kingdom.

Just as during the first dynasties all vineyards were royal domains, it is thought that at first wine was used only for royal and religious occasions. It was always associated with such festivals, but in time it was undoubtedly being made and drunk by the well-to-do at their banquets and parties. Probably it remained beyond the normal reach of the man at the plough at least until the Hellenistic period.

In Egypt unguents for anointing the body were by no means luxury products. The Egyptians were a fanatically cleanly people and in their intensely hot and dry climate the application of oils and fats was essential for the comfort and health of the skin. Everybody used them. The Pharaoh Seti I found it necessary to increase the amount of ointments supplied to his soldiers. When the workmen of Ramessid Thebes struck because their rations were not forthcoming, ointments were among the issues demanded.

Over thirty different forms of unguents appear in the lists, and there is some evidence that varieties used in Old and Middle Kingdom times for ritual and medical purposes tended to be displaced by others manufactured simply as cosmetics.

The bases used for the unguents were oils and animal fats. Probably castor and olive oils were those most generally available to the poor, but many others were also employed. The fats of oxen, sheep and geese were in use from quite early times. Scented or aromatic flowers, seeds, woods and gums were then used to add perfume. This might be done by steeping or warming them in the fats or oils or extracting their essential oils in cloth squeezers similar, on a small scale, to those used for grapes. A charming though late relief shows women expressing oil from lilies in this way. The animal fats scented with flowers were made up into balls and cones of pomade for the head and hair. To attend a party well-oiled in this sense was expected of the well-to-do in New Kingdom society.

That gods, like Christian saints, had their own perfume was well known. When Hatshepsut was about to be begotten by the god Amun, her mother 'waked at the fragrance of the god', which she smelled in the presence of His Majesty. The ancient Egyptian word for a good smell had the meaning 'fragrance of the gods', and it has already been made plain that the use of scented unguents had its religious aspect. The two purposes unite in the use of myrrh and other resins both for incense and for bodily perfumes.

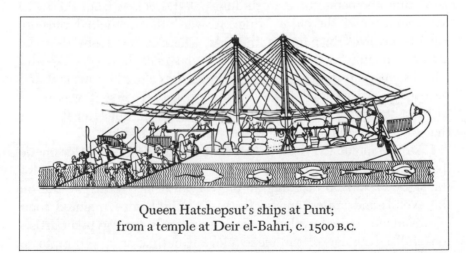

Queen Hatshepsut's ships at Punt;
from a temple at Deir el-Bahri, c. 1500 B.C.

The voyages down the Red Sea to Punt repeatedly undertaken in the most prosperous phases of Egyptian history were first and foremost intended to bring back these precious gums. The reliefs at Deir el-Bahri show 'incense trees' being brought back from Punt by Queen Hatshepsut's expedition, their roots carefully bound, and may represent an effort by the Egyptians to produce their own myrrh. The trees were in fact planted in specially prepared holes in front of the queen's magnificent temple. It is thought that this and subsequent attempts to get the trees to grow in the Nile valley were unsuccessful. It has even been suggested, by one of those guesses that are taken seriously only if they fall from the lips of experts, that the people of Punt deliberately sabotaged the trees in some way in order not to lose the valuable Egyptian market. However all this may be, the expensive and probably sometimes dangerous expeditions to Punt prove the extreme importance the Egyptians attached to the censing and perfuming of their temples, their divine images and themselves.

As with other cosmetics, the history of eye paint was very much involved with both medical and religious usages. It has been given a disproportionate interest by the fact that the decorative palettes on which the minerals were already ground in Predynastic days evolved into splendid ceremonial objects such as the famous two-foot-long palette of King Narmer. This development is itself a proof of the religious associations of eye paints; they were in fact offered to the gods, and they were applied to the divine images. Yet at the same time the name for the grinding palettes comes from the word for 'protect' and therefore brings forward the medicinal purpose equally involved in painting the lids. There is no doubt that the minerals mainly used, galena (black) and malachite (green), did afford some protection against the eye diseases already prevalent and perhaps also discouraged the settling of flies. At first it was usual to paint the upper lid black and the lower green, but later it seems that the complete black outline was the normal fashion.

Like the unguents, the eye paints became increasingly cosmetic in purpose, as is shown by the change from labels such as 'good for the sight' or 'to stop bleeding' to mere beauticians' terms, 'to put on the eyelids and lashes' and so forth. That both sexes painted their eyes is made evident in thousands of portrayals, for Egyptian artists took full advantage of the clear, elegant outline so appropriate to their style.

When they wished to look their best, Egyptian women wore a rouge made from red ochre. They probably also followed the still prevailing custom of applying henna to their nails, and to the palms of their hands and soles of their feet.

It is impossible not to suppose that Egyptian women were more stylish than their Sumerian and Semitic contemporaries. Just as they preferred the idea of straight and slender figures to that of fullness and curves, so they dressed for elegance and seductiveness rather than grandeur. If this was not true of the extreme simplicity of the Old Kingdom fashions, then surely it was for the more sophisticated developments of the Middle and still more the New Kingdom. The impression must, of course, be partly due to the sympathetic manner in which these ladies were painted and sculptured. It owes something to fashionable female society being portrayed at all, for all those scenes of high life are very different from the static figures of goddesses and queens which are almost all the Mesopotamian artists have left for our judgement. Yet when all allowances are made, it seems that the Egyptians had grace and elegance where their sisters at best made do with colour and richness.

The quality of Egyptian dress depended very much on the fine white linen which had been woven since Predynastic times. In imagining any crowd we have to think of almost everyone being dressed in white, and of the white garments contrasting with brown skins. In the Old Kingdom men almost invariably wore a simple loin cloth, those of the gentry sometimes broadly pleated in front, while women wore long-sleeved gowns reaching down to their ankles. Then, as later, the pure white was strikingly relieved by the brightly coloured beads of the broad necklaces or collars worn by both men and women, and by the formal patterns on the headbands of the women. During the Middle Kingdom there were no very significant changes, though the men now more often covered their torso with short sleeved, fitted tunics, and wore their loin cloths longer. As might be expected, change came with the New Kingdom. Already during the eighteenth dynasty imperial contacts with Asia, a wealthier and more pleasure-loving upper class and a prevailing spirit of luxurious cosmopolitanism produced great interest in fashion. There was more variety, more frequent change, and above all, probably from Asian influence both at home and abroad, far more colour.

The adoption of colour was largely made possible by an apparently sudden advance in weaving techniques. Hitherto the Egyptians, with characteristic lack of interest in technical innovation, had kept to the horizontal loom pegged to the ground. This was good enough for the finest linens. With the New Kingdom, vertical, two-beamed looms were introduced to large establishments, and with them men replaced women as the weavers. These looms were held in a heavy rectangular wooden frame, and might be big enough for two men to work at them side by side. These operators squatted on low stools. The *Satire on Trades* tells how uncomfortable this was for them: 'The weaver within doors is worse off than a woman; squatting, his knees against his chest, he does not breathe.'

Vertical looms in the New Kingdom;
from the tomb of Thotnefer at Thebes, c. 1500 B.C.

The new loom was excellent for tapestry weaving, and it is impossible not to associate its use with the appearance of coloured tapestry-work in clothes. The first known examples come from the tomb of Thutmose IV, where they include a robe with alternating rows of lotus and papyrus designs in red, blue and yellow.

Any search through the paintings of the New Kingdom period will discover examples of both men and women wearing coloured gowns and tunics, but it will also prove the continued popularity of white linen, and its far greater charm and seductiveness. The cloth was fine enough to veil, yet reveal, every detail of the anatomy. During the earlier part of the eighteenth dynasty the women's dresses were usually narrow, and left the shoulders bare. Sometimes the right breast was provocatively exposed. Nubile young girls, usually ladies' maids or dancers, might go naked except for an elaborate coiffure and a gold band resting on the hips. (If there was a taste for what would now be called nymphettes it must have been well satisfied.)

Surprisingly, fashions for white linen gowns of a more graceful and less obviously provocative kind came in during the luxurious reign of Amenhotep III and continued with only minor variations until the end of the New Kingdom. They depended on the use of very thin, narrowly pleated linen. The men often wore robes of it reaching to the calf and with short, bell-bottomed sleeves. The women's gowns fell free and softly to their ankles, the pleated cloth often draped elegantly across their breasts and shoulders and sometimes knotted below the breasts. Both sexes introduced colour in the form of very long, flowing sashes.

Wigs were worn by upper class men and women from the very beginning of dynastic times. At first they were simple, but in the New Kingdom they might assume huge and elaborate forms. The men seem to have kept their own hair short, but the women did not. On the contrary they took much trouble to encourage it to grow and to prevent it from greying. One 'recipe for making the hair grow' consisted of 'Paws of a dog, 1 part; kernels of dates, 1 part; hoof of donkey, 1 part. Cook thoroughly with oil in an earthen pot, and anoint therewith.' The truth is we probably do not know when ladies wore their wigs and when they did not. In many of the scenes showing women preparing for, or enjoying, festivities, their hair may be elaborately dressed, but appears to be their own.

Egyptian peasants and workmen grew their hair just long enough to make a thick cap affording some protection from the sun. Barbers sometimes cut the peasants' hair out in the fields. It is a remarkable fact that Egyptian men of almost all times and all classes were clean-shaved. They themselves were evidently very conscious of the contrast with the vigorous, curly growths of the Asiatics, but never had any desire to emulate them. The *Satire on Trades* describes an itinerant town barber, sacrificing himself to 'chins' and going 'from street to street to seek out those whom he may shave'.

No picture of the wealthy Egyptian can be complete without including the jewellery that represented some of the finest work of metalsmiths and stone workers.

The broad banded collar already mentioned as an essential part of the dress of men and women is a remarkable example of Egyptian conservatism. It changed hardly at all from the Old Kingdom down to Ptolemaic times. Broad gold collars were awarded by Pharaoh to those who served him well. There are pictures of Akhenaten and his family handing out collars from the palace balcony, and a well-known picture of Horemhab almost choked by the many collars assigned to him by Tutankhamun.

Fine jewels composed of semi-precious stones were already being worn by the courtiers of the first dynasty, but the very finest work for both craftsmanship and design was made during the Middle Kingdom. In the collections of pectorals, crowns and other ornaments once belonging to queens and princesses of the twelfth dynasty, hundreds of tiny cut stones are mounted in gold to give an enamelled effect. The designs, compounded of religious imagery such as falcons, scarabs and the figures of deities, are masterly. The symbolic jewels with which Tutankhamun's mummy was encrusted seem rather coarse in comparison, yet all are truly sumptuous and the best very good indeed. Here, in the heavy gold mountings, coloured glass was used indiscriminately with semi-precious stones. An example of ornaments that were purely secular and modish are the huge gold earrings much affected by the ladies of the eighteenth dynasty.

As in Mesopotamia, the potters' art so significant in the prehistoric past became a standardized commercial product in dynastic times. The designs of all the wine and oil jars, bowls, cups and cooking utensils were sound but undistinguished. The potters' workshops seem to have been staffed entirely by men. Pivotted turntables were used, and a tall, cylindrical kiln that was filled from the top.

The Predynastic Egyptians were already making excellent stone vessels; in Archaic times this craft attained its finest expression. Bowls, pots and vases were created in lovely shapes and with a

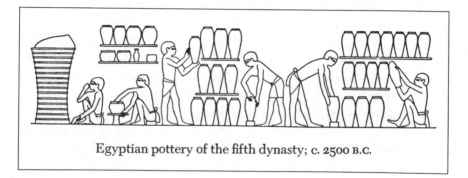

Egyptian pottery of the fifth dynasty; c. 2500 B.C.

perfection of technique that has hardly been explained. As well as alabaster, quite hard stones were used—among them diorite, serpentine, black and white and purple porphyries and rock crystal.

Stone vessels were to remain a characteristic Egyptian product. Hard stones never went out of use, but the most popular material was alabaster, both beautiful and easily worked. It was ideal for unguent jars and cosmetic pots of all kinds and also for large funerary vessels such as the Canopic jars used for burying the viscera. It was a dangerously seductive material, however: the most vulgar objects in Tutankhamun's treasure are made of alabaster.

For many people today, the typical Egyptian antiquity is a figurine or a string of beads in blue-green faience. This substance is, with reason, always known as Egyptian faience, and yet in fact a form of it was first manufactured in Mesopotamia. It seems to have been done in a deliberate effort to imitate the blue of lapis lazuli—itself so highly prized and so rare. The earliest essays, made as long ago as about 4000 B.C., involved shaping the desired object in talc-stone, dusting it with powdered azurite or malachite and heating it in a closed container at a temperature well above that of the domestic fire. The result was to coat the object with a skin of blue glass. During the Old Kingdom period an advance was made that allowed far greater flexibility. The article was modelled out of a mixture of white sand and natron and heated until the substance fused but did not melt. The model could then be glazed with a copper ore just as the talc-stone had been previously. In time it was to be produced on a mass scale, and many other colours were added to the original blue. After about 2000 B.C. it seems to have been experiments in faience work that led on, in both Mesopotamia and Egypt, to the manufacture of true glass.

Faience has a significance in human history greater than its actual uses. For one thing it was the first synthetic substance made by man to satisfy his desires. For another, the original experiments with copper ores and talc-stone may well have led to the discovery of how to reduce copper itself. If so this is a pleasing reversal of Marxist ideology, for here was a purely aesthetic urge leading to an important economic advance.

As practical metallurgists the Egyptians can be said to have started strongly, then shown their usual lack of interest in technical improvement. Copper ores were available in the eastern desert but more importantly in Sinai. As we have seen, expeditions were made there from Archaic times. The veins of ore were usually pursued along shafts driven horizontally into the rock. Smelting was done on the spot, but further refining could be done at home in Egypt. A wide range of tools and weapons as well as hammered copper vessels were already being made during the first dynasty.

Metal working; New Kingdom, c. 1500 B.C.

After this precocious beginning, metallurgy stagnated and Egypt remained in a prolonged copper age of her own. During the Middle Kingdom at a time when true bronze had come into full use in Mesopotamia, it was still exceptional in the Nile valley. It is true that tin was not easily available, yet its import certainly could have been organized. The main reason for not doing so must have been that the Egyptians were accustomed to their dependence on Sinai copper and did not want to change.

The Hyksos probably helped to overcome this conservatism—and they certainly introduced new forms of weapons. By the New Kingdom there was a sufficiency of bronze, and good bellows had at last superseded clay-tipped reeds for raising the heat of furnaces. After about 1200 B.C. the expeditions to Sinai came to an end and instead copper was imported from Syria and Cyprus. It is not known where the Egyptians obtained their tin.

Just as Egypt had lagged behind in producing bronze, she was also late to adopt iron as a working metal. Now, however, a declining people was less able to afford such backwardness. The later New Kingdom Pharaohs were aware of the new metal, for it was in regular use among the Hittites and Mitanni. Yet although some attempts at blacksmithing had begun by 1200 B.C., Egypt did not enter a true Iron Age for another four centuries or more.

Gold was the metal for which Egypt was famous; supplies were supposed to be so abundant that neighbouring monarchs were shameless in asking for gifts. One Mitannian king was most persistent, reminding Amenhotep III that his father had given 'bowls and great pitchers of gold' and demanding ten times as much for himself: 'Let my brother send gold in great quantity . . . for in my brother's land gold is as plentiful as dust.'

It is true, as we have seen, that the Egyptians possessed rich resources of gold in the eastern deserts. In a world where the metal of the sun was not locked up in coin and bullion, its abundance gave Egyptian goldsmiths splendid opportunities. Their work in the royal jewellery of the Middle Kingdom was as exquisite as was ever to be executed by the hand of man, and although there was some aesthetic decline later, a high standard of craftsmanship remained.

Although literary references and considerable numbers of finds had already suggested that Pharaohs disposed of large amounts of gold, tomb robbers had followed their ancient profession so successfully that it was not until their one failure was brought to light that it was appreciated how truly vast those amounts had been. Tutankhamun's grave furniture had used up thousands of pounds of the precious metal in its shrines, catafalques, coffins, mummy mask, furniture, jewellery, weapons and all but innumerable other possessions of the young king. The inner coffin alone contained over three thousand pounds of gold, and the splendid craftsmanship and design of this and of the mask, also in solid gold, are unsurpassed.

Goldsmithing often went together with woodworking, for wooden surfaces were gilded or overlaid with gold leaf or sheet gold, usually with an intervening layer of gesso. Advanced professional carpentry began in early dynastic times as soon as the copper workers had produced the necessary adze and axe blades, pull-saws, chisels and drills.

So inventive were these early carpenters that already during the first dynasty all the main principles of jointing had been perfected, while carving and inlaying with varied woods, with ivory and faience were freely used for enrichment. In this Archaic period the legs of chairs or beds were usually carved in the form of the fore and hind quarters of a bull. Later the legs of lions were preferred. It is truly astonishing that these first designers of civilized furniture should have devised such distinctive conventions that were to persist through classical times down to our own.

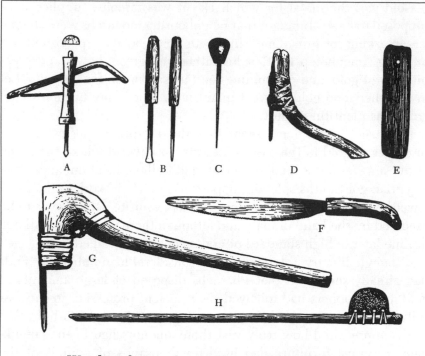

Wood-working tools: (A) bow-drill with copper bit;
(B) copper chisel for cutting mortises (front and side elevations);
(C) copper awl with hardwood handle;
(D) small adze (copper blade lashed with rawhide to wooden handle);
(E) whetstone; (F) small hand-saw (with serrated copper blade);
(G) large adze; (H) large axe (with copper blade lashed into a channel
on the shaft, which is strengthened by a copper ferrule)—all c. 1200 B.C.

This same sense of the astonishingly swift arrival of perfection
is clinched by the elegance and craftsmanship displayed by the
furniture once used by the mother of the builder of the Great Pyramid
—Queen Hetepheres. We have her jewel chest, carrying chair,
bed, headrest, armchairs, all with gold overlays and ebony inlays.
Perhaps most remarkable of all is the gold-sheathed portable canopy
frame, faultlessly proportioned and large enough to enclose the suite
of bed and chairs within its linen curtains. If the queen travelled
through the kingdom with her husband she could be sure of comfort, privacy and protection against insects. The Empress Josephine
could have demanded nothing better.

These items of furniture, together with folding or fixed stools, were to remain the principle products of the cabinet-makers through-out pharaonic times. They are all to be seen again in the more ex-travagant, less elegant, stage of their evolution among the possessions of Tutankhamun. Here, too, the great gilded shrines containing the sarcophagus show carpenters and wood-carvers working together on a large scale.

Furniture making; from a tomb at Thebes, c. 1440 B.C.

Among wood workers the Egyptians distinguished verbally be-tween the carpenter, the carver and the portrait sculptor. However, the carver's skills covered the whole range of woodworking, from large-scale temple equipment—shrines and cult figures, sacred barques, sanctuary doors and so forth—to furniture, palanquins, coffers, containers and coffins. On the other hand the men who executed the finer embellishments may have had more affinity with goldsmiths and jewellers, for one craftsman claimed to have been a master in the working of all materials 'from silver and gold to ivory and ebony'.

Another specialized craft that involved working in wood was, of course, ship-building. From prehistoric times onwards a light boat which fishermen and bird catchers found ideal for use in shallow water and among reed beds was a paddled canoe made by lashing together long bundles of the papyrus reeds that grew everywhere in pools and canals. For going upstream before the north wind they could be fitted with square sails.

Of home-grown timber only the sycamore figs were at all suitable for boat-building, and as they were needed for their fruit, permission for their felling had to be obtained from the vizier. On one famous occasion Hatshepsut ordered sycamores to be cut throughout the kingdom to build the enormous raft, not far short of three hundred

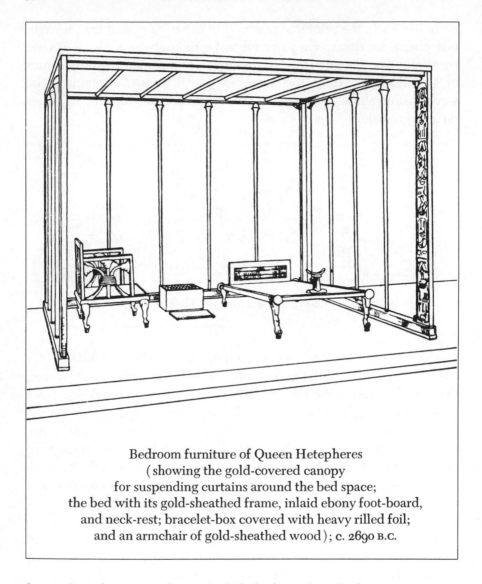

Bedroom furniture of Queen Hetepheres
(showing the gold-covered canopy
for suspending curtains around the bed space;
the bed with its gold-sheathed frame, inlaid ebony foot-board,
and neck-rest; bracelet-box covered with heavy rilled foil;
and an armchair of gold-sheathed wood); c. 2690 B.C.

feet in length, to carry her two obelisks from the Elephantine quarries down to Thebes.

The Egyptians, like the Mesopotamians, looked to Lebanon for their best woods. Byblos was the most convenient port for the transshipment of the timber, and in this way it became at once the harbour for Egyptian ships and the source of the material needed to build them. They could sail there from the Nile mouth in about four days, but it might take more than twice as long to return against prevailing winds and tides. So completely did the Egyptians identify their sea-going vessels with the port that they called them Byblos-ships wherever they were sailing. Indeed, in the end they even trans-ferred the name to Ionian triremes.

To judge from the sketches on pottery, substantial wooden vessels equipped with both oars and matting sails were already voyaging in the eastern Mediterranean in Late Predynastic times. Certainly such transport increased rapidly during the Old Kingdom. The Pharaoh Snefru, for example, built a fleet of no less than sixty ships, and later imported forty cargoes of timber.

There was a great royal shipyard at Perunefer near Memphis, and it was probably thanks to the professionals employed at such places that by the Middle Kingdom the largest ships were 180 feet long and 60 feet in the beam and carried crews of 120. The full development was manifest in the fine ships with their wide sails and curved lotus sterns that Queen Hatshepsut sent to Punt. Even then there was no true keel, and although some tacking was possible oars were still resorted to against head winds.

TRADE

MUCH HAS ALREADY BEEN SAID THAT CONCERNS EGYPT'S TRADING PRAC-tices, both in the previous and the present part. It remains to make the general picture more coherent. The central fact is that all large-scale trading activity was in the hands of Pharaoh; Egyptian texts down to the end of the second millennium contain no mention of professional merchants. The contrast with Mesopotamia could hardly be more complete. It is justifiable in almost every respect to draw the obvious analogy with the present division between the state trading of communist countries and the private trading of the capitalist world.

The methods of obtaining goods and raw materials from lands outside the borders can be roughly distinguished according to the means of acquisition. The first, the obtaining of copper and turquoise from Sinai, cannot properly be described as trading at all. Frequent royal expeditions were sent to the mines, usually led by an official and accompanied by soldiers to ward off or subdue the desert nomads of those desolate regions. Mining communities were installed, sup-plied and defended. Possibly gifts to keep the goodwill of local sheikhs may sometimes have been made, but they were not payments. The second method consisted of acquiring goods brought in by foreign vendors great and small. This kind of trade mainly involved the African hinterland: ebony, ivory, aromatic resins, panther skins and the like were brought to the frontier by caravans of Nubian traders, or in the modest packs of nomad tribesmen. The frontier town of Elephantine got its name as an entrepôt for ivory. There business arrangements and customs duties were handled by officials whose various titles included 'caravan conductor who brings the products of the countries to his lord'. This kind of dealing naturally varied with the political situation. The royal expeditions sent into Nubia during the sixth dynasty involved both forced tribute and genuine purchase. By the Middle Kingdom the establishment of a trading post and factories at Kerma near the Third Cataract made it easier for the African traders to exchange their goods for Egyptian knives, unguents and linens. With the extension of the frontier to Napata the situation must have changed and more goods would have been collected as taxes or tribute. Yet probably the old methods of trade persisted.

The third means of obtaining goods was the most ambitious. This was the despatch of royal marine fleets to foreign ports to deal with the local rulers. The most important line of this kind was the one just described: the timber trade through Byblos and later through other ports of the Phoenician coast. The other consisted of the expeditions down the Red Sea to Punt (Somaliland) that seem to have begun only with the fifth dynasty.

The true nature of the trading relationships between Pharaoh and the merchant princes of the Asian coast is difficult to define. There was always a tendency on the part of the Egyptians to emphasize their superiority by describing as tribute ('bringings') goods that were in fact paid for by a satisfactory exchange. In the high days of the New Kingdom empire much actual tribute was paid, but even then it was probably made good by a shower of royal gifts.

There is no doubt about the commercial nature of the exchange when Egypt had lost imperial control. The prince of Byblos informed poor, bullied Wenamun that while it was true that his own forebears had supplied timber to Egypt it was 'only after Pharaoh had caused to be brought six ships laden with Egyptian goods and they had unloaded them into their warehouses.' In a business-like fashion the prince produced the old account books which proved that a range of payments, including silver, had indeed been made.

Syrians bringing elephants, etc., as gifts to Rekhmire;
fifteenth century B.C.

The voyages to Punt were more hazardous and far longer. In the Old Kingdom period they started from somewhere in the region of Suez. Later the ports of embarkation were shifted further south where they could be approached across the desert by such routes as the Wadi Hammamat and Wadi Quena. The ships seem always to have been assembled there on the Red Sea coast. There is no difficulty in understanding the nature of the trade that went on once the royal fleets arrived at Punt. It was that of a great civilized power trading with barbarous natives. This is made abundantly clear in the artist's record of the most famous of all these expeditions—that of Queen Hatshepsut in about 1495 B.C., which the queen claimed to have been the first mounted since the days of the Hyksos. The Egyptians are tendering strings of beads, axes and weapons in exchange for the myrrh and other resins that were their main objective, though they also took ebony, ivory, gold, monkeys and skins.

Finally we have to spare a thought for the foreigners, either out and out merchants or embassies from the rulers of other lands bearing gifts or 'tribute' to Pharaoh. It seems very likely indeed that Semitic merchants handling lesser goods than the timber of Lebanon —wine and oil for examples—may have been allowed a port in the Delta such as Naukratis became for the Greeks.

Quantities of Cretan and Mycenaean painted pottery have been found in Egypt. Some may have been imported for its own sake, some as containers for scented oils. But the extent of the contacts with the Aegean is best proved by murals in the tombs of no less than five high officials of the earlier eighteenth dynasty. These show 'princes' of Crete and of the 'isles in the midst of the sea' bearing familiar Cretan objects including wine flagons and copper ingots. Trade or an interchange of gifts? It was certainly not tribute, as Egypt had no real authority over the Aegean. The paintings serve as a reminder that in this later Bronze Age world gifts between the monarchs of many lands were on a scale to heighten the wealth and cosmopolitan sparkle of their courts.

2. THE SOCIAL AND POLITICAL WORLD

STATE AND GOVERNMENT

IT IS IMPOSSIBLE TO IMAGINE ANY STABLE MONARCHY POSSESSING A more absolute and universal supremacy than that of ancient Egypt. The vizier Rekhmire put it this way: 'What is the king of Upper and Lower Egypt? He is the god by whose dealings we live, the father and the mother of all men, alone by himself, without an equal.' This was at the height of the great eighteenth dynasty, but such had been the sacred meaning of kingship since the day of Menes the Unifier.

This mystical source of all life, this god incarnate, was also the ultimate source of all authority and all possessions. In the sense that every priest and official, great and small, merely carried out the king's will, he was high priest, chief justice, head of the administration. For the Egyptian, justice was 'what Pharaoh loves', wrongdoing 'what Pharaoh hates'. In theory the entire land of Egypt and its produce was his possession. All surplus grain went into the royal granaries; it would not have come into the ear without him, for it was the king's power that caused the Nile to come down in flood.

On a more mundane level (although always with the same religious connotations) we have seen Pharaoh as exercising a monopoly in building stone, precious materials such as gold, copper and turquoise, and all foreign trade. Pharaoh was also inevitably the supreme war leader—a command which became a very real and

onerous responsibility for the imperial monarchs of the New Kingdom.

As already suggested in Part I, it was in his theological position
that Pharaoh differed most clearly, in principle at least, from his
royal brothers the *lugals* of Mesopotamian city- and national states.
He was no mere Great Man but one of the greatest of the gods:
at the height of his religious power, the greatest of them all.

At the beginning of Egyptian history the palette of Narmer, which
already shows so many of the concepts of kingship that were to prevail for thousands of years—the conquering Horus king from the
north, the divine falcon—is gigantic in stature and wears the tail
and the attached goat beard that had come to him from his pastoral
past. So, too, had the equally ancient crook and scourge (often misleadingly translated as flail), the insignia that symbolized two aspects
of royal power: loving care and coercion.

It was as the incarnation of the sky god Horus that the king's
divine eminence reached its summit during the third and fourth
dynasties. A fine poem illustrates the faith in which thousands toiled
to build the pyramids of Zoser, Khufu and Khaefre.

> *The skies cloud over, the stars are obscured,*
> *The vaults of heaven shake, the limbs of the earth god tremble,*
> *All is still.*
> *When they behold the king in all his divine power,*
> *The dwellers of heaven serve him.*
> *He roves across the heavens,*
> *He roams through every land.*
> *He, the most powerful, who has might over the mighty,*
> *He, the great one, is like a falcon who soars above all falcons.*
> *A god is he, older than the oldest.*
> *Thousands serve him, hundreds make offerings to him.*
> *His lifespan is eternity.*
> *The borders of his power are infinity.*

It seems certain that the Egyptian peasant summoned from his home
to carry out the astounding plans of his lord shared this vision and
pulled on the rope, staggered up the ramp, as a willing servant of
so great a god. It was in the same faith that all Pharoah's kinsmen
served him loyally in their assigned offices and were glad indeed to
prepare their modest tombs at the foot of his eternal pyramid.

One of the lost passages in history most to be lamented is that concerning the decline in the divine standing of Pharaoh that took place during the fifth dynasty. It seems certain that the initiative came from the priesthood of Re at Heliopolis and that the kings themselves accepted the new teaching. Instead of being the most powerful and the oldest god, Pharaoh was now accepted as son of the sun god, Re, who had occupied the throne of Egypt in the beginning. He was still, of course, a god, but one who lavished the wealth of the nation on a temple for Re rather than on his own tomb, and who, so far from making all other gods tremble when he ascended to heaven, had now to approach his father humbly with passports and declarations that he had done no evil.

It is impossible to tell what effect, if any, this demotion had on the status of Pharaoh as ruler of the kingdom, but it may have begun the weakening of the claims of his near relatives to hold all the high offices of state.

The Egyptians had no belief in the need for consistency in religious truths. Over much the same period that saw Pharaoh accept the position of son of the sun god, his original role as Horus the supreme sky god slipped towards that of a different Horus: Horus the young son of Isis and Osiris. From now on it was an essential basis of kingship that the monarch came to the throne as Horus and on his death became Osiris. Both the new doctrines might be said to emphasize the eternal nature of divine kingship in place of the individual king, but while the Re cult was royal and aristocratic the Osiris-Horus resurrection teaching evolved into a popular faith shared by all classes. Pharaoh's acceptance as a personification of the central myth must in the long run have brought him closer to the people and in this way helped to secure the permanence of the monarchy and its lasting esteem.

The political, social and economic breakdown of the First Intermediate period, which saw the fragmentation of the national state into the petty kingdom of the nomarchs, dealt a violent blow to confidence in the divine power and everlastingness of the crown. The sage Ipuwer blames the Pharaoh he is supposed to be addressing for what has happened. 'Authority, Perception and Justice are with thee, but it is confusion which thou wouldst set throughout the land.' Yet perhaps when the strong rulers of the eleventh and twelfth dynasties restored the royal prestige there was a certain benefit from the disasters. Society must have seen in a less mystical and more realistic way that for Egypt prosperity, order and happiness depended upon a strong central government such as could only be brought to them by Pharaoh.

The psychological disturbance and physical suffering of the collapse also brought about a more serious view of life and a deeper, more human sense of the responsibility of Pharaoh towards his people. Thus the Middle Kingdom texts put far more emphasis on him as the good shepherd of the realm. It might be said that the buried historical inheritance of the king as primitive pastoral chief now re-emerged transmuted into spiritual and moral symbolism.

The breakdown of national government of the Second Intermediate period had less effect on the crown than that of the First. It was less total, and the Egyptians were by now more worldly and had lost (it can be assumed) their holy complacency. In the final phase, too, xenophobia and the successful expulsion of foreign usurpers, followed by imperial glory, made it easy for the brilliant kings of the eighteenth dynasty to ride high on a tide of martial patriotism.

There was little change in position and meaning of the kingship, but a tremendous increase in its worldly responsibilities. The conquered lands in Africa and Asia demanded a far more complicated administration and a command of international diplomacy. Even more significant for the position and status of Pharaoh, he was now the commander of a large standing army. The Theban kings could put 20,000 professional soldiers into the field. As national gods the Pharaohs of Egypt were at their zenith in the third and fourth dynasties; as monarchs supreme in a more or less coherent international world this high point was reached in the eighteenth and nineteenth dynasties.

Two lasting features of Egyptian kingship were highly distinctive. One was its dual nature and the other the mode of inheritance.

The substantial physical difference between the Delta and Upper Egypt, and the historical fact that the kingdom was brought into being by the joining together of what had been two rival kingdoms, provided a solid basis for the idea of the King of the Two Lands. Yet undoubtedly there was always a psychological factor. A sense of the significance of opposites appears to be innate in mankind, and the Egyptians, perhaps as part of their love of symmetry, had it very strongly.

The royal iconography and symbolism proclaimed the duality again and again. It appeared in the double crown ingeniously created from the white crown of the north and the red of the south and in the double ceremonial of the coronation. It appeared in the second and fourth of the five royal titles and in many other evocations of the Two Ladies and of the sedge and the bee. In the decoration of royal monuments, furniture, jewels, clothes, these pairs of symbols, to which can be added the northern papyrus and southern lotus, are overwhelmingly dominant. The duality was again manifest in the very administration of the country, and here again was part practical and part symbolic. In the mental as much as in the physical world Pharaoh and his kingdom were strengthened by the polarity, the slight tension, produced by the Two Lands that were One.

As to the succession, there have been almost as many interpretations of the rules determining it as there are Egyptologists who have written on the subject. There is not much doubt, however, that in theory, and usually in practice, the throne descended in the female line. This did not mean that this heiress to the throne ruled, but that she conveyed the right to do so to her husband. The heiress then inevitably became the Great Wife or (in our terms) the queen. Confusion chiefly arises over the selection of the crown prince whose marriage to the heiress would confirm his legal right to the throne. It seems that the theoretical idea was that he should be her full brother, thus maintaining the divine blood at its richest and purest. In practice, however, history shows that sons of lesser wives, or even outsiders, often won the heiress and the throne, perhaps because no full brother existed. Similarly, if the queen had no daughter, a prince was evidently allowed to find his queen in a half sister or from outside the royal family—as was the case with Amenhotep III and Queen Tiy. A number of New Kingdom Pharaohs are known to have married their daughters as subsidiary wives. Probably they were bent on securing the throne through their possession of all possible heiresses.

The pre-eminent right of the heiress appears to be proved beyond dispute by the extraordinary incident recorded by lucky chance in the El-Amarna tablets. Tutankhamun's widow, the heiress daughter of Akhenaten and Queen Nefertiti, wrote to the Hittite king, Suppiluliumas, begging him to send one of his sons to marry her and promising that he would become Pharaoh. Thus she assumed that her hand could raise even a foreign prince to the throne of Egypt. The double edge to this story is that the young widow very probably made this appeal because the elderly and non-royal Ay was trying to secure his own accession by marrying her.

A matter of more political interest is that at the height of their power the priests of Amun at Thebes apparently won some control over the choice of the crown prince by consulting the oracle of Amun. The excellent choice of Thutmose III was made in this way.

The crown prince, once chosen, might be given his own harem and a command in the army. From time to time the succession was further secured by making him co-regent or junior king. It can certainly be said that in spite of all the irregularities, the system worked quite well. Except in times of general breakdown, Egypt was rarely torn by struggles for the succession.

Nor did inbreeding have any ill effects: the eighteenth dynasty maintained it for two and a half centuries. Pharaoh certainly had need of exceptional vigour, for the combination of his secular and religious duties must have been onerous, and he was still expected to make a show as soldier, hunter and sportsman. Those who lacked it may have allowed themselves to be overcome by the heavy pro-gramme of their ritual day and left secular affairs largely to their officials. This was very far from true of the many strong rulers, who, in spite of the thick crust of royal customs and stereotypes, always succeeded in stamping their reigns with their own characters.

As an essentially totalitarian regime, the government of Egypt be-came highly bureaucratic with a vast network of officials, both na-tional and provincial, working at all levels. The chief official under the crown was the vizier, in a sense Pharaoh's human deputy, charged to carry out his wishes in all things. It may be that from the first there were in fact two viziers as part of a duplicated administration of the Two Lands. Undoubtedly this was true by New Kingdom times, when the vizier of the south, with his seat in Thebes, presided from Elephantine to Cusae, while his colleague of the north adminis-tered the rest of the country, probably from Memphis. At this period there was also that third V.I.P., the King's Son of Kush, who as viceroy held the royal signet and controlled the new African province down to Napata.

If in the earlier Old Kingdom the vizier, like other important of-ficials round the king, was always of the royal blood, this inevitably gave way in time to appointment by merit, influence or favouritism. Some high office-holders of the New Kingdom liked to boast that they had risen 'without influential kindred' while others might be king's favourites or relatives of court ladies. Sometimes an office might become virtually hereditary in one family. Nevertheless the civil service was generally open to the talents. A new king appointed his vizier or confirmed the old one in office, and he could always be demoted at the king's pleasure.

In a supervisory way at least, the vizier's responsibilities reached into every area of the Egyptian's life in this world. On the agricultural side they included irrigation works and tree felling, the biennial cattle census and other estimates of national resources, measurement and records of the Nile flood and rainfall, and the related and very exacting business of corvée and the collection of taxes. Among other practical economic concerns was the supervision of royal expeditions, workshops and building projects and (rather surprisingly) of the workshops, stores and estates of the temple of Amun at Thebes. The vizier made or rescinded innumerable appointments—of judges, officials, priests. Militarily he was responsible for the levying and inspection of troops, in foreign affairs for the reception of embassies and tribute. Probably the most onerous of all the vizier's duties, however, were those deriving from his office (under Pharaoh) of chief justice. He presided over the Great Council, mostly hearing cases referred from provincial and local courts; he was archivist for the keeping and consultation of legal and administrative records; all legal documents had to receive his seal. Swarms of petitioners crowded his anterooms. No wonder it was said of the viziership that 'it is not pleasant at all—no, it is bitter as gall.'

There is no doubt that the *taty* was a busy man. He normally started his day by going to the Residence and waiting on His Majesty to offer reports and to receive instructions. In this he was assisted by the royal chancellor, who received him at the entrance to the inner palace. After this he caused all administrative offices to be opened and himself repaired to his Hall of the Vizier to begin his own multifarious duties. Occasionally he went on tours of inspection, but usually relied on his minions—heralds, scribes and henchmen—to keep him in touch with the provinces. When a *taty* was installed, it was the custom for the king to present him with formal instructions concerning his conduct and duties. Much of the above information is taken from versions of these instructions inscribed in the tombs of four New Kingdom viziers. These texts included solemn exhortations as to the conduct of a man who had to be 'the mooring post of the entire land'. But amusing, human and sensible ideas also found a place—such as that petitioners should not be sent away unheard because 'a man with a grievance likes to have his woes listened to

even more than he wants to have them set right.' Again, after warn-
ings against partiality, the vizier was told not to err in the opposite
direction by judging his friends' cases harshly 'for that would be
more than justice'. Then he was advised to 'fly into a rage only when
rage is necessary', for although a judge should be feared, to terrify
people would do his reputation no good.

Not a great deal is known of the constitution of the central government. It seems to have been departmentalized into 'Six Great
Houses'. Of these the most important was probably the Treasury
under two overseers corresponding to the two viziers, with its special
responsibility for the assessment, collection and disbursement of
the grain, oil, flax, hides and other taxes in kind. In Archaic times it
was divided into a White and Red House (and was administered by
the chancellor), but later became the Double White House. Although the royal Treasury itself (and the closely associated national
granary) was centralized, it also worked through a strong provincial
system. Grain and other goods beyond what was needed to cover
direct royal expenses had to be issued to a host of minor officials and
to men engaged in public works throughout the kingdom. For this
purpose they had to be held in stores in every nome, each with its
own staff. At the same time the Treasury had to keep account of just
how much was being held in the provinces. A complicated administrative network was completed by a variety of overseers of
granaries, of cattle and so forth.

The king himself was surrounded by a host of courtiers and officials. Some were influential functionaries—such as the chief steward
of the king, who administered the enormous royal estates and was
very close to the monarch. During the eighteenth dynasty the steward
tended to usurp the functions of the royal chancellor, who had been
responsible for the administration of the Palace and its exchequer,
the organization of the royal expeditions for mining and trade and
the tutoring of the princes. There was also a chamberlain, a courtier
who supervised food, drink and the private apartments, and an
overseer of the harem, who not only had the task of looking after
royal resident ladies in the palaces (of many nationalities) but also
of arranging for the travelling harem that toured with the king.
Protocol was in the hands of the first herald, often a retired soldier.
Among humbler figures close to the king's person were his spokes-
man, scribe, holders of the sunshade and fanbearers.

The provincial administration changed profoundly with the course of history. Although the number varied a little, there were about twenty nomes in Lower Egypt and twenty-two in Upper Egypt. Their rulers, originally loyal appointees of the crown, had grown into the overweening hereditary nobility which did so much to bring about the first breakdown. After the feudalistic regime of the Middle Kingdom in which the nomarchs kept power under the crown, their successful suppression by Sen-Wosret III led immediately to a highly centralized and highly complex bureaucracy.

Under this regime the most important provincial officials were the mayors of the larger towns. Their principal and most unpopular duty was the local assessment, collection and storage of their taxes, for which they were answerable to the office of the vizier. It also fell to them to support local temples, and in this capacity they could be called overseers of prophets.

The mayor must often have been involved in the council or court (*kenbet*) that existed in each town and concerned itself with minor matters of law and order. All important cases were referred up to higher authorities in Thebes and Memphis where, as we have seen, the supreme court was presided over by the vizier (one of his executives had the pleasing title 'Keeper-of-the-things-that-come-in'). The constitution of both central and local courts varied, but included soldiers and priests as well as officials. Pharaoh, as the divine source of all law, was himself the final court of appeal, and he alone could confirm death sentences or exercise his prerogative of mercy.

Pharaoh's position as the fount of law was expressed in terms of Ma'at, the goddess of an exalted concept that can only be expressed through a number of our words: truth, justice and perfect order. It was indeed of the divine king's essence to maintain this universal rightness through his 'Authority, Perception and Justice'. It is, therefore, easy to understand how in contrast with Mesopotamia, Egypt apparently had no written code of laws set up for all to see, but depended upon a body of precedents supposedly expressing the king's will and modified from time to time by royal edict. As in English courts, past decisions might be directly appealed to—even over many centuries.

The actual procedure in the courts does not seem to have differed much from that of Mesopotamia. Testimony was given under sacred oath, with dire penalties for perjury, the plaintiff and the defendant both made speeches, the court passed judgement and the proceedings were noted by a court recorder—who also entered the date and a list of all those taking part.

In certain criminal courts, however, conditions were harsher, with the bastinado (now again a popular adjunct to police examinations) applied to all suspects. Among the most remarkable surviving records are those of the dramatic trials of tomb robbers in the reign of Ramesses IX. For example, an army scribe was called:

He was examined by beating with a stick, and fetters were placed on his feet and hands; an oath administered on pain of mutilation not to speak falsehood. It was said 'Tell the way in which you went to places with your brother.' He said 'Let a witness be brought to accuse me.' He was examined again, and said 'I saw nothing.' He was made a prisoner for further examination.

Without a written code of laws it is difficult to formulate the accepted crimes and punishments. However, certain mortuary texts, 'Protestations of Guiltlessness', refer to the following offenses: blasphemy against a god; violence to a poor man; murder; stealing of tomb offerings; sexual relations with a boy; various forms of cheating with weights and measures. Treason, like murder, was a capital offence, and so, too, was perjury, for it was held to injure the king. The guilty might not only be put to death, but their bodies forbidden burial, which meant they could have no afterlife. For lesser crimes there was mutilation and labour (in terrible conditions) in mines and quarries. Stealing was usually punished by restitution and fines, and all minor offences, particularly the evasion of taxes, by beatings.

There is no doubt that the ideals of impartial justice under Ma'at so finely expressed in the royal instructions to his vizier were often betrayed in practice. Nevertheless they were always there to be appealed to, and the Story of the Eloquent Peasant was composed to show that even a humble man should be able to win his case if he carried it to a higher authority. To counter this Middle Kingdom concern for justice is a sad little prayer dating from the nineteenth dynasty. It is addressed to Amun by a poor man, alone in the law court, where the magistrate and his clerks sit on reed mats. 'The court cheats him of silver and gold for the scribes of the mat, and clothing for the attendants [bailiffs?]. May it be found that Amun assumes his form as the vizier in order to let the poor man off. May the poor man surpass the rich.'

The day to day work of law enforcement was mainly in the hands of the Medjay. This force drawn from the nomad tribesmen of Nubia had originally served as light auxiliary troops. It was in this capacity that the Medjay went with Ahmose against the Hyksos, and spied out the enemy from the cabin roofs of his transport ships. In time they developed into a kind of constabulary or national guard, a semi-military, semi-civilian body of a kind still very familiar. Each town had its own company under a captain, and the whole force was commanded by a chief of Medjay. As well as regular policing they had such jobs as patrolling the cemeteries and the desert approaches.

THE ARMY AND CORVÉE

THE MILITARY HISTORY OF EGYPT FAITHFULLY REFLECTS MANY OF THE features of her general political history. One unchanging factor was that as among most peoples until recent centuries, the king was in fact, and not only nominally, the war leader of the nation. Of course some Pharaohs were very much more soldierly than others, and undoubtedly, too, some of the victorious campaigns attributed to a particular Pharaoh in flowery inscriptions had not in truth been graced by his presence. Yet in general the Egyptian kings did command their armies on foreign campaigns and may often have led them into battle.

During the relatively peaceful isolation of the Old Kingdom there was no standing army of any size, although there would have been a royal guard and a few professional commanders were about the court. When punitive expeditions had to be mounted against Libyans, nomads of the eastern desert or Nubians, levies were recruited from up and down the country, and they were often commanded by civilians turned soldier for the purpose—of whom Weni is a good example.

The fighting that was necessary to establish the eleventh dynasty over a united kingdom naturally increased the number of trained soldiers and the esteem in which the military were held. This more martial spirit survived several generations of the Middle Kingdom, and everyone from peasants to nobles took pride in possessing skill at arms and were frequently buried with their weapons beside them. At this time the national armed forces were largely composed of levies raised from the nomes and often commanded by the nomarchs themselves. There were also Nubian bowmen—as all the world knows from the lifelike models of marching troops dating from this age. The black men carry their double-concave bows and reed arrows, while the accompanying troop of pale-skinned Egyptians are armed with spears. These were the usual weapons, though a rather inefficient type of battle-axe was also in use. The Egyptian hide shield, squared at the bottom and rounded at the top, was distinctive and long remained in favour.

Once again the rule and expulsion of the Hyksos made the great break. As was so often to happen in warfare, the Egyptians had to learn from their enemies how to defeat them. By far the most important innovation due to Hyksos influence was the combination of the chariot and the composite bow, which provided the army with a new kind of speed and fire-power. The Egyptians first copied the Palestinian light chariot with four-spoked wheels, then, showing an exceptional concern for technical improvement, experimented with an eight-spoke type before perfecting a heavier but manoeuverable chariot with six-spoked wheels. These improvements seem then to have had a reflected influence upon the Asians—an unusual success for Egypt.

From the time of the Narmer palette with its decapitated prisoners and death-dealing Pharaoh, the ferocity of war had been celebrated in Egyptian art. Now in the New Kingdom it became a major theme. One favourite subject was Pharaoh standing in his chariot with drawn bow, his plumed horses trampling the bodies of Nubians, Libyans or Asiatics; another was prisoners trussed in a variety of painful and humiliating ways. Some of the most expressive war art is to be seen in the reliefs of Ramesses III at Medinet Habu. They include such details as the pile of chopped-off hands, the equivalent of today's body count. The scene of the great naval battle is grimly dramatic, with enemy ships capsizing and arrow-struck Philistines drowning in shoals.

The new, militaristic spirit of the age and the demands of empire greatly affected all classes of Egyptian society. Under the eighteenth dynasty a large national army was built up with an organized hierarchy of command. This standing army, with its regulars and reserves, was large enough to form a recognized class of soldiers and those liable to conscription. These were free Egyptians, mostly small land-holders or modest professional people and artisans. A career in the army was one of the few ways in which a man lacking scribal education could rise in the world. Soldiers could in fact do very well for themselves. On successful foreign campaigns they were able to keep prisoners as servants, and were given women and other booty and awards known as 'gold of valour'. Afterwards they might be granted plots of land from royal estates which could remain in the family so long as there were sons to continue in military service. In this way congenial settlements of veterans were established up and down the land, and the regular army was assured of a supply of likely recruits.

After about the time of Amenhotep III there tended to be more and more foreigners in the army: Nubians, Asiatics mostly from Palestine and Syria, Libyans and such Peoples of the Sea as the Sherden. Some served as true mercenaries, some as prisoners of war. Foreign prisoners could win freedom and land through army service and the service of their children. Ramesses II used captive Sherden (who wore horned helmets) even in his bodyguard, and many of them settled on the land. After Ramesses III had defeated the Meshwesh of Libya, thousands of them were able to cross the frontiers and join his armies, gaining so much power in time that they were able to take the throne itself.

The army was organized into divisions, perhaps of five thousand men, each named after a great god and commanded by a general assisted in logistics by an adjutant. Under them were combat officers and twenty-five standard-bearers in command of companies of two hundred men. Each division had a squadron of chariots attached under its own commander, but the chariotry as a whole was commanded by a Master of the Horse. As always, this cavalry arm tended to be aristocratic, and was largely made up of young nobles who provided their own equipment. Amenhotep II when still a very young prince had a passion for horses and their training that delighted his father.

There was a separate Home Forces command of the army. It was divided into two, on the lines of the vizierates, one based at Memphis and the other at Thebes. These men garrisoned frontier posts, provided royal escorts and were used to fill up the more esteemed foreign divisions.

It is permissible to speak of an Egyptian navy, yet for the great part of New Kingdom times it existed mainly as a transport and mobile base (both along the Nile and the Syrian coast) for the army. There were always fine royal flag boats known as 'falconships', but all the rest of the vessels were the usual types of merchantmen. They seem to have been sailed by their own crews and skippers, but carried trained marines, the larger ones a full company, under its standard-bearers. Individuals tended to remain with one service or the other, but there are also records of interchange—as when a stable-master of cavalry became admiral of the fleet. The fighting ships must have become relatively more important when the attacks of the Sea People began and they had to be capable of facing such sea battles as that won by Ramesses III at the mouth of the Nile. For this operation, in which land and sea forces were fully co-ordinated, the king claimed that he had 'the river mouths prepared like a strong wall with warships, galleys and coasters' and that they were 'manned completely from bow to stern with warriors carrying their weapons . . . every picked man of Egypt'.

Like other armed forces, those of the Egyptian New Kingdom had their complement of clerks to look after recruiting, commissariat records and so forth. In the amusing nineteenth dynasty *Satirical Letter* in which a scribe mocks his incompetent colleague, a scene in camp is imagined where a motley division including Sherden, Meshwesh and Negroes are full of discontent about heat, late starts and above all rations: 'The number of men is too great for thee, whereas the provisions are too small for them.' Meanwhile the local Bedouin look on murmuring, 'O wise scribe.'

The military scribes were under chief scribes of the army, and they in turn worked with the king's scribe of recruits, an office which apparently exercised some control over all recruited labour, for both military or civilian purposes. This emphasizes the fact that it is hard to draw a line between the two. For particular tasks requiring well organized groups of men such as transporting obelisks or other such royal undertakings, levies of militia were raised, strong young men who were formed into companies according to where they lived. The office of the scribe of recruits kept lists of all men liable to this kind of service and care was taken not to draw too heavily on any one district. Nevertheless, just as in Babylonia, conscription was often resisted, and police were usually present while those chosen were dragged from their protesting families.

Nor was this resistance unjustified, for once drafted, these young men were armed and equipped very much like soldiers, and although they were likely to find themselves in labour battalions working under the supervision of an architect, they might also find themselves fighting alongside regular troops.

If on the one hand these conscript units appeared to have merged with the army, on the other there was overlapping, at least in function, with that other very important forced labour system which Egypt shared with Mesopotamia, the corvée. This was an ancient and essential feature of Egyptian life that presumably had its first great employment in the building of the pyramids and continued down to the end of the nineteenth century A.D.

Corvée labour was supposedly more general in its social range and in the work for which it was raised. In principle even in the New Kingdom only the official class was exempt; priests are known to have been obliged to undertake dirty work in the fields. The really well-to-do, however, undoubtedly avoided the corvée by paying substitutes or buying themselves off. The main burden then as much as later fell on the poorer classes of serfs, labourers, small artisans. Corvées could be called out when extra work was needed in agriculture, such as in the harvest field, during the summer for the repair and development of irrigation works or to fight against high floods. They could also be called, sometimes nation-wide, for unskilled works, such as the transport of building stone, on the great royal undertakings. This kind of corvée was probably limited to the three months of the inundation when farming was very slack. In spite of strict bureaucratic control there were the inevitable abuses: the king on occasion had to issue decrees against those of his officials who marched off temple workers for their own irregular purposes.

THE CLASS STRUCTURE

THE LANDOWNING AND CLASS STRUCTURE UNDERLYING EGYPTIAN SOCIETY was relatively simple in principle, yet some aspects remain elusive. There were many changes with time and an inevitable increase in complexity as civilization itself evolved.

Pharaoh owned the land of Egypt with title deeds assigned to him by the gods; when at his *sed* festival he ran the ritual 'traversing the earth', he was renewing this universal possession. In theory it was never revoked, and even in practice it was never in question that the king had the right to take back any of the lands that he had given to his subjects. Make gifts, however, he did, and had to, on a lavish scale. He made gifts of estates to the gods for the maintenance of their temples, and he made endowments in perpetuity for his own funerary cult. He also made gifts of estates, cattle and servants to those who served him—in the early days largely members of the royal family, but later to other nobles, officials, soldiers.

Large parts of the Kingdom remained under the crown, and there is evidence to suggest that these generally consisted of the best arable lowland, that part of the valley normally watered and fertilized by the inundation. The royal estates might help farmers by the loan of seed corn and the hire of ox teams. It seems that when the king granted holdings to individuals or institutions with special privileges such as remission of tax, it was usually underdeveloped land which they were expected to irrigate (in the valley) or drain (in the Delta).

With the natural acquisitiveness of mankind, those subjects who had benefitted from the generosity of their king wanted full possession of their estates and offices so that they could hand them on to their children, or emulate Pharaoh by entailing a part of their land for their own funerary cults. This was granted to them and their estates became so far their own private property that land could also be bought and sold. Already by third dynasty times an official might own part of an estate in his own name and part assigned to provide the salary of his office. At this period at any rate, private holdings do not seem to have been larger than a few hundred acres, and they were likely to be scattered about the country. This division of estates into widely separated blocks remained common practice and applied to temple as well as private lands. The temple of Khnum at Elephantine, for example, held land in the Delta.

At all times, and particularly in the pyramid age and the later New Kingdom, very large endowments were made for funerary cults by Pharaoh and his land-owning subjects. In effect this was exactly analogous to the endowment of chantries by the kings and nobles and wealthy men of Christendom. Continuing generation after generation, it would have led to the whole kingdom belonging to the dead. In practice, however, it is clear that these endowments were allowed to lapse, or were amalgamated with subsequent ones. Such dispossession of the dead could happen shamefully fast. When Ramesses II on his accession visited his father, Seti's, funerary temple at Abydos he found it abandoned half finished, offerings

and services at an end, and 'the produce of its arable land, its boundaries unfixed, taken and carried away'.

During the New Kingdom very large grants of land together with
livestock and workers were made to temples of gods other than dead
Pharaohs, and most of all to the temple of Amun at Karnak. The
largest were direct royal gifts, but other landowners also sought
divine favour in this way. Ramesses III gave over nine hundred
square miles of land carrying 86,486 people to endow his new foundations at Thebes, and very considerable, although lesser, amounts
to Heliopolis and Memphis, representing altogether something like
10 percent of the cultivable land of the kingdom. This was at least
partly in addition to their existing possessions: perhaps Diodorus
was not so far out when he said that in ancient Egypt one-third of
the land was owned by the temples. This kind of thing did, of course,
give excessive influence to the temples and especially to that of
Amun at Thebes—all the more as it seems that high priests might
have large estates in their own name. Yet the royal endowments
were not without strings: the temples had to provide priestly sine-
cures or administrative posts for crown nominees. It has to be remembered, too, that the temple properties were taxed and administered through the office of the vizier. One way and another the
landed interests of the crown and the temples could hardly be
separated.

There was one large change in the nature of landholding during
pharaonic times. It is of additional interest in that it illustrates the
truth that Pharaoh's divine ownership of the land was more than
purely theoretical. Once again it concerns the nomarchs whose
mounting wealth and independence did most to fragment the Old
Kingdom and who then ruled over the fragments as virtually independent princes. It is possible that some families of this hereditary
nobility were in fact descended from chiefs of prehistoric times and
therefore had their own mystic claim to their lands, but it is thought
that more usually their title came from appointment under the
crown. In either case, when the Middle Kingdom was established
over their heads, they continued to rule as faithful lieges of Pharaoh,
and Egypt had some two centuries of a feudal style of landholding.
Yet when Sen-Wosret III felt strong enough to move against the
nomarchs, and when their liquidation was completed at the opening of the New Kingdom, there seems to have been no great resistance nor difficulties of tenure. The old nobility was swept aside.

Their lands naturally reverted to Pharaoh and fell under the central administration of his vizier and civil service.

The class structure of Egyptian society was probably somewhat simpler and more regulated than that of Mesopotamia, although, like the landholding with which it was associated, it inevitably became more complex with the passage of time. It has been said of Early Dynastic society that it had only two classes, the government and the governed. There is much truth in this for the days when the early kings and their immediate kinsmen and retainers ruled the land as though it were a family estate. Those who believe these rulers, the Followers of Horus, to have been an invading race see the 'governed' as subjected natives racially distinct from the 'governors'.

Even in this Archaic period archaeology has discovered that the situation was not so simple. Cemeteries round Memphis suggest that the citizens were aware of a distinction between the extended royal family and great nobles on one side and something approaching a middle class of a lesser nobility and officials on the other. There were also craftsmen working for this two-level élite who (in death at any rate) were not without social and religious aspirations. Yet it remains true that all these people were privileged when set beside the peasantry which at this time still lived much as it had done in the prehistoric past.

Although in Archaic and Old Kingdom times the cultivators of the soil were accepted as human chattels tied to the soil, they were spared one hard fate suffered by the otherwise more fortunate retainers of the great. We shall find that during the first dynasty craftsmen and other servants were put to death so that they might follow their royal or noble masters into the afterlife.

From the first, then, the sharpest cleavage in Egyptian society was between the educated, any one of whom might aspire to the highest offices, and the uneducated mass who raised the food, did more or less unskilled work—and evade us in their historical anonymity.

A large part of the field workers were serfs employed on royal, temple or other large estates. They probably got a cut from their own harvest reaping as well as rations of all the recognized necessities of life. When land was transferred by gift or sale, they went with it.

During the New Kingdom there seems to have been an increasing tendency for independent farmers to work their lands with paid labour and slaves. By the Ramessid period there was a threat of breakdown in the whole agricultural system, with workers fleeing the land. The main cause of this appears to have been excessive taxation and harsh, sometimes illicit, requisitioning. Wrongful requisitioning was already one of the abuses that Horemhab sought to set right (and we have encountered it far earlier in Mesopotamia). In the nineteenth dynasty an official letter records how two culti-vators on a royal estate had fled because they had been beaten, probably by requisitioners. It continues, 'Now look! The fields lie abandoned and there is no one to till them.' It must have been this kind of situation that we shall soon find causing short supply in the royal storehouses of Ramesses III. The crown and the great temples probably eased the situation by employing prisoners of war.

Perhaps the most elusive class, yet one of importance for the Egyptian economy, is that of the small-holders. Their way of life is portrayed for us in the *Two Brothers* who evidently ran a mixed farm small enough for them to cultivate it on their own. A propor-tion of such small-holders were beneficiaries of Pharaoh and their descendants, the families of soldiers and others who had been granted plots of land for services rendered. The famous ten-metre-long *Wilbour Papyrus,* referring to central Egypt in late Ramessid times, gives a clear idea of the great variety of small-holders who paid their own taxes and were virtually private owners of their land. Most of the plots were of five, ten and twenty *arouras* (an *aroura* being two-thirds of an acre). The holders included many soldiers, priests and scribes, a few craftsmen such as a potter, carpenter, coppersmith and weaver, and two embalmers. There were also many simple cultivators and a large number of women. Though these people were nominally tenants, mostly of temple estates, it seems that they were free to hand on the plots to their children.

We get another glimpse of small-holding through the gradation of the harvest tax. This ranged from a levy of about half the total yield on large estates to less than one-third of this rate on the smallest farms. Altogether there must have been several grades of farmers, owners and tenants, who lived well below the level of those large landlords who could afford fine tombs where they were shown presiding over happily toiling serfs.

The great events of Egyptian history affected the condition of the humblest field workers as well as that of the upper classes. The shock of the collapse after the sixth dynasty as well as the actual social revolution that was a part of it (when, as Ipuwer said, 'Nobles are in lamentation while poor men have joy' and 'Serfs have become the owners of serfs') are thought to have led to some improvement in their lot. There was certainly more concern for the humble among thinking people. It is evident in the idea of Pharaoh as good shepherd and in much of the literature. Typical is the coffin text written about 2000 B.C. and usually referred to as *All Men Created Equal in Opportunity*. In it the sun god tells of his good deeds in the creation of the world. Most important, he made the air for all men alike to breathe, and 'I made the great inundation that the poor man might have rights therein like the great.' Moreover he declares that having 'made every man like his fellow' it was the evil in their own hearts that upset his just intentions.

By the time the New Kingdom was established the class structure had become further divided. We have already seen that it had been affected by the development of a large professional army, and much the same thing had happened with the priesthood. As wealth and land accrued to the temples far larger numbers were needed both for ritual services and for the administration (under the vizier) of the temple estates. As a result priesthood, which had been a lay responsibility, became a profession.

A census official of the eighteenth dynasty divided the people of Egypt whom he was enumerating into 'soldiers, priests, king's servants and all the craftsmen'. To this should be added the royal family, nobility and superior officials at the top, and a growing number of slaves at the bottom. The category of 'soldiers', too, should be expanded. It seems that it included not only serving soldiers but all those belonging to a class also known as 'citizens of the army', who were held liable to military service. This meant the freeman class of small farmers, small traders, petty officials, only a minority of whom were ever called to the standards.

The 'king's servants' comprised not only agricultural serfs but the whole labouring class. There were the miners of gold, copper and turquoise, and the numerous quarrymen, masons, builders and tomb-cutters who must have made such an exceptionally large and distinctive element within the Egyptian working class. There were also the even humbler folk who served the needs of these men as porters, water-carriers and the like. Specialist craftsmen in the work-shops, too, needed their unskilled assistants. Then again in all the houses of the wealthy from the royal palaces downwards, there were domestic servants in the kitchens, pantries, laundries, nurseries.

A wonderfully full picture of the lives of one group of workers and craftsmen has come down to us from western Thebes. These were the royal tomb-cutters whose cantonment at Deir el-Medinah has already been described. The 'crew' usually numbered about sixty men and was divided into a right and a left side, apparently because the organization was based on that of a ship. Each side had a fore-man, and there was also a scribe who kept a detailed day book and also reported to the vizier's office. The officials took a keen interest in the royal tombs and liked to pop along to see how things were going. The crew worked all the year round and their working hours were divided into two equal parts with a rest period between them. They had plenty of holidays, however, one at the end of each of the three ten-day periods into which the Egyptian month was divided, and several days together during the main religious festivals. It was only at these holidays that they could expect to be at home in the village with their wives, for on working days most of them lived in huts up in the harsh valley near the tombs.

The foreman had a plan for the tomb from which to work, and as the shafts were driven beyond the reach of daylight a good supply of wicks and oil was provided. The artists who made the painted reliefs in the completed chambers seem to have been regular members of the crew.

Pay was in wheat for bread and barley for beer issued monthly from the royal granaries. The foremen got larger measures than the others. Everyone also got vegetables, a variety of dried and fresh fish, firewood and a ration of water brought up on donkeys. There were issues of unguents and clothing, while on special occasions the king gave such luxuries as salt, natron for washing, wine and imported Asian beer.

The workers had their own little local sanctuaries for the worship of their favourite divinities and divine Pharaohs where they them-selves served as priests. They also had their own cemetery, where some of the tombs were quite large and well decorated. Most re-markable of all, this community had its own tribunal or *kenbet* for settling disputes. Its membership usually included the scribe and a foreman, but for the rest consisted of workmen and their wives, probably the elders of the village. The tribunal was empowered to determine guilt and punishment, except that capital cases had to be referred up to the vizier. The long life and stability of the Deir el-Medinah village (the crew continued on a largely hereditary basis from the reign of Amenhotep I to late Ramessid times) and the special nature of its work for the royal tombs may have made it a little abnormal. Nevertheless, the discovery of the existence of worker priests and of the *kenbet*, due to the chance preservation of texts, is a warning against the assumption that under a centralized bureaucratic government and ambitious priesthoods the Egyptian workers had no independence, or responsibility for their own affairs.

Equally revealing is the vigorous reaction of this same community when in the difficult days of Ramesses III payments of the workers often fell into arrears. Trouble came to a head in the twenty-ninth year of the reign. The scribe began it: announcing that for twenty days they had received no rations he went off and contrived to extract from a local temple some part of the goods that should have come from the royal stores. This was no more than a temporary easement; five months later the crew marched down from the valley on strike, causing a night of disturbance in the Ramesseum. They protested, 'We are hungry. Hunger and thirst have driven us here. We have no clothes, no oil, no fish, no vegetables. Send word to Pharaoh, our master, or the vizier, our chief, so that we may get something to live on.' After more days of disturbance the arrears were paid, but the next month again rations were not forthcoming and the vizier had to come out in person to try to pacify them. It is interesting that no attempt seems to have been made to use the military or police to crush the workers.

There was one class within Egyptian society that had little hope of such independence of action: the slaves. The class is in practice difficult to define, always being inclined to merge into that of the serfs and other 'king's servants'. In Egypt there appears to have been nothing like the debt slavery of Mesopotamia: practically all slaves were foreigners, most obtained as prisoners of war, but some brought into the country by traders. Probably in the early days nearly all captives had to serve in the army, but it would be surprising if they were not sometimes used beside .corvée labour for pyramid and temple building.

It was in New Kingdom times that slavery began to play a more considerable part in Egypt's social and economic life. Thutmose III and his successors led back very large numbers of prisoners from their Asian campaigns. Some could use their skills as weavers, tailors, cooks in the Palace itself or in the houses of the nobility, but most of these unfortunates were put to work on royal or temple estates. There they are likely to have known the worst conditions of slavery, for they were kept in barracks probably comparable in grimness to the Roman *ergastula*. With the passing of generations, however, they tended to be absorbed among other workers and were listed as ordinary serfs. Ramesses III used large numbers of Syrian prisoners on building work, but later, branded with his mark, they were put into the army. A select few were given to his courtiers and are known to have intermarried with Egyptian servants.

While most Asiatics reached Egypt as part of the royal war booty, some were brought home by individual serving soldiers. Ahmose tells how captives he had taken at Avaris and Sharuhen were granted him by the king, while in his tomb he lists no fewer than ten female and nine male slaves obtained as booty. If Ahmose was at all typical, quite a number of slaves may have entered private households in this way.

The other main source of slaves in New Kingdom times was from the south, from Nubia and beyond. After his southern campaign, Thutmose I gave many Nubian slaves to the temple of Amun at Karnak. These were still Hamitic Nubians, portrayed as darker than the Egyptians but otherwise indistinguishable. Although Negroes occasionally appear in art forms at this earlier date it is only after Thutmose III's extension of the frontier to Napata that they are very often shown in attitudes of subjection, generally in paired opposition with Asiatics. A famous example can be seen in Tutankhamun's carved ivory baton. It is thought very probable that some enslaved Negroes were not prisoners of war but were part of the gifts or tribute sent to Pharaoh by African chieftains, while others may have been obtained through slave traders.

In Egypt as elsewhere slaves could be bought or sold and seem quite often to have been hired out by the day. They were frequently branded by their owners. Evidently they were sometimes offered for sale from door to door. A law case from the reign of Ramesses II is pathetically similar to those of present day housewives tempted by hire purchase touts. A woman was accused of having taken goods from another housewife in order to pay for a 'bargain' offered her in the form of a male and a female slave.

The foreign slaves of Egypt were chattels, but apart from this their living conditions were probably not very different from those of ordinary Egyptian serfs. Like them they were supplied with linen and unguents as well as food rations. In the absence of written law codes little is known of their legal position, but they are thought to have had some rights. That there were laws concerning runaways comparable to those in Mesopotamia is suggested by a model letter used in scribal lessons and purporting to be written by one officer to others concerning two slaves attempting to escape over the frontier into Asia.

In later New Kingdom times and afterwards there are examples of manumission and of marriages into the family of their owners. In the Late period, too, men who had entered the royal service as slave guards and attendants sometimes attained to high positions round the king.

Taken all in all, it seems that slavery was nothing like so essential a part of life in the Nile valley as it was in Mesopotamia—or, indeed, in Anatolia and elsewhere in the ancient world. Egypt was more self-sufficient, in Old and Middle Kingdom times less disturbed by wars than her Asian neighbours. Perhaps more important, as all labourers were 'king's servants' and at his disposal, and as unlimited labour was easily available through the corvée, the need for actual slaves was far less. Although they undoubtedly added to the luxury, splendour and grandiose building projects of the New Kingdom, Egyptian civilization could have been created and maintained without them.

MEN, WOMEN AND CHILDREN

THE VALUES AND INFLUENCE OF WOMEN ON SOCIETY WERE MUCH greater in Egypt than among her Semitic neighbours. While this was most conspicuously true at court and among the rich and educated, it penetrated downward to the professional middle classes. At the bottom of the scale the wives of serfs and slaves must have shared a life experience of endless hard work and child-bearing with their like in Asia, but they may (since these habits usually spread throughout society) have mingled on more equal terms with their menfolk, taken a greater part and had more liberty and fun when occasionally they could escape from grindstone and hearth and enjoy themselves at popular festivals. By the time Herodotus visited Egypt, he was struck by the fact that while the men stayed at the loom it was the women who went to market—always an opportunity for social life, economic influence and some inexpensive drinking.

It may be that this estimate of women's high status and good life has been too much influenced by the record of the visual arts, by the marvellously varied gallery of noble, companionable, graceful, merry, loving and shamelessly seductive women left us by sculptors and painters. In so far as this depends on the Egyptian custom of having scenes of everyday life in tombs and temples and on the chances of preservation there is truth in the argument, yet art and its uses after all express the spirit of society, and the contrast in this respect between Mesopotamia and Egypt cannot be altogether misleading.

The strong feminine presence might be said to start at the highest level among the divinities. Well-placed though Inanna-Ishtar and the other goddesses were, they are by no means so all-pervasive as those of Egypt. The ever recurring names and representations of the Two Ladies of Upper and Lower Egypt and the importance of their symbols among the royal iconography, the equal familiarity of the lovingly protective goddesses Isis, Nephys, Neith and Serket, and the special position of Isis in relation to Osiris and to the throne, the nourishing motherhood so freely represented by Hathor, and, running through everything, the ideals of Egyptian civilization personified in the goddess Ma'at, leave the feminine element in the Sumerian pantheon far behind.

Sharing in the light and breath of these divinities, the queens and princesses of Egypt played a far more conspicuous role on the historical stage than the obscure royal ladies of Mesopotamia. From the Old Kingdom sculptures such as that of the placid Princess Nofret, and of Queen Khamerenebti standing so confidently and affectionately beside her royal husband, right down to the fleshier beauties of the Ptolemaic throne, their figures, their names and titles were everywhere displayed.

Their importance as heiresses of course gave many of these ladies their standing and influence, but again and again in Egyptian history the Mothers, Daughters, Great Wives of the God came to the fore through their own character and ability. Three outstanding queens helped to establish the eighteenth dynasty firmly on the throne. Ahmose described his mother Ahhotep as 'One who cares for Egypt. She has looked after her soldiers, guarded her [Egypt], brought back her fugitives and collected together her deserters; she has pacified Upper Egypt and expelled her rebels.' This queen who saved Egypt in some crisis is a worthy forebear for the girlish-faced and iron-willed Hatshepsut, who was ready to be shown in a king's clothes and ritually bearded. Yet the violent reaction after Hatshepsut's successful reign, when her name was excised from monuments and records, proves that however great their esteem for women, the Egyptians were not prepared willingly to accept their rule.

Another high point was reached with the worldly influence of Queen Tiy over Amenhotep III and their daughter-in-law, Nefertiti's, very different but equally potent relationship with Akhenaten. The new life style that these two caused to flower at Akhetaten is of peculiar interest here. Although it took Akhenaten's genius to give it full expression, it cannot fail to have flowed from liberal ideas already present among the élite. These were wholly consistent: a cult of natural beauty, a new freedom of expression in the arts and an escape from negative morality, went with an open and equal relationship between husband and wife, informality of manners and a permissiveness towards children that allowed the princesses to romp about with their parents, indulge a little in naughtiness and enjoy adult company.

Even after the return to Thebes and to Amun, the life style lingered on, as can be recognized in the tender scenes of adolescent love and affection between Tutankhamun and Ankhesenamun drawn on so many of the young king's possessions. There is the same sense of an equal and free relationship, the same casualness of attitude and immediacy of feeling. The spirited independence later shown by the widowed Ankhesenamun had been fostered by her upbringing and was perhaps encouraged by this experience of marriage.

Stepping down now from the uppermost circle of the divine and royal, there is ample evidence that educated Egyptians greatly respected marriage and motherhood, and also that the wife went about with her husband in their everyday life of work and pleasure. Among the wise sayings of the vizier Ptahhotep, dating from at least as early as the Middle Kingdom, is one: 'If thou art a man of standing thou shouldst found thy household and love thy wife at home as is fitting. Fill her belly; clothe her back. Make her heart glad as long as you live. She is a profitable field for her lord.'

Much later, towards the end of the New Kingdom, Ani recommends a son to marry young to have a son of his own whom he can 'teach to be a man'. On the other hand he warns him, 'Be on your guard against a woman from abroad. . . . Do not stare at her when she passes by. Do not know her carnally; deep water whose windings one knows not is a woman away from her husband . . .' He also expresses this more than formal respect for motherhood:

Double the food which you give to your mother and carry her as she carried you. She had a heavy load in you. You were born after your months but she was still tied to you, for her breast was in your mouth for three years. Although your filth was disgusting, her heart was not disgusted. . . . She put you to school where you learnt to write, and every day supplied you with bread and beer.

In general this wisdom literature is aristocratic in feeling and free from the broad husband-and-wife humour of the Sumerian proverbs. While the tone such speakers adopt towards wifehood tends to be lordly even if respectful, Egyptian artists give a different impression. From Old Kingdom times onwards they show women on terms of equality with their husbands, supervising the work of their estates —of the cattleherds, the harvesters, the craftsmen. Whole families are seen going together to the marshes for such sport as wild fowling. In one well known scene of this kind the party includes a pet cat. At home together, the sculptor Ipy has a kitten on his lap and his wife a cat under her seat; another couple are playing draughts while their daughter looks on.

While words and pictures such as these evoke a picture of happy and respectable married life, many delicious love poems (dating from late in the New Kingdom) tell of the sweetness and pains of romantic love. Unlike the Sumerian love poetry of the sacred marriage, they are very personal, and express the man's desires at least as often as the woman's. They were probably intended to be sung to the strain of lyre, lute or harp and perhaps at those mixed parties of men and women when the guests were plied with food and drink, offered flowers and sweet nard for their hair and entertained by singing and dancing and music. In one such love poem the boy tells how when a stream with a crocodile separates him from his beloved he finds courage to wade across, 'And the waves are like land unto my feet. It is the love of her that makes me steady . . .' Another, coming from the girl's side, must be quoted in full for its poetry,

its erotic imagery and a simple wantonness for which Egyptian
women were noted:

> *My brother, it is pleasant to go to the pool*
> *In order to bathe myself in your presence,*
> *That I may let you see my beauty in my robe of finest linen*
> *When it is wet. . . .*
> *I go down with you into the water*
> *And come forth again with a red fish*
> *Which lies beautiful on my fingers,*
> *Come and look at me . . .*

Herodotus considered Egyptian women led the world in adultery
and told the story of a Pharaoh who could not be cured of his blind-
ness (as the gods had promised) by finding a faithful wife among
his subjects though he tried all from queens to slaves. *The Tale of
the Two Brothers*, hitherto quoted for its happy picture of peasant
life, is in fact centred on the wantonness of the wife who did her best
to seduce her young brother-in-law ('Come let us lie together for
an hour and I will give you two pretty garments') and when
turned down accused him to her husband of being the seducer. As
far as can be judged, the customary and legal aspects of marriage
and divorce were very much the same as in pre-Assyrian Mesopotamia.

While the chief wife was a man's companion and helpmate, there
were only financial limitations on the number of lesser wives, concubines and slave girls a man could possess. All wealthy houses
included a harem, and it seems that few men (other than priests) of
any social pretensions would be content with a monogamous marriage. The status and possessions of the chief wife were, however,
strictly safeguarded. The household goods belonged to her and her
first son was her husband's heir even if he had children by previous
alliances.

Claims that a matrilineal counterpart to the royal heiress existed
in the rest of society and that land always went through the female
line cannot be justified. Property generally descended through eldest
sons, though due provision was made for other children. By the
ordinary course of inheritance, purchase and tenancy, women certainly had a considerable stake in the land of Egypt. It appears to

have been the custom for widows to keep and work their husbands' properties at least until a son was ready to inherit.

The womenfolk of a well-to-do household lived luxuriously, with every opportunity to indulge vanity and possessiveness. As already described, they had their choice of fine linens, cosmetic indulgence of every kind, jewellery, handsome furniture. Their dressing tables were laden with fine jars, mirrors, toilet utensils. They had an unlimited supply of servants and ladies' maids to wait on them, look after their wigs, tire their hair, tie their sashes. The contrast here that existed between rich and poor is touchingly brought out in the *Admonitions of Ipuwer* when he bemoans the social revolution: 'Behold, she who had not even a box is now the owner of a trunk. She who looked at her face in the water is now the owner of a mirror.'

Apart from marriage and the responsibility for estate management that often went with it, the most important career open to women was in the priesthoods. From royal princesses downward many entered the service of the temples, often enriched by holding many offices and local priesthoods simultaneously. When in the Late period the Theban high priests had been virtually ruling Upper Egypt, the Kushite kings arranged that the existing role of God's Wife of Amun should be held by a princess who would represent the royal house, providing a political counter-weight to the lineage of the high priests. Although these ladies worked through a steward, they must have had a firm grasp of worldly affairs and the realities of power.

In the ordinary way, most priestesses were probably concerned with the dancing, singing and instrumental music that were an important part of religious ritual. The temple concubines, thought to have been most numerous in the service of the ithyphallic god, Min, were probably drawn from a lower social level. The same would have been true of another calling open to women, that of professional mourners. These ladies appear in many funerary scenes in groups of about twenty. With their hair loose down their backs they stand wailing to heaven or sit on the ground beating their brows. Evidently novitiates were trained through participation, for at the funeral of the vizier Ramose the mourning party includes girls of various ages, including one young enough to appear naked and clasping her mother's hand.

Women also acted as midwives. Some no doubt relied entirely

on magic, but some were trained in the Houses of Life. Women in labour were described as 'on the bricks', for a primitive manner of delivery was by squatting on two bricks—perhaps with a crossbar. A more advanced contrivance was the delivery chair still used by Egyptian fellaheen. Contraception and abortion were prohibited, and yet there were recognized prescriptions for them. It looks as though the situation was as ambiguous as it has usually been. Women could also become physicians, though probably this rarely happened.

It can be assumed that many court and noble ladies were literate, and that, as always, men disapproved of any such intellectual leanings. One of them scratched a sneering comment on women's literary efforts in the Step Pyramid. Writing palettes belonging to two of Akhenaten's daughters have been found, and although a cultivation of women's abilities may have distinguished Akhenaten's court, it is most unlikely that other well-born girls would not have had the chance to learn to read and write. Some certainly had tutors.

A word for a female scribe existed in the Egyptian language at latest by Middle Kingdom times. There must therefore have been professional women scribes, although we hear nothing of their doings.

Children appear in the art of Egypt far oftener than in Mesopotamia. Several of the happiest examples that come to mind are from Akhetaten, but there are many other family scenes. Sons and daughters are portrayed indiscriminately and with equal affection. Nevertheless it was an accepted precept that every good man wanted his wife to present him with a son who would be 'like unto himself'.

Mothers normally suckled their children until they were three years old. It may have been when they were weaned that they ceased to run about naked. Schooling started a year or two later. Boys were universally circumcised between about the ages of six and twelve, and, as we have seen, were exhorted by the sages to take a wife while they were young. In fact they seem often to have married in early adolescence.

Altogether there is a good deal to suggest that childhood was happier and more free in Egypt than in Mesopotamia. Such a judgement may be subjective, but quite apart from the hints given by literature and the arts, the conditions of the Nile valley and its way of life were ideally suited to children. Towns were smaller and far less congested. For the little ones there were the gardens with their fishponds and kiosks, cats and other pets indoors, and a general love of animals. For older children the river was always quite near with all the wild life of its verges and islands.

In considering the lives of these weaker members of ancient society, its women and its children, it appears that the Nile valley civilization offered them, like its great men of genius, that little extra shelter for the spirit that they needed to fulfil themselves.

3. THE MENTAL WORLD

RELIGION AND COSMOLOGY

"THEY ARE RELIGIOUS TO EXCESS, BEYOND ANY OTHER NATION IN THE world." This was Herodotus's opinion of the Egyptians of his day. If such a detached observer could have visited the land of the Nile two thousand years earlier this judgement would have remained the same. The tenacity of Sumerian traditions in Mesopotamia has been made much of, yet they might be considered wayward if set beside the awe-inspiring constancy of Egypt.

This does not mean that there were not profound changes within the traditional forms. Both social evolution and psychological modifications had their effects. In particular shifts followed both those national breakdowns of the First and Second Intermediate periods. Yet the extent to which the tradition remained the same is witnessed not only by the continuance of the same divine names, the identical divine symbols, over three thousand years, but also by the way that ancient religious texts were copied, studied, glossed and interpreted by some hundred generations of priests.

Much the same bewildering blend of historical, psychological and intellectual elements that formed the elements of religion in Mesopotamia was also present in Egypt. Yet there were two considerable differences. First, there was nothing equivalent to the fusion of the two distinct pantheons of the Sumerians and the Semites, nor of the adoption of foreign deities. Secondly, the intellectual element was much stronger. In discussing the Sumerians it was possible to ask whether theologians could properly be distinguished from mythographers. With the Egyptians from the very dawn of their history there were men wrestling with theological and metaphysical problems and writing down what they believed to be the answers in a manner sometimes worthy of the later Hebrews or Christian Fathers. Not that they normally attempted a logical dogma or consistent faith. Perhaps some priests of Ptah at Memphis dreamed of it in the early days of the Unification, and Akhenaten attempted it some seventeen centuries later, with disastrous results.

The accepted way of looking for the truth, or for illumination, was what Frankfort has called the 'multiplicity of approaches', with a resulting multiplicity of answers. Thus within a single hymn Pharaoh could be evoked as a beautiful child in the arms of his mother, Hathor, and as a divine youth who begot and bore himself. It was a way of thinking that could send a ray on to each of the many facets of human experience and one which led towards tolerance and away from disputation and strife.

Together with the more intellectual concern for theology and metaphysics manifest in the Egyptians went their addiction to formalized religious symbols. The Sumerians and Babylonians had a few simple and visually unstereotyped symbols such as the tree of life, the sun, the star of Ishtar, but the Egyptians had dozens, including such abstractions as 'rule', 'life', 'totality', and 'eternity', which were reproduced line for line over the millennia. They built up into a religious language with signs that were also true symbols. No more elaborate or subtle system of this kind has ever been developed within a general social culture.

It is always said that the early priesthoods were not 'professional', yet to create, propagate and establish such a symbolism and the intricate religious meanings that it expressed suggests that men about the king, or in the great religious centres such as Heliopolis, Memphis and, later, Thebes, must have devoted themselves to meditation and religious questionings and have formed esoteric circles with an influence that was wide and deep. How far through society the language of symbols could be 'read' it is difficult to judge. It was certainly extensively used in the coffins of the men and women of the professional class, but how far did they understand its import?

Many symbols, obviously, could be appreciated at different levels. As an example none is better than the 'scarab', that familiar Egyptian sign and object. The dung beetle, *Scarabeus sacer,* lays its eggs in animal droppings, making them into a ball which it may push up-hill in the sand. Even the prehistoric villagers observed this, and preserved actual specimens of the beetle, probably already seeing in it a symbol of the rising sun and of self-creating life arising from death, an idea that was reinforced by the fact that the Egyptian name of *khoprer* sounds like the word for being or existing. (The Egyptians were much given to seeing significance in verbal like-nesses, a mental process like that underlying sympathetic magic.) Associated with the increasing power and subtlety of sun worship the beetle, now Khopri, became the supreme symbol for the manifesta-tion of god as he 'came into being'. It could also stand for all coming into being; the creator god says, 'I planned in my heart how I should make every shape . . . the myriad forms of Khopri.' So the stylized form of the little beetle appeared everywhere, most gorgeously on jewellery such as Tutankhamun's collar, most massively in noble sculptures such as that standing beside the sacred lake at Karnak, most popularly as lucky charms bought by pilgrims, with most feel-ing, perhaps, when laid on the breast of the dead as the thinking heart, or painted above the mummy's head as a symbol of resurrec-tion. Probably the peasant haggling for his charm at a wayside stall in Abydos would not share many of the thoughts of the priest placing an inscribed scarab upon the exalted dead—yet it was after all the prehistoric peasants who first saw meaning in the creature.

The best example of a symbol deliberately created as a mental act is the rayed sun with hands on the end of its beams, devised under Akhenaten to express the universal life-giving power of the Aten. Suzanne Langer has seen symbol-making as an innate urge of the human mind: no one ever had it more strongly than the ancient Egyptians.

The Egyptians' conventional model of the physical universe was not very different from that devised by the Sumerians. They most usually saw the earth as a disk representing the land of Egypt, with a raised rim of mountains which were the foreign lands. This earth floated upon and was encircled by the primeval waters of Nun, similar in many ways to the realm of Enki. The Nile flowed out from Nun through caverns, and the sun, after its nightly journey below the earth, was reborn daily from the waters of Nun. The heavens covered the earth like a lid which was supported by 'the four pillars of heaven', probably set at the four points of the compass. For symmetry, and because this universe was finite, another 'lid' or underheaven bounded the underworld—though this was probably always most vaguely conceived.

This was the physical model, but in addition there had to be a cosmography of myth. For instance, texts and pictures alike often insisted that the air god Shu supported the upper heavens with his arms, while heaven itself could be the sky goddess Nut arched over the earth, balanced on fingers or toes. Or again Nut's arched body was replaced by Hathor as cow-goddess, while the moon and stars which could sail across the bare body of Nut might equally cross the furry underbelly of the cow; the sun barque, too, followed its celestial course across these heaven-spanning females.

In its cosmogony Egyptian tradition differed from the Sumerian and Babylonian more than in its cosmography, though there were still many ideas in common. Here again there was a 'multiplicity of approaches', due in part to the different teachings of the various religious centres, each with its own supreme deity. It is impossible here to do more than touch on this complexity of subtle intuitions and intellectual elaborations. There was a generally shared view that in the beginning was a chaos of waters, represented by Nun and other aspects of darkness, formlessness and passivity. From the waters there arose, like the fertile soil of Egypt from the receding inundation, the primeval hillock where life, light, activity were to be brought into being by the creator god.

The simple intuition of the emergent hillock of creation was itself to have tremendous creative power. Every sanctuary throughout the land, whatever its divinity, and at whatever date it was founded, could be identified with the original hill. Moreover, as the idea produced its symbol, the hill became a pyramid, the place where the divine king could repeat the first creation and be born into eternal life. There can be no more amazing example of the power of the psyche than this one when the idea of the hillock moved tens of thousands of men to raise millions of tons of stone into pure geometric forms likely to endure as long as mankind itself.

The further acts of creation that were to lead to the establishment of the divine king on the throne of Egypt and of the order of Ma'at were seen in various ways. Of these teachings the most significant were those of Heliopolis and Memphis. At Heliopolis, which was to have so great an influence over the kingship, the original high god or creator was Atum, the Complete One, who in an emergent manifestation was Re, the supreme sun god. In early versions of the story Atum was himself the primeval hill, but later Atum-Re rises *on* the hill, as light, as the first sunrise. Always he was self-created, the 'Becoming One who came into being of himself'.

Atum having created himself as, or on, the hill now went on to produce male and female as Shu, air, and Tefnut, moisture. 'He put his penis in his hand for the pleasure of emission, and there were born brother and sister . . .' This was the primitive interpretation, but Heliopolis also taught a more advanced, though still crude, form of creation by divine utterance: Atum-Re 'conceived with his mouth' and 'Spat forth Shu. Expectorated Tefnut' then embued these off-spring with his spirit (Ka).

Shu and Tefnut gave birth to another brother and sister, Geb, earth, and Nut, the sky goddess, and, as we have seen, Shu inter-vened to lift the sky above the earth. So far this scheme can be recognized as a conventionally devised cosmogony. With their fourth and fifth generations, however, the Heliopolitans drew in divinities of a different kind, gods and goddesses with their own, separate exist-ence in Egyptian mythology and history. These were Osiris with his sister-spouse Isis, and Seth with his sister-spouse Nephys. With their forebears they formed the great Ennead (The Nine) of Heli-opolis. To them has to be added that highly important but infinitely confusing god, Horus. In one aspect he comes up out of the past as a falcon, a glorious sky god whose wings spanned the heaven, whose speckled breast was the sunset clouds and whose eyes the sun and moon. In this aspect he easily fuses with the great sun god, Re himself, becoming Harakte, the youthful early-morning sun. He was addressed as the Great One, the Lord of Heaven, and Pharaoh was his embodiment.

Horus, however, was also the son of Osiris and Isis, the good protagonist of his evil uncle, Seth. There are many versions of the story, but the essential features are that Osiris the good king is drowned by his younger brother. His heart-broken wife, Isis, seeks for his body, finds it, yet Seth is able to tear it up and scatter the parts. Isis and Nephys reunite the body, and although they cannot bring 'the listless one' fully to life they so far succeed in securing an erection that Isis conceives and bears Horus. Reared secretly in the Delta marshes, Horus returns to a long struggle with Seth, life with death. At last the other gods, grown weary of their con-tending, sit in judgement on them and award the kingdom to Horus.

Osiris was essentially renewed life—in the Nile water, in grain, in man. Yet unlike most dying fertility gods (including Dumuzi) he was not himself resurrected but remained supreme in the underworld; it was his son Horus who lived and reigned on earth.

It became the central myth of Egyptian religion and of the Egyptian state that Pharaoh ruled and maintained Ma'at as Horus, but on death became Osiris. Horus was all living kings, Osiris all dead ones. Thus, although these two Horuses may well have had distinct historical origins, they met in the person of Pharaoh—who might in the same literary breath be addressed as son of Re and of Osiris. In this union the ancient royal sun cult of Heliopolis was linked with the equally ancient fertility cult that was in time to bring a hope of life after death to all Egyptians.

Although the Heliopolitan theology always remained dominant and inspired the imagery of countless hymns, prayers and works of art and literature, there were other theologies, and throughout the land the local gods of the nomes could take the place of the high god, often by linking the name with that of Re. When Menes established the capital of the united kingdom at Memphis, its god, Ptah, had a new greatness thrust upon him, and the need was seen to justify it in theological terms. The resulting Memphite theology must be mentioned if only to show to what heights of speculative thought Egyptians of five thousand years ago could rise. Admittedly they set out to give their Ptah precedence over Atum-Re, but they did it in an exalted way. He comes nearer than any other Egyptian divinity to being transcendent rather than immanent. He was seen as a First Principle who brought the universe into being through the thoughts of his heart (which for the Egyptians was the seat of the intelligence) and the authority of his spoken word. When through thought and utterance Ptah had created all gods (of course including Atum-Re), all spirits, all men, and the entire physical universe and having moreover provided justice for good and evil and given 'value to everything' then at last was Ptah satisfied.

Whether the creation of the universe is accepted according to Heliopolis, to Memphis or other theologies that have not been mentioned, it is at once obvious how much it differed from the Mesopotamian cosmogony. It was a reflective scheme rather than a mythological story like the *Enuma elish*. It saw creation as the deliberate establishment of life and order, not as the result of a violent struggle against chaos. It made very little of the creation of man, be-

cause there was no difference of substance between gods and men.
There was the notion that man was fashioned by the ram-god Khnum
on a potter's wheel, but this was hardly more than an image. Where,
however, the subject is touched on more fully it rings with an
Egyptian optimism very different from the Sumerians' sad conviction
that men were made to be slaves of the gods. In the *Instruction for
Merikare* it is declared of the sun god, 'Well-tended are men, the
cattle of the god. He made heaven and earth according to their
desire . . . they who have issued from his body are his images. . . . He
arises in heaven according to their desire. . . . He made for them
plants, animals, fowl and fish to feed them . . .'

We have now to look at the history that lay behind and mingled
with these theologies and also at some of the changes that emerged
among so much that flowed on unchanged.

In the days just before the Unification the royal houses of both
Lower and Upper Egypt were already worshippers and presumably
embodiments of Horus the falcon. On the Scorpion macehead some of
the allies of that successful Upper Egyptian king are shown as followers of Seth coming from the nomes round his native place of
Ombos. It seems that during the second dynasty these followers became so powerful that Seth, usually shown as a fantastic animal,
briefly rivalled Horus as the royal divinity. Those who believe in
the followers of Horus as an invading dynastic race also tend to see
Seth as the leading native divinity. That the god of defeated *in-
digenes* should become a satanic embodiment of death and darkness
is plausible enough. Whatever his origins, Seth was always something
of an odd god out, was worshipped by the Hyksos in the Delta,
and survived to be identified by the Greeks with their monstrous
Typhon.

The cow-goddess Hathor appears with Horus on the Narmer
palette. She must certainly be seen as the main descendant of the
Mother Goddess of the prehistoric cultivators. Because of her nature
she finds no place in the masculine-dominated theologies, yet as we
have seen she and other goddesses always had important roles as
nurses, mothers, protectors of Pharaoh. Hathor in particular was
much beloved, and was concerned with love and joy as well as with
resulting pregnancy and childbirth. So great was she that she could
be addressed as Lady of Heaven, Earth and the Underworld. In the
end she merged almost completely with Isis, in a unity of motherhood.

Re of Heliopolis and Ptah of Memphis were, of course, established by Archaic times. So too were Osiris in his original home of Busiris in the Delta, Thoth at Hermopolis and Min at Coptos. These and other gods of the nomes had already obtained a place in the national pantheon; others again were already enshrined but were always to remain mere local divinities. Amun, with such a tremendous future before him, was not even the chief god of the Theban nome, but was waiting his time in some obscure corner.

Already the afterlife of royalty and their noble kin was being secured by the provision of massive tombs. These were often built in duplicate at Abydos and Sakkara. They were of the type that has come to be known as the mastaba, in which the body and the most precious belongings of the deceased were buried in chambers sunk below ground level and protected by a rectangular superstructure of mud-brick. This might measure up to 170 feet in length, and represented a death-house provisioned with vast quantities of food and drink and other necessaries or luxuries. Near each mastaba was a shelter for the boat in which the owner hoped to voyage with the sun god.

In addition to material goods, the illustrious dead were accompanied by their human retainers. These men and women, who probably took poison, were buried individually in rows of little graves set round the mastaba. At Abydos King Zer had as many as 338 such servitors, most of them women. Their names were inscribed on small, crude plaques. At Sakkara a queen was surrounded by retainers who had been buried with grave goods indicating their calling—paintpots with an artist, model boats with a shipmaster and so on.

As the court became more highly civilized the idea of the immolations evidently became repugnant, for the practice was given up at Sakkara before the end of the first dynasty (it seems to have continued for a time in the south). If our chronologies are correct, this revulsion affected the Egyptians several centuries before the Sumerians. There was, moreover, a significant difference between the practice in the two countries, for while in Sumeria servitors were buried as mere figures in the royal pageant of death, in Egypt they were allowed their own graves and identities. The *idea* of providing service for the next world was, of course, to persist in Egypt, models and *ushabtis* being substituted for flesh and blood.

By the beginning of the Old Kingdom, then, Egyptian religion was already largely in being, with its symbolism, its theologies, its divinities and their rites, and above all its divine Horus kings securely on the throne. The Pyramid Age saw the power and glory of Pharaoh as the Great One, the Lord of Heaven, at its height. Although only royalty could count on immortality, all Egypt must have been confident that the god-king whom with such incredible labour they had placed in the primeval mound had the power to lead them to the life after death which all so passionately desired. Later, in the second part of the Old Kingdom when the priests of Heliopolis built up the might of Re and somewhat reduced that of Pharaoh, the cult of Osiris was already growing in importance and popularity. With the deep and terrible psychological shock of the First Intermediate period, more and more people turned to it, believing that they could no longer depend upon the divine power of an individual Pharaoh but rather on his part in the eternal cycle of death and rebirth. This identification of the dead man with the dead king, Osiris, led to the general use of texts and symbols, such as the crowns and sceptre, once exclusive to the royal dead. Frankfort has called it a 'wholesale usurpation by common men'. In this spirit the Lord of the Underworld could be addressed:

> *They are all thine, all those who come to you,*
> *Great and small, they belong to you.*

With the Middle Kingdom, conceptions of the Underworld of *Dat* tended to become more fearsone, for it seems that, in spite of Osiris, Egyptians now lived in greater apprehension of death. They developed all manner of obstacles such as an awkward ferryman, gates and monsters, and increasingly as time went by men were to depend on spells and formulae to get them safely by. There also began the custom of placing *ushabtis*, answerers, in the tomb, little figures often provided with a hoe who were to answer for the dead man if he was called for corvée in the hereafter.

Side by side with these sometimes debased ideas of the dead passing obstacles, there developed the doctrine of the judgement of the individual soul. In the aristocratic days of the Old Kingdom, Re had been responsible for judging that Pharaoh had not fallen short of the perfection of Ma'at. Now Osiris gradually took over the judgement of all and sundry. By the New Kingdom, when scenes of Osiris weighing the soul in his balance against a feather began to appear in tombs, means for passing the judgement were largely magical, the dead presenting themselves with a papyrus declaring their innocence, and even with a spell to prevent their own hearts from giving away their shortcomings. It was a situation akin to the Christians' sale of pardons and indulgences. Men have always hoped to outwit their gods.

Meanwhile the great change which had taken place as a result of events in the world of the living was the rise to divine supremacy of Amun, brought about by the shift of the capital to Thebes. This god did not belong originally to Thebes, but had already been introduced there during the First Intermediate period. The Theban king Ammenemes I promoted Amun, the Hidden One, probably a divinity of air and the breath of life, to be head of the national pantheon. Heliopolis, however, had by no means lost all influence, and to secure the legitimacy of Amun's rule he was identified with Re and their names were linked. Although it was politically inspired, this union of divine light with divine breath was to produce a subtle theology and one that could still be developed when in the imperialist New Kingdom Amen-Re became the world-renowned king of the gods with his two gigantic temples at Karnak and Luxor and many others throughout the land. Pharaoh was now inevitably son of Amen-Re and might proclaim just how he had been begotten by the god upon the willing person of the queen.

Amenhotep III (who insisted upon a begetting of this kind in a series of reliefs at Luxor) seems deliberately to have inflated his own divinity as Pharaoh by initiating the worship of his living image. He is thought to have built a large temple for this cult at Memphis and he certainly had another far to the south in Kush. So, too, did his queen, Tiy—commoner though she had been. The king's mortuary temple, with the colossal statues of himself before it, was the largest of its kind ever to have been built.

Another religious trend which became conspicuous in the imperial high noon of this reign involved a partial reversion to the theology of Heliopolis. The solar aspect of Amen-Re and his role as creator of the universe was emphasized—with his cult centre at Thebes as the place of creation. At the same time there was a revival of sun worship in the pure and ancient form of Re-Harakte. Some have seen in all this a political purpose, a desire to revalue Heliopolis against the power of the priesthood of Amun. Yet probably the main motive was a higher one: Egypt now saw herself as the apex of a world of many peoples, and the idea of the sun god as lord of all that it encircled was appropriate to this universal view.

An altogether new way of symbolizing this understanding of the sun god, though it had begun earlier, first made itself conspicuous under Amenhotep III. It was the Aten, or sun disk, a divinity conceived as the sheer power and being of the world-encompassing sun, the manifestation of Re in his visible disk.

This was the idea seized upon and transformed by Amenhotep IV, whose famous revolution in name, residence, art and life style in honour of the Aten has already been several times mentioned. It is impossible here even to touch on the controversies concerning Akhenaten and his teaching. All that need be said is that even those modernist scholars who have been most determined to reduce to a pathological freak this man of undoubted genius concede that he created in the name of the Aten, whose beloved son he was, the first true monotheism. Even Osiris, and the entire, vast cult of the mummified dead, were banished from Akhetaten. The dead were to find light and life in the risen Aten.

During the course of his reign Akhenaten's monotheism evolved and became more absolute, leading to his command for the names of Amun and other gods to be struck from temples and monuments and, most significantly, for the plural form of 'gods' also to be erased. Akhenaten's vision of the one true god, whose sole prophet and interpreter he was, had as shattering an effect on the worldly organization of the temples as upon theology. Priests of other gods were largely dispersed, their temples deserted and their revenues diverted to the Aten and the construction of Akhetaten. When the heretic's unique and extraordinary bid had failed and the return to Amun and Thebes had been made, Tutankhamun declared that when he came to the throne 'the temples from one end to another of the land had fallen into ruin; their shrines were desolate . . . overgrown with weeds . . . The land was in confusion for the gods had forsaken this land.'

It is difficult to know how the ordinary people reacted to the effects of the heresy, especially to their deprivation of the comforting hope of Osiris. In the workers' cantonment at Akhetaten itself, cult objects of some of the old gods had been kept. If humble families dared to have such things in their houses in the city of the Aten itself, it can hardly be doubted that old forms of worship were more openly practised elsewhere. Probably very many peasant households throughout Egypt had hardly grasped what was happening at Akhetaten before it was finished and Amun was again king of the gods, his statues decked with jewels.

It is impossible here to follow religious history through the decadence of the Late period. Foreign influences made themselves felt, but for the most part it was a story of conservatism if not stultification in the traditional ways, and of increasing ritualism. There can have been no more fanatically devoted or orthodox followers of Amen-Re than the Kushite rulers of the twenty-fifth dynasty. The remarkable force that still infused Egyptian religions to the very end is evident enough in the building in Ptolemaic times of such imposing temples as those of Horus and Hathor at Edfu and of Isis at Philae. Between the carving of Horus and Hathor on the palette of Narmer and the dedication to them at Edfu there had passed very nearly three thousand years. As for Isis, she had many centuries of greatness still ahead of her.

There must have been many more priests in Egypt than in Mesopotamia to meet the demands of the cult of the dead. From the Pharaoh downwards everyone who could afford it wished to maintain priests to celebrate the daily mortuary liturgy, in temple or tomb, and the numbers involved must have been large. The temple priesthoods were divided into an upper class of prophets of the god and a lower of ordinary priests, each of several grades. As we have seen, priestesses provided music and dancing. During their terms of service all subjected themselves to most rigorous purification, including much ritual washing and the removal of head and body hair, a degree of cleanliness that greatly impressed Herodotus. In Egypt, as in Mesopotamia, the actual image of the god played an important role in the daily service, but it was equalled by that of Pharaoh and his priestly deputies throughout the land. The king and his surrogates had their own ritual levées before unsealing the doors of the shrine to hail, purify, dress and feed the divine image. A closing rite of this daily temple service was central to the whole meaning of Egyptian religion. This was the raising before the god's image of a small figure of the goddess Ma'at as an assertion that rightness, order, justice were established as they had been in the beginning and would be every day.

In all rituals the celebrant priest with his leopard skin cloak officiated, together with the reader, or holder of the roll, with his stole of white linen. There were prayers, litanies and hymns. Moreover, as Ani said of a man's god, 'singing, dancing and incense are his food, and to receive prostrations his property.'

These rites were not seen by the populace, for they were carried out in the holy of holies of the inner temple. Just as in Mesopotamia the opportunity for ordinary folk to participate and to see the sacred images came with the festivals, when the images were carried in their barques for processions on land or water. These festivals, keyed into the seasonal sacred calendar, were legion and must have added immensely to the jollity of life. Always they celebrated the local deity, but those held at the leading holy places—Heliopolis, Abydos, Thebes and several others—attracted pilgrims from far afield, when the cruise itself was a part of the holiday. The most important of all were the New Year (*Opet*) festivities at Thebes, which seem to have lasted over three weeks, and the enactment of the Mysteries of Osiris at Abydos which occupied eight days towards the end of the inundation and roused passionate emotions in the crowds.

Other important festivals which offered a chance for some popular participation and enjoyment centred on Pharaoh. Those of greatest moment were the coronation and the *Sed* festival. From the time of the Unification onwards the long ceremony of the crowning of the new king as Horus was conducted at Memphis. It was a largely duplicated ritual, intended at every step to emphasize the uniting of the red and white crowns. The main chance for the ordinary citizen, however, came before this in the dangerous period between the death of the old king and the crowning of the new. The future king and his entourage travelled by barge to a number of sacred cities and there enacted over several days what has been called the Mystery Play of the Succession. As this was linked with honouring the local god and a feast, there was room for high emotion and jollification.

The *Sed* jubilee may have taken the place of prehistoric ritual sacrifice of the king, and therefore was supposed to induce his rejuvenation. Pharaohs did not always wait the prescribed thirty years for the first *Sed*, and thereafter might celebrate a number. The rites, usually held at the royal capital of the day, involved building a new Festival Hall and much visiting by gods from other temples, Here, too, was an opportunity for rejoicing.

Like their faith in having a high god incarnate on the throne, the Egyptians' concern for their dead and the almost incredible extent to which they lavished wealth upon them is a unique characteristic of their religion. This fact has emerged again and again, but it remains to say something about duties towards the dead, the nature of their survival, and the reasons for the death obsession.

The first duty was the preservation of the body. In Archaic times true embalmment was unknown, but the form of the body was preserved by meticulous wrapping in stiffened linen. Embalming was developed for the élite during the Old Kingdom, and when humbler citizens began to expect an afterlife, they, too, sought preservation of the body, though by simpler and cheaper means. The full process was a prolonged ritual as well as a physical treatment, performed jointly by priests and technicians. The removal of the brain, the evisceration through an incision made with a stone knife, the packing of the corpse in natron for seventy days, the drainage of body fluids on a sacred table, the stuffing, anointing, washing and perfuming of the dried body were all performed by those versed in the technical secrets of the undertakers' guild. It seems, however, that these men performed at least a part of their work wearing dog-head masks of their presiding divinity, Anubis, while a reader priest was present at every stage to recite the appropriate prayers and spells. These were continued during the final stage of bandaging with hundreds of yards of fine, resinated linen. Each bandage had its name and meaning. Even the viscera had their own rituals and were placed in their four Canopic jars under the protection of four gods and four goddesses.

Implicit in the whole proceedings was the reference to Isis restoring the body of Osiris—in whose resurrection the dead man was to share. The final words of the ritual were, according to a late text, 'You live again, you live again for ever, here you are young once more for ever.'

These words 'for ever' introduce the great cosmological dream that lay behind the personal desire for resurrection, the dream that accounts for the Egyptian preoccupation with the dead. Inspired perhaps in part by the regularities of the Nile valley and its seasons, their philosophers saw the maintenance of an eternal cycle, unchanging except within phases of the cycle, as the meaning and purpose of existence. This was what the gods had begun, what Ma'at presided over, and what Pharaoh made available to his people. Yet the death of the individual appeared as an offence against the eternal order, it was a change, and an intensely painful change, that was non-recurrent and therefore meaningless. It can be said, with a rough

Opening-the-mouth ceremony
being performed on the mummy of Hunefer; c. 1350 B.C.

kind of truth, that the concern with death was to defeat it, to counteract a meaningless outrage and to see to it that the dead individual was in fact enabled to take his place in the cycle of the universe.

In the afterlife each man was represented by four distinct entities: the mummified body, the *Ba*, the *Ka* and the *Akh*—all of which except the first have some variety of meanings. The body was so painstakingly preserved, its destruction so great a disaster, because it was felt that an enduring and personal physical basis was necessary for any imaginable form of being. The *Ba* is usually and not misleadingly translated as the soul. It was often shown as a bird with a human head returning into the tomb or hovering over the mummy. Men wanted their *Ba* to remain with them, yet it was also expected to fly to the next world. A spell says, 'Your *Ba* shall not leave your corpse and your *Ba* shall become divine with the blessed dead.'

The *Ka* can appear both more spiritual and more material. Originally it seems to have been the divinity in Pharaoh, his creative genius with which he could have communion during life and be united in death. After the democratization of beliefs every man could have his *Ka*, and it became something between his vital force and his divine alter ego with which he, too, was joined at death. Yet while the *Ba* might flutter to and fro, the *Ka* seems to have dwelt in the tomb with the body, and there had need of nourishment. Its symbol was the strange one of a pair of arms raised in embrace, an embrace that was an embuing with vital force, a spiritual kiss of life. The Egyptian said 'To your *Ka*' where we might say 'Your health'.

As for the *Akh*, it was entirely remote from this world, representing the soul after all the rites of passage as it lived in the afterworld of the Field of Rushes or among the stars.

The tomb itself was of crucial importance as a secure base for the afterlife of the owner. In the Archaic and Old Kingdom mastabas it was very much a dwelling house for the departed, who was sometimes even provided with a lavatory. Later the tomb developed its own architectural plans, but it was always the place where the *Ka* dwelt in association with the mummy and where the *Ba* might visit. As well as the body, the tombs housed statues of the owner, which, once they had been animated by the Opening of the Mouth rite, were alternatives to the mummy as a physical base for the departed. In much the same way the marvellous painted reliefs showing the owner participating in or watching over all the delectable pursuits of country life or the making of all needful possessions, added to or made permanent the actual food and grave goods buried with the dead.

The tomb also provided a place where those living in this world could meet those who were living in the next. We have already seen how, among the well-to-do, endowments of land, men and animals were made to maintain priestly services and offerings at the tomb. In addition to this the family visited the tombs to offer food and drink for the *Kas*, and on feast days of the dead gathered to share a meal with the ancestors. Among the poorer people family tendance was all that could be afforded. They cared for the *Kas* and expected to be helped by them in return. This shared life of the community past, present and everlasting was unlike, yet complementary to, the exalted notions of the existence of the transfigured dead among the gods of the heavens and the underworld.

Where then did the dead live in their aspect as *Akhu*? The answer is too intricate, various, apparently contradictory ever to be fully given. There was the usual 'multiplicity of approaches', there was the historical blend of the Osirian with the solar cult, there was the range from crude to lofty concepts according to the education and understanding of the people concerned. The most usual term was the Field of Rushes, but this could merge into the beautiful ways of heaven or (as a later development) into deep cornfields where the ears grew one cubit long. From very early times the *Akhu* were seen as the 'imperishable stars' circling the northern pole, or again the dead might seek to join the retinue of Re, or to sail in his boat as once only kings had done, rising in the east or sinking back as Westerners into the Underworld and realm of Osiris.

In general, in spite of their increasing apprehensiveness in the face of death and the horrific creatures they invented to make difficult the way, most Egyptians lived and died in the hope that they would fare well on the journey and join the eternal cycle of nature and the universe.

In a tomb of the end of the eighteenth dynasty a 'singer with the harp' tells of the strife-free land of eternity:

> *All our kinsfolk rest in it since the first day of time.*
> *They who are to be . . . will all have come to it.*
> *There exists none who may tarry in the land of Egypt;*
> *There is none who fails to reach yonder place.*
> *As for the duration of what is done on earth*
> *It is a kind of dream;*
> *But they say: 'Welcome safe and sound'*
> *To him who reaches the West.*

Although comparative estimates of such intangibles are dangerous, it appears that from early in their history the Egyptians were far more inclined to link morality with rewards in the afterlife than were their contemporaries in Mesopotamia. This would, indeed, be a natural corollary of their far greater hope of eternal bliss: that great rewards must be earned is a thought not limited to puritans. The prevalence of such thinking already in the Old Kingdom is expressed in many texts. Ideas such as these certainly counted for as much as the idea of the judgement of the dead. Although, as we have seen, men increasingly hoped to gain admission to the next world by the production of carefully prepared passports, the basis of right behaviour in this world was still there, and what appears to us as true morality tended to outweigh mere religious conformities. In the protestations of innocence in the *Book of the Dead*, among the many ill deeds that the applicant states he has not committed are violence against a poor man, defamation of a slave to his master, making anyone weep or suffer, mistreatment of cattle—all this in addition to such things as commercial cheating, thefts or irrigation offences.

Moral values and the ideal of the truly good man changed with the passage of time, though always the principle remained of living in tune with Ma'at. Probably for the peasant or other unambitious people the ideal was for obedience to those above one, for honest dealing and the family virtues. Most of our information, however, concerns men who either held important office or were hoping for promotion. The very high standards of justice expected (though naturally not always obtained) of the vizier and his representatives have already been discussed. When it comes to more personal matters of conduct to be found in the wisdom literature it appears to us far less sympathetic. Particularly is this true of the self-assured men of the Old Kingdom when prevailing ideas might be said to be most fully Egyptian. The advice supposedly given by the sage Ptahhotep of the fifth dynasty to his son and successor as to how to conduct himself in order to succeed in life must strike us as being worldly to near the point of baseness. The first essential for a careerist was an extreme discretion towards those above him in the official hierarchy. 'Bow your back to your superior, the overseer from the palace . . .' 'If he is entertaining you to a meal, take whatever he offers, don't stare and speak only when spoken to.' Moreover, 'Laugh after he laughs and it will be pleasing to his heart and no one can know what you are really thinking.' Meanwhile in his family and community life a man should at all costs avoid ruining his reputation by the pursuit of women but look after his wife as a 'profitable field for her husband'. He should do everything for an obedient and well-conducted son, but cut him off and forget him if he is a liability. It was prudent for a man who had done well for himself not to be miserly among those who had seen him grow rich. There is, however, some advice less objectionable in our ears, such as that the man's own life should be exemplary, that he should not quarrel with a friend or judge him harshly and that in spite of all his attainments he should not be puffed up but should look for greater wisdom even among the lowest for 'it may be found with maidservants at the grindstones'.

Two comments are worth making. One that precepts that now appear to us crude in their worldly wisdom may have appeared as the discoveries of true wisdom in a country where a vast bureaucratic machine was being created for the very first time. The second comment is that the advice given by Ptahhotep is not really so very different from that tacitly accepted by conformist youth today if they intend to do well in a civil service or great corporation. Indeed, some of the wise vizier's sayings find an echo in the musical *How to Succeed in Business Without Really Trying*.

The First Intermediate period of upheaval affected the individual outlook as it did that of society. Ideas of egalitarianism were about, and the very sight of the desecrated and abandoned pyramids and temples made men doubt the value of endeavour and success. The disturbed, even tormented expression which artists imparted to the faces of Middle Kingdom pharaohs must long have been seen among the educated class. Ipuwer declared that crocodiles sank heavy with human flesh 'for men go to them of their own accord'. In a famous literary work of those troubled days, the *Debate on Suicide*, a man argues with his *Ba* as to whether in his state of despair death would not be preferable. 'Death is in my sight today like the odour of myrrh, like sitting under an awning on a breezy day.' This pessimistic work was composed at least a thousand years before a corresponding Babylonian *Dialogue of Pessimism*.

In the *Debate*, the *Ba* at one point counsels 'to pursue the happy day and forget care', and hedonism must have been another mood of the time. Yet just as this discussion ends on an open but rather more hopeful note, so it seems that once established the Middle Kingdom must have offered to all men opportunities of fulfilment on a rather higher level of social concern than those of the Old Kingdom. Frankfort does not doubt that there was a very real revulsion against position and material wealth as the goal of the good man in favour of the social virtues. The idea of Pharaoh as good shepherd was spread through society. As the *Eloquent Peasant* was made to say hopefully to the chief steward, 'You are the father of the orphan, the husband of the widow, the brother of the forsaken, the kilt of the motherless.'

It is curiously difficult to form a clear impression of a distinctive New Kingdom man produced by the imperialist mood. It was certainly an age when there were almost limitless opportunities for young men to rise in the service of the state in both peace and war. Innumerable tomb inscriptions express the pride and satisfaction of important men in their achievements on behalf of Pharoah and the favours he had shown them. On the whole, however, it seems the social ideas of the Middle Kingdom were largely maintained. Yet when the opulence of the time is considered, especially in the Thebes of Amenhotep III, it cannot be doubted that society had its share of extravagant, cynical young men who drank a lot, fornicated happily with equally gay young women and had little thought for Osiris and the ordeal of his balance.

It was in the Late period when the national pride and opportunities of empire had ebbed away that the ideal personality changed again. The 'hot', passionate man had always been to some extent deplored, but now there was a more positive quietism and a submissiveness to the gods. Men were exhorted to 'silence'—to playing it very cool. The vigorous, confident, self-seeking style of the early days had largely given way to one of cultivated meekness. The blessings of poverty were much recommended. Some men had a genuine personal piety while others were more concerned with Fate and Fortune and magical safeguards. The best quality to emerge among these Egyptians of the long decline, living in the sad shadow of former splendour, was a personal conscience and compassion. The *Instruction of Amenemopet*, which tells of many of these qualities, contains the following passage:

> Do not laugh at a blind man or tease a dwarf
> Nor injure the affairs of the lame.
> Do not tease a demented man
> Nor be fierce of face against him if he errs.
> For man is clay and straw
> And the god is his builder.

VISUAL ART AND ARTISTS

EGYPTIAN PAINTING AND SCULPTURE ARE A BOON AND DELIGHT TO US today because in them for the first time we meet individual men and women whom we can see to be, without cavil, exactly like ourselves.

It is exceedingly difficult for students of the past not to put up barriers that make them feel that the long-since dead were never alive quite as they themselves are alive. That is why they are so inclined to pin them out like anatomy-room frogs or dogs, or to pen them into categories, or to ticket them as a type specimen of this or that.

Yet nobody can look at the bust of Ankhaf carved in about 2550 B.C., or at the plump official Ka-aper, or the young royal couple, Menkaure and his wife, without the warm stir of recognition. At its best Sumerian art is powerful, its human representations full of energy, yet it can do nothing to remove the sense of possible otherness. In Egyptian portraiture we see, only a few centuries risen from the prehistoric mists, our brothers, ourselves.

At the opposite extreme many Egyptian works consisted of representations of symbolic acts, attitudes and, of course, accoutrements that had to repeated with only minor variations throughout the millennia. There is no better example than the symbolic set piece of the crowned Pharaoh towering above a vanquished enemy whom he holds by the hair and is about to despatch with his brandished mace. Narmer is shown in this enactment; two thousand years and more later when Egypt was tottering artists reproduced it still.

There were also artistic conventions—a fact which has been true of all forms of portrayal until the coming of the high-speed camera. As the distinctive Egyptian 'form' or style emerged and became set these, too, hardened and must have been enforced from one generation to the next. These included such matters as painting men with a much darker skin than women, kings and other important people much larger than their underlings, the avoidance of space and perspective and the practice of drawing the human torso in the facing position with the head and legs in profile. This last convention, which showed each part in its most characteristic aspect, may have been partly dictated by the idea that a figure foreshortened or with hidden parts would not serve the essential religious purpose, but it also had great advantages in design and solidity and for the Egyptian tendency to combine realistic detail with geometric regularity.

A more significant and even more universal characteristic of the Egyptian style was to show all life at rest and thus taken out of time. In many of the more monumental forms such as seated or standing figures sculptured in the round, positions of rest for the limbs were chosen and formalized, but however active the subject might be—bringing down a mace or hurling a stick at a flying duck, for instance—the movement was shown arrested, frozen. Although more liveliness, more movement might sometimes be allowed for animals, this motionless vision of the world was only once disturbed —by the deliberately revolutionary teaching of Akhenaten. It was certainly in profound harmony with the essential Egyptian world view of all being *sub specia aeternitas*.

In simple materialist terms it is often said that the abundance of Egyptian art and its generally realistic, representational nature was due to two things: the concern for the dead and particular view of the hereafter, and the ready supplies of good stone for both building and fine carving. These things certainly gave the artists their best opportunities, but who shall say that it was not their own response to the dazzling life of the Nile valley and their desire to express it that led to their fulfilment? In the earliest tomb reliefs of the nichestones of the second dynasty the departed were shown seated before the highly conventionalized items of a fine banquet. It must surely have been on the initiative of the artists themselves that they should go on beyond this to portray their patrons enjoying themselves in scenes of everyday life. These employers could no more have ordered them to execute such scenes, never before attempted by the hand of man, than politicians could have ordered scientists to produce the atomic bomb.

The history of the visual arts in Egypt inevitably fell into much the same pattern as most other elements of her cultural life. They attained their finest expression only under the strong central government and royal patronage of the three 'Kingdoms', disintegrated with the social disintegration of the interludes of social breakdown. Each of the three great periods saw something of a fresh start and developed a recognizable character, yet all together belonged to a single conservative evolutionary tradition.

No part of the pattern was more generally characteristic than the marvellously rapid rise and maturing of the visual arts during the first four dynasties. We have seen how Sumerian art influenced the work of Egyptian relief sculptors late in Predynastic times but was soon absorbed. During the Archaic age artists developed almost all the techniques and also the essential style of Egyptian art. To judge from the splendid falcon stele of King Wadji from Abydos and the already majestic, though small, seated statues of Khasekhem and other instances, the best work was executed for the king while much of that done for private patrons was crude. The lasting genius for animal art was already brilliantly manifest though usually on a small scale. Niche stones from Sakkara show the modest start of the painted reliefs of tomb-owners and their worldly joys. The figures are quaint and the colours still primitive.

The steps to mature mastery were taken during the third and fourth dynasties under the leadership of the court artists of Memphis. Here for the first time was a fully civilized and urbane art, an appropriate accompaniment to Imhotep's beautiful if tentative architecture and the sheer audacity of the pyramids of Giza. From a Serdab of the Step Pyramid buildings comes the massively seated figure of Djoser, the first known life-size sculpture of a king. Delicate reliefs of Djoser, together with vigorous portrait reliefs in wood of his 'confidant' and high official Hesire, show at once that the art of bas relief in which the Egyptians were always to excel was already fully mastered. These same reliefs also show the full development of the fine hieroglyphic writing, which like Chinese calligraphy, was always to be an art in its own right as well as a valuable adjunct to sculpture, painting and architecture.

With the pyramid age of the fourth dynasty and on into the fifth comes the full harvest of the Early Dynastic sowing. This included all the individual portraits already mentioned, together with others that have equally become part of the loved and familiar inheritance of mankind—Prince Rahotep and his wife Nofret, Ranufer, the cross-legged scribe, and many more.

Two items coming from opposite ends of the spectrum of subjects perhaps deserve special mention here. One is the valley temple of Khaefre (attached by a ramp walk to his pyramid), a fine building lined with slabs of red granite which originally housed twenty-three slightly over life-size seated statues of the king including, or similar to, the surviving example in which the royal head is protected by the Horus falcon. Here is the best early example of what again was to be characteristically Egyptian: the association of architectural forms with large-scale figure sculpture. The second subject is the small painted stone carvings of girls at the grindstone and other servants which in the fifth dynasty were often placed in tombs to serve the owners' needs. The greater liveliness and informality with which they were portrayed reveals that already artists were looking for an outlet for self-expression of a more light-hearted kind than was allowed them by the royal, noble and dignified. Servants, peasants, boatmen and the 'underprivileged' generally were always to provide it.

The preposterous sphinx of Giza, probably a representation of Khaefre, is not a work of much art but certainly proves that in the Old Kingdom already sculptors as well as architects could work on a colossal scale. It also illustrates the spontaneity that was still possible, for someone must have had the bright idea of utilizing a rock mass left in quarrying stone for the Great Pyramid—and have been given his head.

When to all else is added the charm of the painted wall reliefs of chief architect Ti and other great men, where the studies of hunting in the marshes for the first and only time almost attain to landscape, there is every justification for those who judge that Egypt never again equalled this glorious summer of Memphite art.

The nomarchs of Upper Egypt, whom the rash generosity of the crown had enabled to live in princely style during the later Old Kingdom, employed artists who followed the Memphite school. When the kingdom split up these petty courts became the centres of provincial art of a kind. Often it was of a crudity only too appropriate to the simultaneous collapse in the standards of fine craftsmanship. Some specimens of tomb painting have the quaint vigor and bright colouring of folk art at all times. The First Intermediate period is a sad proof that without wealthy and fastidious patronage at the top the high arts of civilization cannot be maintained.

Memphis itself certainly shared in the general cultural disintegration, although it is just possible that artists contrived to keep some tradition of a better kind alive. Very little material in fact survives. The revival seems to have begun, as would be expected, at Herakleopolis and at Thebes during the period of their rivalry. After Menthuhotep's final victory the building of his highly original pyramid tomb and temple at Deir el-Bahri (later to inspire Queen Hatshepsut's architect on the neighbouring site) must have provided a tremendous stimulus for the court artists.

The sculptors of the early Middle Kingdom certainly studied Old Kingdom monuments as their models, and so hastened their return to excellence. Thebes added a touch of more primitive harshness and vigour. Perhaps it is because so much has been lost that we get the feeling that artists of this first Theban age of the Middle Kingdom never settled down to form a coherent style comparable to that of ancient Memphis. As we have seen, the age is chiefly noted for sculptured portraits of the kings of the twelfth dynasty that show an exceptional concern to reveal the inner conflicts of their subjects. At the other extreme the minor arts of jewellery and hieroglyphs show a clear, brilliant perfection of design, as well as superb craftsmanship.

Nomarchs continued to patronize local talent for as long as they were allowed to rule. Princes of Elephantine, for example, showed ambition if no great style in their tombs. Far more remarkable was the fine work executed by Egyptian artists in the remote African outpost of Kerma. It is thought that when Prince Hepzefa of Asyut was sent there as governor he took his artists and craftsmen with him and that one of them was responsible for carving a portrait of his wife Sennuwy from a local stone. As a study of the tranquil aspect of woman, it is one of the most appealing and lovely ever to have been made. Found as it was in the barbaric burial mound of Hepzefa, it epitomizes the mingling of Egyptian with African elements that produced remarkable hybrid styles in minor arts such as pottery and furniture.

The cultural breakdown of the Second Intermediate period was much less complete than in the First. Nevertheless the later eighteenth and seventeenth centuries B.C. was certainly a time of little opportunity for artists, with no major public building, princely tombs few and small and no tombs of officials at all. Yet after the expulsion of the Hyksos, painters and sculptors were able to resume the old traditions of forms and subjects almost as though there had been no interruption. It must be true to say that no other civilized people has had this ability of the Egyptians to go back and pick up apparently broken threads and continue the web to the same design.

With the enormously increased number of works of art made in, and surviving from, the New Kingdom, it is impossible to do more than touch upon a few salient points. There is, first of all, the matter of foreign influence in the arts. It might be thought that the presence of the Hyksos themselves followed by all the imperial contacts would have led to many Mediterranean and Asian borrowings. Already in the Middle Kingdom decorative arts had made use of such foreign motifs as the (probably Cretan) running spiral, and trifling infiltrations of this kind were resumed in the imperial age. Trifling, however, they remained. Egyptian artists reveal an interest in the peculiarities of foreigners—as for instance the people of Punt in

Hatshepsut's reliefs and the tribute-bearers in the vizier Rekhmire's tomb paintings—but there was no question of allowing alien ideas to break their own set forms. Herodotus observed that 'the Egyptians keep to their native customs and never adopt any from abroad'. This was already, and was to remain, equally true of their art.

The pure traditions of the Middle Kingdom were maintained and refined down to the end of the reign of the conqueror Thutmose III. There was never a happier combination of architectural genius with brilliant sculpture and painting than in Senmut's creation at Deir el-Bahri. At Rekhmire's tomb, where the scenes are painted on hard plaster without relief carving, painters can be seen taking a new pleasure in their medium, rather than regarding it as an enhancement of relief or a cheap substitute for it. After this something of the old purity and all the old austerity gave way before the tide of imperial wealth and grandeur. Painters and sculptors sought more elaborate, sumptuous effects, which were soon to be manifest also in gigantic and grandiose building. It is as difficult to imagine the Theban temples when walls, columns and roof timbers were brilliant with colour as it is in the case of Greek and Gothic buildings.

Some former greatness and virtue were lost, but it would be an ascetic critic who could refuse to enjoy the best of the middle eighteenth dynasty art. Nearly all of it was still intended to secure satisfaction for the dead, but what unbounded enjoyment it expresses of life in this world. The fantastic hunting scenes with giraffes, ostriches and all manner of wild creatures; the parties with their music, dancing and acrobats; chariot driving and archery; beyond everything the delectable young girls, the ideal now more slender and willowy below the huge wigs—what an exuberant parade it is!

Of all the tombs of Theban grandees where these scenes were drawn, none has better work than that of Ramose, vizier late in the reign of Amenhotep III. The reliefs on three walls of the main hall show the style of the reign at its highest pitch of sensual refinement. Then, on the fourth wall, appears one of the most dramatic transformations in the history of art; scenes dashingly outlined in the revolutionary new style of Akhenaten. There had been some slight signs of the coming revolution earlier in the reign, but this sharp change in Ramose's tomb shows how abruptly the final step was taken.

What centuries of foreign contacts had failed to do, one fiercely committed young Pharaoh accomplished at a stroke. The traditional mould of Egyptian art was broken, frozen figures moved, time was let in. It seems that Akhenaten himself did much to initiate the revolution in the visual arts. One of the first sculptors employed by him proclaimed that he was 'the assistant whom His Majesty himself had taught'. This man, Bak, was a son of a court sculptor of Amenhotep III and would have been trained in the traditional style, yet he was able and willing to work in the new mode.

Atenist art was at its most extreme while Akhenaten ruled in Thebes and for the first years at Akhetaten; towards the end of the reign its most excited mannerisms were modified—as all the world knows from the Nefertiti portrait heads and other work from the studio of Khamose. Egyptologists have been surprisingly ready to believe that the distortions in head, face and body form of the entire royal family seen in the noble statues of the king from the Aten temple in Thebes and in all the lively family scenes from Akhetaten derived from the physical abnormalities of Akhenaten himself. He probably had some feminine characteristics, but for the rest there is no more need to believe in these abnormalities than that El Greco's subjects were not only elongated but crooked. It was surely an exuberance of mannerism celebrating the revolt from ancient disciplines.

The Atenist revolution had a more lasting effect on the visual arts than elsewhere. The art of Tutankhamun's tomb furniture is now much disparaged, yet many of the scenes between the young king and queen with their inheritance from the movement, the informality and personal relatedness of Atenist art, have a charm, a touch of idyllic romance even, unique in Egyptian art. Atenist ideas had their more austere sequel in the tomb of Horemhab.

In the late New Kingdom much good work was done but there were no fresh departures. Quality depended very much on individual artists. Thus Seti I employed first-class relief sculptors and painters at Abydos when much rather mechanical stuff was being produced elsewhere. As for Ramesses II, all visitors to Egypt know that his statues and buildings prevail in sheer size and numbers over all else. Much of the sculpture is dull and heavy, reminding one of the totalitarian art of Stalin and Hitler, yet there are portrait statues of this Pharaoh that do not fall far short of those of Thutmose III. The massed battle and hunting scenes of Ramesses II and his successors at least show an ambition suitable to a late imperial regime.

Working after the end of Egyptian greatness, the artists of the

Late period were even more uneven in quality and erratic in purpose. It is worth remembering, however, that it was precisely at this time that Egyptian art had most influence abroad—as seen in the charming Phoenician and Assyrian ivories. The sophisticated disillusion of post-Ramessid society is perfectly expressed in satirical paintings on papyrus in which the follies of men are transferred to animals. The Kushite rulers both at home in Napata and in Egypt succeeded to a remarkable degree in reviving traditional forms. When first discovered, some works of this age were mistaken for the Old and Middle Kingdom models on which they had been based. The last dynasties also produced some really splendid realistic portrait heads. It was wholly characteristic of the long life of Egyptian art that to the very end it was concerned to resuscitate past achievements and held out with almost complete success against conquering Assyrians, Persians, Greeks.

It is usual to write of Egyptian art almost as though it were an exudation of each age rather than the work of individual men. In fact a great deal is known, and far more could be learnt, about artists and their place in society. It is obvious that architects, sculptors and painters were far more important in Egypt that they ever were in Mesopotamia, and it is appropriate that we should know the names of dozens of them, whereas in Asia they perished in their anonymity.

Painters and sculptors at work;
from a tomb at Beni Hasan, c. 1900 B.C.

Architects, men who planned and directed the work of builders and masons and gave employment to artist-decorators, could be at the very top of the social tree. Imhotep and Amenhotep, son of Hapu, were exceptional in being great men and sages as well as architects, but there were others—such as Hemon, who probably built the Great Pyramid, and the brilliant Senmut—who were certainly close to the throne. Was there a wide gap between them and the dirty-handed men who had to wield hammer and chisel and paint-brush, men who had no title equivalent to artist and might have been classified among 'all the craftsmen'?

It is often said that socially the painters and sculptors belonged to this humble class, yet such a notion offends against all that is probable in human relationships and most of the existing evidence. There would have been numbers of mere craftsmen in the studios, but the men of genius and talent must have lived at least on the fringes of the court. Great men, sometimes even the king, sat for them; architects must have worked closely with them and become their friends. It is true that decorators lived among ordinary tomb-cutters in Thebes, but then artistic work in the valley tombs is very poor. For the reign of Akhenaten there is certainty. Bak, Dhutmose and other artists had good houses in the fashionable parts of Akhe-taten; Queen Tiy must have known the sculptor Yuti, from whom she commissioned portraits of her daughter. A little earlier two sculptors at Thebes could afford tombs that show them to have lived in luxury and respect.

Luckily we know from the testimony of a Middle Kingdom sculptor that artists were not humble-minded nor inclined to regard them-selves as mere craftsmen. He declared:

I was an artist skilled in my art, pre-eminent in my learning. . . . I knew how to render the movements of a man and the carriage of a woman . . . the poising of an arm to bring the hippopotamus low, and the move-ments of the runner. No one succeeds in all these things save only myself and the eldest son of my body.

A glowing dusk by the Nile makes as fine a setting for popular music as any in the world, and music must in fact always have added to the enjoyment of life for all Egyptians high and low. Yet native secular musicianship remained very simple. The sistrum, particularly associated with the cult of Hathor, always remained in use, a small flute and kettledrums were played, and for strings, an upright harp. Probably these few instruments were seldom played for their own sake but as an accompaniment to singing and dancing. The harp and flute seem also to have been played in the temple.

It is thought that the Egyptian failure to develop musically may have been another result of their mathematical weakness. The Meso-potamians, with their grasp of geometric progression, mastered more advanced stopping. However this may have been, there is no doubt that the Egyptians learnt much from Asia—at first through the Hyksos and later through the imperial contacts of the eighteenth dynasty. Larger and more varied harps were introduced, also lyres, an elegant long-necked lute perhaps of Kassite origin, pipes of a shriller kind and Asiatic drums. Sachs has said, 'A new kind of noisy, stimulating music seems to have taken possession of the Egyptians.' This description certainly fits several party scenes in New Kingdom tombs where banquets are accompanied by music on wind and strings, or young girls dance naked to an accompaniment of pipes and hand-clapping. Nakht's tomb (middle eighteenth dynasty) is of particular interest in showing a little orchestral group: three girls playing the double pipes, lute and big standing harp. Temple music is finely represented in a Sakkaran tomb of the age of Tutankhamun, where behind a priest offering sacrifice squat a blind harpist and a flute player. Armies had their trumpets—long narrow instruments that must have sounded harsh and shrill.

Although high-born ladies were sometimes responsible for temple music, to be a musician in the world of pleasure did not carry a high social status. Instruments are usually seen in the hands of either girl entertainers or blind men. Evidently, however, the harpist was more esteemed than the lyre player, for Ipuwer gives as one of the signs of social upset that 'He who knew not the lyre is now the owner of a harp.' There are no signs that musicians ever moved in court circles as artists occasionally did.

INTELLECTUAL LIFE

TO BE A MASTER OF THE IMMENSELY DIFFICULT SKILLS OF READING AND writing was probably even more admired and desired in Egypt than in Mesopotamia. Probably, too, a rather smaller proportion of the population was literate. To encourage young pupils struggling to learn the hieroglyphic and hieratic scripts they were put to copying various texts that told how enviable was the life of a scribe in comparison with that of any other calling. Unfortunately they mangled their work so much that translation has proved difficult for the modern scribe. The *Satire on Trades*, already several times quoted, was a text of this kind, vilifying other occupations in comically scathing terms. The opening passage tells how these words were addressed by a father, Khety, to his boy with whom 'he was journeying upstream to the Residence City, to put him to the writing school among the children of officials.' He goes on to say, '. . . you should set your heart on the pursuit of writing. . . . As for the scribe every place is his at the Residence City, and he will not be poor in it. . . . I shall make you love writing more than your own mother.'

Another text also often copied by school boys, known as *In Praise of Learned Scribes*, put its emphasis on learning as a means to immortality in the sense of being remembered in this world. 'Be a scribe, desire that your name may [endure]. More effective is a book than a decorated tombstone. . . . A man is perished, his corpse is dust, all his relatives are come to the ground—it is his writing that makes him remembered in the mouth of the reciter.' (Incidentally, these and other lines in the same text make it clear that Egyptians were not thinking only of survival in the next world when they lavished wealth on their tombs.)

Less is known of Egyptian schools than of the Sumerian *edubba*, but they seem to have been very similar—with boys starting at about the same early age and being encouraged with frequent beating. A type of senior college was known as the House of Life. It is thought that these may always have been attached to temples. Teaching was largely oral, and it appears that very eminent men—princes, viziers and other high officials—might teach in them if they had the vocation. This is in harmony with the view that there were no set courses or regular examinations, but that the Houses of Life were academies, with scriptoria, libraries and teaching in a number of special subjects. Among these was medicine. The statue inscription of a physician notes that he was sent to 'Re-establish the department of the House of Life devoted to medicine' and that he 'provided them with everything that could ensure their mastery, and with all the instruments indicated in the writings.'

Although a large proportion of scribes and learned men undoubtedly came from educated families, so that learning like so many other things tended to be hereditary, bright boys might have their chance to schooling and so to success in life. It seems, for example, that Khety was of humble social origins. Just as in Mesopotamia, the product of the schools might remain a scribe in the sense of secretary, attending on soldiers and other eminent men, or as clerk in the administration, or he might have acquired his education in order to become a priest, administrator or professional man.

The Houses of Life as institutions performed special services for Pharaoh and his government, such as fixing the dates of feasts and seasons and generally supervising the calendar, maintaining dynastic records and composing official inscriptions.

Although royal children, including princesses, were probably most often taught at home by tutors, even Pharaohs might attend an academy. Ramesses IV boasted that he had studied all the written texts of the House of Life to discover the secrets of the gods. The honour paid to learning and education is further shown by the reverent allusions to such sages as Imhotep, Hardehef and Amenhotep, son of Hapu, by kings praying to be scribes to the high god and by the many statues portraying great men as scribes— often seated crosslegged with their open papyrus roll, inks and brushes.

As we have seen, the cursive form of writing known as hieratic had already been developed from the pictorial hieroglyphic script in the Archaic period, but as hieroglyphs remained in use for ceremonial and other formal uses (generally incised in stone or painted on carefully prepared surfaces) a fully competent scribe had to be master of both forms. In the eighth century B.C. a still more simplified cursive form known as demotic was introduced for everyday use. When the space to be filled recommended it, hieroglyphs might be written from top to bottom, or from left to right. Normally, however, the Egyptians wrote from right to left. Papyrus paper was made by slicing the fresh pith of this sedge into strips, superimposing two layers at right angles to one another, then beating, pressing, and finally drying them. Long rolls could be made by pasting sections together: the splendid *Harris Papyrus* of Ramesses III was no less than 133 feet long. It probably originally belonged to the archives of the temple of Medinet Habu; most large temples must have had libraries and record offices for the storage of texts of all kinds.

Writing was usually done with a rush, one end being cut obliquely and the fibres teased out to form a brush. Scribes often made use of little cakes of both red and black pigments—for much the same purposes as a modern typist employs the red and black registers of her ribbon.

There is no doubt that the Egyptians valued eloquence and the skilled use of words for their own sake. One of the most remarkable expressions of this comes from the *Instruction for Merikare* when the writer tells his son, 'Be a craftsman in speech so that you may be strong . . . speech is more valorous than any fighting.' More literary and subtle are the desires uttered in the *Complaint* of a twelfth dynasty writer: 'Would that I had words that are unknown, utterances and sayings in a new language that has not passed away . . . not an utterance that has grown stale.' In the introduction to his *Instructions,* Ptahhotep writes of his own 'good speech' (or 'beautifully expressed utterances') and of teaching it to others for his own advantage. In the Middle Kingdom *Prophecy of Nerti,* Pharaoh asks for someone 'who may say to me a few fine words or choice speeches, hearing which My Majesty may be entertained.' It is most remarkable, too, that in the *Eloquent Peasant* the chief steward reports to Pharaoh, 'I have found one of those peasants who is truly eloquent', whereupon the king replies that the man shall be made to linger, his case spun out: 'To keep him talking, be thou silent. Then have his speech brought to us in writing so that we may hear it.' (To prove that he has a social conscience as well as a taste for oratory, the king orders not only that the peasant shall be fed but that food be sent to his family in the country.)

This civilized love of language makes it all the more unfortunate that owing to the Egyptian system of writing without vowels very little is known of the vocalization. We are almost equally ignorant of the rules of prosody.

While many of the literary forms of Egypt can be approximately paralleled with those of Mesopotamia—especially such temple compositions as hymns, prayers, ritual texts—there are also expected differences. Tomb inscriptions produced not only voluminous texts concerning the hereafter, but also many proud essays in autobiography. General comparisons are unwise, but it does appear to be true that on balance the Egyptians were more prosaic, much of their literature coming from the conscious mind, in contrast with the powerful promptings from the unconscious evident in the best Sumerian poetry and myth. The Egyptians did, of course, compose delightful poetry. The high quality of love poems has already been proved, and there is nothing from Mesopotamia to equal the nature poetry of Akhenaten's famous *Hymn to the Sun.* This poetry, however, tends to be light and lyrical. The Egyptians had neither the epic power nor profundity of *Gilgamesh.* Nor had they the urge to mythological expression found in this great epic or in the Akkadian *Creation Epic.* Instead we have to look to such colloquial, sometimes bawdy, folk versions as the *Contending of Horus and Seth* on the one hand, or to such remarkable intellectual works as the *Memphite Theology* on the other.

It is in keeping with the love of realism shown in their visual art that the Egyptians should have been successful innovators in largely secular narratives full of details of everyday life. The *Eloquent Peasant*, although its message was the importance of social justice, begins in a sound, matter-of-fact narrative style. It is not surprising that the *Story of Sinuhe* was very popular in ancient Egypt, for it has some elements of the genuine adventure story—as when the hero hides, slips across the frontier and is saved from death by a nomad sheikh. Moreover the scene where he returns to Egypt as an old man and is welcomed home by Pharaoh and the royal children is both vivid and touching. (It is typical, too, in that Pharaoh very often plays some part in literary works, whatever their subject.) The plot of the *Two Brothers* and the style of its telling prove that it was intended for popular entertainment, while the *Journey of Wenamun* is picaresque narrative with some mordant humour. These two last works both date from very late in the New Kingdom when popular literature had emerged and was being written down.

There was certainly more humour in Egyptian than in Mesopotamian writings, some of it satirical, some much broader. In this, texts like the *Satire on Trades* and the *Satirical Letter* relate to the comic strip type captions that sometimes accompany pictorial scenes. If fun was usually at the expense of 'the lower orders', this was a state of affairs that was to prevail everywhere until very recent times.

The difficulty of dating literary works known only from later copies is only a little less in Egypt than we found it to be in Mesopotamia. So far as a correct chronology can be established, it seems fairly clear that literary history does not follow the same trajectory as so many other cultural elements—that is to say of a swift rise to a summit of achievement in the Old Kingdom followed by elaboration and refinement, then by some degree of ossification or decay. Literature and the influence of writers appear to have been at their height after the fall of the sixth dynasty, helping to lighten the prevailing gloom of the First Intermediate period and shining out in the Middle Kingdom.

Most of the known works of the Old Kingdom are royal and religious: the Memphite and Heliopolitan theologies and, by far the most extensive, the magico-religious spells and prayers inscribed in the fifth and sixth dynasty royal tombs and known as the Pyramid Texts. These mainly derive from the sun cult of Heliopolis but also contain really primitive material, such as the *Cannibal Hymn,* handed down from the rituals of prehistoric chieftains. In the feudal period, beginning probably at Herakleopolis, the Pyramid Texts were modified to suit the funerary needs of commoners; because they were usually inscribed on coffins they have been named the Coffin Texts. With the further democratization in the New Kingdom a third recension of this funerary literature took shape as the *Book of Coming Forth by Day,* now usually called the *Book of the Dead.* It is full of spells of a most feebly superstitious kind; long or short versions were often written on papyrus and buried with the corpse. The wealthy might face the dangers of the next world equipped with a long and elegantly illuminated roll, while the poor had to make do with a few spells on a papyrus scrap.

Returning briefly to the history of a more genuine kind of literature, it appears that the movement that was to flower in the Middle Kingdom began at Herakleopolis in the days when her rulers were re-establishing ordered government but before they were overwhelmed by Thebes. That thoughtful writing should have developed in those relatively impoverished conditions may be analogous with the fact that literature has been the one art successfully practised by women. With some cheap paper and ink and a quiet room anyone can become an author.

In order to balance an impression that may have been given of Egyptian writers as lyricists or cheerful extroverts, it is as well to recall the very different works evoked by the experience of social tragedy. There is the grim picture of the tragedy itself left by Ipuwer, the disillusioned melancholy of the *Suicide* dialogue and the beautiful *Songs of the Harper.* Already in the *Instruction for Merikare* a hope for the return of good times is implicit and can be read as pointing the way to the actual restoration that came with the Middle Kingdom. In that age itself not only were noble works concerning social morality and justice written, but also such a human and enjoyable novella as the *Sinuhe.*

If the New Kingdom produced no new major works but rather fed on the classics, there must have been some lively story-telling, and also some remarkable advances in style. One passage from *Wenamun* is enough to prove this. The hero is going for his difficult interview with the Prince of Byblos: 'And I found him sitting in his upper room, with his back turned to a window, so that the waves of the great Syrian sea broke against the back of his head.' That is a description that could not have been written in the Old Kingdom and could have been written today.

How far were the Egyptians historically minded in their attitude to the past and their records for posterity? Almost everything that was said on these subjects in relation to Mesopotamia is applicable also to the Kingdom of the Two Lands.

There were, of course, differences. In spite of the religious motives involved in tomb biographies, there is no doubt at all that the people concerned wished also to leave some account of their deeds and honours to be appreciated by posterity. Then again the fact that Pharaohs built great stone temples and loved to cover walls and columns with illustrated records of their victories and other achievements, or to set up large steles for the same purpose, vastly increased the enduring historical record. The temples of East and West Thebes taken together provide a history of the New Kingdom quite unrivalled in pre-Assyrian Mesopotamia. The campaigns of Thutmose III including the tactics of the battle of Megiddo, Hatshepsut's great expedition, Ramesses II and the battle of Kadesh, Ramesses III's repulse of the Sea People are only outstanding records among much more.

One distinction that follows from the complete dominance of Pharaoh over a unified kingdom is manifest in the Egyptian dating system. Instead of naming years after events or persons as in Mesopotamia, the Egyptian scribes numbered the regnal years of each reign, beginning afresh with each accession. Unhappily for future historians they still saw no need to draw each regnal series together into a comprehensive chronological system.

The Egyptian devotion to the idea of eternity and the unchanging cycle of being can be supposed to have given them a reverence for the past beyond even that of other ancient peoples. The sense of changelessness had some curious effects on the conception of history, in particular the exact copying of the recorded deeds of past kings by their successors. Thus, for example, Piopi II, last king of the Old Kingdom, inscribed his Sakkara temple with reproductions of the reliefs and texts celebrating the Libyan victories of Sahure a century earlier. In the same way the list of cities captured by Thutmose III was used by later rulers as their own.

We have seen how even the recipe for a cosmetic might enhance its value by being attributed to a queen of long ago. Texts of various kinds were quite often said to have been taken from some ancient work, while the lifetimes of great men might be shifted back to earlier prestigious reigns—quite often to that of Snefru. This reverence for the past finds its best expression in the *Merikare*. Referring to the man who has made himself a master of fine words it says: 'Truth comes to him fully brewed in accordance with the sayings of the ancestors. Copy thy father and thy ancestors. Behold their words remain in writing. Open, that you may read and copy their wisdom. In this way the skilled man becomes learned.'

The Egyptians were always sympathetic and careful observers of animals, birds and fish. From Archaic times onwards artists sculptured, modelled and painted the species. The records of Thutmose III at Karnak include studies of foreign plants and animals supposedly brought back from a Syrian campaign. Here, however, the sculptor's version of the trees and flowers does not seem to have been botanically correct. At Akhetaten the cult of nature was evidently wholly aesthetic. Floors and walls in some royal rooms were covered with beautiful and natural-looking paintings of plants and foliage, but they are not in fact true to nature. No doubt the inmates of the aviary and zoo in the North Palace were more admired and revered than studied.

When imperial conquests widened their horizons, the Egyptians observed foreign races to an extent that could at a stretch be called anthropological. Although there was always some tendency for them to become stereotyped, artists made life-like and unbiassed portrayals of the physical characteristics and dress of Negroes, Asians, Libyans and Cretans.

In almost all departments of special knowledge Egyptian intellectuals were inclined to settle happily into ruts. Once they had established procedures that worked fairly well for practical purposes, they liked to make do with them and to avoid theorizing. This was conspicuously true of mathematics, where after the usual capable start in the Old Kingdom, Egypt lagged far behind the Old Babylonians and seems to have made hardly any advance thereafter.

The system of numeration was a decimal one in the sense that it consisted of a sign for unity and for each power of ten up to a million. There were no separate signs for numbers between one and ten or for multiples of ten, so that signs had to be repeated the requisite number of times and were then strung together, from right to left. This made it possible to reduce addition and subtraction to the collecting together and counting of the simple signs representing units, tens, hundreds and so on. Multiplication was usually done by doubling the given number the appropriate number of times and adding up the results. Fractions were used, but in all cases except two-thirds, which had its own sign, they had to be reduced to units with a numerator of one. The *Rhind Papyrus,* which surprisingly dates from Hyksos times, expounds many of these methods and also gives space to the properties of the triangle, rectangle and trapezium. Egyptian mathematicians had arrived at a very close approximation to *pi,* probably by empirical means.

Essentially, it seems that the system was an additive one. It was also a business of written manipulations, without general principles, in which every problem had to be worked out separately. Yet as we know it served wonderfully well for all the practical problems for which it was intended—simple matters such as the division of rations, the calculating of field areas or volumes of grain or of stones —all the small problems confronting administrators, tax collectors and architects.

Surveyors measuring a field; from a tomb at Thebes, c. 1400 B.C.

These elementary methods also worked well enough to enable the Egyptians to build their pyramids with an amazing degree of accuracy (they knew how to calculate the inclination from a given base and height). They also usually oriented the sides very precisely to face the cardinal points of the compass. So precise, indeed, was the siting of the Giza pyramids that it is thought that calculations based on the rising and setting of stars on an artificial horizon must have been made. There are some hints that the Great Bear, or Ox Leg, was used for the purpose.

The weakness of the mathematical system was an obstacle also to the development of astronomy. It could not cope with the type of calculation necessary to make the advance from mere observation to prediction. The Egyptians only learnt of such possibilities at a late date from the Babylonians. Observe the stars of course they did. They mapped the constellations and gave them names, but the most practical result of their studies was for the measurement of time. The heliacal rising of particular stars was identified with the periods of ten days into which the month of the civil calendar was divided, while the sequential rising of these so-called 'decan' stars were used from Old Kingdom times to make a star-clock giving the 'hours of night'.

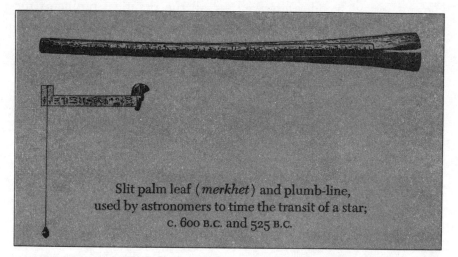

Slit palm leaf (*merkhet*) and plumb-line,
used by astronomers to time the transit of a star;
c. 600 B.C. and 525 B.C.

The most important of all heliacal risings was that of Sirius, which the Egyptians called after a goddess later identified with the Greek Sothis. This event was observed to coincide with the first rapid rise of the inundation, a coincidence which caused Sothis to be addressed as 'Bringer of the New Year and the Inundation', and moreover to be used as a check on the civil calendar.

The calendar certainly needed checking—which was bad luck, for the wise men of the kingdom had very early devised a calendar which was the best of its kind in the ancient world, and which

Herodotus still considered superior to the Greek. Lunar months had inevitably been recognized from prehistoric times and they continued to be significant for the religious year and its festivals. The Egyptians, however, were very soon able to see that twelve of these months did not correspond with the solar year. In spite of slight irregularities it did not take long to observe that the average interval between inundations was 365 days, and already by the pyramid age a calendar divided into twelve months of thirty days plus five feast days had been adopted for the whole kingdom. This 'Nilotic Year' saved Egypt from all the inconsistencies of Mesopotamia and remained in use until the Julian calendar was imposed in Roman times.

It would take several lifetimes before it could be realized that the calendrical seasons were getting out of line with the natural ones— owing to that extra day that we compensate with leap years. It is very typical of the Egyptians that they resolved not to meddle with what was established, but allowed the error to advance until, after 1460 years, the calendar's New Year again coincided with the rising of Sothis and the Inundation. As there is a Roman record of the beginning of one of the Sothic cycles, and earlier records of 'goings up of Sothis', the Egyptians' stubborn adherence to their 365 days has been a boon to modern chronologists.

If the Egyptians lagged behind the people of Mesopotamia in mathematics and astronomy, just as they did in much technology, they appear to have been ahead in medical knowledge and treatment —and more particularly in surgery. The practice of mummification had always encouraged free handling of the corpse, and knowledge, if very imperfect understanding, of its parts.

The practice of medicine was held in high respect. There was a tradition that the second king of the first dynasty was a physician and wrote a treatise on anatomy. Knowledge of healing was attributed to famed sages such as Imhotep—and this great man may in fact have been Djoser's physician. Many men were proud to name themselves as chief physician to the Palace or to the king, and they were well rewarded. Akhenaten's doctor, Penthu, had himself portrayed being hung with gold necklets given him by the king.

We have seen that medicine was one of the special subjects that could be studied at the House of Life, and that special apparatus might be provided there. The libraries in these academies were probably quite well stocked with medical texts of one kind and another. Nine such papyri have survived—though there is much overlapping between them and some are almost entirely devoted to magic.

In general there was much the same blend of practical medicine with magic and religion that we have found in Mesopotamia. There was the same tendency to regard any affliction that had no obvious external cause as due to the entry of some evil thing, and the same attempts to drive it out by incantation and ritual act. Possession might be attributed to particular gods, a demon or human enemy, or to the dead. There does, however, seem to have been far less dependence on omens in Egypt than in Babylonia.

The pharmacopoeias of the two lands also had much in common, although the mineral drugs prescribed in Egypt may have been more varied and of greater real curative value. Yet the texts often recommended spells and the use of charms and images to make these drugs more effective.

Some sections of the papyri are devoted to special subjects such as gynaecology (including pregnancy tests), stomach diseases, ailments of the anus and rectum, skin diseases, fractures and burns and so forth. By far the most remarkable of all the medical compilations is the main section of that known as the *Edwin Smith Papyrus:* it is also the oldest, having probably been originally written as early as the first dynasty, and certainly not later than the fourth.

What is most remarkable about this oldest of surgical text books is that it is entirely free from magico-religious elements. Starting with an essay on the heart, there are forty-eight sections concerning wounds and fractures set out according to the topography of the body. Each section is divided into the same five parts: the nature of the hurt; examination of the symptoms, diagnosis, prognosis and treatment. We do not know much about the doctor's visiting practice or bedside manner, but the headings 'If thou examinest a man having' and then 'Thou shouldst say concerning him' show that a thorough examination preceded the diagnosis. Doctors sometimes claimed to be 'gifted in the examination with the hand'. As for the prognosis, there were three possible choices: 'An ailment which I will treat' (certain cure); 'an ailment with which I will contend' (possible cure); 'an ailment not to be treated' (a fatal case). The last, cautious, decision suggests that there may have been penalties for surgical failure. Quite a range of equipment is mentioned, flax being used like lint for absorbent pads and plugs, and of course for the bandaging at which the Egyptians were highly skilled owing to its use in mummification. Adhesive plasters, sutures, cautery and padded splints are also mentioned. Although they find no place in this text, surgeons did in fact possess quite a range of special implements—such as scalpels, lancets, forceps and saws.

The rationality of the *Edwin Smith Papyrus* cannot be entirely attributed to the fact that it is surgical and therefore not concerned with ailments of unknown cause. One item in particular is significant, a case of partial paralysis due to brain damage. The text explicitly states that this condition was caused by something in the patient's own body and not to any invading evil.

The lion-headed goddess Sekhmet was the chief patron divinity of medicine, although Thoth as god of all learning was also much concerned; Isis was considered helpful in therapeutic magic (having resuscitated Osiris); Horus and Douaou of Heliopolis had a special interest for oculists, and Ta-urt, the gross hippopotamus goddess, for women in childbirth.

It seems that practitioners of medicine in good standing could be divided into the priestly and the secular, although a number of leading physicians might be qualified in both forms of healing. All had to be fully literate. The priestly class possessed the higher status, and as priests of Sekhmet they had their own hierarchy through which they could rise to be chief of the priests of Sekhmet—which was likely to mean being a physician to the king. The lay physicians no doubt had their own range of social standing and financial reward. They were expected to work closely to the ancient books. The calling became very much a hereditary one and many doctors got their practical training from fathers and uncles. some of the lore was probably always kept as a professional secret. There were women physicians, but the evidence suggests they were rarities. Herodotus observed that there were many medical specialists in Egypt and this may always have been so. Yet many of the highest placed physicians were undoubtedly 'general practitioners' prepared to work with anything from an amulet to an enema.

It would be very interesting to know how much had been done to institute a national health scheme of the kind associated with the modern welfare state. The evidence is shaky, but the state does seem to have taken an interest in the health of its people and may have supported lay doctors to attend the army, and all the various groups of civil servants and workmen engaged on state projects.

Some Egyptologists have seen the rational philosophy and deductive methods of the *Edwin Smith Papyrus* as the best evidence for the prevalence of a true scientific spirit at the dawn of Egyptian history. This may be going too far, but there must have been a ferment of energy, enquiry, technical, intellectual and artistic endeavour that was to lift the civilization of the Nile valley so swiftly to the heights of the Pyramid Age. Such a man as Imhotep could only have been produced by a society that did not fear freshness of vision, originality or change.

Was it unfortunate that this youthful freedom rather quickly set into the hard mould of maturity? All individuals and societies tend to form venerated habits and customs, but the Egyptians went further than most, making changelessness an underlying philosophy of life. This had its heavy disadvantages: it certainly checked any possible flowering of the scientific spirit or ideas of progress. Instead it produced a strong, enduring society that probably had more influence on the growth of ancient civilization and the inheritance of the Greeks than can ever be precisely defined. It ensured a stable creativeness that produced wonders. Herodotus gave Egypt a great place in his history because, as he said, 'of the number of remarkable things which the country contains, and because of the fact that more monuments which beggar description are to be found there than anywhere else in the world.'

CHRONOLOGY OF
MESOPOTAMIA AND THE INDUS VALLEY

THE SUMERIANS HAD NO FIXED POINT, SUCH AS THE BEGINNING OF THE CHRIS-tian era, from which dates could be calculated. The *King Lists* gave the se-quence of rulers and the lengths of their individual reigns. Within reigns, scribes identified years by their outstanding political or religious events. From the tenth century B.C. the Assyrians named years after high officials.

For the Early Dynastic period and before, the *King Lists* are chronologi-cally useless (pp. 63–7) and the nearest approach for a fixed date is made by the works of art related to those of Protoliterate Sumer that have been found in Late Predynastic contexts in Egypt. Dates assigned to Early Dynastic I and II are therefore rough approximations; for Phase III greater solidity is given by contemporary records of the eight kings of Lagash (omitted from the *King Lists*). For the stretch of over seven hundred years between the beginning of the First Semitic Empire of Sargon of Akkad and the fall of the dynasty of Hammurabi before the Kassites, the succession of kings and the lengths of their reigns is well established except for minor uncertainties caused by the Gutian conquest. Unfortunately, however, the absolute date of this long historical period cannot be fixed because of the chronological 'dark age' lying between the Kassite seizure of Babylonia and about 1450 B.C. Attempts have been made to obtain fixed points from Babylonian observations of the Venus periods of sixty-four years, but there is as yet no certain correlation. This book adopts the 'middle chronology', which dates the beginning of the Kassite period to c. 1595. Some scholars prefer either to raise or lower this date, and all those dependent upon it, by a Venus period of sixty-four years. After 1450, Babylonian and Assyrian *King Lists* enable dates to be fixed with a margin of error of not more than ten years. For the late Assyrian Empire after 900 B.C. dates are accurate within a year or two.

MESOPOTAMIA AND THE INDUS VALLEY

B.C.	PERIOD	RULER
5000	Chalcolithic	
		Early rulers of city-states
3500		
3300	Protoliterate	Semi-mythical 1st Dyn. of Kish
2900	Early Dyn. I	
	Early Dyn. II	Mebaragesi (Kish)
		Agga (Kish) Gilgamesh (Uruk)
2600	Early Dyn. III	Kings of the Royal Tombs of Ur
		Ur-Nanshe (Lagash)
2500		Mesanapeda (Ur)
		Eanatum I (Lagash)
2400		Lugalzagesi Urukagina
		(Umma) (Lagash)
	1st Semitic Empire	Sargon (Akkad)
2300		Naram-Sin (Akkad)
2200		Shar-kali-sharri (Akkad)
		Gutian
		Gudea (Lagash) Kings
		Utuhengal (Uruk)
2100	Third Dyn. of Ur	Ur-Nammu (Ur)
		Shulgi (Ur)
		Ibbi-Sin (Ur)
2000	Isin-Larsa Period	Ishbi-Erra (Isin)
1900	Old Babylonian	Sumuabum (Babylon)
	Period (until 1595)	Rim-Sin (Larsa) Shamshi-Adad (Assur)
1800	2nd Semitic Empire	Hammurabi (Babylon) Ishme-
		Dagan (Assur) Zimri-Lim (Mari)
		Samsu-iluna
1700		Succeeding kings
		of the House of Hammurabi
1600	'Dark Age'	Kassite kings rule Babylonia
		through four centuries

EVENTS	B.C.
Settlement of the Lower Valley	5000
Arrival of the Sumerians?	3500
	3300
	2900
First walled cities	
	2600
Semites in Mari and spreading southward; rise of Indus cities	2500
	2400
Lagash sacked by Umma	
Foundation of Akkad	
	2300
Arrival of Gutians in the north	2200
Gutians expelled	
Empire of Ur established Hurrian attacks Fall of Ur	2100
Rise of early Assyrian kings Assyrian settlement at Kanesh	2000
Foundation of royal house, Babylon Hurrians invade Assyria	1900
	1800
Hammurabi completes conquest, 1760 Kassites invade the mid-valley	
Indus civilization in decline; rise of Hittite kings	1700
	1600
Mursilis I, the Hittite, sacks Babylon, 1595	

MESOPOTAMIA AND THE INDUS VALLEY (continued)

B.C.	PERIOD	RULER
1500		
1400	Mid-Assyrian Period begins	
1300		Shalmaneser I (Assyria)
1200		
1100	1st Assyrian Empire	Tiglath-Pileser I (Assyria)
900	2nd Assyrian Empire	Assurnasirpal II (Assyria) Tiglath-Pileser III (Assyria) Sargon II (Assyria)
700		Sennacherib (Assyria) Esarhaddon (Assyria) Assurbanipal (Assyria) Nabopalassar (Chaldean, of Babylon)
600		Nebuchadnezzar II Nabonidus

EVENTS	B.C.
Rise of Mitanni (Hurrian)	1500
	1400
Collapse of Mitanni	
	1300
Attacks by the Sea People; collapse of the Hittite Empire	1200
	1100
Babylon falls to the Assyrians Aramaeans settling in the Valley	
	900
	700
Conquest of Egypt; Memphis falls, 671; Thebes sacked, 663	
Medes sack Nineveh, 612	
Jews deported to Babylonia	600
Babylon falls to the Persians, 539	

CHRONOLOGY OF EGYPT

LIKE THE SUMERIANS, THE EGYPTIANS HAD NO FIXED ERAS BUT DATED EVENTS according to the regnal years of each Pharaoh. Although for orderly times under strong dynasties it is possible to place all the Pharaohs in sequence and add up their regnal years to make a correct block total, there are many uncertainties in the dynastic lists (p. 286) and the denser obscurities of the two Intermediate periods. There is also the problem of tethering the floating blocks of reigns to absolute dates. This has been partly accomplished by astronomical means based on the heliacal rising of the star Sothis (our Sirius), which had been accepted as marking the first day of the Month of Inundation—New Year's Day. As the Egyptians made no intercalary device, such as our leap year, to cover the six hours of the year beyond 365 days, their civil calendar fell out of time with the solar year. It was only in cycles of 1460 (365 × 4) years that the two coincided once more and Sothis duly rose just before the sun on New Year's Day. It is known that there was one such synchronism in A.D. 139. There are also several records in which the heliacal risings of the star are related to the regnal years of Pharaohs. Two of the most exact and useful are the ninth years of Amenhotep I (1536 B.C.) and the seventh of Sen-Wosret III (1872 B.C.). Dates before the Middle Kingdom become progressively less secure. Although Carbon 14 dating is not yet sufficiently accurate to be very helpful, recent revision of the system tends to favour the earlier historical estimate of c. 3200 B.C. for the Unification rather than the later estimates made by some historians.

EGYPT

EARLY DYNASTIC or ARCHAIC PERIOD

THE OLD KINGDOM

FIRST INTERMEDIATE PERIOD

* Figures in parentheses refer to the number of kings in each dynasty.

EVENTS	B.C.
	5000
	4000
	3600
Asian influence on Egypt; arrival of the Dynastic Race?	3400

EARLY DYNASTIC or ARCHAIC PERIOD

Unification of the Two Lands	3200
	2900
Dominance of Seth cult Re-unification under the "Peace-maker"	

THE OLD KINGDOM

Building of the Step Pyramid complex	2700
The Pyramid Age; Pharaohs at height of their sacred power	2600
Decline in absolute power of the Pharaohs	2500
Harim conspiracy; Weni defeats E. Bedouins	
Harkhuf's expedition to Nubia	2300
	2180

FIRST INTERMEDIATE PERIOD

Social revolution; Asians holding the North	
	2100
Fighting between nomes Eastern frontier secured against Asians Struggle between Herakleopolis and Thebes	

EGYPT (continued)

B.C.	PERIOD	RULER

THE MIDDLE KINGDOM

B.C.	PERIOD	RULER
	Dynasty XI	Menthuhotep I
2000	Dynasty XII (8)	Amenemhet (Ammenemes) I Sen-Wosret (Sesostris) I
1900		Sen-Wosret III
		Amenemhet III
1800		Queen Sebekneferu (last ruler of Dyn. XII)

SECOND INTERMEDIATE PERIOD

B.C.	PERIOD	RULER
	Dynasties XIII–XIV	Many ephemeral kings, perhaps ruling from Ittawi and the West Delta
1700	Dynasty XV (6)	Hyksos kings, ending with Apopi (Apophis)
1600	Dynasty XVII	Kamose

THE NEW KINGDOM

B.C.	PERIOD	RULER
	Dynasty XVIII (16)	Ahmose Amenhotep (Amenophis) I Thutmose (Thothmosis) I & II
1500		Hatshepsut Thutmose III
1400		Amenhotep (Amenophis) III Amenhotep IV (Akhenaten) Tutankhamun & Ay Horemhab
	Dynasty XIX (9)	Ramesses I Seti I
1300		Ramesses II
		Merenptah

THE MIDDLE KINGDOM

Two Lands re-united under Thebes

                                                                                          2000

Capital moved north to Ittawi
Peace and prosperity fully restored

                                                                                          1900

Campaigns in Palestine and Nubia;
    nomarchs suppressed
Development of the Fayum

                                                                                          1800

SECOND INTERMEDIATE PERIOD

Asians establish stronghold at Avaris
    and gradually annex Egypt up to Cusae

                                                                                          1700

Rule from Memphis

Kings of Thebes emerge as Dynasty XVII   1600

THE NEW KINGDOM

Expulsion of the Hyksos
Reoccupation of Nubia begun
Victorious campaign against the Mitanni (Nahrin)

                                                                                          1500

Great expedition to Punt, c. 1495
Seventeen Asian campaigns; battle of Megiddo, 1468

Height of Imperial prosperity   1400
Atenist revolution; capital at Akhetaten
Return to Thebes; old gods restored
Administrative reforms

Reconquest of Asian territories begun

Asian campaigns; battle of Kadesh, 1286;   1300
    capital moved from Thebes to Pi-Ramesse
Sea People repulsed

EGYPT (continued)

B.C.	PERIOD	RULER
1200		Queen Twosre (last ruler of Dyn. XIX)
	Dynasty XX (10)	
		Ramesses III
1100		Ramesses IV–XI

THE LATE PERIOD

B.C.	PERIOD	RULER
	Dynasty XXI	Kings of Tanis and High Priests of Thebes
1000		
	Dynasties XXII–XXIII (Libyan)	Shoshenk (Shishak)
900		
800		
	Dynasty XXV (Nubian)	Piankhi
700		
		Taharka
	Dynasty XXVI	Psammetichus I
600		
		Psammetichus III
500		

| | 1200 |

Victory over Sea People on the Delta, c. 1170

| Loss of Asian territories;
    rise to political power of High Priests
    of Amun at Thebes | 1100 |

THE LATE PERIOD

| Cache of royal mummies made at Deir el-Bahri
 Palestinian campaign; pillage of Jerusalem | 1000 |

| | 900 |
| | 800 |

| Princes of Kush
    rule Egypt;
    attempt to restore
    ancient virtues
 Assyrians conquer and rule Egypt, c. 671–52
 Assyrians expelled with help of Lydians
 Victorious campaign to Carchemish ends in defeat, 605 | 700 |

| | 600 |

Persian conquest of Egypt; battle of Pelusium, 525

| | 500 |

SELECTED BIBLIOGRAPHY

GENERAL

Adams, R. M.: *Urban revolution. (International Encyclopedia of the Social Sciences.)* New York, 1968.

Bottero, Edzard, Falkenstein, and Vercoutter: *The Near East: The Early Civilizations.* London, 1967.

Forbes, R. J.: *Studies in Ancient Technology.* 6 vols. Leiden, 1955–8.

Frankfort, H. et al.: *The Intellectual Adventure of Ancient Man.* Chicago, 1946.

Hawkes, J., and Woolley, L.: *Prehistory and the Beginnings of Civilization. (History of Mankind,* Vol. I; UNESCO.) London, 1963.

Neugebauer, O.: *The Exact Sciences in Antiquity.* Providence, 1957.

Pritchard, J. B.: *Ancient Near Eastern Texts.* 3rd, expanded, edition. Princeton, 1969.

Singer, C., Holmyard, E. J., and Hall, A. R., eds., *History of Technology,* I. Oxford, 1954.

MESOPOTAMIA

Diakonoff, N. M.: *Society and State in Ancient Mesopotamia.* Moscow, 1959.

Frankfort, H.: *Kingship and the Gods,* II. Chicago, 1948.

Jacobsen, T.: *The Sumerian King List*. Chicago, 1939.

————: "Primitive Democracy in Ancient Mesopotamia," *Journal of Near Eastern Studies*, 1943.

Kramer, S. N.: *History Begins at Sumer*. New York, 1959.

————: *The Sumerians*. Chicago, 1963.

Laessøe, J.: *People of Ancient Assyria*. London, 1963.

Leemans, W. F.: *Foreign Trade in Old Babylonian Times*. Leiden, 1960.

Mallowan, M. E. L.: *Nimrud*. 2 vols. London, 1966.

Oppenheim, A. L.: *Ancient Mesopotamia*. Chicago, 1964.

Parrot, A.: *Sumer*. New York, 1961.

Saggs, H. W. F.: *Everyday Life in Babylonia and Assyria*. London and New York, 1965.

Woolley, L.: *Ur Excavations*. 4 vols. London, 1954.

————: *The Sumerians*. London, 1954.

THE INDUS CIVILIZATION

Fairservis, W. A.: "The Origin, Character and Decline of an Early Civilization," *American Museum Novitates*, No. 2302 (1967).

Gordon, P. H.: *The Prehistoric Background of Indian Culture*. Bombay, 1938.

Khan, F. A.: "Excavations at Kot Diji," *Pakistan Archaeology* (Karachi), No. 2 (1965).

Kosambi, D. D.: *The Culture and Civilization of Ancient India*. London, 1965.

Marshall, J.: *Mohenjo-daro and the Indus Civilization*. 3 vols. London, 1931.

Piggott, S.: *Prehistoric India to 1000 B.C.* Harmondsworth, 1950.

Wheeler, R. E. M.: *The Indus Civilization*. 3rd edition. Cambridge, 1968.

EGYPT

Aldred, C.: *The Egyptians*. (*Ancient People and Places*.) London, 1961.

Baumgartel, E.: *The Cultures of Prehistoric Egypt*. Oxford, 1947.

Breasted, J. H.: *Development of Religion and Thought in Ancient Egypt*. New York, 1912 and 1959.

Cambridge Ancient History. Revised edition in fascicules. Cambridge, 1963.

Caton Thompson, G., and Gardiner, E. W.: *The Desert Fayum*. London, 1934.

Černý, J.: *Ancient Egyptian Religion*. London, 1952.

Drioton, É., and Vandier, J.: *L'Égypte*. (*Les Peuples de l'Orient Méditerranéen*, Vol. II; 4th edition.) Paris, 1962.

Edwards, I. E. S.: *The Pyramids of Egypt*. Harmondsworth, 1947; London, 1961.

Emery, W. B.: *Archaic Egypt*. Harmondsworth, 1961.

Frankfort, H.: *Kingship and the Gods*, I. Chicago, 1948.

Gardiner, A.: *The Wilbur Papyrus*. 4 vols. Oxford, 1941 and 1948–52.

———: *Egypt of the Pharaohs*. Oxford, 1961.

Ghalioungui, P.: *Magic and Medical Science in Ancient Egypt*. London, 1963.

Glanville, S. R. K., ed.: *The Legacy of Egypt*. Oxford, 1942.

Hayes, W. C.: *The Sceptre of Egypt*. 2 vols. New York, 1953 and 1959.

Kees, H.: *Ancient Egypt: A Cultural Topography*. London, 1959.

Lucas, A.: *Ancient Egyptian Materials and Industries*. 3rd edition. London, 1948.

Montet, P.: *Everyday Life in Egypt*. London, 1958.

Reisner, G.: *The Development of the Egyptian Tomb*. Oxford, 1936.

Simpson, W. K., ed.: *The Literature of Ancient Egypt*. New Haven, 1972.

Smith, W. S.: *The Art and Architecture of Ancient Egypt*. 3rd edition. London, 1948; Harmondsworth, 1958.

Winlock, H. E.: *Excavations at Deir el-Bahri*. New York, 1942.

INDEX

A NOTE ABOUT THE AUTHOR

Jacquetta Hawkes, holder of two degrees from Cambridge University, has done archaeological research and worked on excavations in Palestine, Britain, France and Ireland. She is the author of *A Land* (1951), *Man on Earth, Journey Down a Rainbow* (with J. B. Priestley, 1955), *Providence Island* (1959), *Man and the Sun* (1962), *History of Mankind, Volume I* (with Sir Leonard Woolley, 1963) and *The World of the Past* (1963). She lives with her husband, J. B. Priestley, near Stratford-on-Avon, England.